Tricks of the
UNIX® Masters

Tricks of the
UNIX® Masters

Russell G. Sage

The Waite Group

HOWARD W. SAMS & COMPANY

A Division of Macmillan, Inc.

11711 North College, Suite 141, Carmel, IN 46032 USA

International Standard Book Number: 0-672-22449-6
Library of Congress Catalog Card Number: 86-62477

Acquisitions Editor: *James S. Hill*
Editor: *Katherine Stuart Ewing*
Technical Editor: *Harry Henderson*
Designer: *T. R. Emrick*
Illustrator: *Don Clemons*
Cover Artist: *Kevin Caddell*
Compositor: *Shepard Poorman Communications, Indianapolis*

Printed in the United States of America

Contents

Preface

UNIX is more than just an operating system. It's a whole working environment. Learning about UNIX involves peeling back layer after layer and discovering new facilities and techniques, a process that can and does take years.

Tricks of the UNIX Masters is a look at UNIX *by* a professional *for* professionals, including system programmers and system administrators. Although this book presents a solid conceptual foundation for thinking about UNIX, it goes beyond the introductory and intermediate levels to the master level, sharing tools, tricks, and tips that you would gain otherwise only through years of experience and exploration.

Our approach is to look at each area of functionality and determine what we as UNIX professionals need and want to be able to do in our daily work. We then develop, present, and fully explain tools to meet these needs. Particularly extensive coverage is given to

- management issues
- files and file systems
- devices
- communications
- administration and security issues

Acknowledgments

I would like to thank Jay Bayne, my advisor and professor at Cal Poly, for believing in me when no one else did. It really made a difference. I would also like to thank Waite Group editor Harry Henderson for doing an excellent job in editing the manuscript and making important contributions to the writing. If it weren't for you, the book wouldn't be what it is today.

Introduction

The continuing price and performance gains in contemporary and soon-to-be-produced micro and super-micro computers are making the power of UNIX available to many more users. UNIX or UNIX-like systems run on everything from PC-XT level systems to ATs and beyond, with some configurations costing less than an 8-bit micro system cost only a few years ago. The availability of large amounts of RAM and powerful microprocessors has led to increasing interest in multitasking, multiprocessing systems, an area in which UNIX has a solid reputation.

Getting the most out of UNIX isn't easy, however. People have complained for years that it isn't "user friendly," and this is a reasonable criticism, although UNIX indeed contains the tools to build interfaces of whatever level of sophistication is desired. The most important reason why UNIX is hard to use effectively, though, is that it uses concepts which are *powerful but unfamiliar to many people who have worked with simpler operating systems*. UNIX also offers far more tools, much greater flexibility, and many more options than, for example, the popular MS-DOS, as a quick comparison of their respective manuals readily reveals.

If you're like most of us, you probably started by learning just enough UNIX to do whatever you needed to do on your system, whether it was word processing and text formatting, programming, or running statistics packages. After a while, you probably picked up (from others or on your own) a small bag of tricks, perhaps including some experience with simple shell programming.

Although this is a natural course of development, given UNIX's more than 200 commands, you may have overlooked or missed many powerful and useful ideas. More importantly, you may not have the perspective that comes from fully understanding how the different parts of UNIX work and the concepts that underlie them.

This book shows many useful tools and tricks that you can put to work right away to significantly increase your productivity with UNIX. Unlike some books that simply present a collection of scripts or other tools, we go into the details of how each program works and some of the directions you can take to adapt the programs to your own particular needs. This combination of tools, concepts, and problem-solving techniques will help you become a UNIX master.

What You Should Already Know

To benefit from this book you should have some basic experience with UNIX. You should know the general aspects of the file system, such as directories, nesting, and pathnames. You should know how to use one of the UNIX editors to enter shell scripts, and know at least a little shell programming. We have made few assumptions concerning what you should know about a given command or feature of UNIX. Each command or concept is explained when it is introduced, and an occasional trip to your UNIX manuals can clear up any obscure areas. Keep one thing in mind: There are so many commands with so many options that even we masters have to "go to the book" on occasion.

If you're just beginning to use UNIX, the book *UNIX Primer Plus* by Mitchell Waite, Donald Martin, and Stephen Prata (SAMS, 1983) gives just the comprehensive introduction you need. If you're beyond the basics but still rather fuzzy about the inner workings of the shell and shell programming, another book, *Advanced UNIX—A Programmer's Guide* by Stephen Prata (SAMS, 1985) can give you a thorough grounding. In fact, that book makes an ideal companion and reference as you follow the advanced explorations that make up this book.

Which UNIX?

There are, of course, many "flavors" of UNIX. In addition to the major families of UNIX implementations (AT&T System V, Microsoft XENIX, and Berkeley [BSD]), several different shells are available, of which the two most widely used are the Bourne shell and the C shell. All scripts in this book were tested under both System V and XENIX using the Bourne shell, except as noted. *Most* of our scripts also run under the Bourne shell in BSD, although a few commands in System V are not found in BSD, and vice versa. We try to point out the areas where the two systems differ significantly and give some alternate approaches for BSD users.

Most of our scripts also can be rewritten to run under the C shell after taking into account syntax differences. If you are a Bourne shell user who would like to experiment with the C shell, the previously mentioned *Advanced UNIX—A Programmer's Guide* is a good introduction.

If one of our scripts doesn't run on your system, don't panic. Please check:

- Which version of UNIX do you have? Have we mentioned something in regard to it?
- Which shell are you using (Bourne, C, other)?
- Do you need to change a pathname because something is in a different part of your system?
- Do you lack permission to access a particular file? Do you need to su to another user uid or be root?
- Does the script use a previously introduced script that you haven't put on your system yet?

Most of these are pretty obvious, but it never hurts to take a deep breath and think systematically before diving into a debugging session.

Chapter Overview

Let's take a quick look at what we cover in this book so that you get an idea of its scope as well as where to find a given topic.

Chapter 1 introduces the UNIX environment as a whole, the ways users relate to different parts of it, and how your development as a UNIX master will enable you to get the most out of all aspects and features of the environment.

Chapter 2 looks at the most pervasive feature of the UNIX environment, the file system, and introduces tools for exploring file structures and file contents.

Chapter 3 provides tools for the practical day-to-day file management tasks of copying and backing up files and discarding unwanted files.

Chapter 4 looks at the kinds of files that are important for software documentation and offers tools that make it easier for you to manage your growing collection of software tools.

Chapter 5 focuses on your home environment and personal management. This involves managing your scheduling and tasks. Several helpful tools are presented to aid you.

Chapter 6 provides ways that you can learn about other users and tools for maintaining the security of your workspace on the system.

Chapter 7 looks at some of the nuts and bolts of UNIX devices, especially terminals and disks, with some example tools. Included also are tools for dealing with file systems.

Chapter 8 looks at UNIX communications, an area growing rapidly in importance. This material helps you deal with uncooperative modems as well as the security and management problems that come up in dealing with cu and uucp. Tools help you deal with both UNIX to non-UNIX and UNIX to UNIX communications. Practical examples of hardware configurations are also provided.

Chapter 9 introduces system administration and security. You can find information here that you could obtain on your own only with years of reading and experimentation. As UNIX becomes more prevalent in the "real world," security becomes a very important issue. We present concepts, tips on what to watch for, and tools to help you watch.

Chapter 10 closes the book with a potpourri of UNIX tricks, including one or two line commands that do unexpectedly powerful things.

A set of appendixes provides information useful in shell programming and debugging.

Because some of the tools use scripts introduced previously in the book, you should work through the book in chapter sequence when implementing the scripts on your system. It won't hurt for you to browse a little first, though.

The author is interested in hearing from you about your experience with this book and your own applications and extensions to the tools we present. He is planning on setting up a bulletin board system for UNIX masters to share ideas and so that he can distribute software presented and not presented in this book. For more information, write

Russ Sage
P.O. Box 1186
Cupertino, CA 95015-1186

1

The UNIX Environment

The spectrum of environments and where we fit in
Our home directory and how to make it feel like "home"
Theories of relativity à la UNIX
Some metaphors for the UNIX world

The UNIX
Environment

Introduction

This chapter looks at the environment that exists within and around UNIX. To approach all aspects of the UNIX environment would be a monumental task at best and is beyond the scope of this book. Even individual utilities such as `fsdb` and `sdb` need their own books to do them justice. What we attempt to do is give the reader the background, philosophy, and feel for UNIX that underlies the many explorations and tools presented in this book.

In conjunction with reading this chapter, you might want to read (or reread) profile(4), environ(5), term(5), termcap(5), and termio(7) in the UNIX manuals to familiarize yourself with the mechanisms UNIX provides to set up a working environment.

Many different subenvironments exist within UNIX. Together they make up the pieces of the overall picture that we think of as a UNIX system. This book is aimed at the most important aspects of the UNIX environment to give you the groundwork needed to understand the entire system. This gives you a context within which to see your own work with the system, whether as a user, programmer, or system administrator.

The areas we look at in this chapter are the different environments in computers from a theoretical point of view, the home environment and how to set it up, ways to use relative notation, and the overall global environment.

The "Environment Spectrum"

Each computer system supports a number of different environments. These environments are used as building blocks to create functional working systems. The different levels are needed to both reduce the amount of work it takes to operate the machine and to build up an interface so that we can use the computer at a relatively high, human-like level.

We are looking at this model because it helps to put into perspective the levels at which we can operate. By knowing more about where we are in the system and how it operates around us, we can more easily build increasingly abstract models on top of the ones already in place. Computers are really working models of abstractions, so the more we understand about the models, the more we can use them to make our work easier and faster.

The spectrum model in Figure 1-1 shows the various levels that operate inside a computer. The bottom layer is the starting point from which the spectrum grows upward. Each level builds on the preceding one and is used to support the one above it. For each level up, the environment is larger and more "virtual" in the sense that fewer arbitrary limits apply. The upper levels use the lower to function and thus hide the details needed to run those lower levels. We can make high level models that run on the lower level machine without having to know anything about the lower levels.

Let's take a brief look at the levels in the model and talk about which ones this book operates in.

Figure 1-1
The Computer Environment Spectrum

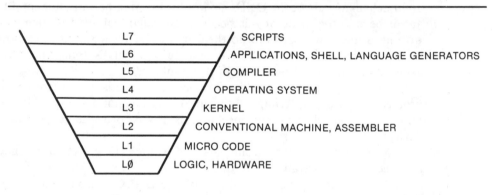

L7	SCRIPTS
L6	APPLICATIONS, SHELL, LANGUAGE GENERATORS
L5	COMPILER
L4	OPERATING SYSTEM
L3	KERNEL
L2	CONVENTIONAL MACHINE, ASSEMBLER
L1	MICRO CODE
L0	LOGIC, HARDWARE

Level 0—Hardware

At the lowest level are the hardware and logic circuits. This level defines the way data is stored and processed throughout the hardware. As technology in silicon chip manufacturing continues to advance, this level becomes physically smaller and denser whereas storing and processing speeds continue to increase. The components at this level are the CPU, memory, support chips and the system bus.

Notice that although advances at this level continue, very little change at the top layer of the pyramid ensues. The UNIX philosophy is to isolate the lower level hardware layer and provide uniform interfaces to it that don't need to change "at the top." The top layer should not even know about the bottom layer. This is not to say that what happens in the world of hardware isn't important in the real world because real-world constraints affect overall speed and capacity, not to mention cost of resources.

Level 1—Micro-Code

This level is much like a programming language. It is the tool that a system architect uses to create a native machine language. Machine language tells the hardware what a specific instruction should do.

In the beginning of CPU development, most instruction sets were hard coded. This means that when the CPU fetched an instruction, decoding and execution were done directly by the circuits in the silicon chip. With advancements in CPU technology, some chips have the capability of being programmed at the instruction execution level, which allows designers to create and implement new instruction sets with minimal work.

Level 2—Conventional Machine

This level provides the translation from assembly language mnemonics into machine language op codes and data. Assembly language is a somewhat more English-like notation that makes it easier for humans to understand and control the execution of computers.

The conventional machine is supported by the assembler. The assembler can turn higher level ideas into strings of numbers that then can be executed. Along with the assembler, models are used to assist in the utilization of the computing hardware. Now we can define things like stacks, interrupt vectors, and peripheral I/O.

Level 3—Kernel

The kernel is the next logical upward movement and is a conceptualization that can now be implemented in software on the conventional machine. The kernel provides an environment that supports even higher abstractions than the ones used so far. The two most important are process management for multiprogramming and multitasking, and the file system, which manages the file storage, format, lookup, etc. With these two areas intertwined, we have the base function of a multiuser machine and the core of an operating system.

One of the most important areas that the kernel manages is security. The user identification checks are done in the system calls inside the kernel. Mechanisms are used by the kernel to handle file, device, memory, and process security. The only way to deactivate them is to modify kernel source code and recompile the whole system, which is very unlikely. Other mechanisms, such as the file system, are also subject to security breaches.

Level 4—Operating System

This level builds on the kernel to create a total operating environment. Needs for more functions in the system can be satisfied by making standalone programs that are aimed at specific areas. Thus, the total of all the specific functions defines the operating system.

Level 5—Compilers

The compiler is a tool (or program) built on the operating system to further develop higher and more powerful environments. The new environments can assume even larger abstractions than those at the lower level and make more assumptions about what already exists. This makes higher level symbolic constructs such as data and control structures possible. The result is the applications program.

Using a compiler, we can define a completely new language and make it a working reality on the computer by writing a compiler program that reads this new language. This opens up whole new areas in human-machine interfacing. High-level languages can embody different approaches to problem-solving, such as the procedural model or the object-oriented model, and eventually perhaps can approach the expressive power of a human language like English.

Level 6—Application Programs

Application programs can mean lots of different things these days. We can assume that any program which sits on the compiler is an application program. Some examples of possible application programs are the next generation of languages, interpreters, and applications generators. The interpreter is a program written in a common high-level language that can decode and execute another syntax (or language). The example that concerns us in UNIX is the shell. It is a C program written to read shell syntax and have it executed.

An application generator is a program written in a high-level language. It is designed to get enough information from the user about his or her application that it can use a compiler-level language such as C to write an applications program to implement what is wanted. The user does no programming. The output of the generator is a working program.

UNIX doesn't particularly hold to such distinctions between levels. Some facilities such as pipes are part of the kernel at a low level. A command such as `cat` performs a pretty simple function at the operating system level. Something like `ls` is like a simple applications program with relatively few options. Large programs like the `roff` family are definitely fullblown applications, and facilities like `sed` and `awk` are actually miniprogramming language interpreters. The remarkable thing about UNIX is the uniformity it brings to this whole range of functions.

Level 7—Shell Scripts

This top level is a language interpreted by the program /bin/sh (in the case of the Bourne shell). Its syntax supports a complete programming language. Although this language lacks the range of built-in structures and functions of a modern high-level language, it has all the essentials for writing useful programs. The big plus is that the shell language has available as extrinsic functions every facility, utility, and program that exists on the UNIX system. This means the shell language can express algorithms in twenty lines that might take a hundred lines or more of a low-level language like C, at a penalty in performance, of course.

Your Home on the System

Because UNIX was designed to be a multiuser system, there are many provisions for making the system secure and personal for each user. You are given a specific area in the file system (or on the disk if that's the way you look at it) that is all yours and nobody else's. You can lock your area so that no one can see inside, or you can leave it open for other people to read and or write into.

In addition to defining your place on the system, the home directory can be tailored to your exact specifications. Home is not just the file storage area, but is your whole environment. Shell variables can be set up to define paths throughout the system. Tools can be built to aid you in your work.

What Is the Neighborhood Like?

Many older minicomputer and microcomputer environments have a "flat" file system, which means that all the files reside in one huge holding area and there are no logical divisions to separate them. The lack of divisions results in a mass of files that must be waded through when you want to find a specific item. Some systems had group divisions in their file systems, but usually these divisions were different flat file systems. Time has shown that this kind of environment (or model) is not a very good solution.

The solution that UNIX uses is the inverted tree model. The root of the system is at the top, and the branches fork out and down. There is one and only one root at the top. The branches may go out in any direction and extend down any depth. In addition, you can have remote branches that can be taken off the system and put back on later. They are mounted on the existing tree structure in the system.

When you login, you can be placed anywhere in the system tree structure. The login point is defined in the passwd file and is referred to as $HOME, which is one of the predefined "shell variables" for your use. You can now have your personal tree structure under that directory name. It is totally yours and can be made impermeable to everyone except root. You can design $HOME any way you want.

Prototype Directory Layout

Once your $HOME has been attached to a specific spot on the tree, you have total control over the structure that exists below it. You can leave it flat, or make it like a minitree in itself. The structure really depends on your needs and your enthusiasm in setting up your own area. The biggest gain available to us is when we can use our home environment to support us and take away much of the burden of manual work. The next two chapters present a variety of tools that can operate on your personal file system.

Figure 1-2 contains a prototype directory tree structure for your $HOME environment. This layout presents an environment skeleton that you can fill in with appropriate information.

As you grow in your use of the system, you will need these types of areas in which to compartmentalize information. You will find also that our backup scripts are designed to move through or *traverse* trees, so you are guaranteed to benefit from using a hierarchical construction.

Figure 1-2
Prototype $HOME Directory Tree Structure

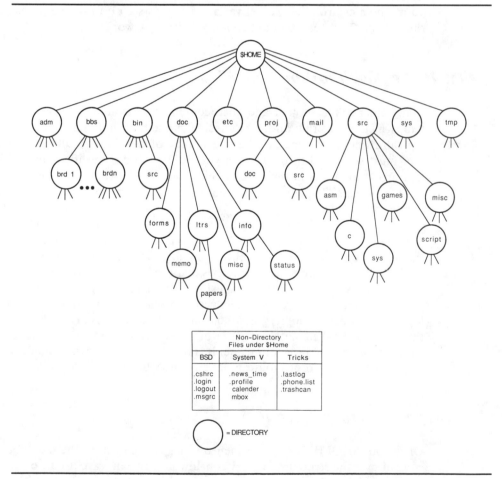

Let's go through this example structure and define what the pieces are. The structure includes a lot of files and directories, but they are all there for a purpose. You may not want to use these exact names, but you get an idea of what kinds of categories can occur and how to use the system to support this structure.

The root of this tree is $HOME, which is defined in the fifth field of the file /etc/passwd. Usage of the passwd file is described in passwd(4). An example of the author's passwd entry is

```
russ:.pDIPADYfIXBY:103:101:Russ Sage:/usr/russ:/bin/sh
```

From left to right you see the user name (russ), password (.pDI...), user id (103), group id (101), a personal comment, the name of the home directory (/usr /russ), and the shell obtained upon login (/bin/sh).

Files in $HOME

The files discussed in following text fall into three areas: Files that normally occur on your system if you are on System V, files that normally occur if you are on Berkeley 4.2, and files that occur from using programs in this book.

System V Files

The first file is .news_time. The date on this file is the last time you read the news. To read news, use the news(1) command.

The next file is .profile. This file is executed at every login shell and can be used to tailor your own environment. We look at this file in more depth in following text.

The next file is calendar. This file holds dates and messages. The calendar(1) command reads the file for dates very close to the current date. Then the messages are printed or mailed to you.

The last file is mbox, your default system mailbox. When you save mail using the mail(1) command it goes into mbox by default.

4.2 BSD Files

The first file here is .cshrc. This is the first stage of profiling done by the cshell. In UNIX, any file named "rc" means "run commands" or "run on boot up."

The .login file is synonymous with the sh .profile. This file contains customizations that you want when you log on.

The next file is .logout. This is executed when you log out. For example, you could use it to print accounting information such as how long you have been logged on, how much disk space you are using, etc. System V has no file like this.

The next file is .msgsrc, which is for the Berkeley command msgs(1). The .msgsrc file contains the last read message file. The message files are stored as sequentially numbered files in the /usr/msgs directory.

Tricks of the Masters Files

These are programs and files you can develop in the course of using this book. The .lastlog file holds the dates of each time you login on your account. The program that manages this file is called lastlog and is presented in Chapter 5.

The next file is .trashcan. This is a directory that temporarily holds files you have deleted. When you know for sure you don't need them, they can be removed forever. This facility is presented in Chapter 3.

The last file is .phone.list. This is your personal phone list database. It is managed by the phone command in Chapter 5.

Directories

The first directory is adm. It holds administrative files that you might have, such as schedules, employee information, meetings, etc.

Under the bbs directory are subdirectories for each bulletin board you call. As you call systems, you have a place to put all the associated files and data. This way you don't get the files from boards mixed up with one another. Information you need is menus for the system, help text, program downloads, and general information that you capture.

The bin directory holds any tools that you have. These might be shell scripts or object modules from compiled programs. A subdirectory called src is optional. This holds the C source code for the object modules in bin so that the source for quick fixes and updates is handy.

The doc directory is the root of all kinds of documentation. Subdirectories here would be forms, letters, memos, miscellaneous information, and status reports. Each subdirectory holds the specific files in these areas.

The etc (pronounced et-see) directory contains any system or administrative commands and files that you use. If you have administrative responsibility, a typical inclusion in this directory would be a backup of the current configuration files that the system is using. Files you want to back up include

```
/.profile
/etc/bcheckrc
     brc
     checklist
     gettydefs
     group
     inittab
     motd
     mountable
     unmountable
     passwd
     profile
```

```
        rc
/usr/lib/crontab
/usr/lib/uucp/L.sys
    USERFILE
    uudemon.day
    uudemon.hr
    uudemon.wk
```

or any other bits and pieces of information about the system.

The proj directory is for any special projects that you have. Rather than proj, you might call the directory by the name of the project, like dev for development, or qa for quality assurance. All data, correspondence, documentation, and source code for each job goes under the project main directory name. Of course, you could have more than one project directory.

The next directory is mail. This is a good place to put your mail correspondence from other people that use the system. The file names in this directory are user names. For example, if I received mail from Bob, I would have a file called bob and in it would be the mail I received from him.

The src directory is for all source code. Logically group your source code into subdirectories to make it easier to find in the future. Possible subdirectories are asm for assembly code, c for C source code, games, misc, script for shell scripts, and sys for any system related source code. (If you keep your personal tool source in /bin /src, you might want to duplicate it here.)

The sys directory is a catchall for system-related information. This ranges from critical system file backups, documentation on areas of the system, or bits and pieces of command output from who, ps, logfiles, uucp, or whatever.

The last directory is tmp, which is a scratch area in which to put temporary working files. Basically everything in tmp is something you can remove at any time, and the can tool described in Chapter 3 helps you do just that.

Notice that $HOME has a minimal number of regular files. This reduces the confusion that can occur with flat file systems. Every file should be in its place, but it doesn't have to be placed only there. If any kind of task arises where files associated with that task could get mixed up with other files, create a directory for it.

Analysis of an Example System Profile

The file .profile functions, as its name suggests, to set up and initialize the way you want the system to be. This includes setting up terminals, defining variables, running programs, and basically configuring the run-time system. A sample profile is found in profile(4). The following .profile is one that the author uses. We are including this at this early stage to encourage you to touch on concepts that are explored in more detail later in this book. Don't worry about understanding how every part works. For now, make a mental note of the possibilities. Your .profile may be simpler, and it almost certainly will be different.

```
1    # @(#).profile v1.0   Defines "home" on the system   Author: Russ Sage
2
3    CHOICE="ushort"
4    case $CHOICE in
5    ufull)   PS1="'uuname -l'> ";;
6    ushort)  PS1="'uuname -l¦cut -c1-3'> ";;
7    graphic) PS1="^[[12mj^[[10m ";;
8    esac
9
10   LOGNAME='logname'
11   HOME='grep "^$LOGNAME:" /etc/passwd ¦ cut -d: -f6'
12   MAIL=/usr/spool/mail/$LOGNAME
13   export LOGNAME HOME MAIL
14
15   HA=$HOME/adm
16   HBB=$HOME/bbs
17   HB=$HOME/bin
18   HD=$HOME/doc
19   HE=$HOME/etc
20   HM=$HOME/mail
21   HP=$HOME/proj
22   HSR=$HOME/src
23   HSY=$HOME/sys
24   HT=$HOME/tmp
25   HDIRS="HA HBB HB HD HE HM HP HSR HSY HT"
26   export $HDIRS HDIRS
27
28   P=/usr/spool/uucppublic/$LOGNAME; export P
29
30   CDPATH=.:..:$HOME:$HDIRS
31   PATH=.:/bin/:/usr/bin:/etc:$HOME/bin
32   SHELL='grep "^$LOGNAME:" /etc/passwd¦cut -d: -f7'
33   export CDPATH PATH SHELL
34
35   case "'basename \'tty\''" in
36   console) eval 'tset -m ansi:ansi -m :\?ansi -r -s -Q';;
37   tty00)   eval 'tset -m ansi:ansi -m :\?ansi -r -s -Q';;
38   tty01)   eval 'tset -m ansi:ansi -m :\?ansi -r -s -Q';;
39   esac
40
41   echo TERM = $TERM
42   TERMCAP=/etc/termcap
43   export TERM TERMCAP
44
45   HZ=20
46   TZ=PST8PDT
47   export HZ TZ
```

```
48
49   umask 0022
50
51   echo "\nTime of this login : 'date'"
52   lastlog -l
53
54   RED="^[[31m"
55   GREEN="^[[32m"
56   YELLOW="^[[33m"
57   BLUE="^[[34m"
58   CYAN="^[[35m"
59
60   case "'date|cut -d' ' -f1'" in
61   Mon)      echo "$RED";;
62   Tue)      echo "$GREEN";;
63   Wed)      echo "$YELLOW";;
64   Thu)      echo "$BLUE";;
65   Fri)      echo "$CYAN";;
66   esac
```

How .profile Is Run

When you log onto the system, the login program execs the shell with the '-' parameter (for example, -sh). This alerts the shell that this is login time and the profile should be executed. First /etc/profile, the general profile set up by the system administrator for all users, is executed, then the user's .profile. Each shell after that does not run these setup programs again. The /etc/profile file is an interesting file to check out for machine-specific information and to see what defaults have been set up for you. If you want to execute your .profile anytime after logging in, type ". .profile".

To support your home directory, create shell variables to facilitate ease of movement and reduce keystrokes when working with pathnames. Shell variables are always strings, and once defined, don't disappear until you log off.

When created, shell variables are local to the currently running shell. They can be passed on to deeper level shells by "exporting" them. Therefore, if you create a shell out of vi, all your exported variables are still defined for that shell. For a comprehensive list of the default shell variables used by the system, see Appendix A.

Note that in our example profile for every first-level subdirectory we have in our home directory, we also have a shell variable assigned with that name. Thus, we can reference the different areas of our $HOME with little trouble.

Example Profile, Line by Line

Lines 3-8 do a tricky setup of the primary prompt, variable PS1. Line 3 initializes the choice that selects the prompt. The value ushort is hard coded in the file, but you could always prompt for it or set it up dependent on a file.

The first choice is ufull, used to set the prompt as the full uucp node name on the local system. You choose this if you use several machines and use another machine to access this one. The distinctive prompt reminds you which machine you are using. Note that the prompt is the same number of characters, whether the string is short or long. If you still want the uucp node name but not a long string for a prompt, you can opt for ushort, which is the first three characters of the node name. As line 6 shows, the name is obtained by using `uuname` to get the local node name (-l option). Then this name is passed through `cut`, which cuts out characters 1 through 3. The result is assigned to the prompt variable.

The last choice is for those of you who have graphics characters. The assignment made in line 7 is a Greek character. Obtain it by using special escape sequences that instruct terminals to print special characters. The ^[characters are the representation in vi of the literal escape character. You can get this character by typing `control-v`, then `ESC` in vi. The sequence ESC[12m means print the next character from the graphic character set. The j is the character that is your prompt and is mapped into a graphic character that ends up on your screen. By using different characters from the alphabet, you can have as your prompt just about any graphic character. The ESC[10m sets your terminal back to regular text so that all characters printed after you type ESC[10m are normal.

If you wish to keep your custom prompt for all subordinate shells, export it. Otherwise you get a $ for lower level shells.

Line 10 sets LOGNAME to the output of the `logname`(1) command. The `logname` command is a regular UNIX command that prints your login name from the /etc/passwd file. This variable is usually set for you by the system, but this example shows how you can set it up manually.

Line 11 initializes the HOME variable. This, too, is set for you by the system, but we want to show how to do things intentionally, not by default. First we look for the passwd entry, as defined by LOGNAME. We search from the beginning of the line for the name ended by a : character to ensure that only the correct user name is matched. Then the whole entry is sent to `cut`, which cuts out the sixth field, the home directory. The advantage of this strategy is that $HOME is automatically changed if the entry in /etc/passwd is changed.

Line 12 initializes the MAIL variable. By defining MAIL, you specify that you are to be notified when new mail is sent to you while you are on line. Line 13 exports these variables so that they are available to us in child shells.

Lines 15-24 define all the first-level directories in our home directory prototype layout. Most names are two letters, some are three. Now we can do commands like:

```
$ cd $HD
$ ls -R $HSR
$ cu -ltty00 dir | tee $HBB/board/session$$
```

Line 25 sets HDIRS to all the directory variable names, which makes it easier to include all the directories without typing their names again. Also, we can run through all the directories and print the amount of disk usage:

```
$ for DIR in $HDIRS
> do
```

```
> echo "disk usage for $DIR: 'du -s $DIR'"
> done
```

Line 26 exports the variables so that we can always use them. Note that we exported $HDIRS and HDIRS. Before the export executed, $HDIRS was expanded to all the different variable names. Therefore, we really exported all the names plus the HDIRS variable itself.

Line 28 initializes P to be your directory under PUBDIR, or /usr/spool /uucppublic. Now we have an easy way to reference our files while doing uucp tasks.

Line 30 sets up CDPATH. This is the path that is checked when you do a cd. First the current directory (.) is checked to see whether that is the name of the directory that you want to go to. Next .. is checked. After that your home directory name is checked. The last assignment to CDPATH is $HDIRS, which includes all the subdirectory names. What these names do is allow cd to look in that directory for the name you typed.

For example, if you were in /etc and typed "cd doc", you would end up in $HOME/doc because CDPATH had the root $HOME in it. Likewise, if you had a subdirectory $HOME/doc/status and typed "cd status" from somewhere out in the system, you would go to $HOME/doc/status because the root $HOME/doc was in CDPATH.

The order of the lookup in the directories is the same as declared in the CDPATH variable. If you type a directory name that occurs in more than one place, you go to the first one that is encountered in the sequential lookup. For example, if you said "cd sys", you would go to $HOME/sys before $HOME/src/sys.

Table 1-1 is a sample of equivalent cd commands expressed in the three different forms UNIX understands. Which one you use depends on what feels most comfortable and requires the fewest number of keystrokes.

Table 1-1
Three Ways To Use cd

Absolute	CDPATH	Variable/Relative
cd /usr/russ	cd	cd $HOME
cd /usr/russ/src/asm	cd asm	cd $HSR/asm
cd /usr/russ/doc/paper/conf	cd paper/conf	cd $HD/paper/conf
cd /usr/russ/tmp	cd tmp	cd $HT

Line 31 initializes the PATH variable. PATH works in the same way as CDPATH. It looks for programs to run in each directory in the PATH variable. If the name is not found in any of these directories, the message <file-name>: not found is printed.

Because we can set our PATH as anything, we can point to all the weird places executables "hang out" in the system. When we want to execute them, we won't have to look for them and type in the whole pathname. To add more to PATH, type something like this:

```
PATH=$PATH:/usr/lib/uucp
```

The `paths` command presented later in this book uses $PATH to tell us which directory an executable resides in.

Line 32 initializes the SHELL variable. At most, one or two utilities may use this variable. It is usually set by the system when you login. Line 33 exports the variables.

Lines 35-39 are a tricky way to set up the terminal definitions. Line 35 starts with the innermost command, the `tty` command, in grave accents ('...'). The output of `tty` is "/dev/tty00". Then we take the basename of this string, which is "tty00". Next we use a case structure based on this value to see what we want to do for each specific terminal. The tset commands shown here are from the XENIX environment and may not be applicable to your environment.

Line 41 echoes the TERM value to the screen, which is done to show you what your terminal type is in case you need it. This value is available if the previously described `tset` command set TERM for you as part of its normal job.

Line 42 sets TERMCAP to point to /etc/termcap. This is the normal way to set TERMCAP up. An alternate way is to set TERMCAP to the actual cryptic string that resides in the termcap file. When TERMCAP is set to the cryptic string, vi doesn't have to do the file I/O to get your terminal capabilities. Line 43 exports these values so that they are accessible at any shell level.

Line 45 sets up the hertz variable. This variable is from XENIX and is probably also on System V. It is used to to set up time information.

Line 46 sets up the time zone information as needed in `ctime`(3) library call. By having a TZ variable, you can override the default time zone when accessing the time from a C program. Line 47 exports these values.

Line 49 sets up your umask value. This controls the default permission for all files that you create. The system subtracts the umask value from 777. The result becomes the file permission, in this case, 755. When you create a directory with permission 755, that directory is shown under "ls -l" as rwxr-xr-x. When you create a nondirectory file with permission 755, that file is shown as rw-r--r--, which is equivalent to 644. Nondirectory files don't have the x bit so that they can't be executed. Directories, on the other hand, need the x bit set so that they can be accessed with `cd`.

Lines 51 and 52 tell you about your login session times. Line 51 tells your current login time, and line 52 calls a script called lastlog, which prints the date of your last login time and is presented in Chapter 5.

Lines 54-58 initialize variables to generate colors on a color monitor. The escape values are standard ANSI values. These work on a XENIX system and may work on yours. Having multiple colors for UNIX is interesting. Bit-mapped graphics aren't available, but character graphics and varied foreground and background colors are. The foreground colors are in the 30s and the background colors are in the 40s.

Lines 60-66 are just a bit of fun. They are a tricky way to set a different color on your screen every day. Line 60 starts by running the date command and piping the output to the cut command. The first field is cut out, which is the day of the week. Next we create a case structure based on the day string, performing a different action for each day. By echoing the escape sequences, the monitor reacts immediately. This is totally configurable and you can do anything you can dream up.

Theories of Relativity Inside UNIX

Now that we've looked at the range of the home environment, the next step is to go to environments just outside $HOME. For example, what other directories are at the same level as your $HOME? Who else is out there? How can you access their directories easily? Can you run programs in someone else's directory? These kinds of questions and actions relate to other people on your system.

The only way to answer these questions is to look around for yourself. No one is going to tell you everything about what the system is like. You have to explore it for yourself and find out where you can and can't go. The system is finite, so you can help yourself by making listings of all the directories and files.

The point being made is that you can maneuver in UNIX using a relative notation. Because the system tree is built with directories, the . and .. notations allow us to traverse up and down the tree. At any point, .. means the parent directory of the current directory that we are in.

Some example relative commands are shown below.

- `ls -l $HOME/..`   lists files in my parent directory
- `cd ../../..`   assuming current directory is /usr/russ/src/c, makes my current directory /usr.
- `ls .`   lists files in the current directory
- `ls ..`   lists files in my parent directory
- `$HOME/../../bin/ls`   runs the ls in /usr/russ/../../bin, or /bin/ls.
- `../fred/bin/ls`   runs the ls command in Fred's bin directory that is in the same parent directory as I am, or /usr/fred/bin/ls.

The Overall System Environment

The system environment is not just *in* UNIX, but *is* UNIX. As we see throughout this book, the whole system—UNIX, C, commands, files, etc.—is just a logical approach to operating a computer. Each hardware box operates differently. The software is what defines the system to the end user. Therefore, we no longer have to worry about hardware constraints or side affects. We can view each machine running UNIX as the same, and treat each UNIX the same. We anticipate that the reaction of the machine will be the same every time.

We can regard UNIX in the same way as we do physical laws. We are bound by them, but we are also free to apply these laws to situations and areas that we have never encountered before. We can trust these laws and assume that they apply wherever we go. Such is the UNIX system, at least ideally.

The system has many environments. An understanding of what they are, how they interact, and what they can be used for is essential. Just as

$$programs = data\ structures + algorithms$$

so does

$$UNIX = file\ tree + utilities$$

The UNIX environment is a combination of two essential things: the file tree and the system call interface. The tree allows infinite expansion possibilities by providing the capability of mounting external disk regions at any point in the file system. The tree also aids in the collection of logically related files, which keeps the system more organized.

The system call interface provides a toolset with which most other functions can be built. The definition of the System V interface is in published book form and can be found in bookstores. The adherence to this standard guarantees compatibility with the ever growing AT&T System V.

The Overall File Tree

To get a better grasp of this UNIX world of ours, look at the sample printout of the UNIX structure in Figure 1-3. This is a pictorial view of the entire root file system tree. Any other extensions to the file system are mounted on this file system. The

Figure 1-3
UNIX File System Tree

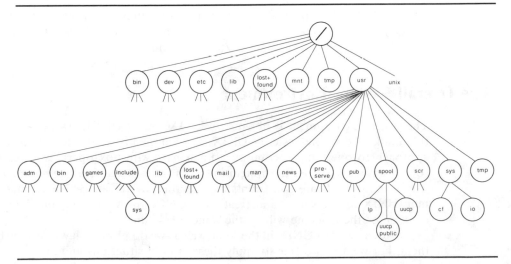

temporary mount point is /mnt. More permanent mount points need to be created, such as /0, /1, and so on, or /usr1, /usr2, and so on. The permanent mount points are really up to the administrator.

First Layer

The leftmost directory is /bin, which holds all the major binary utilities. This is the biggest of the two major bin directories.

The next directory is /dev, which is where all the device files reside. Device files are the access points to peripherals connected to the system. The file is linked to the peripheral by the kernel and device driver.

Administrative utilities and configuration files are stored in /etc. Examples are `getty` and `gettydefs`, `init` and `inittab`, and the password file (/etc /passwd).

Next is /lib, which is where libraries for the compiler reside. Other types of libraries can be kept here too.

The /lost+found directory is used by `fsck` (the principal file system maintenance facility) to store files that are thrown away. If you really want to keep these files, they can be retrieved from this holding area after the file system is cleaned up.

The next directory is /mnt. This is a temporary mount point for file systems. We often mount and unmount file systems just to run a quick check on something. This is a good place to do it.

The system's major temporary working directory is /tmp. Many utilities, such as vi, fsck, shell scripts, and backup programs, use /tmp to store working files.

Next is /usr, which is used as a mount point. The file system mounted there contains additional system information and users' directories. This split between the boot file system and the user file system was made to balance the load on the disk. If all important files were on one partition, it would get larger than is desirable. Performance might be impaired if all the action was directed at one logical area of the disk. By splitting the whole system into two, each file system maintains a reasonable amount of free space. We look at the major changes in /usr in a moment.

The last file is the kernel itself, /unix. All /unix really is, is a large a.out (compiled object file). The kernel is made by running `ld` on a bunch of libraries, which are loaded in turn into a huge run-time module, known as /unix. The machine bootstraps from the first 512 bytes of the root file system. The bootstrap program found there loads a larger boot program, sometimes called /boot. /boot loads and runs /unix.

Second Layer

The second layer of directories resides under /usr. As mentioned previously, /usr is used as a mount point for another file system. That means all the files that are under /usr are on a different partition of the main boot drive or are on a different disk altogether.

The first directory is adm, for administration. It holds the accounting files and the log file for `su`, as well as other administrative files.

The bin directory has executables that are less frequently used than those in the root-level bin directory (/bin). Between the two, almost every executable is accounted for. Other executables are scattered throughout the system, like /usr/lib /uucp/uucico and /usr/lib/ex3.7preserve.

Next is games. UNIX comes with an assortment of interesting games. Most are text-based, but a few graphic types of programs, like worm, worms, and rain, are provided.

The include directory contains all the header files. Header files are used in C programs to define structures and system equates useful for programming. A sub-directory here is sys, which contains all the system-related header files. A lot can be learned about UNIX from reading the header files.

The next directory is lib, which contains library files for all sorts of "stuff": printer files, vi support files, other languages, and uucp. The /usr/lib directory seems to be a catchall for whatever libraries, other than the compiler libraries, that the system contains.

The lost+found directory is here for the same reason as the one is provided at the root level. Each file system needs to have this file. Without it, fsck has no temporary place to put semitrashed files, so it throws them away forever.

The mail directory is where your system mail box is. When you run the mail command, messages are queued here. Under usr/mail, each file is named after a user. The user's mail is held in that file until he or she reads it.

The man directory is for the online manual pages. Not every system has this. Having instant access to man pages is a nice feature. However, these pages take up a lot of space, and access can take quite a lot of time on a heavily-loaded system.

The news directory is where all the news files are kept. The files are named according to the order in which they were entered into the directory. The command news(1) looks at the date of $HOME/.news_time file to tell which ones you have not read.

The preserve directory is for vi files. They are put here when you are in the vi or ex editor and the power to the machine is lost, or your login session is disconnected as in a hangup. When the system powers up, /tmp contains ex files. A utility called /usr/lib/ex3.7preserve is run from /etc/rc, which sees /tmp, converts it to a preserve file, and places it in /usr/preserve. When you login, you have mail that says you have a preserved editor file that you can recover. Next to not having the power go off in the first place, that's pretty user-friendly.

The pub directory does not contain much, usually just some information files, like an ASCII table and the Greek characters.

The spool directory is the main entry point for all spooled files in the system. In this directory are many subdirectories that hold specific types of spooled files. Some typical subdirectories are lp, uucp, and uucppublic. In the latest System V, more files are being put under /usr/spool, such as mail, cron, and at files.

The src directory is where the UNIX source code is kept if the system has it. Under this directory, many levels branch out: commands, libraries, kernel code, machine language code, and standalone utilities. Many times, source code for the local machine is kept under /usr/src also.

The sys directory has traditionally been where the files necessary for generating a new kernel are stored. These files are header files, the configuration file, the libraries, and a makefile that makes a new kernel from all these files.

The last directory is tmp. This is a secondary temporary holding area that is not used as much as /tmp. Sort, however, uses it.

The UNIX Life: Some Metaphors

UNIX is very much a life and world of its own. Its social structure mimics real life, with a government containing a ruler (root), a support staff (bin, cron, lp, sys), and the masses (/usr/*). The masses don't have access to the ruler's power except by pre-established means (/bin/su) or by becoming a criminal and circumventing the security measures. Like all societies, a large multiuser UNIX system has limitations on, and freedoms for, its users.

When logged into the system, the user "has a place in the world" ($HOME). This place is dependent on what came before (the parent directory, ..), and future places depend on what happens later ($HOME subordinate directories).

Work is segregated into organizations and hierarchies depending on its function in society (all users in /usr, all in-transit files in /usr/spool, all security functions in /etc). Look around your system to become familiar with your world. You can then choose either to participate in a part of that world or ignore it.

The movement of people is even paralleled in UNIX. Some areas (/tmp) are accessible to anyone, and some areas are heavily policed to keep most people out (/etc/passwd). Transportation services can move our belongings (transferring files through uucp networks). We can even take public transportation to different parts of the city (rlogin to other systems, BSD only).

Different paths through the UNIX world are available to us. These paths help form our destiny (disk partitions mounted elsewhere on the file tree). When a disk pack is mounted, it is available to us. When it is unmounted, we no longer have access to it.

When processes run, they proceed through different stages of their life. They are born (forked), grow up (become scheduled and placed in process table), and finally become productive workers in society (get to run state and execute).

All processes have a family tree. A child process always has a parent, and parent processes can spawn many children. Depending on the application, there can be grandparents and/or grandchildren. Processes die as easily as they are created. The one peculiar thing in the UNIX world is that children almost always die before their parents.

The government (kernel) enforces the parameters of the environment in what would be a rather totalitarian fashion if done in the real world. Only a certain number of workers are allowed in the workplace at one time (max # of slots in process table). Workers are limited in the number of children they can have (max # of processes per user). As workers accumulate material goods, they are limited to the amount of goods that can be put into a room of their houses (maximum file size or ulimit). Although no limit is fixed on the number of different files (rooms) of maximum size that can exist, the whole system has a limit (df showing free space), and one overconsuming person has an impact on everyone around him—a sort of ecology.

Just as the computer age has ushered in automatic electronic surveillance, so does UNIX keep tabs on all the users' activities. The accounting mechanisms are handled by the government (internal to the kernel) and always record the actions of each user. However, this is a free society to the extent that you may get a printout of your credit standing (using `acctcom` to print accounting records).

Although UNIX has negative aspects (as does our society), it also has some very positive features. The flexibility of the system and the richness of the tools gives us a very productive and elaborate work environment. Our productivity in this sense is limited mainly by our own imagination. When a job becomes too tiresome or tedious, we can always create tools to do the job for us. This is a free-enterprise environment where good ideas can lead to considerably increased productivity.

2

File Accessibility

Exploring the file tree
Combining powerful ideas
Finding files

    `tree`   visual display of a file tree
    `thead`   print the head of each file in a tree
    `tgrep`   search for strings in a file system tree
    `paths`   find the path to an executable, with special options

Listing file information

    `lc`   list file information in columns
    `ll`   list file information in long form
    `kind` list files of same kind
    `m`   easy access to `more`
    `mmm`   `nroff` processing with manuscript macros
    `pall` print all files in a tree

File Accessibility

Introduction

In Chapter 1, we presented a broad outline of the generic structure of a UNIX system and showed how its various parts interact. That is like introducing geography by showing a world globe and pointing out the continents and major bodies of water. This information, although a good foundation for your general knowledge, does not tell you the best way to drive from San Francisco to Los Angeles. A further level of detail is necessary, and that detail consists of names of communities, freeways, particular freeway exits, streets, and specific addresses.

A UNIX file system is like a continent that has many cities and, indeed, addresses within cities. Directories and various levels of subdirectories may be compared with the routes between places. Individual file names are like addresses. The sheer number of paths and destinations can be rather daunting, yet by its regularity and consistency, the UNIX file structure makes getting from place to place easy, once you understand a few principles.

As UNIX users, we all have learned how to use basic file information commands like `ls` with various options. We know how to move between directories and copy or move files. However, finding what we need to know about our files in all the mass of available detail isn't easy. What we need to do is create tools that use the tree structure of UNIX files to find what we are looking for, and, as appropriate, display information about files, print listings of file contents, and so on.

This chapter presents tools that make it easy to find and access files in the system. Files can be accessed in many different ways, so the techniques and styles vary from script to script. For example, sometimes we might want to find the names of *all* files in a given tree segment, whereas at other times we might be interested in only files of a particular kind, such as text files in general or C source files in particular.

Combining Powerful Ideas

Two concepts are common to nearly all useful file tools. The first is the idea of *recursive* lookup, which means that several UNIX commands (`find` is a good example) go through a complete file tree beginning at a specified starting point (or with the current default directory). If a subdirectory is encountered within a directory, that subdirectory's contents are examined. If a sub-subdirectory is found in the subdirectory's contents, the sub-subdirectory is examined, and so on, down to the lowest sub-sub-subdirectory. Thus the path to every file in the whole tree is traversed.

Standard UNIX commands provide only a limited number of basic functions that can operate recursively on a file tree. Our strategy in designing the tools in this chapter is to take advantage of this recursive lookup and extend it to many other functions.

The second key idea related to useful file tools is the capability of combining commands with pipes and controlling the flow of data with redirection. You have probably encountered these features in your own work with UNIX and used them effectively. What you may not realize is that by combining the recursive lookup offered by some standard commands with specific functions offered by other commands, we can create commands that automatically traverse vast file trees and obtain information. (In the next chapter, we go beyond displaying and listing to manipulate the files so that we can copy, remove, and back them up as needed.)

Finally, as you read through this and following chapters, observe how we often use our newly created tools as components of other tools.

For convenience, we group the tools into two sections: finding files and listing file information. It makes sense to present them in this order because you have to find files before you can look at or manipulate their contents.

Finding Files

This section concentrates on finding files wherever they are located throughout the file system tree, displaying selected information, and looking for strings within the files.

The first program, `tree`, traverses a file tree and prints all the file names in a visual tree format. It descends recursively into each subdirectory and finds all its files, thereby providing a global view of file areas and their nesting depth.

Another tool is `thead`. `Thead` prints the first few lines of text files that are in a file tree segment. Looking at the "head" or first few lines of a file can give you enough information to identify the contents of the file. A directory can be specified explicitly when invoking `thead`, or a list of pathnames can be piped into `thead`. This makes `thead` a filter, which is a special kind of UNIX command that we discuss later.

The next tool is `tgrep`. As the name suggests, it is another tree-related command that uses the `grep` utility. `Tgrep` searches for a string in every file that resides in a file tree segment: It also is a filter, so pathnames can be piped into it.

For our last project in this section, we turn to the use of directory paths as a means of navigating the file system. First, we describe the basic algorithm for a utility that checks each file in a list of file names to see whether that file is in any directory in the specified search path. We then build `paths`, a utility that adds useful options to the basic searching strategy.

Listing File Information

This section contains tools involved in the displaying of file names and the contents of files. These kinds of tools are useful because they can reduce the amount of typing required as well as bundling more functionality into a single command.

The first two scripts are front-end processors to the `ls` command. `Lc` lists file information in a column format, and `ll` lists files in a long format. Hardcoded in these scripts are extra options for `ls` to make the printouts more informative. Because the `ls` command is used so often, packaging the most used keystrokes into scripts makes sense. Packaging reduces the amount of typing required and makes the commands easier to use by eliminating the need to remember detailed syntax.

The third tool is `kind`. `Kind` is another preprocessor type script, using the UNIX `file` command. `File` reads the specified file, then reports whether it is text, archive, or executable. Because the `file` command's printouts don't select files of a specific kind, we create a utility to do this. `Kind` manipulates `file`'s printout. `Kind` displays only the names of files of the specified kind.

Another script is `m`, which makes it easier to use the standard UNIX `more` command by reducing the amount of typing required and making the interface much easier to use. The script does this without sacrificing flexibility: Just as you can use `more` on a file or pipe data to `more`, so also can you `m` a file and pipe data to `m`.

The next script, `mmm`, is a one-liner, pregenerated command line for the UNIX `nroff` command. There are many ways to call `nroff` and lots of different options possible. If you don't use `nroff` often, you can become frustrated trying to remember the specific options you need. Remembering is no longer a problem when you have `mmm`: Determine what options you normally use, and put them in a script. You then have access to your custom `nroff` at the touch of three keystrokes.

The last utility is `pall`. `Pall` traverses a file tree looking for specific types of files, and prepares these files for the line printer. The UNIX `pr` command is used to page all the files together and provide headers. This command submits one large file to the line printer and is most useful when you have multiple directories of text files or source program files.

Having reflected on our strategy and the direction it is going to take us, let's start looking at the tools.

Name: `tree`

tree   Prints a visual display of a file tree

Function

Finds all files in a file tree and prints the names in a visual format showing the hierarchical tree structure.

Synopsis

tree [dir]

27

Sample Call

$ tree $HOME

Print a visual tree of my entire home directory

Code for tree

```
1    :
2    # @(#) tree v1.0   Visual display of a file tree   Author: Russ Sage
3
4    if [ "$#" -gt 1 ]
5      then  echo "tree: wrong arg count" >&2
6            echo "usage: tree [dir]"      >&2
7            exit 2
8    fi
9    if [ "$#" -eq 1 ]
10     then  if [ ! -d $1 ]
11             then  echo "$0: $1 not a directory" >&2
12                   echo "usage: tree [dir]"       >&2
13                   exit 2
14           fi
15   fi
16
17   find ${1:-.} -print | sort | sed -e "1p" -e "1d"          \
18                                    -e "s¦[^/]*/¦     /¦g"  \
19                                    -e "s¦^ */¦/¦"            \
20                                    -e "s¦/\([^/]*\)$¦\1¦"
```

Description

Why do we need tree?

As we noted, the entire UNIX system is designed around a file system that resembles a tree. The tree that we work with in UNIX is upside down: The root is at the top, and the branches and leaves grow downward. The physical structure of real trees and that of the UNIX file system are very similar: one root (starting point) and a trunk. How deep or how long a branch can get away from the trunk is not limited by anything other than physical limitations. Similarly, the number of leaves that a specific branch may contain is virtually unrestricted.

Much of UNIX is designed to accommodate the tree structure. Some commands traverse the tree and report on its components, but their outputs usually are not in the most human-readable form, which is where scripts have the potential to become very powerful tools. Taking the raw, unfriendly output and massaging it into nice, informative output is so easy.

Tree is a combination of UNIX commands that show the logical file structure in a visual form. This command is useful for getting the global picture of files, their place in the hierarchy, and the way they are nested in directories and subdirectories.

What does tree *do?*

The tree command is a postprocessor for the UNIX find command. Find looks through a file tree segment and prints out the pathnames of all files that fit the specified criteria. Tree uses the UNIX sed facility to turn the output of find into a visual printout.

The input to tree is a directory name, which can be any form of absolute pathname, such as /usr/spool/uucp, or a relative pathname, such as ../../bin. If no directory name is specified, the default is ., which is the current directory.

The directory name is the beginning (or root) of the tree that is displayed. All files subordinate to this directory are displayed in an indented form to represent the depth of the tree. Between successive layers, a slash (/) character is printed to show the file nesting that is taking place.

Let's look at an example directory structure. The root is /tmp, with two directories, a and b. Under a is subdirectory aa, which contains file1, and under b is subdirectory bb, which contains file2. The find command generates a printout like this:

```
# find /tmp -print

/tmp
/tmp/a
/tmp/a/aa
/tmp/a/aa/file1
/tmp/b
/tmp/b/bb
/tmp/b/bb/file2
```

From this listing, we can see that the files a and aa are directories and file1 is at the bottom of the file tree. Compare this output with the output the tree command creates using sed.

```
# tree /tmp

/tmp
/       a
/       /       aa
/       /       /       file1
/       b
/       /       bb
/       /       /       file2
```

The root directory of this listing is the /tmp directory. The slash characters are only printed where the tree is expanded to a deeper level. The first level is /tmp. Under this level are the files a and b, then their respective subdirectories aa and bb.

From this one picture, we deduce that two files are in the first level directory (and these files are actually directories) and that two files are in subordinate directories. Note that we can tell aa and bb are actually directories only because file1 and file2 are present.

Compare this format with the output of the "raw" `find` command. The output of `tree` eliminates the distracting repetition of path elements in each entry. This makes the *significant* information immediately apparent. That's what we mean by making the UNIX interface more human readable.

Examples

1. `$ tree`

Use the default directory (current directory, or $ tree .) to start the file tree.

2. `$ tree /`

Print a tree listing for *every* file on the whole system. `Find` starts at the root of the file tree and generates a list of every file in the system.

3. `$ tree $HOME/..`

Show the tree format for all other users on the system (assuming that all the user directories reside in the same directory, such as /usr/*).

Explanation

Line 1 has just a colon (:), the "null command." The reason is that all the scripts in this book are designed to be run under the Bourne shell. Our version-identifying comment in line 2 starts with a pound (#) sign. The C shell looks for a # as the first character in a script. If it finds #, it tries to execute the script. Otherwise, the C shell passes the script to the Bourne shell. Therefore, we don't want the first line to start with a #. We could have left the first line blank, but blank lines are invisible and easy to delete accidentally. As appropriate, we use blank lines elsewhere for setting off significant portions of the code.

Line 2 is the version-identifying string. The character string @(#) is a special sequence in a comment line that is recognized as the "what" string. The UNIX `what` command reads a file and prints the message that follows the "what" string. To identify the version of this script, type

```
# what tree
```

and the message printed is

```
tree:
        tree  v1.0   Visual display of a file tree   Author: Russ Sage
```

Lines 4-7 check to see whether too many arguments were passed on the command line. This is done by examining the $# variable, which is the count of the number of positional parameters on the command line. If more than one parameter is counted, the appropriate error message is printed to standard error and the program exits with a bad value status.

Note that the `echo` command normally prints to stdout. We can redirect stdout to another file descriptor by specifying which descriptor to print to. In this case, we are going to print to the standard error. The syntax translates to "echo this string and redirect it to the file descriptor (&) of standard error (2)." Printing error messages to standard error gives the script a consistent behavior regardless of the environment in which it is run.

Note also that exit status codes in the shell are opposite to those used in C programming. In C, a true value is 1, a false value is non-1. In shell programming, a good exit status (true) is 0, and a bad exit status (false) is non-0.

You might wonder why we bother to return the false exit status if the script is simply going to print an error message and die. The reason is that all UNIX tools should be designed to communicate with other commands and processes in which they may be embedded. Another command may need to call `tree` and verify that it ran correctly. Part of good software tool design is anticipating and allowing for the many uses to which a tool may be put.

Lines 9-15 verify that any parameters passed on the command line are truly directories, as specified in our syntax. Remember that only one directory can be placed on the command line. If we are using only one parameter and that parameter is not a directory, we print an error message and leave. The test statements thus ensure that either no parameter is used or the one parameter used is a valid directory.

We get to the heart of the `tree` command in lines 17-20. The driving force is the UNIX `find` command. The directory being searched is determined when the command is run. The syntax ${1:-.} is a form of parameter substitution. This syntax says that if $1 (which is the first positional parameter) is set (that is, an argument was passed on the command line and it was not null), use its value. Otherwise use the directory . (the current directory). This type of substitution gives us the capability of defaulting to a specific directory when no file is passed on the command line, which is often useful behavior for a file tool.

The `find` statement prints out every pathname it encounters. No qualifying options are used to select subsets of files, so every name is printed. Then the pathnames produced by `find` are sorted for easier reading. Sorting takes a little more time to execute, but the readability of the printout makes the time well spent.

Next, the sorted pathnames are piped to the UNIX `sed` command. `Sed` is the "stream editor," a very versatile facility that can be used to identify and act on a variety of patterns in text. The -e options are the editing phrases applied to the incoming data. The first statement simply tells `sed` to print the first line, then delete line 1. This is done to print the line representing the root of the tree being examined. This line requires no further modification because it doesn't have any additional path elements that need to be transformed into slashes to show indentation. Then `sed` is told to delete this line because it is no longer needed for processing.

The second editing phrase is a substitute command. It changes every nonslash

(↑/) character (up to the first /) to a sequence of blanks and then one / character. This gets rid of the intermediate directories in the front of the path list. The *g* at the end of the phrase means to do this globally (or all occurrences on the line). Thus, the line now consists of the initial path element and one or more sequences of spaces followed by slashes. The backslash (\) character at the end of the sed edit phrases are continuation characters that tell sed to continue to the next line in the current batch of editing phrases.

The third editing phrase (line 19) is also a substitution command and changes all nonblanks (up to a /) into "no characters" and one /. This statement removes the blanks from the previous edit and slides the character to the leftmost position. This creates the nesting indication that we see in the preceding example printout.

The last editing phrase (on line 20) changes as / and all nonslash characters (to the end of the line) to just the nonslash characters. Notice that this removes the rightmost / from the find listing. What remains is the subordinate file name extended to the right.

Note the sed syntax \1, which is a tag that refers to the first (in this case, only) regular expression in parentheses that precedes it. In this case, it tells sed to pass through only the characters matched by the regular expression, which are the characters other than /.

Name: thead

thead   Prints the head of files in a tree

Function

Traverses file trees and prints the first few lines of each file. If no directory is specified, thead acts as a filter.

Synopsis

thead [dir ...]

Sample Call

$ find $HOME/src -name "*.c" -print ¦ sort ¦ thead

Prints the head of all my C source files

Code for thead

```
1   :
2   # @(#) thead v1.0   Prints head of files in tree   Author: Russ Sage
3
4   if [ "'echo $1¦cut -c1'" = "-" ]
5     then  echo "$0: arg error"
6           echo "usage: $0 [dir ...]"
7           exit 1
8   fi
9
```

```
10   case $# in
11   0)   while read FILE
12        do
13                if file $FILE | fgrep text >/dev/null 2>&1
14                  then  echo "\n:::::::::::::::::::::::"
15                        echo " $FILE"
16                        echo ":::::::::::::::::::::::"
17                        head -15 $FILE
18                fi
19        done;;
20   *)   for NAME in $*
21        do
22                find $NAME -type f -print | sort | while read FILE
23                do
24                        if file $FILE | fgrep text >/dev/null 2>&1
25                          then echo "\n:::::::::::::::::::::::"
26                                echo "$FILE"
27                                echo ":::::::::::::::::::::::"
28                                head -15 $FILE
29                        fi
30                done
31        done;;
32   esac
```

Environment Variables

FILE	Holds the name of each file
NAME	Directory name from the command line

Description

Why do we need thead?

As explained earlier in this chapter, the hierarchical file system is very much a part of UNIX. However, only a few commands in UNIX deal directly with recursive file lookups. The only way to make the system grow to accommodate our needs is to create new recursive file-management utilities. In the case at hand, we combine our tree-searching strategy with the UNIX head command to make easy the identification of the contents of all files in a specified tree segment.

Sometimes we might want to see files in more than one directory. Large software development projects typically create files in multiple hierarchical directories. Thead can accommodate paths from all over the system and output the "heads" in a continuous stream.

What does thead do?

Thead is a preprocessor to the UNIX head command. Head is very primitive in its scope, but by adding control structures and logic, we can create a very useful tool not available in the standard UNIX environment.

For example, we might want to look at the head of all text files in our home directory. If we have many subdirectories, we need to go to them and look at their files, too. We can do this with the command:

```
$ thead $HOME
```

If we want to look at just the C source files (*.c) however, this syntax doesn't work. It does not have the wildcard flexibility. We need a way to specify (or qualify) the files in $HOME before we look at them. Because thead can accept pathnames, we can use a command like this:

```
$ find $HOME -name "*.c" -print | sort | thead
```

The UNIX find command generates a list of .c files, which is sorted and fed to thead one at a time from the pipe.

You can see that it is useful for a script to be able to receive its input either from the command line arguments, as in the first example, or through a pipe, as in the example just shown. Being able to use a pipe enables you to apply whatever other UNIX commands may be appropriate to selecting the data you want your script to operate on. A command with this dual-input capability is called a *filter*. Among the standard UNIX commands you find quite a few filters, such as wc, awk, and sort.

These two ways of supplying input to programs make the interface to scripts very flexible. We can tailor the software to our needs instead of tailoring our needs to the software.

The arguments to thead are directories. There are no hyphen (-) options, just directory or pathname arguments. Thead knows which way the command is being used through the syntax. If the command line has a file name, thead loops through all the positional parameters. If the command line has no file names, thead reads the stdin and stops when an EOF is encountered. (This would be the case when thead is receiving input from a pipe.)

For every file that thead processes, a check is made to verify that the file is text only. Doing a head command on an executable prints weird characters to the screen and sometimes may cause the head command to trigger a core dump.

Examples

1. `$ thead /etc`

Print data from each text file in the /etc directory. A very useful command because most of /etc is executables. It is handy to be able to isolate text files quickly.

2. `$ thead /usr/include`

Scans through all the include files (*.h), even down in the sys subdirectory.

3. `$ find $HOME -ctime 0 -print | thead`

This sequence finds all the files in your home directory that have been changed in the last 24 hours. Each file name is checked to see whether it is text and printed if it is.

Explanation

Lines 4-8 perform the error checking. Because `thead` does not have any options, any positional parameters that begin with a hyphen (-) are invalid. If the first character of the first positional parameter is a -, the "argument error" message is printed with the usage statement and `thead` exits.

Some shell programming techniques used here are frequently encountered in this book, so stop a moment and review them.

Let's analyze line 4, working from the inside out. The processing going on inside is that the `echo` command is outputting the contents of $1 (the current command-line parameter), and this is being piped to the `cut` command. `Cut` is used to extract specific characters or groups of characters from a string. In this case, the option -c1 is used to get only the first character.

A `cut` *for BSD*

The `cut` command isn't available in BSD, but the following script cuts out the first nonblank field in the current argument.

Assume we are using a command to generate a series of strings. (In this case it is the `who` command):

```
for NAME in 'who | sed "s/^\([^ ]*\).*/\1/"'
do
done
```

For each line (argument) encountered, `sed` is told to substitute the second string for the first string. The first string is the line to cut up. We look from the beginning of the line (^) for a nonblank ([^]) followed by any number of nonblanks (*). This sequence is broken by reaching a blank. The nonblank sequence is bounded by \(and \), which is referred to later as \1. The .* means that after a blank is found, match each character until the end of the line. We are really only after what is in the \(\) pair. By grouping the first set of nonblanks, we have in effect done a "cut -f1".

At this point we come to the grave accents (') surrounding the expression. These take the output resulting from all the commands they enclose and provide it to the next larger structure in our nested expressions. This next bracketing is indicated by quotes. The quotes turn the character into a string so that it can be compared to "-". The next layer is the brackets indicating the condition for an if statement. This results in a zero (true) or nonzero (false) condition being generated, and that controls whether the *then* part of the if-then statement is executed.

We aren't going to have to analyze many lines of code in this much detail, but we wanted to show you how to read an expression or a whole line of code so that it makes sense.

The rest of the script is one huge case statement. The argument used for branching is the number of positional parameters on the command line. In lines 11-19, a while loop is activated when no positional parameters are used. Notice that the while loop does a read statement but does not specify where its input is to be taken from. This is because the default input is stdin. For each file name that is read through stdin, the UNIX `file` command is run. The output of `file` is piped to `fgrep` (rather than `grep`, which increases speed) to see whether the file is a text file.

The actual output from `fgrep` is redirected to the null device (an infinite bit bucket) because we don't need it.

What we are interested in is the return status of the whole pipeline execution. If the `file` command and the `fgrep` command are successful, the return status is zero. This is the true value, so the *then* portion of the loop (lines 14-17) is executed. If the file does not exist or is not a text file, the return status is nonzero and the if statement terminates. This takes us to the bottom of the loop so that the next iteration of the while loop occurs and we look for the next argument from stdin.

Now let's look at the then processing (lines 14-17). For each file that is a text file, a line of colons (:) is printed around the file name, and the UNIX `head` command prints the first 15 lines. This scenario continues until stdin has no more data.

Look at the other alternative covered by the case statement. This handles the situation where there are some positional parameters (indicated by the * in the case statement). A for loop runs through each parameter (line 20). The asterisk (*) in the case statement says "match any other value that hasn't been matched." It's the catchall option. The for loop uses the argument $* for its input. This means the value of all positional parameters, which is really the whole command line, excluding the name of the utility.

`Find` is used to search for all regular files in the directory. "Regular" files does not mean "text files only," so we check for these later. The output of `find` is piped into the `sort` command to make it more readable. The sorted list is piped into a while loop that puts the file name into the variable FILE (line 27). The file is verified as text, then printed with the `head` command.

If we compare lines 13-18 and lines 24-29, we see that they are the same code. In most programming languages, this would indicate that we should make the lines into a procedure and call it when we need it. The shell programming language, although quite powerful, doesn't have a good way to implement procedures. The latest System V shell has functions which do solve these problems.

Notice that the inner while loop iterates on each file that exists in a specific directory, and the outer for loop goes from directory to directory.

Modifications

To increase flexibility, a nice feature would be to have more options that you could pass directly to the `find` command within `thead`. Useful arguments would be -name to isolate patterns of file names, or -ctime to pick up time-related changes.

Another nice feature would be to add option parsing (based on -), then a -n option to specify that n lines should be printed from the `head` command.

Explorations

What is the difference between the following two statements?

```
$ find $HOME -name "*.c" -print | thead
```

and

```
$ find $HOME -name "*.c" -exec head {} \;
```

They look very similar and they are. They process the same files and print the
same data from each file. The biggest difference is that the line which uses thead
prints a nice banner around the file name whereas the straight find command
prints a continuous stream of text so that which file you are looking at is very
difficult to determine.

Name: tgrep

tgrep   Search for strings in a tree of files

Function

Traverses a file tree and looks for a specific string in each file. If no directory is
specified, tgrep acts as a filter.

Synopsis

tgrep [-c¦-h] string [file ...]

Sample Call

tgrep "profanity" /

Find profanity anywhere in the system (root is on the warpath again!)

Code for tgrep

```
1    :
2    # @(#) tgrep v1.0   Search for strings in tree   Author: Russ Sage
3
4    OPT=""
5
6    for ARG in $@
7    do
8            if [ "`echo $ARG|cut -c1`" = "-" ]
9              then  case $ARG in
10                    -c)  OPT="-name \"*.c\""
11                         shift;;
12                    -h)  OPT="-name \"*.h\""
13                         shift;;
14                    *)   echo "$0: incorrect argument"            >&2
15                         echo "usage: $0 [-c¦-h] string [file ...]" >&2
16                         exit 1;;
17                    esac
18            fi
19    done
20
```

37

```
21   case $# in
22   0)   echo "$0: argument error"                    >&2
23        echo "usage: $0 [-c|-h] string [dir ...]" >&2
24        exit 2
25        ;;
26   1)   while read FILE
27        do
28                grep -y "$1" $FILE /dev/null
29        done
30        ;;
31   *)   STRING=$1; shift
32        eval find "$@" -type f $OPT -print | sort | while read FILE
33        do
34                grep -y "$STRING" $FILE /dev/null
35        done
36        ;;
37   esac
```

Environment Variables

FILE	Holds each file name
OPT	Holds special options for find
STRING	Temp variable to hold the search string

Description

Why do we need `tgrep`?

As can be seen from the two previous utilities, recursive file lookup is very useful. It saves time by avoiding a manual search of files, and it creates tools that can be used in larger utilities. The more tools that we build, the more we have to build with. The only problem is that you have to be aware of dependencies (which utilities or tools need or affect which others).

Another area where UNIX does not have a "native" recursive command is string processing. The `grep` family is great, but it only works on fixed path file names. What we need is a preprocessor for the `grep` command. Then, we can make queries about all the files in the entire system or any subset of our choice. Trying to do this by hand means a lot of typing and possible mistakes in syntax. You also have to remember the exact way you constructed your command line the next time you want to do the same task. Why do the dirty work? That's what the computer is for.

By creating a script to automate the file tree traversal, we are free to spend our energies on greater things, instead of getting tied up in matters of specific syntax. Once we've created enough powerful file access tools, we can spend our time writing programs that manipulate the file data to solve problems.

What does `tgrep` do?

The main purpose of `tgrep` is to provide a more versatile and easy-to-use `grep` facility. The syntax is exactly the same as greps, except for the type of file that is allowed. In the UNIX `grep` command, the file argument can be just about any file, but text files make the most sense. In tgrep, text files could be used but directories make the most sense because we are looking for file names. The find command wouldn't work very well trying to squeeze many file names out of a text file. Multiple directories can be on the command line because they all are used as starting points for a find statement.

By default, tgrep finds all regular files. This routine includes no checking for text files because we are not trying to print everything to the screen. Therefore, we search for strings in all types of files, from archive to executable.

If you want to qualify file names, use the two options -c and -h. The -c option forces the UNIX find command to look for file names of the form *.c. Likewise, -h stands for *.h files. These options might be useful for C program management, which we address in more detail in Chapter 4. These options aren't all that important, but they do show how easy it is to add options to the script.

If any options other than the ones provided for are used, an error message is printed and the script stops. Like thead, tgrep is a filter.

Examples

1. `$ tgrep unix $HOME`

Look for any occurrence of the word unix in all the files of my home directory.

2. `$ tgrep -c "^sleep()$" $HOME/src`

Look for the expression (beginning of line, string, end of line) in all of the C source files in my source directory (-c option).

3. `# find /usr/src -name "*.c" -print ¦ tgrep "ioctl"`

Look for any calls to ioctl in C source code files under /usr/src. (Note that I'm root as shown by the fact that I'm looking in a restricted part of the system, the source distribution, and that the prompt is "#".)

4. `$ tgrep "¦ more" 'find . -type f -print'`

Look for the vertical bar (¦) character followed by the word *more* in the list of files generated from the find statement. Find prints all file names from the current directory and all subdirectories that are regular files.

5. `$ tgrep trap /bin /usr/bin /etc`

Look for the trap command in all of the shell scripts that reside in the three directories.

Explanation

Line 4 initializes the variable OPT, which holds optional commands for the find statement, to a null string.

Lines 6-18 perform the error checking. The first character of each positional parameter is checked against a -. If the test is successful, the argument is checked for correctness. The possible options are -c and -h. Anything else triggers the error message and exits the program. Notice the valid options are shifted off the command line, which is done so that the expression $@ can be used later to access only the string and the path arguments. The $@ expression is another form of $* in that it expands to all the positional parameters. However, in following text, we see one big difference.

Another trick is involved in the assignments to the OPT variable, such as in line 10. To the variable, we need to assign a value that includes a pair of quote marks because the quotes need to be part of the string that eventually is used with find. However, the second quote encountered normally *terminates* an assignment statement, which we don't want to happen in this case. The solution is to use the \ character, which removes any special meaning from the character following it. In this case the special meaning would be to end the assignment string.

Thus, the quote before the asterisk in line 10 is assigned as part of the value of OPT instead of terminating the assignment. The next quote mark encountered also has to be kept in the value to terminate the string being stored there, so it is quoted with a \, too. The last quote in the line isn't quoted with a \. This quote follows its normal shell function and terminates the assignment statement.

You need to experiment with quoting in order to understand it. When things don't seem to be running right and everything looks great, check for quoting errors.

The rest of the script is a case statement (lines 21-37), based on the number of arguments on the command line. If there are no arguments, an error message is printed, and we quit. We can't do any grepping if we don't at least have a string to look for.

If only one argument is included, it should be the string to search for. Also, it means that there are no files on the command line, so we read from stdin, acting as a filter. A while loop (lines 26-29) starts reading from stdin for each file we grep for the string. The -y option to grep is for case insensitivity. Using this option gives us the best odds of hitting the string that we are looking for.

Another interesting feature of this loop is the grep commands in lines 28 and 34. Not only are we looking for the string in the file, but we look for it in /dev/null. Seem kind of strange? It is. The problem is in the grep command itself. Grep knows when more than one file is on its command line. If there is more than one, the file name is printed before the string that is found. If only one file is on the command line, the file name is not printed because it is assumed the user would remember what it is. This creates a problem in scripts where you have lots of files but process them one at a time. We are processing them one at a time because if we used file name metacharacter expansions, there are likely to be too many file names to fit on one command line to grep. So instead of coming up with some elaborate scheme to divide up the arguments, we avoid it by looping on the files one by one. Because we are really looking at lots of strings, we want to see the file names where things are found.

By putting /dev/null on the grep command line, grep always prints the file name before the string for our loop because it now has two file names in its arguments. Of course, nothing is found in /dev/null because by definition, it is empty.

The last pattern in the case statement (line 31-36) is the catchall. This matches any number of positional parameters over one, which allows us to have a variable number of directories on the command line.

Even though we can put multiple directories on the command line, the first argument is still the string. There is no easy way to say "from the second parameter on", so we save the string and shift it away. Now we can access the rest of the command line as $@.

Let's look at what happens when we reference $OPT to get our options for find. For example, suppose we call tgrep with the -c option. When we assign the value of OPT, we put the c string "*.c" inside double quotes because we didn't want the shell to expand the string (that is, replace it with the names of all files matching the pattern) at that time. Now, as $OPT is referenced in the find command, the value of OPT is *.c, which means find a file literally named *.c. To disable the literal interpretation, we have to use the eval command. Before the find command executes, eval forces the shell to reparse the command with respect to variable expansion. This pass makes the "*.c" turn into *.c, which lets the file-name generation take place so that all the files are searched.

By stating $@ in the find command, we can search for all the directories at once. Thus, we only need to call find once, which conserves CPU usage. One interesting problem that arose when developing this script was that $* did not work. An error kept arising from the find command. Even running the shell in -x (execution flag on) mode did not reveal the problem. Changing the syntax seemed to fix it right up. It turns out that the reason is that $* expands to "$1 $2 ...", whereas $@ expands to "$1" "$2" (that is, separate arguments). What happened was that $* was handing off multiple directory names to the find command as one string. Find couldn't locate a file of that form, so it died. When $@ was used instead, the find command received multiple independent strings. This sat well with find and everything worked. The small things are the ones that always take time to learn!

Explorations

What is the difference between these two statements:

```
grep "$1" 'find "$2" -print'
```

and

```
find "$2" -print | while read F
do
        grep "$1" $F
done
```

They look pretty similar, but are different in one major way. The first statement is one call to grep. The arguments are many file names supplied by the find command. If find generates too many file names, the whole command dies. No warning is issued when too many file names are generated, but too many file names is fatal. So we must treat this syntax as unreliable for general use.

The second statement is a loop. It runs slower and calls grep many times, which chews up CPU time. But the good thing about it is that the loop reads from a pipe, which has virtually no limit to the amount it can hold. Our code never dies unexpectedly.

Name: paths

paths   File path locator with special options

Function

Prints the directory location of a file, a long listing of the file, or looks for setuid bit files in directories on the specified path.

Synopsis

paths [-l] [-s] file [file ...]

Sample Call

$ paths -l ed ex vi

   Print a long listing of the editors ed, ex, and vi

Code for paths

```
1    :
2    # @(#) paths v1.0    Path locator with special options    Author: Russ Sage
3
4    FORMAT="path"
5
6    for ARG in $@
7    do
8            if [ "`echo $ARG | cut -c1`" = "-" ]
9              then  case $ARG in
10                    -l)  FORMAT="ls"
11                         shift;;
12                    -s)  FORMAT="set"
13                         set "1";;
14                    *)   echo "$0: arg error"                        >&2
15                         echo "usage: $0 [-l] [-s] file [file ...]" >&2
16                         exit 1;;
17                   esac
18           fi
19   done
20
21   IFS="${IFS}:"
22
23   for FILE in $@
24   do
25           for DIR in $PATH
26           do
27                   case $FORMAT in
28                   path)  if [ -f $DIR/$FILE ]
```

```
29                      then   echo $DIR/$FILE
30                      fi;;
31              ls)     if [ -f $DIR/$FILE ]
32                      then  ls -l $DIR/$FILE
33                      fi;;
34              set)    echo "\n::::::::::::::::::::"
35                      echo "$DIR"
36                      echo "::::::::::::::::::::"
37                      ls -al $DIR | grep "^[^ ]*s[^ ]*";;
38              esac
39          done
40   done
```

Environment Variables

ARG	Holds each command line argument
DIR	The directory element in PATH
FILE	Holds each file from the command line
FORMAT	The type of output desired
IFS	Shell environment variable, interfield separator
PATH	Shell environment variable, paths of the executable directories

Description

Why do we need paths?

In our shell environment, a variable called PATH contains directory names separated by a colon (:) delimiter. Every time you type a command at the shell prompt, the shell starts with the first directory in PATH and sees whether the command you typed resides in that directory. If it does, the command is executed. If it doesn't, the shell goes to the next directory in PATH and so on until all directories are checked. If the command still is not found, you get the following error message:

```
$ whatchamacallit
sh: whatchamacallit: not found
```

This command lookup is automatic, but the system does not tell us *where* the command is located. We need a utility that searches and displays the path to a specific file. Once you have such a utility, you can use many short cuts and play lots of tricks. You can combine a command like this with other commands to create more powerful actions. Other UNIX commands you can combine with path are more, ls, file, and cd. You will probably discover others as you experiment.

A command something like what we're looking for resides someplace in the System V world. For example, the AT&T command is where. On Berkeley UNIX, the command is which (a csh script) or whereis (an executable). Whereis gives additional information, such as the location of source files (in /usr/src). Once you see how we create our own path-searching command, you can modify it to provide features found in some of the other commands and tailor things to your needs.

Before we get too fancy, let's take a quick look at a barebones `path` command. The entire program looks like this:

```
IFS="${IFS}:"
for FILE in $@
do
        for DIR in $PATH
        do
            if [ -f $DIR/$FILE ]
               then  echo $DIR/$FILE
            fi
        done
done
```

The overall idea is very simple. We first append the colon (:) to the field separator. We need to keep the default values (blank, tab, newline) so that we still can process the command line with spaces as delimiters. The : enables us to parse out each separate path in the PATH variable.

The whole program is two for loops. The outer loop runs through the file names passed on the command line. The inner loop iterates on the directories in the PATH variable. For each file, every directory is checked to see whether that directory contains a file by that name. The full pathname is a combination of the prefix directory and the file name (referred to as the dirname and basename, respectively). The shell's built-in test command is used to determine whether a file exists in a certain directory.

If your PATH variable looks like this

```
PATH=.:/bin:/usr/bin:/etc/:$HOME/bin
```

the inner loop would go for five iterations: ., /bin, /usr/bin, /etc, and finally $HOME/bin, in that order. If the call was "path ll" to look for a utility that we create later in this chapter, the output might look like this

```
/usr/bin/ll
/usr/russ/bin/ll
```

indicating that the ll command was found in two places in your set of search paths.

What does `paths` do?
Now that we know how the barebones path works, we can appreciate the added features of the special path or `paths` command. `Paths` has three basic functions.

It can perform like the barebones `path` we just looked at and give the pathname to executables. It can do a long listing of the path file. It also can list all setuid bit files that are in your path directories. (See Chapter 8 for more discussion on setuid bits.)

The syntax varies a little bit with the different options. To use the path format or the ls format, the command line syntax is

```
paths [-l] file [file ...]
```

as in the commands "paths ls who date" or "paths -l ll". The syntax that looks for setuid files has no file names on the command line. The whole command is like this:

```
paths -s
```

The setuid format and the path -l formats are mutually exclusive. This is because the assumption is that you want the computer to tell you what and where the files are rather than you guessing at the file names.

If any other options are included on the command line, an error message is printed to stdout and the script exits. The options set up the format flag to one of the three formats. All further output from the script is driven by the output format selected.

Examples

```
1.  $ paths ls more who paths
    /bin/ls
    /usr/bin/more
    /bin/who
    /usr/russ/bin/paths
```

Find the path to the commands `ls`, `more`, `who`, and `paths`. The output shows absolute pathnames. Notice a newline is printed at the end of each file name to create a file-per-line printout.

```
2.  $ more `paths gettydefs termcap paths`
```

If you have /etc in your PATH, this example works. If you don't, the first two files won't be found. The `paths` command is run first and its output is put in its place on the `more` command line. When `more` runs, it doesn't know that its arguments came from another command. After the subexecution, the more command becomes

```
    more /etc/gettydefs /etc/termcap /usr/russ/bin/paths
```

with full pathnames to each file. This shows how you can set up `paths` to do all the work of finding and showing you the files you want to see.

```
3.  $ ll `paths ll`
```

This lists in long format each file named `ll` that path finds. (We introduce our version of an `ll` command a little later in the chapter.) As before, the path information is generated first and placed in the command line, then the `ll` command is run.

4. `$ m 'paths paths'`

This generates the pathname to this script and passes it to the m script, which uses more to print it. (We show you this script later, too.)

Explanation

In line 4, FORMAT is initialized for the path type of lookup. This makes the default action exactly like the barebones `path` we discussed previously.

In lines 6-19, all the arguments on the command line are checked for validity. The criterion for an argument to be an option is a hyphen as the first character. Note that this does not allow the use of the syntax "-xyz". It forces you into the syntax of "-x -y -z". Although this point may seem trivial, it is important. A trade-off must always be made between developing a script quickly, and accepting the disadvantage of a rigid syntax, versus allowing a flexible format at the expense of additional coding and testing and slower execution speed. Which you choose to do depends on your priorities, how many people use your tool, and how critical execution speed is. Of course, if speed is critical, you probably want to use C anyway. We leave the handling of concatenated options as an exercise for the reader.

The for loop runs through every positional parameter. If the first character of that argument is a "-", it is checked against the legal option list by the case statement in lines 9-17. The "-l" option alters the format variable, then is shifted out of the picture. This is done to free up that position so that the end result is just file names on the command line.

The "-s" option also alters the format variable. Instead of shifting out, however, it destroys the current command line and replaces it with the character "1". This makes the for loop go through only one iteration because only one parameter is on the command line. By manipulating the command line like this, we don't need a different loop: we can use the same loop as the barebones path with no modifications. Because the s option expects no file names, we don't want to look at the command line any further.

If an option is used that is not a l or an s, that option is matched by the asterisk (∗), and an error message is printed to standard error. The script then exits.

We could have simply checked the first command line parameter to see whether it is an option, and if so, set it. Because only one option can be used at a time, we could assume the rest of the stuff on the command line was file names. The loop, however, allows for easy addition of other options that could be run in addition to the single one. It's a matter of preference and doesn't affect performance that much.

In line 21, we add the colon (:) character to the other IFS characters. We need to append the colon, not make IFS a colon only. If we did the latter, it would mess up the parsing of file names on the command line.

The major loop is listed on lines 23-40. This is the double for loop driver. The outer loop runs through each file on the command line, whereas the inner loop runs through each directory in your PATH variable. Notice that the outer loop is the file names, not the directory entries. If we switched the two, the printout would have file names out of order because it would search through directories first.

Therefore, for each file and directory name, the action is dependent on the format wanted. The path format prints a pathname, the ls format does the ls command, and the set format doesn't look up specific file names but checks permissions and looks for setuid files.

Notice that the path and ls options are clones. The ls option is an addition that reduces the amount of work for the caller. Having a lookup and ls combination relieves the caller from having to make a substitution command. The old and new commands are like this:

```
ll 'path ll'      ←Find the path to ll, then run ls -l on it
paths -l ll       ←Find the path and instead of printing it do an ls -l on it
```

The setuid format in line 32 leaves the "single file at a time" approach and becomes a directory machine. Because the outer loop is set to one iteration, the inner loop becomes the main driver. For each directory in PATH, a banner and the directory name are printed, which makes a pleasant, informative, and readable printout.

The key command is the ls-grep combination. Every file in the directory is listed in a long format, then scanned for the setuid bit. The model is as follows: The command ls -al $DIR prints

```
-rws--x--x   1 root      bin        16235 Sep 13  1985 /bin/su
```

The argument to grep "^[^]*s[^]*" says to search from the beginning of the line for a nonblank followed by one or more nonblanks, followed by an s, and followed by a nonblank and more nonblanks. This expression restricts the search to the permission bits at the beginning of the line. If there is an s character anywhere in the permission (either setuid or setgid), grep is successful and the whole line is printed.

This kind of setuid search is somewhat "lightweight" in that only the PATH that you have is searched. Setuid files might reside in directories that are not in PATH. As implemented however, this option provides a quick reference to your locally accessed setuid files.

Modifications

This script is open to many different types of modifications. The finding of a pathname is a very fundamental need in file-management software. This capability allows us to build on the paths program itself or to use paths as a portion of a larger program.

One thing to note for your own program development is the flexibility of paths as expressed in the differences among formats. The first two formats use individual files, whereas the set format uses directories. Future additions to `paths` could follow either of these lines or maybe combine them. If the need exists, the software can accommodate it.

Name: lc

lc   List files in column format

Function

Prints file information in column format, showing directories and executables. The listing can optionally be sent through `more`.

Synopsis

lc [-m] [ls options] file [file ...]

Sample Call

lc -R $HOME

List all files in all subdirectories of my home directory

Code for lc

```
1    :
2    # @(#) lc v1.0   List files in a column   Author: Russ Sage
3
4    if [ "$1" = "-m" ]
5      then  MORE="¦ /usr/bin/more"
6            shift
7      else  MORE=""
8    fi
9
10   eval "/bin/ls -a $@ ¦ /bin/pr -5t" $MORE      # pre System V
11   eval /bin/ls -aCF $@ $MORE                     # System V
```

Environment Variable

MORE   Holds the pipe to the `more` command

Description

Why do we need lc*?*

In the world of computers, some people create a wheel and other people recreate it. If the first wheel is not the right size or right color, another is made. In our particular situation, the original wheel is the UNIX `ls` command, which is somewhat defective in its earliest incarnations. It prints good information, but it only prints file names in one column, which can waste space, and make it hard to read file names. Therefore, we create a version of `ls` that displays listings in multiple columns.

As can be seen from the preceding listing, lc has two forms. One is pre-

System V and the other is System V and later. The reason is that the System V release 2 has a new ⎣s command that *does* do what we want. Berkeley also has a version of ⎣s that defaults to multiple columns when outputting to a terminal. But for XENIX and earlier System V, we have to do it ourselves. The point, though, is that although your version of UNIX, XENIX, or whatever, might lack commands found in other versions, you usually can build what you want. It might take some work, and it might not run as fast or as efficiently, but you *can* gain the capability.

For users of csh and the latest sh with functions, this whole scenario could probably be replaced by making ⎣c an alias. Use the alias facility to assign a name to any valid UNIX command line (such as a call to ⎣s with specified options). This is easier than writing a script, but restricts you to working with already established commands and options. It is faster since no extra processes are created.

With the plain old sh, we have to go through the usual procedure of making a script and placing it in a bin directory. As an aside, the SCO XENIX System V solved this problem by linking these same names (lc, lf, l) to the usual ⎣s and using the calling name to determine the form of the printout.

Thus, there are often lots of alternatives. UNIX masters, when confronted with a problem, don't start struggling with C or a shell script. Because they are familiar with existing UNIX resources, they can look at the problem and devise a strategy using the least complicated facility that gets the job done with an acceptable level of performance. In order of general complexity this could be an obscure but existing command and/or option, an alias, a shell script, or a C program.

What does ⎣c *do?*

The general strategy for making this command is to bundle some options together and make a new command with a more powerful interface. To capture this power, we can make either a front-end or back-end processor for a regular UNIX command.

The primary task here is the printing of columns, so we look at ⎣s options to bundle in. Of course, we include the -C option. What other ⎣s options do we want? Well, UNIX normally does not print dot files, such as .profile unless you say ls -a. It's hard to remember to look for these important files, so we design our command to print them by default. No files hide from us. For System V and BSD users (or anybody who has the -F option), the listing is enhanced by printing "/" after a directory name and "*" after an executable file. The early UNIX ls command did not have the code to print in this manner. Note that this usage of the term "executable" means that the permission flags have the "x" bit showing rather than that the file type is an a.out with a magic number. This distinction is an important one that makes our script more generally useful.

If the printout is going to be long, which recursive directory listings usually are, you want to have **more** available. We build in the **more** command so that it can be activated using the -m option. The string -m must be the first option after the command name due to the way it is checked inside the program. If it is passed after the first option, it is passed to the UNIX ls command and interpreted as printing in stream format. This format is where all the names are on lines separated by commas (,). Again, you could make the script's interface more flexible at the expense of more coding.

Examples

1. `$ lc 'path lc'`

Get the pathname to `lc` and list the file information in columns.

2. `$ lc -m -R /`

Print a column list of *all* files on the system by recursively going down through the system tree hierarchy, piping the printout through `more`.

Another little trick: This syntax was used to create another command called `expose`. The script command line would be "lc -m -R $@", which would recursively list every file in whatever directory you choose and give you a nice paged format.

3. `$ lc -m -R /usr/lib`

List recursively starting from /usr/lib all the files in all the directories and pipe the listing through `more`.

4. `$ lc -m . ¦ more`

List files in the current directory and pipe the listing through `more`, then pipe all that through `more` again. Does this work? No way. Everything gets confused and the interrupt key is usually the best way to get out.

Explanation

In lines 4-8, the command line is checked to see whether the first argument is -m, the `more` option. If the option is found, the MORE variable is loaded with the pipe and `more` command. This establishes the postprocessing to be done with the `ls` output. Next, the option is shifted off the command line. This is done so that the rest of the command line can be passed on to `ls` without causing unwanted effects. If the first option is not -m, the MORE variable is set to null, which makes it get parsed out of the command line later on.

Line 10 is the command line you would use if you are running on an old UNIX machine, like Version 7 or System III. It does not have the built-in option of printing slashes (/) and asterisks (*), nor does it have the capability of printing in columns. You have to sacrifice the first options, but multiline printouts can be achieved with the UNIX `pr` command. `Pr` is used with the "-5t" option, so it prints in five columns (usually acceptable, but may be too many columns if long file names are involved) and omits the header and footer. By leaving the header off, the 24-line page format isn't forced on you.

Note that the eval command is used here. Eval is a special built-in shell command that forces a reevaluation of the current line to be executed. The shell reparses the line to expand the value of variable names onto the command line and let them be recognized as such. Here we are eval'ing the MORE variable. Remember that we put a pipe into it. If we don't eval the line, `pr` tries to open files called "¦" and "more", which do not exist. To get the shell to take these characters as literal pipes and programs instead, eval is used.

Line 10 has one more twist to it. The command line already has one pipe. How does the shell know when to interpret the "¦" character as a file name or a pipe? By quoting the argument to the eval command, which tells eval to keep everything that is in quotes the same but expand MORE and put it at the back of the quoted command line. Pretty obscure, but if you think about it for a couple of years, it really makes sense.

For those of you who have the new ls (System 5, release 2, or BSD 4.2), we don't need two pipelines in the command. As line 11 shows, we get the column format right from ls itself, along with showing all files and the special characters / and * for directories and executables. The $@ includes everything from the command line, which is your extra ls options and the file names you want to list. By doing this, we create a base point (options a,C,F) and you can build on top of it (using options R,t,...). A neat trick to get ls to print the option string is to call it with a bad option. Most commands don't use z or ?, so the call "ls -z" or "ls -?" results in:

```
ls: illegal option -- z
usage: -1ACFRabcdfgilmnopqrstux [files]
```

All these options definitely keep you busy. If you use any of them often, put them into the script lc and you have your own tailored command.

Did you notice that all the regular UNIX commands used in our script had full pathnames? This might seem a little strange, but the reason for specifying full pathnames is that when the shell runs that command, it does not have to go back through your PATH shell variable and look up where the command is. If you reference the commands relatively, the file lookup time has massive overhead. When you call lc, the shell looks it up, then lc calls ls, which has to be looked up. If the results are then piped through more or pr, more lookups are required. Full pathnames, on the other hand, are recognized immediately by the shell (by looking to see whether the first character is a /), and the referenced command can be called directly. The lookup overhead is just one, for lc.

Using pathnames, of course, requires that you know where the utilities you want to reference reside in your system. You may have to use paths to get the correct pathnames to hard code into your script, and you may have to rewrite the script if you move to a different system. That's just another illustration of the universal trade-off between speed and efficiency on one side and flexibility and portability on the other.

Name: ll

ll   List files in a long format

Function

Prints files in the long format (-l). The printout can optionally be piped through more.

Synopsis

ll [-m] [ls options] file [file ...]

Sample Call

ll *.c   List all C source files in long format

Code for ll

```
1  :
2  # @(#) ll v1.0    Long listing of files    Author: Russ Sage
3
4  if [ "$1" = "-m" ]
5    then MORE="| /usr/bin/more"
6         shift
7    else MORE=""
8  fi
9
10 eval /bin/ls -al $@ $MORE
```

Environment Variable

MORE   Contains the pipe to the more command

Description

Why do we need ll?

The reasons for building a command like ll are similar to those we discussed previously for lc. We can use ll for a number of purposes. It reduces the amount of typing we have to do, avoids the need to remember special options, and, in general, customizes the system to our needs rather than our having to accommodate the system.

What does ll do?

The foundation for this command is the familiar command "ls -l". This, you recall, provides extensive information about each file, including permissions, links, name of owner, size, and so on. (By the way, C programmers can get this information through stat(2).) Because such a list is liable to overflow the screen if there are many files, the -m option is provided. This pages the output through more. Note that this option must be the first option if it is used. The option string gets removed so that it does not interfere with file names and regular "ls" options that are passed as arguments.

Following -m (if present), ll accepts any other ls options that are legal. Also any combination of file names can be used. The usual file name generation applies here: * matches everything, ? matches one character, and [ ] match ranges. Thus in effect, we have provided an ls that defaults to "ls -l", invokes more with a simple option instead of having to have a pipe on the command line, and still preserves all of the flexibility of ls.

Examples

1. `$ ll /etc/*mount*`

List all files in the /etc directory that have the word **mount** anywhere within them (like mount, umount, unmountable).

2. `$ ll -i 'who¦awk '{print "/dev/" $2}''`

First does a **who**, then pipes it to **awk**, which cuts out the device name and prefixes it with /dev/. The result is that a list of full pathnames to all the terminal devices currently logged on is placed on the command line of the ls -li command. The printout shows all the inode information for each terminal device.

3. `$ ll 'kind -a /lib'`

Print a long file listing of all the archive files in the /lib directory. This directory contains all the compiler libraries for the languages on UNIX. (The kind command, which selects files by type, is introduced in the next section.)

4. `$ ll -m -i /dev`

List all the usual information plus the inode number for all the files in the /dev directory. Put the listing through **more**.

Explanation

In line 4, if the first positional parameter is -m, the MORE variable is initialized to include the pipe and the /usr/bin/more program. (For a discussion of why an absolute pathname is used, see `lc` in the previous section.) Then, the -m string is shifted off the command line. If the first option is not -m, the MORE variable is set to null, which is parsed out in the "eval" reparsing (line 10).

In line 10, eval is used to build the final command line. **Ls** is called with our command defaults of -al (list all files in long format). The arguments on the command line (minus the first argument if it was -m, which we shifted off) arc then supplied. These arguments can be additional options to `ls` plus file or directory names. Finally the contents of MORE provide the pipe to the **more** command if -m was specified. Otherwise, the contents of MORE are null and have no effect on the command line parsing.

What would happen if the user puts -m as the second (or subsequent) option? In this case, the -m gets passed to `ls`. **Ls** considers this option as meaning "stream output", which isn't what we want. However `ls` is also being called with the -l option, which overrides the -m by design. You wouldn't get your **more**, but your output would still be in the correct format.

Name: kind

kind   List file names that have types of the same kind

Function

Selects and outputs the names of all files in the specified path(s) that are of the specified kind. If no file type is specified, text files are selected.

Synopsis

kind [-a] [-d] [-t] [-x] [file ...]

Sample Call

more `kind /etc/*`

More every text file in the /etc directory

Code for kind

```
1    :
2    # @(#) kind v1.0    Prints files of the same kind    Author: Russ Sage
3
4    if [ $# -gt 0 ]
5      then if [ `echo $1 | cut -c1` = "-" ]
6            then case $1 in
7                 -a)  KIND='archive'
8                      shift;;
9                 -d)  KIND='data'
10                     shift;;
11                -t)  KIND='text'
12                     shift;;
13                -x)  KIND='executable'
14                     shift;;
15                *)   echo "kind: arg error"                        >&2
16                     echo "usage: kind [-a] [-d] [-t] [-x] [file ...]" >&2
17                     echo "       -a  archive"                     >&2
18                     echo "       -d  data"                        >&2
19                     echo "       -t  text, default"               >&2
20                     echo "       -x  executable"                  >&2
21                     echo "       if no args, reads stdin"         >&2
22                     exit 1;;
23            esac
24       fi
25   fi
26
27   : ${KIND:='text'}
28
29   case $# in
30   0)  while read FILE
31       do
32           file $FILE | fgrep $KIND | cut -d: -f1
33       done;;
34   *)  file $@ | fgrep $KIND | cut -d: -f1;;
35   esac
```

Environment Variables

FILE   Holds the file name as it is read from stdin
KIND   Contains the string defining the type of file

Description

Why do we need `kind`?

The UNIX file system is very uniform in its treatment of files. There are three kinds of files: regular file (text, data, executable), directory, and device. Each kind of file has its special purpose and usually has specific commands or data files that operate with it.

Let's look at how some of the existing UNIX commands treat file types. The `ls` command distinguishes between directories and other files, so it can be useful. The other important command is `file`. It tells you what type a given file is, which is potentially useful, but too restrictive. To get any usefulness out of it, you have to pack some code around it. What we really need is a hybrid of `ls` and `file`, a utility that prints all the names of files of a specific file type.

An example of the usefulness of this kind of utility is in analyzing directories. Take the /etc directory, for example. It contains programs, data files, and text files. Each one of these requires its own type of analysis. Programs are analyzed with `ls`, `size`, `nm`, and `file`. Data files are analyzed with `od`. Text files are examined with `more`, `wc`, `head`, `tail`, and others. Thus, you normally want to work with one kind of file at a time.

What does `kind` do?

`Kind` is a tool that prints out file names of all files of a specified kind. It has an ls-type interface where you can pass options and file names, or file-name expansion characters. Pathnames are expanded and reflected in the output if they are specified, but you can avoid clutter by first doing a `cd` to the directory you want to use. For example, if I were in my home directory (/usr/russ) and I typed

```
$ kind -d /etc/*
```

the output would look like:

```
/etc/mnttab
/etc/utmp
/etc/wtmp
```

That is, all the data files are listed. If I did this sequence, however

```
$ cd /etc
$ kind -d *
```

the output would reflect the path used in the calling sequence and print like this:

```
mnttab
utmp
wtmp
```

Then this kind of output can be used in an outer command to list and examine file information.

The options that are allowed are -a for archive files, -d for data files, -t for text files (which is the default), and -x for executable files. The definition of these types is in accordance with the UNIX `file` command. Note that `file`'s criterion for an executable is different from that used by `ls`: `ls` looks for x bits in the inode, whereas `file` checks to see whether the first few bytes of the file contain the "magic number." The magic number is an identifier in the a.out structure (see /usr/include/a.out.h) that says "I'm a compiled C program."

The file names come after the options on the command line. These names can be generated by any standard UNIX method. If the command line has no file names, `kind` becomes a filter and reads stdin for the list of file names. (Notice I said no files. Options can be used because they are shifted out as they are encountered.) Thus, you can use other commands to pipe a list of files to `kind`. It filters out and prints only the ones that are of the type you are looking for.

Examples

1. `$ od 'kind -d /etc/*'`

Seems like it should work, but `od` does not work on multiple file names. It can only handle one file name at a time.

2. `$ ll 'sh -x kind -a /lib/*' ¦ m`

This is a long one. List in long format all the archive files that are in the /lib directory. We ran the shell in debug mode so that you can see each command line before it is executed. The resultant output is piped through more.

3. ```
find / -print ¦ kind -x ¦ while read FILE
> do
>   ll $FILE
> done > /tmp/filelist
```

This loop finds all the truly executable files. For each one, it does an "ls -l" listing. Note here that `ll` is called for every file name.

You might come close to the same operation with this `find` statement

```
# find / -perm -0111 -exec ll {} \;
```

but the perm option here is looking again at the inode permission bits and not at the a.out structure for the magic number, as described in preceding text. By the way, for
```

you to be able to run the file command (and thus kind) successfully on system files, you must have read permission so that you can read for the magic number.

```
4.  $ for F in 'kind /bin/* /usr/bin/* /etc/*'
    > do
    >       fgrep "trap" $F /dev/null
    > done
    $ fgrep "trap" 'kind /bin/* /usr/bin/* /etc/*'

    $ find /bin /usr/bin /etc -exec fgrep "trap" {} \;
```

Three ways to search for the word "trap" in all the text files.

Explanation

The options that can be passed must be in the very first argument ($1). This creates a more rigid syntax by which to trap errors. It restricts the flexibility somewhat. As noted previously, you can make your own trade-off by adding code if you wish.

In line 4, we check to see whether any parameters are included. If some are included, they are processed. If no parameters are used, nothing is done and execution falls through to line 27.

If arguments are used, and the first character is a minus sign, a case statement is used to determine which kind of file is being specified. The KIND variable is set to the appropriate file type and the parameter is shifted off the command line. If the argument isn't matched by any valid option, it is matched by the * and must be an error. The appropriate error and usage statement is printed to standard error and kind exits with a failure execution status.

In line 27, the KIND variable is checked to see whether it is set or equal to null. If it is equal to null, it gets set to the string "text." If it is already set, it is not changed. This makes a nice default assignment statement. Thus, the user doesn't have to specify -t on the command line. If -t is specified, however, it is matched in the case statement.

The rest of the program is in lines 29-42, which is another case statement that checks the number of arguments remaining on the command line after error processing. If an option was passed, KIND was set and the option was shifted away. The only arguments left on the command line are file or pathnames. If there are zero arguments by the time we are ready for final processing, no names were specified on the command line.

In this case, lines 30-33 set up a loop, read the file names from stdin, run the file command, use fgrep to find whether the type reported by file matches the type we are interested in (as stored in KIND). We then use cut to extract the output we want. The normal output of file has the file name, a colon, then the description. We only need the file name, so we cut out field one using the delimiter of :. When no more data is coming in, the while loop terminates, and we fall through to the end of the case statement and exit.

If arguments *are* found on the command line, the branch of the case statement at line 34 is executed instead. By using $@, all the file names from the command line are included in the file command. Thus, no loop is needed. Otherwise, processing is identical to line 32.

Modifications

One really nice thing that kind could do is to mix the kinds of output. This means having multiple options on the command line, like -a and -d. You would need a collective string where each piece would be separated by the | character. Then this string would be used in egrep. An example is "egrep 'archive|data'". You would have to loop on the command line instead of using fixed positions, and make sure that when only one option is given, you don't get a stray pipe floating around.

Name: m

m   Easy access to more

Function

Provides a fast and easy way to page output.

Synopsis

m [more options] [file ...]

Sample Call

m *   More all the files in the current directory

Code for m

```
1   :
2   # @(#) m v1.0   Easy access to more
3
4   /usr/bin/more $@
```

Description

Why do we need m*?*

UNIX is heavily line based in its operation. There is usually lots of text and data. Going through tons of data requires a lot of typing if you have to control the paging manually or invoke more repeatedly. We need software tools to help us make the job faster. One of these tools is m: It's very short and simple, but that doesn't mean it isn't useful.

There are basically two ways to get data to the screen. The first way is by direct command, as in "more datafile". You order data to the screen by the command itself. The second way is to use a command to generate data, then have more at the end catching it, as in "od -c . | more". In both these cases, we typed a lot of characters. By making more a one-character invocation, we could have reduced the last two commands by six keystrokes. In a whole day, that saves quite a bit of keyboard pounding! (If your system supports aliasing, as mentioned earlier, you could use an alias in this case:

```
"alias m more".)
```

What does m *do?*

Hopefully, each of your systems has the more command, or at least a substitute. Paging of text output is essential when working with lots of code.

All options and arguments are passed through on the command line. You can put options to the more command on the m command line. These are passed on just as they are. Also, files are optional. If they are used, more prints them. Otherwise, data is expected on the stdin stream. Thus, m can be used as a "catcher" or as a filter just as more can.

In case you are not up on your more options, two really neat ones are 1) jumping in to vi right where your cursor is on the more listing and 2) escaping from more to run a shell command and returning to where you left off. The first option is activated by typing "v" at the more status line. (That is, when more has displayed a screenful of text and paused.) The second option is run by typing ":!cmd" or "!cmd". When the command is done, more picks right back up. As you can see, this is an ex command line syntax. More actually has quite a bit of the ex editor hidden in it. You can perform many of the editor commands at the more status line prompt.

A typical session looks like this:

```
m `path termcap`                      ←find termcap and more it out
            .
            .
            .
--More--(5%)                          ←more status line prompt
v                                        vi /etc/termcap
vi +210 /etc/termcap                  ←automatic command line from more
            .
            .
:q                                    ←quit vi
--More--(5%)                          ←resume in more
:!sh                                     fork a shell
$ date                                   run the date command
Wed Apr 23 07:15:04 PST 1986
$ ^d                                  ←kill the shell
--More--(5%)                          ←back to more
:f                                       print out the name of the file
                                         being more'd
"/etc/termcap" line 54                   output of the f command
--More--(5%)
f                                     ←more command to skip screenfuls
  .skipping 23 lines
            .
            .
--More--(9%)                          ←skipped and printed more text
q                                        quit the more listing
```

Examples

1. `$ ll -R / ¦ m`

Starting from the root directory (/), list in long form (ll) all files (-a implicit in ll) in the entire system (-R) and page the output to the screen (¦ m).

2. `$ m 'path inittab rc passwd'`

Locate and `more` the system files inittab, rc, and passwd. A gotcha here is that path more than likely matches /bin/passwd before /etc/passwd (because /etc always gets stuck at the end), which means that you may try to `more` an executable. Depending on which version of `more` you are running, this can mean anything from crashing your terminal to getting a nice little message from `more` that it wasn't a text file.

Explanation

Because there is not a whole lot of code here, things are pretty straightforward, with no error checking, no extra padding. Just plain old `more`. The reason the entire pathname is specified here is for speed purposes, as we've noted previously. You should double check the location of `more`. On Berkeley systems, it might be in /usr/ucb/more. Type `path more` to find out and put the appropriate path in place of ours.

By the way, a trick to getting that string into your script file is to go into the editor and issue the following command:

```
:.!path more
```

This escapes to a shell and runs the `path` command (:!), then places its output (which is the entire pathname) in the editor buffer on top of the current line (.). Then you have the data in your editor file and you can edit it as necessary.

Name: mmm

mmm   `Nroff` command line for manuscript macros

Function

Calls the `nroff` text processor with specific options that initialize the manuscript macros.

Synopsis

mmm file [...]

Sample Call

mmm memo   Process my memo through `nroff` and display it on the screen

Code for mmm

```
1   :
2   # @(#) mmm v1.0   Nroff command line with mm macros    Author: Russ Sage
3
4   if [ "$#" -eq 0 ]
5     then  echo "mmm: wrong arg count"  >&2
6           echo "usage: mmm file [...]" >&2
7           exit 1
8   fi
9
10  LIST=""
11  for ARG in $*
12  do
13          if [ ! -f $ARG ]
14            then echo "mmm: $ARG is not a regular file" >&2
15            else LIST="$LIST $ARG"
16          fi
17  done
18
19  nroff -r00 -mm $LIST
```

Environment Variables

ARG   Holds each positional parameter on the command line
LIST   Holds the list of verified file names

Description

Why do we need mmm?

One of the facts of the business world is paperwork. We produce memos, letters, contracts, documents, manuals, and more. If you are involved with the UNIX style of documentation production, your text files mostly are in some sort of nroff format.

But various formatting packages meet different needs. There is regular nroff, and nroff with additions, like the ms and mm macros. For graphics and typesetting, troff comes in. AT&T has a whole environment called the Writers Workbench, and Berkeley has similar facilities.

Most of our writing tasks can be boiled down to a few standard formats, such as letters, general manuscripts, manual pages, and so on. It's not easy to remember the nroff (or other command) options to use in a given case, and we shouldn't have to. Our mmm command serves as an illustration of a package that we can run whenever we want a particular format. You can create several versions that meet your own writing needs.

Using "canned" commands means that we can do useful work even when we haven't done a particular kind of work for some time. We also save repetitious typing. UNIX masters periodically retire to their mountain retreats where they study the manuals, looking for useful but obscure options that can be built into workaday tools. Relying too uncritically on your current toolkit can lead to missed opportunities.

What does mmm *do?*

Mmm is a front-end processor for the `nroff` command. By "front end," we mean that it processes the calling command line and sets up all the options to call the `nroff` program. Some of the options to `nroff` are hard coded into the call. These options initialize portions of the `nroff` program.

If you include no arguments, mmm recognizes an error and prints the usage statement. Notice that if you pass mmm an argument like -z, that argument is looked on as a file name and not an option to be passed through, which again triggers an error. The second error is not fatal, but the first error is.

After processing all the arguments, the `nroff` program uses the file names as input data files. The output is by default the stdout. This is normally your screen but can be redirected or piped to the line printer or whatever.

Examples

1. `$ mmm nroffile ¦ m`

Run `nroff` on nroffile, put the output to the screen and pipe it through `more`. Useful for learning `nroff` and experimenting with various commands and observing the output.

2. ```
$ for F in proj.?
  do
          mmm $F > $F.rf
  done
```

Loop through all the file names that have the string "proj." followed by a single character. This would match the proj.1, proj.2 sequence all the way through the character set to proj.z, proj.{, proj.¦, proj.}, and proj. ~ , assuming that you have file names which use these characters. Process each file and redirect the `nroff` output for the file to its own name, appended with .rf.

3. `$ mmm status[12] ¦ lpr -o5`

Nroff the files status1 and status2. The output to standard out is piped to the `lpr` program. Lpr is a filter and accepts either file names on the command line or data piped to it directly (but not both). The -o5 option tells `lpr` to offset the page 5 characters.

## *Explanation*

In line 4, the number of arguments on the command line is checked to see whether it is equal to zero. If so, the error message is printed to the standard error. The usage statement is also printed, and mmm exits with a failure status.

The variable LIST is initialized to null in line 10. Shell variables usually start out as null anyway, but it is good programming to preset the value.

Next we process each argument on the command line with a loop (lines 11-17). All the arguments should be file names, so each one is checked to see whether it
```

exists as a regular file. If it is not a file, an error message is printed to standard error. The program does not exit, though. We don't have to abort the whole thing just because the name is not a file. We skip it and go on to finish all the arguments. Especially if the command is being used in the background while other work is being done, the user would rather get most of the work done than none at all. This is a design decision that you can change if it is inappropriate to your situation.

If the name is a valid file, it is added to the list of good file names. This list becomes the master list for the nroff command.

After all the arguments have been verified, we build and execute the `nroff` command line in line 19.

The -rO0 option for `nroff` tells the manuscript macros (mm package) to set the register that deals with the offsetting of the text to offset by 0 characters. This means all the text is against the left margin, or left-justified. From experimentation, I have found that left-justifying the `nroff` text and offsetting the line printer gives the most reliable printout. Otherwise if you offset the `nroff` text and offset the line printer, it can be a real hassle to dial in exact columns on the page. You might want to change this if your output routines or devices behave differently. The -mm option tells `nroff` to look through the library of manuscript macros and see whether any are being used in the input document. These macros are very large and eat up lots of CPU time. If you need to use them, you also need a large computer or a dedicated one to get good turnaround time.

The last argument is $LIST. In this variable is a string of file names delimited by a blank. These names are placed on the `nroff` command line. Be assured that there are no errors.

Modifications

Because of all the arguments being treated as file names, we have no way to pass in extra `mm` commands. Having this capability would be beneficial because as you are experimenting with `nroff`, you need to try the options to see what they do. It would be a lot of work to keep editing the `mmm` script to add one-time options that you might never need, or ones that you have to change constantly.

One way to provide more flexibility is to see whether any of the arguments have a hyphen as the first character. If so, pick up that option and shift it off the file name list. Then you would have a list of options to include and file names to process.

Note that the "slot" occupied by mm in our script could be filled instead with other macro packages available on your system, such as -ms and -me, depending on the formats you desire. Avoiding a search for things you don't need speeds up processing: See your `nroff` or `troff` documentation for details.

Name: `pall`

pall   Print all files in a directory tree

Function

Finds all the files in a given directory according to some criteria, paginates the files, and puts the result in one file ready for the line printer.

Synopsis

pall [-t¦-d] directory

Sample Call

pall /usr/lib

Print in paged format all the text files under /usr/lib

Code for pall

```
1   :
2   # @(#) pall v1.0   Print all files in a tree   Author: Russ Sage
3
4   if [ $# -eq 0 -o $# -gt 2 ]
5     then echo "pall: wrong argument count"  >&2
6          echo "usage: pall [-t¦-d] dir"     >&2
7          echo " -t text (default)"          >&2
8          echo " -d dev (.c,.h,.mk,.s)"      >&2
9          exit 1
10  fi
11
12  NAME=""
13  if [ 'echo $1 | cut -c1' = "-" ]
14    then  case $1 in
15          -t)     NAME=""
16                  shift;;
17          -d)     NAME="-name \"*.[chms]*\""
18                  shift;;
19          *)      echo "pall: invalid arg $1"    >&2
20                  echo "usage: pall [-t¦-d] dir" >&2
21                  echo " -t text (default)"      >&2
22                  echo " -d dev (.c,.h,.mk,.s)"  >&2
23                  exit 1;;
24          esac
25  fi
26
27  echo "creating output file: /tmp/lpr$$"
28
29  eval find $1 -type f $NAME -print | sort | while read FILE
30  do
31          if file $FILE |
32             egrep 'exec¦data¦empty¦reloc¦cannot open' >/dev/null 2>&1
33          then  continue
34          else file $FILE > /dev/tty
35               pr $FILE
36          fi
37  done >> /tmp/lpr$$
```

```
38
39   echo "\nSend /tmp/lpr$$ to line printer (y/n): \c"
40   read CMD
41   if [ "$CMD" = "y" ]
42     then lpr /tmp/lpr$$
43   fi
```

Environment Variables

FILE   Holds each file name as it is processed in the while loop
NAME   Contains the find string to locate specific file names
CMD   Holds the command to put the results to the printer

Description

Why do we need pall?

This utility combines the concepts of file tree traversal and the display of file contents. When files are tucked away under subdirectories, we still want to be able to find them. We need a utility that traverses a tree structure, finds the kind of files we want, prepares them for printing, and queues the job to the printer.

This kind of facility is especially useful when source code or documentation files are kept in a tree hierarchy. To complicate the matter, these text files are usually mixed with executable files (compiled programs), data files, and possibly archives. You must be able to filter out all nonprintable files and just prepare text files, and all files must be checked so that none are missed.

To perform this whole process manually requires you to cd to each level in the tree, find the text files, process them (usually with the UNIX pr command or some other text manipulator) and print them. After doing all this work, you still have to put the individual printouts together into a coherent order. This is a lot of work and is prone to human error. Why not let the machine do the work? We now have the concepts and tools we need to build this utility.

In addition to file handling, pall is also useful for printer handling. Usually, each job queued to the printer has a header printed first. This means that if you queue ten jobs individually, each job has two to three pages in front of it that have to be manually torn off. Multiply this by hundreds of files, and you have reams of paper that must be thrown away.

Pall eliminates the waste because all the processed data ends up in one large text file. When all processing is done, the one file can be queued for printing or saved for some other task. The only limitation to this model is the maximum size of files you can create. This value is calculated by multiplying the ulimit value times the block size. For example, my ulimit is 4096. The block size here is 512, not 1024. The max file size is 2097152. You can calculate this from the keyboard as follows:

```
$ ulimit
4096
$ expr 4096 \* 512
2097152
```

That's large enough for most purposes.

What does pall *do?*

Pall is designed to find specific files, process them through the UNIX pr command, and collect all the output into one file. After all source files have been pr'd, you are asked whether you want to queue the file for line printing. The resultant file is retained in the /tmp directory where it can be used for other purposes or removed.

The options to pall are -t and -d. The -t option is the default and does not need to be specified. It exists for documentation of the command line to more clearly show the action being performed.

If the text option is chosen, all files are found in the tree structure, then filtered for text-only files. If the -d or development option is chosen, only program development file names are looked for. Then the files are filtered for text only. Development files are considered to be file names that have the form *.c for C source, *.h for header include files, *.mk for makefiles, and *.s for assembly source files. If any other matches are needed, the characters can be easily placed in the program.

Prior to doing the file lookup, the temp file name is displayed on the screen so that you know how to reference it after the command is finished. All output generated from the files is redirected to this one file. Pall also prints to the screen while it is processing files. The file output is performed in real time as the files are being processed. The printout is from the regular UNIX file command. By printing, you get an idea of what kind of files are being processed. If a nasty file slips through, you know where it is located and what type of file it is. It makes debugging a lot easier.

The processing performed on the files is the default action of pr. This paginates the file and prints a header at the top of every page. The header has the date, the file name, and the page number. There is no way to pass a header into pall as it is running because it is assumed you want to know the name of each file as it is on disk. Changing the header line would only cause confusion and more work.

How pall is called affects the format of the file name in the header. If you call pall using an absolute directory name, the printout uses full pathnames. If you call it with relative pathnames, the printout uses these. The internals of pall use the UNIX find command. Find uses data from the command line, which is what the user types. The output changes depending on what is on the command line that find used. If you call pall using the following command line, the header file names have the full pathname:

```
$ pall /usr/include

May 5 10:39 1986 /usr/include/a.out.h Page 1
                     .
                     .
                     .
```

```
May 5 10:39 1986 /usr/include/ar.h Page 1
                            .
                            .
                            .
```

If you call pall using a relative notation, the file names also have relative names, which is not so good. If you have multiple directories with similarly named files, you don't know for sure whether you are looking at the right printout. Here is what it would look like:

```
$ cd /usr/include
$ pall .

May 5 10:39 1986 ./a.out.h Page 1
                     .
                     .
                     .

May 5 10:39 1986 ./ar.h Page 1
                    .
                    .
                    .
```

Examples

1. ## $ pall /usr/include

Print *all* the header files. This includes those under the sys subdirectory and any other directories that might be under /usr/include. This is the reason that pall was written. It creates one huge listing of all the header files, in sorted order, with the page header printing the entire pathname.

2. ## $ pall $HOME/src

Traverse all the directories under the source directory and print all the files.

Explanation

First the error checking is done on the command line. If there are no arguments or there are more than two, an error message is printed, the usage statement is printed, and the program exits with an unsuccessful return status.

In line 12, the NAME variable is initialized. This is the default action, so this line provides the ability to not specify an option on the command line. The if statement in line 13 says, "If the first character of the first argument is equal to a dash", check to see which option it is.

If the -t option is set, the NAME variable is initialized to null, which is the same as the default action, so nothing has really changed. Then the option is shifted off the command line.

If the -d option is set, the NAME variable is initialized to the find string that singles out the file names that have extensions appropriate to program development.

Notice that the double quotes inside the statement are quoted, or enclosed in slashes. The shell accepts the quotes around the find string in the first parsing phase without aborting the assignment, thus leaving the double quotes for the `find` command later on.

If the option is anything else, the error message is printed and the program exits.

In line 27, a displayed message indicates which file holds the results. This statement does not create the file. It just prints the same file name as the name of the file that is created later on.

Lines 29-43 are the main loop of the whole program. The `find` statement has to be eval'd because the NAME variable has data we need. If there was no eval, the string substitution would not work right. Notice that the NAME variable does not need to have quotes on line 24. They are already in the NAME variable and get eaten on the eval pass.

The `find` statement finds only f type files, or regular files. This means no directories or character and block devices. Being a regular file still means it can be data or an executable. If the NAME variable is null, it is parsed out of the command line. If it has the development file characters in it, they become part of the `find` command during the eval pass. This limits which files `find` matches. When the files are found, their names are printed to stdout. The stdout is piped to the `sort` command, which puts the file names in order. This helps immensely in sorting out the mountains of output. Reading foot-thick printouts that are not in sorted order can drive anybody crazy.

The sorted names are piped to a while loop that reads the file names one at a time. Notice that the stdout for the entire while loop is redirected to the temp file, which makes it easy to capture all the output at one point instead of redirecting each command call to a file.

For each file that qualifies, a test is made in lines 31-36. The test is started by running the `file` command. The output of `file` is piped to `egrep`, which looks for any file type matching a set of multiple expressions. If any expressions are matched, we don't want to process the file. They are nontext files and are not compatible with line printers. Many times, data files contain mass quantities of form feeds, which eject a page for every couple of characters. If you are not around when the job is printing, you can end up with a listing that is half a box of paper and does the forests no good whatsoever.

We do not want the output of the `egrep` command, just its return status. If `egrep` finds one of these expressions, it exits with a successful status, or 0. This triggers the if test to execute the then statement, which in this case, breaks us out of the if-then-else and continues with the while loop, thus skipping the file.

If the `egrep` did not find one of these strings, execution falls through to the else statement, which does another `file` command and redirects it to the device /dev/tty. This device is an all-purpose device name that is guaranteed to make it to your screen. /dev/tty is provided by UNIX to bypass any redirections that might be on the process at the time. Because stdout is already redirected for the entire while loop, we need to go to /der/tty so that output goes to the screen and not into the lpr file. Displaying the file name as it is processed lets the user know the file will be added to the printout.

Assuming that the file meets our criteria, it is processed with the `pr` command. The output goes to stdout, which is redirected by the while loop so that all output goes right into one file. Note that we need to append (> >) the output. Otherwise we would keep overwriting the lpr file with the last file processed.

After all the files are processed, you are asked whether you want to put the result file to the line printer. The prompt asks for a yes or no answer, but the code only checks for the positive yes answer. This means any keystroke means no, except for y, which is yes. The command is read from the terminal and checked to see whether it is a y. If yes, the file is queued to the line printer. If not, the test falls through and the script exits.

Note that the prompt for the line printer came out of standard output. The redirection only lasted for the while loop, then went away. It did so because the while loop was actually a subshell: any redirected loop is. A bug appears when you set variables outside the loop, then change them inside the loop. After the loop, they are still their original value, not the updated value. The updated value was a subshell variable that disappears when the shell dies. Shell variables can only pass values down to children processes, and children cannot pass variables up to the parent. Usually variable passing is handled by using a file name to store any data that is to be passed between parent and child.

Handling Huge Output Files

As we noted, the total size of the output file is limited. Remember that find goes down to the bottom of all subtrees from the command line directory name. If you are at the top of a very deep tree, literally hundreds of files can be processed. Because you are limited to the maximum output file size, you can process a limited number of files. Of course, how many files you can process is also related to how big the input files are.

If the output file is pushed to its maximum, all data appended is lost. Losing data is very frustrating, and it usually takes quite some time for it to occur. On a slow system trying to process a large tree, like all the UNIX source code, it can take an hour or longer for the output file to fill up. This means you have to hang around and keep watching it until the point where it overflows. If it does overflow, you have to trash the whole thing and start over. This also means you have to move down in the tree. This can be a problem in balanced trees.

For example, look at /usr/lib. This directory holds many files at the first level and contains many first level directories. If we could not process all of /usr/lib in one shot, we would have to go down inside of /usr/lib. To manually try and pall each subdirectory would take a long time and would invite human error. Also pall only accepts one directory name at a time, which makes for a lot of printouts that are confusing to sort out.

What is the solution? The ultimate solution is to raise your ulimit. You can do this either with a C program using the ulimit system call, or by the shell ulimit command. We present techniques for this purpose in Chapter 7.

Modifications

You probably want to add your own touches in a few areas. The first area is the characters used to look up development file names. The characters we used are the most commonly used suffixes in UNIX. If you use languages other than C and assembler, you can add the appropriate characters.

The next area where additions can be made are the options that `pall` can accept. You may have a specific need for certain named files or certain types of files, like nroff files. These options can be added to the case statement very easily and would enhance the command.

The last area is what kind of files you want to skip. The `egrep` string here covers most of the important nontext file types. There may be specific kinds on your system, or the names may be different. If you need to add more strings, go ahead. `Egrep` can handle quite a few. I don't know what its limit is. You could probably find this out by looking through `egrep` source code. If the line gets too long to fit on one screen, that's okay. A wrap won't hurt, as long as it does not go over 255 characters. The dangerous thing is to put the if string redirection to null on a line by itself. Everything seems to run correctly, but it doesn't. The redirection must be on the same line as the egrep.

We've covered a lot in this chapter. More importantly, we've given you lots of ideas that you can use in exploring your environment and looking at files of all sorts. In the next chapter, we get down to the nitty-gritty of daily file management, and put to work the tools that we're learning so that they make our lives easier.

3
File Maintenance

File housekeeping
Moving files

    `cptdir`   copy a directory tree
    `can`   move files to a trash can
    `dosflp`   wildcard access for MS-DOS files

Backup techniques

    `autobkp` automatic file backup
    `cpiobr`   backup and restore

Backup verification

    `dsum`   dual directory sum
    `log`   view file backup logs

File Maintenance

Introduction

Even a "small" UNIX system with a handful of users generates hundreds of files in the course of normal operations. While programming, you can create many files for various versions of your programs. Saving mail and writing with vi contribute more files to the heap. Utilities like uucp, lp, and others add still more files. If you have a micro-based UNIX system, your hard disk starts to get full. On a larger multiuser system, space seldom seems a problem, but in fact, files always seem to expand to fill available storage. Thus, each user should take responsibility for not wasting space. (If you pay for disk storage, you may have a financial incentive as well.) However, what you want to keep, you want to *keep*. That's where the job of backups begins.

File Housekeeping

In the last chapter, we developed some tools for finding and displaying information to help us keep track of all our files. Now we're going to turn to the essential housekeeping chores that give us a fighting chance against chaos and disaster.

File housekeeping means getting rid of files we no longer need while making regular backups of those we want to keep. It requires the ability to use a variety of available storage media. Housekeeping also implies a set of regular, repetitive tasks —and that means we can create UNIX tools to automate the process.

Housekeeping Operations

File housekeeping involves two kinds of operations: backups and garbage removal.

Backups are the homage we pay to the fragility of physical data at the hands of Murphy and the other gods of entropy. A good backup tool is fast, flexible, and easy to use, which encourages users to back up critical files frequently. In subsequent text, we present a variety of backup methods suitable for various system configurations and kinds of media.

"Soft" and "hard" are the two kinds of backups. Soft backups are backups to another file or directory in the same file system, or another file system (that is, partition) on the same or another hard disk. This kind of backup is very easy to do, and guards against self-inflicted accidents, such as unintentional file deletion. Our cptdir tool is used for this kind of backup most often. The main shortcoming of soft backups is that you still are vulnerable to any problem that affects the physical medium (usually a hard disk), such that both the original and backup areas are destroyed.

A hard backup is a backup to a different device, or even a different UNIX system. Tools presented later in the chapter handle this kind of backup and provide the tools you need to implement the frequency and type of backup that suits the size of your installation, its level of activity, and the criticality of the data involved.

Hard backups are always somewhat tedious because disks or tapes have to be mounted (or communications set up with another system), and the operation takes more time. The advantage, of course, is that you are no longer dependent on the integrity of any one device.

By automating our backup procedures, we strive to make them as painless as possible. By making our backup tools reasonably intelligent, we can select only those files that need to be backed up, and save time and space. The best way to ensure that backups get done on a regular basis is to minimize the time and effort involved. Finally, creating tools to verify that our backups were done correctly brings peace of mind.

Garbage removal can be automated by identifying and preparing for removal the files that are likely to be temporary or other sorts of work files created (but not necessarily destroyed) by compiles, pipes, and other operations. You also may be able to identify files peculiar to your own operations as being "not for retention."

File Moving Tools

The first group of tools is simple, general-purpose file movers. The program cptdir can copy a directory (and any subordinate directories below it in the tree) to a destination directory. The destination is typically a directory designated as a backup for some ongoing project.

Can takes care of a chore that is necessary, if not fun—taking out the garbage. It allows you to select types of temporary files that should be removed periodically. By putting them in a "trash" directory, can gives you a chance to review your discards and recover anything you really want to keep.

Dosflp allows wildcards to be used in copying selected files from an MS-DOS formatted floppy disk to XENIX. This simplifies the operation of copying and reduces keystrokes.

Backup Tools

Next, we present the workhorse backup tools. Autobkp uses a script of pathnames to determine which portions of the file system should be examined. It then backs up those files in the selected areas that have been added or modified in the past 24 hours.

Cpiobr provides an interactive front end to the UNIX cpio command. It allows you to back up files from a hard disk to a floppy and to restore them from the floppy to the hard disk if necessary.

Tools for Verifying Backup Operations

Making a backup won't relieve your anxiety until you know that you've backed up everything you should have and that the backup ran correctly. Dsum uses a checksum to verify that the original and backup directories contain the same files. Log displays the log file to show what the automatic backup did at 4:00 a.m. while you were (hopefully) asleep.

As we create these tools, we review some important UNIX commands and find new ways to use them. When you have worked through everything in this chapter, you will know how to work "with the grain" when using the UNIX file system. You will be able to automate another large area of your computer workday. You should be able to create custom backup and verification utilities to meet your needs. You will have put your system to work ensuring its own survival. (We leave it to the philosophers to determine whether that gives your computer a primitive form of life!)

By the way, many of the tools in this chapter take advantage of the recursive tree searching methods that we developed in the last chapter. You might review that material if you have trouble understanding something presented here.

Moving Files

Name: cptdir

cptdir   Copy a directory tree to another location

Function

Copies a file system tree under a directory to another directory in the system. It is not limited to any specific directory or hard disk.

Synopsis

cptdir [-s] srcdir destdir

Sample Call

cptdir $HOME /bkp

Copies every file from $HOME to directory /bkp

Code for cptdir

```
1   :
2   # @(#) cptdir v1.0   Copy a directory tree   Author: Russ Sage
3
```

```
 4   if [ $# -lt 2 -o $# -gt 3 ]
 5      then   echo "cptdir: argument error"           >&2
 6             echo "usage: cptdir [-s] srcdir destdir" >&2
 7             echo "           -s  silent mode"         >&2
 8             exit 1
 9   fi
10
11   if [ "$1" = "-s" ]
12      then  OPT="-pd"
13            shift
14      else  OPT="-pdv"
15   fi
16
17   SRC=$1
18   DEST=$2
19   umask 0
20
21   if [ -d $DEST ]
22      then  echo "\""$DEST\"" already exists. Remove it? (y/n): \c"
23            read CMD
24            if [ "$CMD" = "y" ]
25               then rm -rf $DEST
26                    mkdir $DEST
27            fi
28      else  mkdir $DEST
29   fi
30
31   if [ "`echo $DEST|cut -c1`" = "/" ]
32      then  cd $SRC
33            find . -print | sort | cpio $OPT $DEST
34      else  PWD=`pwd`
35            cd $SRC
36            find . -print | sort | cpio $OPT $PWD/$DEST
37   fi
```

Environment Variables

CMD	A command read from the user
DEST	The destination directory to copy to
OPT	Options that are passed on to `cpio`
PWD	The current working directory
SRC	The source directory to copy from

Description

Why do we need `cptdir`?

We have pointed out the need for more commands that recursively traverse the tree-structured UNIX file system. In the older UNIX systems one command, `tar`, could handle tree movements. In the newer systems, this has changed and we have the -r option to cp, which does a cp recursively (only available in the latest version of System V) and the cpio command. The latter is a multipurpose copy command that can handle both stream and file system formats.

The problem with using even these enhanced standard UNIX commands is that you have to specify much detail and make sure that you are using the syntax correctly. Typing errors can lead to wasted time or, even worse, unintended side effects. Some of these side effects involve permission and ownership changes, inode order allocation, the location of destination files, and the resultant pathnames. This is a lot to remember and must be recalled every time you do the copy. Because copying of this sort is not done frequently, it is hard to remember all these details. We address this problem by automating the details of the process while giving the user flexibility and control over the results. We create file management tools that put better handles on the basic UNIX commands.

What does cptdir do?

Cptdir copies a directory (and the tree below it if it exists) to another directory in the system. Because directories involve logical access and are not hardware-dependent (as are device names), you can copy files easily to another location on the same disk or copy them to another disk entirely without invoking special syntax or options.

You can specify whether you want the names of the files being copied to be displayed. If you do not want file names shown, use the -s (for "silent") option. The default is "verbose" mode, which displays the names as the files are copied.

Note that this is a copy, not a move. A disadvantage of copying as opposed to moving is that if the destination is a directory on the same disk, you need extra space on the disk to hold the second image. You also need enough inodes to hold all the files. On the other hand, you have no chance of trashing your original files.

The command line accepts a source directory name and a destination directory name. The only option allowed on the command line is "-s": Any other options bomb the command without causing any damage. You can, of course, add code to check the option and print the usage message if something other than -s is used. Beyond what is required to prevent damage to data or the system, the amount of error checking you do is a matter of personal preference. Minimizing error checking makes for more compact, faster scripts suitable for experienced users.

If the specified destination directory does not exist, it is created. If the destination directory already exists, a message is displayed to that effect, and you are asked whether you want to clean it out. If you respond "yes," the directory is removed and created again with nothing in it. If you respond "no," the directory is left as is and the copied files are simply added to those already in the directory. This could create some confusion, especially if some files with duplicate names already exist in the destination directory. In most cases, however, you won't want to append a backup to an existing directory.

However it is created, it is necessary that the destination directory exist for the cpio command to operate correctly. If it is not there, cpio does not run and displays an error message.

Cptdir begins the copying by going to the source directory and generating a list of the files that reside there, recursively going down the tree. This may result in more copying than you had planned, so you need to know the extent of the file structure you want to copy. Then the files are copied to the destination directory. The source files are not modified or altered in any way (except the access date may be modified).

While the copying is taking place, the output on the screen is from cpio, which displays the final path to the destination files. This path should agree with the one you put on the command line or something is wrong.

Examples

1. ```
$ cd /mnt
$ cptdir /bin .
```

Go to another mounted disk pack (commonly mounted on the /mnt directory) and copy all the /bin files to the current directory. Note that the resultant files are /mnt /*, which may not be what you want.

2. ```
$ cd /bin
$ cptdir . /mnt/bin
```

Like the preceding command, but notice the dots changed location. The command says to copy all the files in the current directory to the destination /mnt/bin. All files are then /mnt/bin/*, which sounds more reasonable.

3. ```
$ cptdir /bin /mnt
```

Same as example 1.

4. ```
$ cptdir /bin /mnt/bin
```

Same as example 2.

Explanation

In lines 4-9, the error checking is done for the command line arguments. If less than two arguments are used, there aren't enough. At least a source directory name and a destination directory name must be used. More than three arguments are too many. At the most, there should only be -s, a source directory, and a destination directory.

In lines 11-15, the options are set up for the cpio command. The default is pdv, which means "pass" for copying in file system format (as opposed to raw data stream), "directory" for creating directories if needed, and "verbose" for printing the file names as they are copied. If the first positional parameter is -s, which tells cptdir to run in silent mode, the cpio options do not include the verbose option, and thus the file names are not displayed.

Lines 17, 18, and 19 set up the "from" and "to" directories, and force the umask to 0. The umask determines the default permissions for all files created by our shell. We want to change the umask to ensure that all files are copied into the destination tree, and none are locked out due to not having read or write permission. A side effect is that all directories have rwxrwxrwx permission, and all files have rw-rw-rw- permissions, which may be areas where your security needs will force changes. The change to the umask is only in effect while the script is running. When cptdir dies, the umask of your calling shell is still intact.

Lines 21-29 do the checking of the destination directory. If it already exists, you are prompted to remove it and remake it. If it does not exist, it is created for `cpio`.

Lines 31-36 do the actual copying. Before explaining what is going on here, let's see how `cpio` works. Because the `find` statement is generating the file list for us, we need to be aware of how its output can affect the performance of `cpio`.

If we say "find . -print", the list of file names ends up with a dot in front, like this:

```
./dir
./dir/file1
./dir/file2
```

This is the relative notation, which is very useful to use when you don't want your files going to an absolute pathname but want to preserve their relationship with each other. If they are referenced according to "dot", the destination can be anywhere. However, if we said "find /dir -print", the list would look like this:

```
/dir
/dir/file1
/dir/file2
```

In both cases, we are referencing our current directory, but the use of /dir forces the pathname to start at "/" and does not allow any relative notation to be used. Passing this same information to `cpio` can radically change the destination of your files. For example, if I said "cd /src; find . -print ¦ cpio -pdv /dest", the final list is

```
/dest/./dir
/dest/./dir/file1
/dest/./dir/file2
```

which is probably what we wanted in the first place. However, if I said "find /src -print ¦ cpio -pdv /dest", the final pathnames would be

```
/dest/src/dir
/dest/src/dir/file1
/dest/src/dir/file2
```

79

which isn't good because it has created an unnecessary directory level. Notice that the directory name "src" got caught in the printout. This is because find printed it and cpio thought src was part of the destination name.

Always using the . notation may cause us to lose information that we already have. For example, if I said "cd /nowhere; find /src ....", the destination would get the wrong pathname. We should be able to use this kind of notation and not get trapped by the syntax. This is what cptdir does for us.

In line 31, the destination directory is checked to see whether the first character is a slash (/). If it is, we know right away that the destination directory name was expressed as an absolute pathname, so we can change directories without losing any information about our current directory. In line 32-33, we change to the source directory and copy the files.

But if the first character of the destination directory is *not* a slash, the notation used is relative. This means that if we change directories, we lose the information about where we were when the script was run. To avoid this, we get in line 34 the current directory by capturing the output of the pwd command and assigning it to a variable so that we can restore it later. We then change to the source directory and copy the files, using the absolute path prefix from the pwd, then the relative suffix from that location.

The reason for doing all this is to use the dot notation in the find statement. As can be seen in the preceding description, not using the dot notation can mess up the destination pathnames. To always use dot in find, we need to make sure where we are going to put the files. Again remember that the cd command only holds for this "lower" level shell, so it doesn't affect the shell that started the script. In general, a script should leave users in the same condition they were in before the script ran, except for accomplishing the job requested, which includes not changing the current directory.

When cptdir dies, control returns to the calling shell, which still maintains its own current directory. Remember that each time you go down a shell level, exported variables are passed down, but *nothing* is passed up.

Modifications

As currently implemented, no additional options are allowed to be passed in to the cpio command. What if you wanted to link all the files or have file dates modified by the copy? Neither capability would be possible.

We easily can add the capability of passing in further arguments. They should be recognized as arguments, saved, then shifted off the command line.

A loop something like this should work:

```
for ARG in $*
do
      if [ "`echo $ARG¦cut -c1`" = "-" ]
        then   CPIOARG="$CPIOARG $ARG"
               shift
      fi
done
```

Then the variable CPIOARG can be passed on to the `cpio` command.

Another area where changes could be made is in the handling of file permissions. As explained earlier, the umask 0 forces all permissions to be writeable. If this is not suitable to you, the `find` statement can be altered to copy (and change permissions) selectively.

For example, let's say you have a directory with two files in it. If the statement "find /dir -print" were executed, the list of files is

```
/dir
/dir/file1
/dir/file2
```

Note that the directory name occurs first. A problem arises when the directory name is not owned by you, or you do not have write permission. What happens is the directory name gets copied first, the permissions are established (locking you out), then file1 and file2 cannot be copied into dir. The solution we used in `cptdir` is to alter the umask so that you always have write permission. This is somewhat of a kludge, but it works.

An alternate way is to change the `find` statement. The statement "find /dir -depth -print" has the following effect on the file list generated:

```
/dir/file1
/dir/file2
/dir
```

Notice that the directory name is *last!* That's right. The -depth option reverses the file list so that the directory name is printed last.

What does this do? Well, magically, file1 and file2 are copied first, then the directory permissions are officially established. You can write the files into a directory for which you don't have write permission. Because the files are copied first, you do not have to worry about what kind of permissions the directory name carries. Unfortunately the -depth option of `find` is not supported on all versions of UNIX.

Name: can

can   Maintain a file trash can

Function

Moves files to a trash can to simulate file removal. By doing so, allows restoration of files after their simulated removal.

Synopsis

can [-l] [-r] file [file ...]

Sample Call

can junk   Put the file junk into the trash can

Code for can

```
1    :
2    # @(#) can v1.0   Maintain file trash can   Author: Russ Sage
3
4    CAN=$HOME/.trashcan
5
6    if [ ! -d $CAN ]
7       then mkdir $CAN
8    fi
9
10   if [ "`echo \"$1\"`|cut -c1`" = "-" ]
11      then case $1 in
12           -l)    echo "$CAN:"
13                  ls -al $CAN
14                  exit 0;;
15           -r)    echo "removing $CAN/*:"
16                  rm -rf $CAN/*
17                  exit 0;;
18           -z|-?) echo "usage can [-l] [-r] file [file ...]" >&2
19                  exit 0;;
20        esac
21   fi
22
23   mv $@ $CAN
```

Environment Variables

CAN   The directory location of the trash can
HOME   The directory location of your home directory

Description

Why do we need can?

In the final analysis UNIX, for all its splendors, is simply a framework for storing and manipulating data in files. As we noted earlier, one ends up with hundreds of files. Some files you want to keep indefinitely, whereas others have served their purpose and are cluttering up the disk. Unfortunately it's easy to throw away something you really wanted to keep. The unadorned rm command is an incinerator: Throw something in and it's gone (unless you have a backup, and restoring backups is a pain). Here are some classic ways that you can go wrong with rm:

`rm * /tmp` ←Remove all files in the /tmp directory

We really meant to say rm /tmp/*. What this did was to remove all the files in the current directory first, then try to remove /tmp. The latter failed since tmp is a directory. In fact, we've removed everything we wanted to keep and kept everything we wanted to remove! This syntax is similar to other UNIX statements like "grep * file": a nasty boo-boo.

`rm -rf / tmp` ←Remove the tmp directory with all its files

We really meant to say rm -rf /tmp but accidentally put a space in the command. What this did is remove *every* file in the whole system (if we let it run long enough) because we told UNIX to remove root and all her children! You should watch the `rm` command. If it looks like something is wrong, kill this command right away. It could be killing you.

Mistakes like this only need to happen once to ruin your whole day. After it happens you become cautious for a while, then ease off as time goes on. If you don't watch out, the mistake comes back to haunt you.

What we want is a trash can rather than an incinerator. That way, you can go back and retrieve something that you threw out by mistake. You also want to control when the garbage collector comes, makes his pickup, and removes the trash for good. What you can do is to review the contents of the trash can periodically, then clean out the can when you're sure that you don't want to keep anything in it. You don't want the can to get too full because it's using up disk space.

What does `can` do?

`Can` is designed to manage a trash can for your files. By using `can`, you can minimize the accidental loss of your work and even can retrieve files later if necessary.

`Can` not only places your files into the trash can, but shows you what is currently in the trash can and empties it when you want to.

The only options that `can` recognizes are -l and -r. The -l option lists what is in the trash can, and the -r option removes all of its contents. Remember that once you remove the trash, you won't be able to retrieve it.

The process of placing files into the trash can is done by the UNIX `mv` command. Options meant for `can` must be the first argument on the command line. If you want to pass options to the `mv` command, they can be placed on the command line in any position. The only options that give the usage statement are -z or -?. These are meant to be flags that are for error processing only. By having specific error processing flags, `mv` options may also be placed first on the command line without affecting `can`. in the "help" facility. If you design your scripts so that these options always produce the usage statement (that is, are never valid options), you have a consistent way of getting help on syntax. Many (but alas not all) standard UNIX commands give a usage statement when fed -z or -?, a useful thing to remember next time you're stumped.

If no options are passed to `can`, the default action is to move all the specified files into the trash can that resides in your home directory, named $HOME/.trash-can. If this directory does not exist, it is created automatically the first time `can` is run. This lets you run the command without having to set up any special locations. If you use the -r option, just the files in the trash can are removed, not the trash can itself.

Examples

1. `$ can *.c`

Move all files that end in .c to the trash can.

2. `$ can -l`

List all files that currently reside in the trash can.

3. `$ can -r`

Remove all files from the trash can.

4. `$ can -q *`

Lets the -q option be passed on to the `mv` command. This is not a valid `mv` command, so `mv` prints its error message and exits.

Explanation

Line 4 sets up the location of the trash can so that it resides in your home directory under the name of .trashcan. Notice that naming it with . first makes it an unlistable, or hidden, file. The only way to see these files is to use the -a option for the UNIX `ls` command.

Lines 6-8 check to see whether your trash can directory is currently defined. If it is not, it is made. Note that because it is made by you, it has your full permission for reading and writing in the home directory.

Lines 10-21 check to see whether the first positional parameter starts with a dash (-). If such a parameter is found, it is checked to see whether it is an option meant for can (-l, -r, -z, or - ?). Notice that to use double quotes inside of double quotes (line 10), you must quote the quotes. The backslash (\) character is used for this purpose.

If the option is -l, a reminder of the trash can directory's name is displayed, the files in the trash can are listed via the UNIX `ls` command, and `can` exits because only the listing was wanted.

If the option is -r, a message is given naming the trash can directory to be removed and the files in the trash can are removed by the `rm` command. This is destructive and removes your files forever. After the removal, `can` exits. You could add code to prompt for confirmation first if that would make you feel more comfortable.

If the option is either -z or -?, the usage statement is printed and `can` exits, which is sort of a kludgey way to do this, but we can't use * to match any other option because the option may be meant for `mv` rather than for `can`. By using a select few error processing arguments, we can let all other arguments pass. If an option isn't one of `can`'s options or one of our specified error options, it is passed to `mv`. If the option is invalid for `mv`, that command issues its own error message and quits. You could, of course, modify the script so that it checks for valid `mv` options at the "outer" level. Then it could issue an error message and quit if any option that isn't valid for either `can` or `mv` is used. The question is whether more complete control over error processing is worth extra coding and execution time.

Line 23 does the actual moving of the files into the trash can. Note that it is executed only if no `can` option is specified because this is `can`'s default behavior. The parameter $@ is used here. By including all the parameters on the command line, any options meant for `mv` are passed on to it. This way we can alter the way the files are moved into the trash can.

Name: dosflp

dosflp   Wildcard functionality for copying files from a DOS floppy

Function

Copies files from a DOS floppy (in XENIX) to the hard disk. Provides the capability of using wildcard notation for files on the floppy, where such notation does not normally exist.

Synopsis

dosflp [-a] [-c] [-dDRIV] [-eEXP][-h] [-l] [-r] [-sDIR]

where
    -a means copy files matching *.asm
    -c means copy files matching *.c
    -d selects drive name DRIV from A,B,X,Y (A is default)
    -e uses expression EXP to `grep` file names
    -h copies files matching *.h
    -l lists files only
    -r removes files instead of copying them
    -s specifies DOS subdirectory DIR on floppy

Sample Call

dosflp   Copy all files from A: to the current directory

Code for dosflp

```
1    :
2    # @(#) dosflp v1.0   Wildcard copies from DOS floppy   Author: Russ Sage
3
4    EXP=.\*
5    DRIVE="A:"
6    OP="c"
7
8    if [ "$#" -gt 0 ]
9      then  for ARG in $@
10           do
```

```
11              case "$ARG" in
12              -a)   EXP='.*\.asm$';;
13              -c)   EXP='.*\.c$';;
14              -d*)  DRIVE="'echo $ARG | cut -c3-':";;
15              -e*)  EXP=''echo $ARG | cut -c3-'';;
16              -h)   EXP='.*\.h$';;
17              -l)   OP="l";;
18              -r)   OP="r";;
19              -s*)  DRIVE="$DRIVE'echo \"$ARG\" | cut -c3- '/";"
20              *)    echo "dosflp: arg error"
21                    echo "usage: dosflp [-a] [-c] [-d] [-e] [-h] [-l]
[-r] [-s]"
22                    exit 1;;
23            esac
24        done
25   fi
26
27   case $OP in
28   c)   echo "\nCopying files from $DRIVE to 'pwd'";;
29   l)   echo "\nListing files on $DRIVE"
30        dosdir $DRIVE | more
31        exit;;
32   r)   echo "This option removes all the data on the floppy."
33        echo -n "Do you want to do this (y/n): "
34        read RSP
35        if [ "$RSP" = "y" ]
36          then  echo "\nRemoving files on $DRIVE"
37          else  exit
38        fi;;
39   esac
40
41   dosls $DRIVE | tr "[A-Z]" "[a-z]" > /tmp/doslist
42
43   for FILE in 'grep "$EXP" /tmp/doslist'
44   do
45            echo $FILE
46            case $OP in
47            c) doscp $DRIVE$FILE .;;
48            r) dosrm $DRIVE$FILE;;
49            esac
50   done
51
52   rm /tmp/doslist
```

Environment Variables

ARG   Holds arguments from the command line
DRIVE   Drive that accesses the DOS floppy

EXP	Expression that simulates wildcard action
FILE	Holds each file name to be acted on
OP	Option that defines what action to take

Description

Why do we need dosflp?

This command is for the XENIX system only. XENIX, being a product of Microsoft, has the facilities to talk to an MS-DOS file system. As background for those who do not know about the use of DOS with XENIX, let's review the basic parameters.

Each hard disk can have a maximum of four partitions. This is a DOS limitation that carries over into the XENIX world. It is not too bad, until you start to work with large hard disks. With a 70M disk, for example, you might configure four equal partitions, each containing approximately 17M. You could create a smaller partition, but then another one would have to be bigger. The practical consideration of how much of your software and data is to be used primarily under MS-DOS and how much under XENIX may dictate a different configuration.

The one big advantage to XENIX/DOS is that XENIX can reside on one partition and DOS on another. How to do this is to run the program "fdisk" under each operating system. That means XENIX can talk to a DOS partition by accessing the device pathname that leads to a different partition. The driver for reading the DOS partition must know what DOS looks like (that is, what is DOS's file system). Once this is done, the files can be listed and copied back and forth. Unfortunately, DOS has no provision to read XENIX partitions.

In the case of a floppy disk, you only have to deal with one partition. This again is a DOS restraint. Some UNIX systems allow as many partitions on a hard disk or floppy as you want, but this is not so in the DOS world. By definition, a DOS floppy is formatted under DOS, which does a low-level format and places a DOS file system on the disk.

Under XENIX, a floppy can be either a file system or a raw sequential device similar to a tape. For dosflp, we are using only DOS formatted floppies.

Now to the matter at hand: Assuming you have a DOS system and you have files stored on a DOS disk, you can read and write files to the floppy from XENIX. But some restrictions apply to the copying that are not very user friendly. For example, you can say "doscp *.c a:". This copies all files in the current directory that end in .c to the DOS floppy in drive a. One side effect of doing a doscp is that all newlines (or line feeds) are turned into carriage return/line feeds because DOS treats end-of-line differently than XENIX. Likewise, when you copy from a DOS floppy to XENIX, the extra carriage returns are stripped out.

The thing that you can't do is say "doscp a:*.c .". The doscp command does not accept *.c when copying from the floppy. This is because the shell expands metacharacters (*,?,[]), and the shell cannot read the DOS partition directly. Therefore, you cannot use wildcards when copying from the DOS floppy.

Note that many more side effects are possible when dealing with DOS floppies. First, the length of the file name is limited. DOS allows up to eight characters plus a three-character extension. The result is that after copying all your XENIX files to a floppy, many of them may not have the same name as they had under XENIX. This is a pain when trying to do backups to DOS floppies because you may no longer be sure how to refer to the files when copying them back from the floppy. Also, because the extension in DOS is only three characters, a file called "spreadsheet.finance" could end up on the DOS floppy as "spreadsh.fin", which might be hard for you to find.

That's not all. When the file is copied from XENIX to DOS, *all* file names under DOS are stored with capital letters in the file name. If you have file names that mix upper- and lowercase, you are going to lose some readability. If you use uppercase letters when you copy the files back to XENIX, they are not converted back to lowercase. The result is that all your files end up in uppercase under XENIX. Not too good again.

What we need is a tool so that we can specify which files to copy from the floppy to the hard disk, and have them copied while still preserving the case of the file name. All this is done by `dosflp`.

What does `dosflp` do?

`Dosflp` tries to eliminate all the negative aspects to XENIX/DOS file copying. This is a tall order but one that is achievable. Briefly, the approach of `dosflp` is to get a list of the file names from the floppy, convert the names to lowercase, pick the files from the entire list that match your wildcard criteria, then copy each file, one by one, to the current XENIX directory. To do this requires more XENIX dosxx commands as well as various XENIX commands.

In addition to copying, `dosflp` also lists the files that reside on the DOS floppy and removes files on the floppy. These functions are easy to implement because once the access procedure is written, adding new commands to operate on the files is straightforward.

We usually want to handle certain types of files as groups. These include assembler source files, C source files, and C header files. So that you don't have to enter wildcards for these file types, we have hard coded them as options to the `dosflp` command. For example, the -a option copies only files that end in .asm, so you don't have to remember the expression notation for copying these files. Similarly, -c copies all files that end in .c, and -h copies files ending in .h.

As we see later, the hard coded expressions that we are talking about here are `grep` expressions. The full power of `grep` is available for specifying patterns of file names.

Use the -d option to specify which floppy drive to copy from. The default drive is a:, or A:. The case of the drive character usually is not a problem. To be sure, check the file /etc/default/msdos. This file contains the match between the drive character and the XENIX pathname. An example file might look like this:

```
A=/dev/fd048ds9
B=/dev/fd148ds9
C=/dev/hd0d
D=/dev/hd1d
X=/dev/fd096ds15
Y=/dev/fd196ds15
```

As you can see, the pathnames are usual device names—nothing special here.

The engine used by `dosflp` is the `doscp` command. This is the utility with the brains to understand the DOS file system format. `Dosflp` passes the drive designator and other options to it via shell variables. For example, the option "-dB:" changes to drive B from default drive A.

If the hard coded expressions are not what you want, you can define your own wildcard expressions by using the -e option. Remember that the expression has to conform to the `grep` syntax. If you need to refresh your memory, see grep(1) in AT&T UNIX, or grep(C) in XENIX. For the full regular expression syntax, see ed(1). This is the basis of most regular expression commands, like `sed` and `grep`.

For example, if you use the expression "*test*", the grep expression would be ".*test.*". This could be altered a bit depending on what you want on either side of the test string. The syntax specifies all characters (.*), followed by the string t-e-s-t, followed by any string (.*). The option then would be "- e.*test.*". This looks kind of bizarre, but it fits the syntax. (The double quotes are not actually included in the command.) The backslash (\) character is used to quote the asterisk. If you don't quote it, the shell expands it with all the file names from your current directory, which isn't what we wanted. Quoting it allows the actual character to be passed on for `dosflp` to use in the `grep` string.

The -h option is another one of the hard coded options. Let's take a brief look at its syntax inside `dosflp`. It is ".*\.h$", and it specifies any character followed by one or more occurrences of any character (.*), a literal period (\.), and the h character followed by the end of the line (h$). You could type this using the -e option but -h makes it a lot easier.

The -l option changes the basic operation of the `dosflp` command. Rather than copying files, the command lists files. This is done using a different dosxx command, in this case `dosdir`. The list option is useful in `dosflp` so that you can get a list as part of deciding what to do next, and you won't have to remember `dosdir`.

The -r option also changes the basic operation of the `dosflp` command. In this case, the files are removed instead of being copied. If you type this option, a message is printed to ask you to confirm that you want to remove the specified files. You can simply reply "n" and abort the removal if you typed the option by accident. Remember that the removed files, or in the case of -l, the listed files, are selected by the hard coded or user-specified `grep` expression. By default, `all` files are matched. For the -r option, this is analogous to saying "rm *".

The last option, -s, provides the capability of accessing files that reside inside a subdirectory on the DOS floppy. If you reference only the drive name, -s defaults to the topmost directory on the floppy. If the file you want is in a subdirectory, you must use proper notation to get to it. One difference between XENIX and DOS is in the character used to separate elements in a pathname. XENIX uses the normal UNIX style notation, /x/y/z. Under DOS, the character used is the backslash, \x\y\z. But if you want to use the XENIX commands on a DOS floppy, you must use the normal XENIX notation, a:/x/y/z. Kind of confusing, but that's the way it is.

By default, `dosflp` wants to copy files from the floppy to your current directory on the hard disk. If you change the operation to listing or removing, it performs these actions on the floppy.

Examples

1. ```
$ dosflp -dB: -c -l
```

List all files *.c on the DOS floppy in drive B. This does not go down into subdirectories but only involves files that reside on the top directory level.

2. ```
$ cd /destdir
$ dosflp -ssrc -e.\*src.\*
```

Change to the directory where the files are to be put. Copy the files from the DOS floppy in drive A, subdirectory src, to the current directory. The files to copy are *src*. In UNIX notation, it would look like "cp A:/src/*src* .".

3. ```
$ dosflp -r -stmp
```

Remove all files that reside in the tmp subdirectory on the DOS floppy in drive A. Notice that this does not remove the directory itself. In UNIX notation, it would be "rm A:/tmp/*".

4. ```
$ sh -x 'path dosflp' -dB:
```

This runs the dosflp tool in "execution" debug mode. The one restriction when invoking the shell this way is that the data file you pass to it (in this case dosflp) must be a full pathname. The shell does *not* do a path lookup for the file, which is why we need to find the path to dosflp first, then feed this path to a shell running in debug mode, as well as pass dosflp an argument on the command line. Notice that calling dosflp this way does not alter the value of $#, which only recognizes the -dB: as an argument.

Explanation

Lines 4-6 do the default initializations by storing the values in the appropriate shell variables. The default expression wildcard matches every file, signified by the grep expression .*. The backslash is required to quote the asterisk, so it is not expanded by the shell. The default drive is A:. The default operation is to copy files; indicated by the value "c" for the option variable.

In lines 8-25, the setting up of options and error checking are performed. If the command line has some arguments ($# -gt 0), we iterate through each argument and check it. If a valid option is found, variables are set up according to the option. If an invalid option is encountered, an error message is printed and the program exits with a bad return status.

There are essentially two kinds of options. The options that set hard coded file type selections simply set the variable EXP according to the option. Similarly, the options that set the kind of processing to be performed by the script simply set the variable OP accordingly. The other options must be processed by extracting one or more characters from the command line following the option flag by echoing and piping the current ARG to the cut command to extract the character(s) starting with the third character in the argument, then assigning the output of this operation to the appropriate variable.

A consequence of the way we do this is that spaces cannot be allowed between options and the characters following them. For example, the -d option has to get the drive name from the option. The syntax must be -dB:, not -d B: because the B: would be interpreted as another ARG in the for loop, which throws everything off.

In lines 27-39, the operation to be performed is determined by another case statement. If copying is to be done, the "copying" message is printed and execution continues following the case statement. If the files are to be listed, a message indicating the drive whose contents are to be listed is printed, the listing is done by running dosdir and piping its output to more, and dosflp exits.

If the files are to be removed, the user is prompted to continue. If the response is "yes," a displayed message indicates from which drive the files are to be removed. If the response is "no," dosflp exits.

The rest of the script is concerned with the mechanics of copying. Line 41 is the first step in bridging the gap that resides between the two types of media. The dosls command is used to get a clean listing of files from the floppy. Before we put this list into a temporary file, we pipe it through the tr (translate) command, which converts all the characters to lowercase so that when the files are actually copied, the filenames used are in lowercase, which results in the copy being placed on the XENIX disk in lowercase. If you have files that are uppercase or mixed, you have to change them by hand after the copy.

Lines 43-50 do the actual copying. A for loop is run to access each file individually. This is a constraint imposed from the dosxx commands. You have to access files one at a time because this level has no wildcard capability. The file names that the for loop uses are determined by using grep to select names according to the expression set up earlier.

The name of each file selected is echoed first so that the user can see whether the command is performing as expected. At this point, we can be doing one of two things: copying files or removing them. The operation is determined by the case statement in lines 46-49. If the operation is to copy files, the file is copied from the drive-file combination to the current directory. Note that in the DRIVE variable, the subdirectory is included if it was specified from the command line. This explains the extra "/" character at the end of the assignment to the DRIVE variable in line 16. The full effect would be like this: B:/subdir/file. If the operation is to remove files, the drive/file combination is removed via the dosrm command. As an aside, the pathname is somewhat flexible (or sloppy, depending on how you like to look at it) in that you can say A:subdir, or A:/subdir. Either way works. After all the files have been processed, the temp file is removed.

Modifications

One area where you could customize dosflp is in expressions. The expressions are already included for .asm, .c, and .h, but you could change these or add more options for any string that you use a lot.

Backup Techniques

Name: autobkp

autobkp   Automatic incremental file backup

Function

Searches file trees for files that have changed in the last 24 hours and transfers them to another system (via uucp) or moves them to another area on the hard disk.

Synopsis

autobkp [-c] [<pathlist] [> >logfile]

-c copies files to another area on disk instead of using uucp

Sample Call

autobkp < filelist > > bkplog

Back up all files specified in the file named filelist and record the file names in the file named bkplog

Code for autobkp

```
1    :
2    # @(#) autobkp v1.0   Automatic file backup   Author: Russ Sage
3
4    if [ $# -gt 1 ]
5      then  echo "autobkp: argument error"                       >&2
6            echo "usage: autobkp [-c] [<pathlist] [>>logfile]"    >&2
7            exit
8    fi
9
10   if [ "$1" = "-c" ]
11     then  COPY=on
12     else  COPY=off
13   fi
14
15   echo "\nBACKUP DATE   'date '+%a %m/%d/%y %H:%M:%S''"
16   echo "----------------------------------------"
17
18   SYSTEM=''        # destination system uucp node name
19   : ${SYSTEM:='uuname -l'}
20
21   echo "Source system:\t\t'uuname -l'\nDestination system:\t$SYSTEM"
22
23   while read SRCDIR DESTDIR FILES
24   do
25         if [ ! -d $SRCDIR ]
26           then  echo "autobkp: $SRCDIR is not a directory"
27                 continue
28         fi
29
30         cd $SRCDIR
```

```
31          echo "\nFinding files in: $SRCDIR"
32
33          for FILE in 'find . -type f -ctime 0 -name "$FILES" -print'
34          do
35                  case $COPY in
36                  off) uucp $FILE $SYSTEM!$DESTDIR;;
37                  on)  cp $FILE $DESTDIR;;
38                  esac
39                  echo " Transferred  $FILE  to  $DESTDIR"
40          done
41   done
```

Environment Variables

COPY   Flag to determine whether uucp or cp command to be used
FILE   Each file found from the source pathlist
FILES   Wildcard to specify which files qualify
PATH1   Source pathname
PATH2   Destination pathname
SYSTEM   Destination system name for uucp

Description

Why do we need autobkup?

As we've remarked, UNIX files breed like rabbits. The more files we create, the longer keeping them organized takes. It's easy to get lazy or acquire a false sense of security and neglect regular backups.

You can approach file backups in several ways. The most common strategy is to do *incremental* backups, where the whole system is backed up at some starting date (and sometimes again at regular but infrequent intervals). At frequent intervals (usually daily), the file system is examined for files that have been modified or added in the last 24 hours. These files are backed up, so the backup as a whole is kept up current.

Where to place backup files is another issue and depends on the configuration of your system, the amount of storage available, and the criticality of the data involved. Let's consider some of the options.

A standalone micro or supermicro system may have only one hard disk. If the disk contains enough space to hold a separate partition, you can back up to that partition. A partition can also be used as a raw device rather than a file system and treated like a tape or floppy. Alternative storage options may include a second hard disk, a cartridge device, or a tape backup device. If you have none of these options available, you can always back up to floppies. This is a rather tedious manual process, but it can be handled with cpio or tar.

If you also have access to another, larger system like a corporate mainframe, you can back up files by sending them to that system via uucp. Even if you have enough storage on your own system to hold your own backups, you might very well want to send a copy of any critical files to the mainframe because that gives you an off-site backup. Fires, floods, and other disasters do happen.

What we need is a mechanism that usually is run automatically (by `cron`, or with the aid of the `at` tool we present in Chapter 5). First, it finds all the files that have been changed in the last 24 hours (assuming that you already have an initial copy of everything). It starts looking for files from specified directories and copies the qualified files to specified destination directories. It copies the files with the utility that best fits the configuration which you are currently using. All these things are accomplished by our `autobkp` script.

What does `autobkp` do?

You list paths, and `autobkp` finds the files in those paths and copies them to the destinations you specify. You can specify file names with patterns such as *.c, *.h, or whatever. With `autobkp`, you can back up critical files without backing up all files. It is sometimes advantageous to omit files from backups. Typical files you may not want to back up are very large files that aren't critical, like core and data files; temporary files, like *.o, which are recreated with each new compile; and executables, where you have the C source and can compile to get a new executable. By omitting these types of files, you can reduce the size of your backups by megabytes.

The default backup is copy via `uucp`, which assumes that you are a satellite system to a mainframe and backs up your files to the larger system. If you want to copy the files to another area on the hard disk, or a second hard disk, use the -c option to copy with `cp` instead of using `uucp`.

Throughout the backup process, status messages are displayed to stdout. This makes it easy to collect all the messages by redirecting stdout while doing the backup. If you use `autobkp` manually, the messages go to the screen. The first message is a banner that prints the day, date and time. It looks like this:

```
BACKUP DATE    Fri 05/23/86 17:33:35
```

The second message identifies the source and destination systems. The output appears below. In this example, the source system is russ and the destination system is vax.

```
Source system:   russ
Destination system: vax
```

As each source location is visited, the following message is displayed

```
Finding files in: src_dir
```

where the word "src_dir" is the location from which files are being supplied to the copy loop. Notice that the first name should be a directory. This is because `autobkp` starts from that location to find the files. If the first name is not a directory, the program prints an error message and continues with the next set of source/destination backups.

For each file that is found, the following message is printed after the copy has been made

```
Transferred file to dest_dir
```

which specifies that file "file" has been copied to the destination directory dest_dir.

The PATHLIST File

To make the interface as flexible as possible, `autobkp` reads the stdin. By redirecting stdin, you can maintain different lists of files that need to be backed up and switch them on the command line. You might have one pathlist for system files, another for source files, a third for personal files, a fourth for product files, and so on. A pathlist for each of these sets of files is created and fed as input to `autobkp`. The input is read for three fields: FROM, TO, and TYPE. The FROM field is the source directory. All backup files are found from this location. Remember that `autobkp` traverses down to the bottom of the file tree from the specified directory.

The TO field is the destination directory, where all the files found for this entry in the pathlist file end up on the destination machine or partition.

The TYPE field is the wildcard specifier that tells `autobkp` which files to look for. Values here can be *, *.c, *src*, and so on. As we see later, this wildcard is fed to the UNIX `find` command, which actually does the file lookup. You can use any expression in the TYPE field as long as it conforms to the syntax of `find`.

To summarize: Any files that have changed in the last 24 hours are found in the FROM list using the TYPE qualifier, and are copied to the TO area.

Below is a typical pathlist file. It specifies multiple directories to use in looking for files. Note that these directories are under the home directory: If you wanted to back up *all* your home directory, you could specify that directory, but here we want to single out specific directories.

```
/usr/russ/bin      /pack1/russ/.bkp/bin        *
/usr/russ/doc      /pack1/russ/.bkp/doc        *
/usr/russ/src      /pack1/russ/.bkp/src        *.c
/usr/product1      /pack1/russ/.bkp/product1   *.[ch]
```

The entries back up the bin, doc, and src directories on the author's local machine. In the case of the src directory, we've specified that only C source files (*.c) are to be backed up. Some product information also is being backed up, from another area on the same system. Only files with the extensions *.c and *.h are backed up.

The destination (hard coded in the autobkp script) is another UNIX system. The destination is some mounted disk pack, the home directory, and a backup subdirectory.

Using Cron

Now that autobkp knows what to find, let's tell it when to find it. Cron, the always resident time keeper, can do this job easily. Cron entries usually are set by system administrators (or whoever has write permission on /usr/lib/crontab), so you might have to ask the administrator to put an entry in cron's data file for you. To get more information on cron entries, read cron(1M) in the Administrators Manual. Briefly, the fields in /usr/lib/crontab are minute, hour, day of month, month of year and day of week. By using *, we can force many of these fields to be all possible values. A cron entry to back up my home directory at 4:00 a.m. every day of every week of every month of the year would look like this:

```
0 4 * * * /usr/russ/bin/autobkp.cron
```

Notice that the cron entry calls a driver script instead of using autobkp directly. There are several good reasons for writing a driver script to wrap around the basic autobkp utility. First, cron does not print diagnostic information to your terminal, so if anything goes wrong you never hear about it. Second, it is easier to maintain a stripped-down version of autobkp and add bells and whistles to the driver script. You can make your own modifications to the driver script and not worry about messing up the real utility. The driver script can be as sophisticated as you want it to be. The one presented here is functional but can be added to easily.

```
# Cron-driven autobkp driver
echo "backed up: 'date'" > /dev/tty00
/usr/bin/autobkp < /usr/russ/bin/autobkpath
                 >> /usr/russ/bin/autobkp.log
```

This driver puts a message to the terminal, fires off autobkp, uses the pathlist file in the bin directory for input, and places all output to the log file. Notice that the terminal device name is absolute (tty00), which only works if you have a hard coded terminal connected to the system. Using the terminal device name allows the message to appear on that CRT even if no one is logged in on it. This is kind of nice because you can see the message on your screen the first thing in the morning. If you do not have a hard coded terminal, maybe you can do something different, like mailing the message to yourself.

Examples

1. `$ autobkp`

Run the program without passing it pathlists or log files. Because stdin is looking for FROM, TO, TYPE, type these three fields by hand. When you press the carriage return, autobkp goes off and does its thing, prints any information to the terminal screen, and waits for more input. To stop, enter ^d (it makes the read statement return with a nonzero status).

2. `$ autobkp < pathlist`

Get all input data from pathlist, but print all backup logging information to the terminal screen. Autobkp terminates when it has read all the data in pathlist.

3. `$ autobkp >> logfile`

Again, the pathlists must be input from the keyboard. All output goes to the log file rather than to the terminal screen. To terminate autobkp, type ^d.

4. `$ autobkp -c < pathlist >> logfile`

Copy the files from one area of the hard disk to another (determined by the destination directory in pathlist). Use the input from the pathlist file and put all output to the file logfile.

Explanation

Lines 4-8 do the error checking. Autobkp can be called either with no options or with one option (-c, for using cp). Remember that redirection is *not* considered to provide arguments because the shell interprets the redirection symbol and what follows it before calling the command). Thus, if the number of positional parameters is greater than 1 ($# -gt 1), an error condition results. Then the error message and usage statement are echoed to standard error and the program exits.

Lines 10-13 check to see whether the -c option has been used. Notice that we don't check to see whether $# is equal to 1 or try to cut out the first character to see whether it is a "-" because such tests fail if no option was passed (which is valid syntax as noted previously). If we said

```
if [ $1 = -c ]
```

and did not pass in the option, the test command would bomb out, displaying a message about "no argument in the statement." But when we quote it like it is

```
if [ "$1" = "-c" ]
```

the quotes allow for a null value in the argument, so test correctly evaluates a missing $1 as "is null equal to -c?" This is false, so everything is okay.

97

As a side note, look particularly carefully at the test command. You can test values two ways. The first is string comparison and the second is number comparison. Shell variables are *always* stored as strings. You can, however, force the system to see those strings as numbers and interpret their values as such, like the BASIC language statement number = val(STRING$). You tell the system to change its way of seeing the strings by altering the syntax for the comparison. For strings, the comparison is

```
str1 = str2
```

but numerical comparison is like this:

```
num1 -eq num2
     -lt
     -gt
```

Check it against the manual. If you try to mix strings with numerical comparisons, the comparisons do not work. It took me many months of shell programming to finally notice this slight difference. Without seeing something like this, bugs seem very elusive, but explanations can be found for why things don't work.

Returning to the option checking code, if the -c option is passed, the COPY variable is set to on, meaning "Yes, we are going to copy with `cp` rather than use `uucp`." If the -c option is not used, COPY is set to off.

Lines 15-16 print the banner message for the backup session that is going to take place. Note that we buried the UNIX `date` command inside the `echo` statement, reducing the amount of data capturing that we would have to go through to get the date directly.

Watch for the quotes in this statement. The outer quotes are double to bundle the complete argument for the `echo` statement. The grave accents (') enclose the date command so that it is "subexecuted" and its output captured for our use. The single quotes inside the `date` command are used to pass a format to alter the arrangement of the values for a more readable banner. At the end of the `echo` statement, all the quotes are next to each other. This does not present a problem, as there is no potential ambiguity in the nesting. You do have to remember to watch for situations where you and the shell might disagree on what is wanted, that is, when you have to go to the \" type of notation.

Line 18 assigns the name of the remote system you are `uucp`ing to the variable SYSTEM. Here it is null, which later triggers another action to provide a default. If, however, you always want to `uucp` to a particular other system, modify this line to assign the name of that system. If line 18 is left so that it assigns a null, line 14 picks this up and assigns to SYSTEM the name of your current system. In other words, if you leave line 18 as it is and call `autobkp` without the -c option, you `uucp` to yourself, which is perfectly legal. For reasons of efficiency, you probably would want to do an `autobkp -c` for making local backups, however.

Line 19 illustrates a concept used very often in shell programming. Let's look at it a piece at a time.

The first character is ":". In this case, we are interested in what takes place in the test rather than in the return value, so we let the colon ("do nothing") command receive the results as an argument. The text following the colon is interpreted like this: "If the variable SYSTEM is not set or is set to null, set it to the value that follows." The value in this case is the output from the command uuname -l. What this does is set as the destination system the same system as the source system if the destination was not hard coded earlier.

The reason we use uuname -l rather than the regular uname -n is for compatibility. Uname -n gets the node name right from the uts structure in the kernel, but not all XENIX systems use the kernel uts structure node element. Instead, they put the name in the file /etc/systemid, which accommodates the micnet that was designed for XENIX by Microsoft. The uuname -l command is the local name (or source machine) for the uucp system and returns the correct value on both UNIX and XENIX. It makes sense to use something that always works!

Line 21 prints the values of the source system name and the destination system name. This message adds information to the record of what is going on, so you can see how you have the script set up by the output. Again, we are burying the uuname command inside the echo statement. We don't need to save the source system name because it is always available to us through the uuname command. Because we've only used this name twice, we decided not to assign it to a variable.

Lines 23-41 are the entire loop that drives autobkp. The control loop is a while statement that reads values from the stdin. Note that you can read more than just one value in the read statement. This is nice when you want to read more than one value but don't need to parse out each piece of input to figure out whether it is the first, second, or third data item. We read them all at once, and they are assigned to the specified variables. Because the read is from the stdin, we can redirect stdin when we call autobkp and the read statement never knows the difference. If we don't redirect input, then we have to type it in from the keyboard. The loop terminates when the end of file is read; in this case, the end of the pathlist file or a control-d (^d) from the keyboard. So the driving loop says "while there is still more data to read in, read a set, process it, then read another set."

Lines 25-28 check to see whether the source directory is really a directory. If it is not, an error message is displayed and the continue statement forces the next iteration of the while loop.

Line 30 actually changes directory to the source directory. This is so the output of the find command is relative to . (dot). If we did not do a cd, the pathname would end up being absolute, which would be carried over to the destination system. Then the path starting from the destination directory would have an extra absolute path under it.

Line 31 prints the directory where the source files are being found. This is nice to have in the log file because you can read and follow more easily where autobkp is going.

Lines 33-40 do the actual copying of the files. The loop here is a for loop that reads file names from the output of a find command. Note that this automatically limits the total number of files that the loop can handle. This has been explained earlier in the book, but let's look at it again. If find produces a list of hundreds of files, the word list of the for statement overflows and bombs out your shell (or at least this command). The assumption here is that you won't have that many files in the source directory. You could avoid this by breaking up the source directory into smaller pieces and putting them in the pathlist file. If you want to make this a really robust loop, change it to look like this:

```
find . -type f -ctime 0 -name "$FILES" -print | while read FILE
```

By using this type of loop, the limit of file names has now been changed from the input limit for the shell to the size of a pipe in the system (which is very large, infinite for practical purposes). Changing this one line does not affect any other part of the loop.

Let's look at the details of the `find` command. First, we tell it to look for files in the current directory (.). This makes all pathnames relative to dot. Next we tell it to find all files of type f, which means regular files rather than directories or device files. We don't want to back up those kind of files. Next we tell it to look for files that have changed. By "changed," we mean accessed or modified. (To see which commands alter the access, change and modify times and look at stat(2). By telling find to look for "ctime 0", we mean all files changed in the last 24 hours. The explanation that `find`'s documentation gives on these numbers is kind of bizarre, so take it with a grain of salt.) Then we tell it to find only files that qualify by having their name fit the path specified in the $FILES value we read in. At this stage, we can filter out files we don't want (as explained previously) or select files that we do want. Finally we tell find to print the file names of all files that fit the criteria. The file names then are fed to the for loop. In other words, the output of the `find` command becomes the argument to the enclosing for loop.

In lines 35-38, the case statement determines what type of backup we are going to do and issues the copy commands. If COPY is set to off, we `uucp` the files. Notice here that the destination is SYSTEM. If we leave SYSTEM null in line 18, SYSTEM is our own system and we `uucp` files to ourself. If COPY is on, regardless of the value of SYSTEM, we copy (rather than `uucp`) the files to another directory in the current system. This directory could be on the same hard disk, or it could be another mounted file system. After the file has been copied, a message is echoed that tells which file got transferred to where. This is also nice for the log file to have so that we are able to track where your backup files were shuttled to.

The `find` loop cycles until all files in the current tree segment are done. Remember that find is recursive, so make sure you aren't asking for more of the tree than you want to deal with. If you say backup from /, every file in the system could be transferred. When the for loop is done, the outer while loop goes to its next iteration. When all input data has been processed, the program exits.

Some Considerations for `uucp`

When using `uucp`, the destination path must have the "x" or execution bit on for group "others" for all intermediate directories to the file. This would look like:

```
--------x
```

The very last directory must have "wx" permissions, so `uucp` can write the file in the directory. Then the file is owned by uucp. If you need to be owner, copy it (use cp rather than mv) to a different file name, and ownership is yours. If you mv it, you are only changing the name associated with the same inode. But when you cp it, you create a brand new inode. This new inode (created by you) has your uid and gid, so you own it. If you are root and copy a file (using cp, not mv) on top of another existing file, the inode information does not change, only the data that the inode accesses.

When uucp forces the preceding file permissions on all intervening directories to be writeable by everyone, the final directory has *no* security. Allowing anyone to have write access means that anyone can remove or alter the files in that directory. Not everyone wants to open themselves up to this. If you copy the files to the normal uucp public area (/usr/spool/uucppublic/$LOGNAME) instead, you have to watch them closely. Many systems have a script that runs from cron, which finds files in this directory that have not been accessed in a certain number of days and removes those files—so much for your backups. If the retention period is longer than your backup cycle time, you might be all right. Like many other things, it depends on your circumstances and security needs.

Development Discoveries

The original design of the pathlists had the TYPE argument at the end of the FROM argument, as in /usr/russ/bin/*. This presented a problem (besides showing your author was not a master yet!) because when the * was stripped, it was expanded into all the file names instead of the literal character. The easy solution was to make it a separate field, as it is now. The masterly solution is to quote the metacharacter to keep it literal. As the * is being stripped from the pathname, the \ keeps it in the * form instead of letting it become expanded. An example would be:

```
TYPE='basename \"$FROM"'
```

This puts the character * into the variable TYPE instead of making TYPE a list of all files that fit the metachar. Then when find is called, the TYPE variable must be quoted so that the metachar is not expanded by the shell, but by find itself.

Name: cpiobr

cpiobr   Cpio stream backup and restore

Function

Provides a menu interface to the cpio command and the facilities for backing up and restoring files. The output to the media is in sequential stream format.

Synopsis

cpiobr

Sample Call

cpiobr   Call up the main menu to back up, restore, or list files

Code for cpiobr

```
1    :
2    # @(#) cpiobr v1.0    Cpio stream backup and restore    Author: Russ Sage
3
4    if [ "$#" -gt "0" ]
5       then  echo "cpiobr: too many arguments"
6             exit
7    fi
8
9    while :
10   do
11              c
12              set `date`
13              echo "
14
15   $1, $2 $3                        $4
16
17         Cpio Backup & Restore
18         ---------------------
19      Backup to removable media
20      Restore from removable media
21      List files on media
22      Long list files on media
23      <cr> to exit
24
25      Press b,r,f,l, or <cr>: \c"
26
27         read CMD
28         if [ "$CMD" = "" ]
29           then break
30          fi
31
32          ABORT=off
33
34          while :
35          do
36                  echo "
37
38    Enter media type:
39       Raw System V floppy drive (/dev/rfp021)
40       Raw XENIX floppy drive    (/dev/rfd0)
41       Tape drive                (/dev/rmt0)
42       Any device                (/dev/???)
```

```
43        <cr> to exit
44
45        Press s,x,t,a, or <cr>: \c"
46
47                    read MEDIA
48                    case $MEDIA in
49            s|S)    DEV=/dev/rfp021
50                    break;;
51            x|X)    DEV=/dev/rfd0
52                    break;;
53            t|T)    DEV=/dev/rmt0
54                    break;;
55            a|A)    echo "enter full pathname (or <> to exit): \c"
56                    read DEV
57                    if [ "$DEV" = "" ]
58                        then  continue
59                          else  break
60                    fi;;
61            "")     ABORT=on
62                    break;;
63            *)      echo "cpiobr: invalid command \"$MEDIA\"";;
64                    esac
65          done # while get media
66
67          if [ "$ABORT" = "on" ]
68             then continue
69          fi
70
71        case $CMD in
72        b|B)    echo "\nEnter the source directory name: \c"
73                read SRC
74                cd $SRC
75                echo "\nPlace floppy in drive and hit <cr> ...\c"
76                read CMD
77                find . -print | sort | cpio | -ocBv > $DEV
78                echo "\nhit <cr>\c"
79                read CMD
80                ;;
81        r|R)    echo "\nEnter the destination directory name: \c"
82                read DEST
83                cd $DEST
84                echo "\nPlace floppy in drive and hit <cr> ...\c"
85                read CMD
86                cpio -icBvdmu < $DEV
87                echo "\nhit <cr>\c"
88                read CMD
89                ;;
```

```
90              f¦F)    cpio -icBt < $DEV
91                      echo "\nhit <cr>\c"
92                      read CMD
93                      ;;
94              l¦L)    cpio -icBtv < $DEV
95                      echo "\nhit <cr>\c"
96                      read CMD
97                      ;;
98              *)      echo "cpiobr: invalid command \"'$CMD\'""
99                      ;;
100             esac
101     done
```

Environment Variables

ABORT	Flag that determines whether to abort
CMD	Command read in from user
DEST	Destination directory during restore
DEV	Pathname to device for media
MEDIA	Holds type of media to be used
SRC	Source directory during backup

Description

Why do we need cpiobr?

We've already gained a measure of convenience and control over backups with autobkp, but we haven't dealt with "raw devices" yet. These are devices that do not contain a file system, but simply have data put on them as a stream. Tapes and sometimes floppies are used in this fashion. As noted earlier, you may not have the hard-disk storage or off-site system to do a backup in file system format. Instead, you may need to use a stack of floppies or a tape device. Even if you have other backup options, there are times when a backup to a tape or floppies might be warranted as an added precaution, because then you could store the tape or floppies off site.

A problem is that there is a wide variety of cpio syntax to use in these backups, depending on the format and device to be used. If you switch devices, you have to try to remember (or you have to look up) the appropriate syntax—or do you? One solution is to hard code the various cpio variations and call them in response to a menu that simply asks the user what type of media is to be used. This is our approach in designing cpiobr. Another advantage of the menu system is that you might be able to turn the chore of making this kind of backup over to a less experienced operator or clerical person who needs to know only how to mount the tapes or other media and to answer the menu prompts.

What does cpiobr do?

Cpiobr is a menu-driven interactive backup and restore utility. It is really a front end to the cpio UNIX command. Functions performed from the menu include backing up files from a hard disk to a floppy, restoring files from the floppy to the hard disk, listing the file names of the files stored on the floppy, and listing the file names with optional extra information (similar to ls -l). The floppy here is the primary target media, but other target media can be used, such as a large tape or streamer tape.

When the action to be performed is determined, the next choice is which device should be used. Cpiobr can be used on AT&T UNIX machines (/dev /fp021), IBM type XENIX machines (/dev/fd0), streamer tape (/dev/rmt0), or any other device pathname that you need (/dev/???). Usually the device name determines which type of media the device uses. Because this utility is for any and all UNIX machines, some choices are nonexistent on your machine, so you are allowed to choose any device name you need.

Once the device name is chosen, if you are doing a backup or restoration, you are asked what the source or destination directories are. Give directory names from the point of view of your current directory or absolute pathnames from /., so cpiobr cds to that directory, then uses relative pathnames from there on. This avoids any problems due to absolute pathnames becoming part of the backup itself. If you type in a relative pathname, make sure it is from your current directory so that cpiopbr starts at the right place in the file tree.

When files are copied to the desired media, the pathnames given to cpio start with "./". This means that no directory prefix names are on the floppy. Therefore, when restoring files, be sure to give the complete, final pathname. All files coming off floppy are put directly under the destination directory you give cpiobr.

Examples

(These indicate responses to the main menu, submenu, and additional information prompts in that order.)

1. b
    x
    $HOME

Back up files to the XENIX floppy, starting from $HOME.

2. r
    a
    /dev/rmt0
    $HOME

Restore files from a device of my choice (/dev/rmt0, a mag tape) and put the files in my home directory.

3. l
    s

List in long format all the file information that resides on floppies for a UNIX PC machine.

Explanation

Lines 4-7 check for error conditions. The only error condition here is whether you passed any arguments to `cpiobr`. Because this is a menu-driven utility, there are no arguments to pass.

To get an overall idea of how this utility works, let's think about what needs to be done. First, we have to find out what action needs to be performed. Once we get this information, we need to know which device is to be used. What invalid choices are entered by the user? We need to cycle through the choices until correct input is entered.

After the two pieces of information are obtained, we need to find out where to find or put files. After this, we can do the `cpio`.

To execute this scenario, we need only two loops: one for each input stage. In this case, we used two "while forever" loops. To get out of the loops, we use the break shell command, which forces us out of the current loop. But we see a problem with this approach a little later.

The main, outermost, driving loop starts at line 6 and ends with the last line of the program, line 87. The purpose of this outermost loop is to control the operation of the program as a whole, getting the menu option from the user, and ultimately exiting when the user indicates he or she is finished. Of course you still can exit by using the normal interrupt character, but the menu has an exit option (CR). It's better to provide an explicit option, particularly for inexperienced users.

Starting on line 11, we set up the screen for the main menu. The command here is "c", which is explained later in this book. It stands for "clear screen" and can be substituted for the regular UNIX clear command, which you can use for now if you want.

Line 12 forces the positional parameters to be set to the output of the UNIX `date` command. This syntax is a little rare but very useful indeed. If we didn't do it this way, we would have to capture the entire date output in one variable, then cut it up into small pieces and place each piece in a separate variable. This would require lots more instructions and variables in the program. By using our syntax, we force the first positional parameter to be the first field of the date output, the second positional parameter to be second field, and so on. To get at any specific field, we use the $n notation, where n is the positional parameter number.

Lines 13-25 are one huge `echo` statement that prints the main menu. Putting everything in a single `echo` statement is preferable because it minimizes the overhead encountered in processing multiple statements, so it is fast. If we used an `echo` statement for each and every line of the main menu, it would print very slowly and be choppy. The UNIX `cat` command also could have been used in this fashion, utilizing here documents (embedded text). An example of this would be

```
    cat <<-EOF
Main Menu Information
    EOF
```

But a major problem occurs when you actually print the prompt. To make the cursor wait at the end of the prompt line requires echoing "\c", and `cat` cannot do this. You end up with `cat` to print the menu and `echo` to print the prompt, which makes for another choppy display of the entire screen. Consistency and speed is what we are looking for. Learning these tricks helps you even more in writing larger programs that do a lot of menus and other text display.

Using the `echo` statement in this manner has some disadvantages, but they are fairly trivial. First, the body of the `echo` statement must contain the exact output you want on the screen, which requires absolute positioning inside the `echo` statement to produce correct spacing. Usually the positioning is not aligned with the indentation that the code is currently using, so the visual flow of the code is broken for the length of the menu, then returns after the menu. This can be somewhat distracting when reading the code.

Another small detail is that `echo` does not like to echo tab characters. If you put a real tab character inside the `echo` quotes, it usually prints as a blank. To get `echo` to print tabs, you have to talk to `echo` in its own language, with a "\t", or \\t when not quoted. So the menus in `cpiobr` are padded with spaces. This also makes it easy to move a menu left and right by small amounts for proper positioning on the screen.

One issue relating to menus is where they should be put on the screen. Totally left-justified looks funky, but center-justification won't be retained when any other output goes to the screen (like from cpio). This input is not center-justified but left-justified. A good compromise is to place the menu about three to five spaces in from the leftmost column. As with most such matters of aesthetics, you may disagree.

Back to our specific menu: To make the main menu screen both aesthetically pleasing and informational, parts of the date output are displayed on the screen. (Note that the main menu is cleared each time before it is used.) A sample of the screen follows.

```
Wed, May 28                    13:18:49


        Cpio Backup & Restore
        ---------------------
    Backup to removable media
    Restore from removable media
    List files on media
    Long list files on media
    <cr> to exit

    Press b,r,f,l, or <cr>:
```

The top left corner has the day of week, month, and day of month. These are the fields 1, 2, and 3 from the `date` command. The top right corner has the current time. This is field 4 from the `date` command. All this data makes for a nice, balanced, informational screen.

After the menu is printed, line 27 reads in the user's command. Note that one of the options causes an exit if only the carriage return is pressed. How do we check for that? We *quote* the input variable so that test recognizes the null value (see lines 28-30). If a null was input, we break out of the current while loop. This puts us at the end of the program, which then exits properly. If the input was not null, we continue and do the error checking on the input command later.

Line 32 initializes the ABORT variable to off, which is explained in detail later. For now, we just say that this variable exists because of a conflict between the way the break command works and the structure of this program (that is, a fully menu-driven utility).

Lines 34-65 are the nested while loop that processes the submenu. The reason we use while-forever loops is because they keep going until we get good input. When the input is good, we break out of it. A very easy way to process menus.

In lines 36-45, we again are using the `echo` statement to print the entire submenu. This menu asks for the device name that is used in the backup/restore commands.

Line 47 reads the user input into the variable MEDIA. The value of MEDIA is then evaluated in a case statement. Notice that the patterns being matched for include both the lower- and uppercase forms of the characters. This makes life easier for the user, and makes for a little more robust programming, reducing the amount of error checking we have to do. Also note that each pattern match ends in a break statement. When valid input is matched, we want execution to continue past the end of the while statement, which is accomplished by the break statement. The variable DEV is now set as the path to the chosen device.

The "a" option on lines 55-60 requires further processing. We are going to prompt users for the device name of their choice. If users forget the name or decide not to use this option, they can enter a carriage return, which is recognized as a null and the continue statement is executed. This forces the next iteration of the current loop, which reprints the submenu. Another carriage return then can be used to exit the submenu and return to the main menu. On the other hand, if users enter a non-null value, the break statement is executed, so the menu loop is left with the specified path in DEV.

If users input an illegal value, an error message is printed and the submenu is printed again. Note that entering only a carriage return to the submenu sets the ABORT variable to on. Why do this? Now we come to the part where the shell language fails for our application. The scenario goes something like this: We are on the submenu. We decide we don't want to make a selection here, so we want to exit this menu and return to the main menu (or previous menu). If we break out of the while loop for the submenu, we fall into the outer while loop and continue processing with prompts for source and destination directories.

If we attempt to solve the problem by using a "break 2" statement, we break out of both while loops (putting us at the bottom of the program) and exit, leaving us out in the cold. Again, not what we want. What we really want is to break out of the current (inner) loop and continue with the next iteration of the outer loop to get the main menu again. There is no way to tell the shell to do this, so we create a flag variable to simulate this action and call it ABORT. If we set ABORT to yes, we want to *not* continue with the main menu command but abort its action and return to the main menu. This really means to do a continue, so lines 67-69 check for this. If the ABORT flag is on, the submenu was exited intentionally and the continue forces the main menu to be printed again instead of trying to execute any half-baked backup specifications.

In line 71, we get to the checking of the original (main menu) command and the obtaining of the information needed for processing it. The four basic commands are backup, restore, list files, and list files with long information. If any other command was entered, an error message is displayed and the main menu is displayed again. The only way to exit the main menu is to press a carriage return without any text preceding it, and line 28 breaks out of the loop.

The backup and restore commands use relative naming. They first query for the specific directory, then change directory there. The echo statement and "dummy" reading of CMD prompt the user to put the floppy in (or mount the tape or whatever) and press carriage return when ready.

In the case of backup, the `find` command is used to find *every* file that resides in the file tree starting from the current directory. The `find` list is sorted, so the files are sorted on the backup media. Then the sorted file list is piped into `cpio`, with the options -ocBv. This means "stream output, character headers used, block size of 5K, and verbose" to print out the names as they are copied to the backup media.

In the case of restore, the options -icBvdmu are used. This means "stream input, using character headers, with 5k blocks, verbose to print file names as they are restored, creates directories when needed, files retain the original modification date, and all files are unconditionally copied."

If the files are to be listed only, the options are either -icBt to print a table of files backed up (table is `cpio` notation for "ls") or -icBtv to print a table of files with extra verbose information (`cpio` notation for "ls -l").

At the end of processing each main command, the message

```
hit <cr>
```

is printed. This is because when the main menu is printed, it clears the screen. If you wanted to get a list of files as described previously, and didn't stop execution, the list would be printed, execution would reach the outer "done", the outer loop would restart, and the screen would be cleared for the redisplay of the main menu. Poof, there goes the list, before even an Evelyn Wood graduate could read it! To delay clearing the screen, we prompt for a keystroke. Whatever is typed is read into a variable, then never used again. It is just a dummy variable.

Backup Notes

You can back up files many ways, but let's look at some differences between the `cpio` and `tar` command. The original UNIX backup command was `tar`. This tape archive utility was meant to maintain tape archives and do the actual copying.

It works but has a few peculiarities. First, each file put to tape (or whatever media you use) is aligned on a 1K boundary. This means that if your file has one byte in it, `tar` allocates 1K minimum to your file, which can be a massive waste of space if you have lots of small files and you are copying them to tape. However, `tar` has some nice aspects, too.

For example, you can tell it what blocking factor to use, and you can also tell it how big the backup image is, so you can chop up large backup streams into lots of small pieces (for example k=360 for low density XENIX floppies). One strange aspect of `tar` is that the backup occurs in one long, continuous stream, but the restore is a unique format for each medium. For example, say you have 10M of data to back up. You better have enough floppies formatted and ready to go before you start the `tar` stream. If you run out of media, you have to break off the command and start over. A sample command would look like this:

```
cd $HOME
tar cvefbk /dev/fd048ds9 18 360 .
```

This says to backup *all* files (recursively down the tree) from the current directory (.) to the specified device file, with blocking factor of 18K and a total image of 360K bytes. One interesting point here is that when `tar` recursively goes down a tree, it gets file names in inode allocation order, which is *not* normal sorted order. You *cannot* get a sorted file list onto a tar backup unless you make a duplicate copy of all the data you wish to back up and force the inode allocation into sorted order. How do you do this? Like so:

```
cd $HOME
find . -print | sort | cpio -pdv /bkpsort
```

This makes new copies of all your data and allocates the file names in sorted order. Then when you cd /bkpsort and do tar ., the files go onto the media in sorted order.

Let's suppose that the backup took 15 disks. When you restore this entire bunch, you must type the following command 15 times because each one of the disks is a unique backup image.

```
tar xvf /dev/fd048ds9
```

This repetitious typing is a pain, but it can be a life saver as we see shortly.

The `cpio` command is the next generation backup command. Its overall action is similar to that of `tar`, but there are some major differences. First, you must generate a list of files for `cpio`, which means using `find` to generate the list. Because we can pipe the `find` list through the `sort` command, we do not have to recopy all our files to get a sorted list.

Next, `cpio` does not align on 1K boundaries. It packs all the data contiguously, and has a magic number in the header to specify the beginning of a new file. `Cpio` also does not have a command to tell it how big the media image is. How does it know? The device driver should recognize the size and send the appropriate signal back to cpio, which then stops and prompts for the next floppy. This is fine until you are on a system where the drivers are trashy, like XENIX. XENIX drivers do not recognize when to stop, and keep on going right off the end of the floppy disk. The cpio code should perform alike on all systems, but it does not perform correctly on XENIX machines.

One major difference between tar and cpio is in the resultant backup images. Because cpio does not have definite boundaries between the separate media, files get split between two floppies. This means that when you try to back up these 15 floppies, they are *one* continuous stream of input, just like the one continuous stream of output to create them. What happens when floppy #2 dies? *All* your files after #2 are useless. You just lost your entire backup image. Because tar backs up as separate images, when #2 is lost you can still back up 3-15 with no problem.

One other nice aspect of cpio is that it can operate in both file system format and stream format. File system format (-p option for pass) talks to block devices like hard disks, and the stream format talks to raw character devices (-i and -o), such as tape or low-level formatted floppies. Cpio is a nice utility to use to copy file trees around the system on the hard disk.

How does 4.2 BSD handle this? For years, it was the tar in/out shuffle as documented in the tar(1) manual pages. Not the most elegant approach, but it does work. Now they have a -r option (for recursively going down trees) for the regular cp command. I still think Cpio is better.

Backup Verification

Name: dsum

dsum   Dual directory sum

Function

Displays the output of the UNIX sum command for two copies of a file from two different directories on the same line. This allows quick visual scanning to see whether the files have identical contents and can be used to verify a copy.

Synopsis

dsum [-c¦-o] control__dir backup__dir

Sample Call

dsum $HOME/bin /mnt

> See whether any files have changed while being copied from my home directory bin to the floppy mounted on /mnt

Code for dsum

```
1   :
2   # @(#) dsum v1.0   Dual directory sum   Author: Russ Sage
```

```
3
4    if [ $# -lt 2 -o $# -gt 3 ]
5      then echo "dsum: invalid argument count"              >&2
6            echo "usage: dsum [-c|-o] control_dir backup_dir" >&2
7            echo "  -c = C source files, -o = object files"   >&2
8            exit 1
9    fi
10
11   case $# in
12   2)      FLIST=*;;
13   3)      case $1 in
14           -c) FLIST=*.c;;
15           -o) FLIST=*.o;;
16           *)  echo "dsum: invalid argument $1" >&2
17               echo "usage: dsum [-c|-o] control_dir backup_dir"  >&2
18               exit 1;;
19           esac
20           shift;;
21   esac
22
23   for FILE in $1/$FLIST
24   do
25           BASEF='basename $FILE'
26           if [ 'expr $BASEF : '.*'' -lt 7 ]
27             then echo "'$BASEF:   \t''sum $FILE | cut -d' ' -f1'\t\c"
28             else echo "$BASEF:\t'sum $FILE | cut -d' ' -f1'\t\c"
29           fi
30           sum $2/$BASEF | cut -d' ' -f1
31   done
```

Environment Variables

BASEF	Holds base file name from a long pathname
FILE	Holds each file name that is checked
FLIST	Holds the qualifier of what types of files to check

Description

Why do we need dsum?

In a software development environment, there are always tons of files. These files hold just about everything: source code, relocatables, object code, data, and text. Another aspect of software development environments is that files are usually spread out among many different machines (or groups, as the case may be). There always seems to be a lot of file pushing, too. Move these files from this system to that system, modify some, move them back, etc. Sort of like digging holes in the Army: You do it because they tell you to.

When you are moving many files, what is the best way to assure yourself (or anybody else, for that matter) that the copies you have made are *exactly* the same as the original? If you introduce a mistake into the first copy, then propagate that error through many copies, or even overwrite the original with a modified copy, you may never be able to return to the original state.

One way to monitor copies is with the UNIX sum command. Sum reads the data and prints a number that is a sort of checksum. Other UNIX utilities that do something like this are cmp for comparing object files and diff for finding differences in text files.

The author used to think that sum would report a difference of just one bit, a sort of cyclic redundancy check, but that was quite wrong. Recently there was a 35K-byte file that contained long listings of files that had been backed up. Actually there were two files, one that was sorted and one that was not. They were the same size, and sum reported the same number for both files. When a cmp was done on the two files, the 39th byte was revealed to be different. How do we explain the fact that sum saw these two files as being exactly the same? Possibly sum folded the data in such a way that the sums were the same even though one file was sorted and the other was not.

This implies that sum does not do a true checksum on each bit. Examining the algorithm in the source code is the only way to find out for sure. Of course, in most cases, if a file is different than the original, it is not a mere permutation of the order of the data so that sum still is quite useful.

What does dsum do?

Dsum is a utility that does post-copy verification. It assumes that files are copied from a source directory and to a destination directory. The source directory is called the control directory because it controls which files are compared. For each file in the control directory, the name is printed along with its sum value and the sum value of the copied file in the destination directory. All this information is displayed on one line.

The benefit of having dsum print all the information on one line is that the two files can be visually checked very easily. You don't have to look in another location for the information you need.

The alternative to dsum would be a scenario something like the following.

1. Copy your files to another directory.
2. Sum all the files from the control directory and put the resulting list into a file.
3. Sum all the files from the backup directory and put the resulting list into a file.
4. Diff the two files to see whether any copies are not the same.

This does not even give you a nice visual display of what is going on.

Dsum does not traverse down the file tree because most copies are directory to directory, not tree segment to tree segment. Because it does not traverse, the complexity of the program is greatly decreased.

By default, *all* files are compared. This assumes that you copied all files to the backup directory. In some instances, you may only want to copy specific files, like

*.c (for all your source files), in which case, the control directory has lots of files but the backup directory only has files ending in .c.

To handle such cases, the options -c and -o are included. The -c option only uses *.c files from the control directory. Then it only checks *.c files in the backup directory. The -o option does the same things for files matching *.o.

Examples

1. ```
   $ mount /dev/fd0 /mnt
   $ cp /usr/include/* /mnt
   $ dsum /usr/include /mnt
   ```

Mount the floppy disk on the /mnt directory. Copy all the header files in /usr /include to the floppy. Verify the backup using dsum on the original directory and the backup directory.

Note: By copying *, we don't go down into /usr/include/sys at all.

2. ```
   $ dsum . ..
   ```

Using as the control files the files in the current directory, sum each file against one of the same name in the parent directory.

Explanation

Lines 4-9 perform the error checking. If there are less than two arguments, the control and/or backup directories were not specified and an error results. If the number of arguments is greater than three, there is something else besides a -c option and the two directories, which is also an error. Anything else (two or three arguments) is treated as valid.

Lines 11-21 initialize the FLIST variable. FLIST is the controlling variable that determines what file names to look at. If the command line only has directory names on it ($# = 2), FLIST is assigned the default value of * (all files) in line 12. The * is assigned to FLIST and is not expanded at assignment time (this is a feature of the shell). If there was an option included on the command line ($# = 3), the first variable is checked and FLIST gets the appropriate value, *.c or *.o. If the option was neither of these, an error message is displayed and the program exits.

Lines 23-31 do the work. The loop is powered by a for loop iterating through the word list created by the control directory as qualified by the FLIST variable. Line 23 is where FLIST is actually expanded from the * to each file name. This gives the for loop some data to use. The FILE variable is then the entire path to each file in the control directory.

Line 25 sort of undoes the expansion of line 19. The BASEF variable gets the basename of the entire path that is in FILE. The reason we do this is because we need just the file name later on when we reference the backup directory. (The UNIX basename command returns the last element in a specified path: that is, the filename itself when the path contains intermediate directories.)

Lines 26-29 print the first part of the output. An if-then statement is included because we need to alter the output depending on how many characters the file name has. Line 26 looks at the length of the file name by using expr. Expr can be used to compare two strings and get a count of the number of characters matched. Comparing the file name to "all characters" thus returns the length of the string. (You might want to consult expr(1) for other tricky uses of this multipurpose command.)

This returned value is used in the test statement to see whether the filename is less than seven characters: possibly only one or two characters. In the latter case, if we tab, we only get to the first tab stop. To get past the first tab stop, we echo seven characters to get into the range of the next tab field. (If there were 3-6 characters, we still end up in the second tab field, so that works, too.) Then a tab is echoed to put us at the second tab stop, which is what we want.

If the length of the file name is greater than seven characters, we are already on or after the first tab stop. Thus the next tab printed puts us at the second tab stop. The effect is that all the columns line up no matter what the size of the file name (unless it is really large). This gets rid of the "creeping column blues." That is when the columns move around depending on the size of what is displayed. An example of this is the regular **sum** command. Its output looks like this:

```
4243 3 autobkp
247 1 can
25167 6 cpiobr
186 3 dosflp
56864 2 dsum
2782 1 log
```

On the other hand, **Dsum**'s output is very clean and aligned, not creeping all over the screen. Creeping just makes the output look junky and makes it difficult to quickly scan the information.

The magic of the one-line output is done in line 27 (for file names less than 7 characters) or line 28 (for longer file names). Inside the **echo** command in each case, we bury other commands but still control the way their output is printed to the screen. First, the file name by itself is printed from the base name extracted earlier. Notice that the file name does not include the information about which directory it is from. Then we move over a little bit and print the first field of the sum output for that file (the sum itself). This is the sum from the version of the file in the control directory because the FILE variable was generated from that directory. **Sum** prints three values (the sum, the number of blocks of storage for the file, and the file name itself). We need to get just the first one, which is extracted by executing **sum** and piping it to **cut**, which returns just the first field. After the sum value is printed, we use the echo character \c to suppress the newline. This keeps the cursor on the same line.

Line 30 then picks up from there. It generates the sum of the same file in the backup directory ($2 from the command line) with the current file name, cuts only the number out, and prints it right after the cursor on the same line.

The loop terminates when all files from the control directory have been summed.

Modifications

A nice modification would be to have dsum not only print the values like it does, but also print a flag at the end of the line when the two files are different. That way we would not have to look at the numbers closely. We look for the flag and see right away when something goes wrong.

To make your job a little easier, a solution to the problem of printing the flag follows. It was not included in the tool as presented previously so that things could be kept relatively simple. You can make the modification yourself as an exercise. The following code does it:

```
for FILE in $1/$FLIST
do
        BASEF='basename $FILE'
        S1='sum $FILE 2>&1 | cut -d' ' -f1'
        S2='sum $2/$BASEF 2>&1 | cut -d' ' -f1'
        if [ "$S1" = "$S2" ]
          then M=""
          else M="<---"
        fi
        if [ 'expr $BASEF : '.*'' -lt 7 ]
        then  echo "$BASEF:      \t$S1\t$S2       $M"
        else  echo "$BASEF:\t$S1\t$S2    $M"
        fi
done
```

The approach is different than the current dsum solution because you cannot just generate the sum on the fly. You have to capture the output of sum and use it later. The concept we are looking for occurs in the sixth line. If the two sum values are different, the M variable gets set accordingly. If the files are different, M gets the arrow that points out the bad copy.

Name: log

log	Menu access to backup logfiles

Function

Provides a menu interface to logfiles produced from the autobkp tool.

Synopsis

log

Sample Call

log

Code for log

```
1    :
2    # @(#) log v1.0   Menu access to backup logfiles   Author: Russ Sage
3
4    c
5    set 'date'
6    echo "
7
8    $1, $2 $3              $4
9
10            Logfile Menu
11           ------------
12       1 - list all log file names
13       2 - display log of home backup
14       3 - display log of product backup
15       <cr> to exit
16
17       Enter command (1-3,<>): \c"
18   read CMD
19
20   case $CMD in
21   "")    exit;;
22   1)     echo "\nLogfile names:"
23          sed -n -e "/more/s/^.*more \(.*\);;$/\1/p" $HOME/bin/log;;
24   2)     more $HOME/bin/autobkplog.home;;
25   3)     more $HOME/bin/auto2.bkplogm;;
26   *)     echo "log: $CMD is not a command";;
27   esac
```

Environment Variables

CMD   Command read in from user
HOME   Your home directory on the system

Description

Why do we need log?

If you have read sequentially through this chapter, you have already seen the autobkp program. The output of autobkp is very informational and should be retained as part of your backup procedures. This is even more important when you have things running from cron. At times, little things can go wrong that blow away your backup procedures and the only way to track the little things down is through log files. Cron log files have some information, but the autobkp log file has the most.

A problem arises when you start to have multiple autobkp jobs. You may not want to lump unrelated file backups into the same pathlist file, so you create multiple pathlist files, multiple cron jobs, and multiple log files. If you end up with five or ten jobs, how do you keep track of their log files, remember their names, and make it easy to look through them? This is all solved in `log`.

What does `log` *do?*

`Log` is a menu-driven utility. The menu allows you to see the actual file names of the log files so that you do not have to remember them. The rest of the commands are entry points into the logfiles, using the `more` command to view them.

When we looked at `cpiobr`, we saw how menu-driven programs run. Log is a little simpler in that it makes only one pass. In addition, log is a "living" program. It is not static but must be constantly altered to match your backup procedures. Through this modification, log can tell you what the real file names are.

`Log` is sort of a self-referencing program. To display the real file names, it looks inside of itself and filters out (using `sed`) the names of the log files from the `more` commands that print them. As you keep adding log files, log can keep current because log looks to itself as the definition of what is correct. Doing the lookup procedure this way relieves us from having to keep a separate datafile around with the names in it or using some naming convention to accomplish the same task. Log's self-referencing allows you to add an infinite number of log files to the list, and you have the freedom to name those files anything you want.

You can probably see that the strategy used in `log` can be used to provide a display of any set of files (notes, documentation, or whatever) you wish. All you have to do is code them following the `more` commands and add as many command numbers in the main menu as you want.

Explanation

Line 4 clears the screen using the `c` command presented later in this book. (Again, you can use `clear` instead if it is available.)

Line 5 sets the positional parameters to the output of the `date` command. This is the same thing that we did in the `cpiobr` program.

Lines 6-17 print out the menu. One echo statement is used, as described in cpiobr. Line 13 reads the command from the user.

Lines 20-27 do the major work of the program. If the input was just a carriage return (treated as null), the program exits. In line 23, `sed` looks in the file $HOME /bin/log. This requires that you put `log` in your home bin directory. If you put it somewhere else, you must change this line of code. `Sed` uses -n, which suppress all output except what it is explicitly told to print. The -e string is the magic that finds the file names.

This approach uses the substitute function in `sed`. In this way, we can substitute everything except for the file name, then just print that. The syntax goes like this: First we search for more (/more/), which finds all the lines in log that have the word "more" in them. By definition, each log file is printed to the screen using `more`. As you add log files, each new line should have `more` in it, so the files are found automatically by the sed expression.

Next, we tell `sed` to substitute. The first expression consists of the beginning through the end of the line, but we use parentheses to mark within it the pattern .*, which refers to the part of the line between the space following "more" and the first semicolon at the end of the line. If you look at any of the lines in log that start with "more", you see that this corresponds to the file name we are looking for.

We then tell sed to substitute pattern 1 for the whole line. Pattern 1 is sed notation for the first marked or "tagged" expression. In other words, we substitute the file name for the line as a whole and tell sed to print the result, thus displaying the file name.

This works for as many more statements as you have. The more log files you have, the more files sed processes. Note that the sed statement looks in any number of characters from the beginning of the line to find the word *more*. By not hard coding a specific number of characters to indent, you are free to pick your own indent levels.

If the command entered was not a valid command, an error message is printed.

This program has no loop, so execution just falls through. If you want to run it again, you have to type log again.

Example

```
$ log
    1
```

Run the program and the menu is displayed. Enter number 1 to see all the log file names.

Now that we've learned how to identify and manage files in general, let's look at some systematic ways of managing *information* in files. We start in the next chapter with files that are important to us as programmers.

4

Programming Documentation Management

Documentation management

stripc	strip C file documentation header
stripf	strip C function documentation header
strips	strip shell script documentation header
ctags	C function tag cross reference

Programming Documentation Management

Introduction

You decide to take a chance. The product is three months late for production, and it needs only a tiny fix. You're sure you know how the function that opens an input buffer works. You've used it before. You increase the buffer size in the function call and run a quick test. Everything's fine, so you compile the final disk and send it to production. A month later, reports from angry consumers start arriving. It seems that if the word processor, spreadsheet, and database are all open and active at the same time (one of your product's big selling points), the new buffer is just large enough to clobber a key section of memory and turn a high flying marvel of integrated software into a flaming wreck.

Why didn't you check the documentation on that function? Finding which file the documentation is in would take quite a while, and because documentation is so hard to maintain, everyone else's is out of date anyway. Nevertheless, debacles like this don't have to happen.

Programming is hard work, but it's only half the job. Good documentation is essential if you are going to be able to maintain your code, but managing all the documentation associated with a large software project is also hard work. There are constant revisions and usually a lack of uniformity in approach. Documenting C source files both as a whole and on a function by function basis is a good first step, but the documentation isn't very useful if you have to hunt through dozens of files to find out how a particular function is called or what functions make up a given module.

If you would like to examine another tool related to development, see the `cg` program in Chapter 10.

Programming and Documentation Management

This chapter presents a set of shell scripts for extracting documentation information from source code for C programs and shell scripts. Two strategies are used. First, by following a standard "documentation model" in source code, you can devise scripts that simply "pull" the up-to-date header information sections out of the source code files and assemble them into a new file. These files serve as the framework for a program's documentation. This means that, provided the source code headers are updated by various programmers in a standard way, a simple UNIX command can extract a completely new manual framework.

The scripts that implement this approach are `stripc`, `stripf`, and `strips`. `Stripc` and `Stripf` provide listings of file-level and function-level documentation blocks from your C source files, whereas `strips` extracts documentation from shell script files.

The second approach is to access specific kinds of structures (such as C functions) in the body of the code itself. This is how you can find out exactly how a given function is called without poring through a mountain of listings. The `ctags` script is both a useful tool and a model for applying this approach to other kinds of program structures.

`Ctags` combines its output file with vi/ex, to provide an easy way to access any given function and examine, copy, or edit it into the current program. `Ctags` does this by providing vi tags for each function found in any of a specified set of files so that you can use a simple editor command to get at what you want. You don't have to worry any longer about which file contains which function. `Ctags` is an excellent example of using the powers of UNIX to their fullest.

With these tools you can avoid reinventing the wheel because you can easily search for and extract the tools you need for a particular application. Did you already write the code to drive a Trantor TR-101 terminal? Use `ctags` and find out. Moreover, the self-documenting printed file and function documentation produced by these scripts gives other programmers a head start in understanding what you've done. It might even impress your boss a little.

How in general should we approach designing such scripts? We have some potential advantages in providing this kind of access on UNIX systems. First of all, source files aren't different from other text files, so we can use all of the UNIX searching and pattern matching tools (`sed`, `awk`, and so on) to find things. Second, we've mastered the techniques for traversing file trees and operating on selected types of files, as seen in the previous chapters. Our approach is to combine these facilities so that access is provided to structured documentation contained in program files.

Name: `stripc`

stripc   Strip C documentation header from source file

Function

Prints the first block of comment lines in a C source code file so that you can quickly identify a C program's purpose.

Synopsis

stripc file [...]

Sample Call

stripc prog*.c > header

Strip out the initial comment blocks of all files and place in one file called header

Code for stripc

```
1   :
2   # a(#) stripc v1.0   Strip comment header   Author: Russ Sage
3
4   if [ "$#" -eq "0" ]
5     then  echo "stripc: arg count error"  >&2
6           echo "usage: stripc file [...]" >&2
7           exit 1
8   fi
9
10  for FILE in $a
11  do
12          if [ ! -s $FILE ]
13            then  echo "file \"$FILE\" does not exist" >&2
14                  continue
15          fi
16
17          awk '/^\/\*/, /^ \*\// { if ($0 != " */")
18                                        print
19                                  else {print;exit}
20          }' $FILE
21          echo "^L"
22  done
```

(Before typing in this code, note that line 21 should have a real control-L entered between the two quotes where we have ^L, for reasons explained later.)

Environment Variable

FILE   Holds the name of the file from the command line

Description

Why do we need stripc?

On large software development projects, documentation tends to take a lot of time to process. There are program files to document, functional specs to write, and ultimately manuals and reference cards, glossaries, indexes, and so on. The actual program code must have its own in-line documentation, or managing the code becomes very difficult.

To avoid confusion, a documentation model must be created, then made into a standard for all programmers to follow. Whether or not the model is absolutely perfect, having one is the first step in creating an environment that you can control.

The next two tools presented follow the documentation model described in following text. This model is consistent and clear, and it can be added to or modified to suit your particular needs.

What does `stripc` do?

`Stripc` prints only the first comment header block from the beginning of a C source file. This block would contain all the important information about the file: its official name, what it is for, who created it, when it was created, and so on. Within the file might reside one or more functions or even a main program. This model assumes that your overall code has very few "mains" and lots of independent modules.

To see what kind of information we need to extract from source files, let's look at the model source file.

```
/*
 *  This is the documentation header for
 *  a C source code file.
 *  It explains what the file contains (programs, function
 *  libraries, etc.) and identifies the project.
 *
 *
 */ This bracket marks the end of the header comment.
^L  Control-L is used as a delimiter by the extraction tools.
/*  This is the documentation header for the main portion of the program.
 *  The main label should explain what this program is and what it does.
 *  The author, date, and revision history can go here also.
 */
main()
{
        /* main C program goes here */
}
^L
/*  This is the documentation header for the specific function
 *  that follows. The calling sequence, the input and output, and the
 *  general purpose of the function is documented.
 */
func1(arg1,arg2)
int arg1;
char arg2;
{
        /* function code goes here */
}
^L
/*  Likewise this comment block documents the next function.
 *  Having the documentation already with the code reduces the
 *  amount of overhead when reading and modifying the code.
 */
func2(arg1,arg2)
```

```
int arg1, arg2;
{
        /* function code goes here */
}
```

As stated previously, the "main" is optional and probably occurs in only one or two files, depending on what kind of programs you are writing. One file can have as many functions as you want, but the recommended maximum number is one to three depending on how the functions are related. Deal with only one programming idea and its implementation per file.

When you examine the model, you see that three levels of documentation are provided. The header at the beginning of the file is extracted by `stripc`. The header pertains to the file as a whole. The header at the beginning of the main program refers to the program as a whole and is handled by `stripf`. The header for each function pertains to that function: These headers are handled by `stripf`, which is discussed later.

Notice that between each function is a form feed (ASCII control-L). We indicated this key combination with the symbol ^L in the preceding listing so that our word processors wouldn't produce extra pages in formatting the manuscript for this book. You need to put a real control-L in place of ^L in each case when putting the comments in your files and when entering the source code for this and the following scripts. The form feed character is used in the header model to mark the top boundary of the first function in the file and to eject printer pages for a clean printout with a function appearing on each page.

At the beginning of every major label (either a main or a function name), a documentation "header" should exist. This header usually reflects the most recent changes in that module and can be counted on more reliably than a header in a document that was printed weeks or even months ago.

The input to `stripc` is a sequence of source code file names. Each file on the command line is checked to see whether it exists and has a size greater than zero bytes. If it does not meet these criteria, an error message is printed and the next file is checked. Each file is read from the first byte, and a starting comment character string (/*) is looked for. When this is found, the information up to the ending comment character string (*/) is output to stdout one line at a time. If the right characters are not found, nothing is printed, but no error message is displayed to mess up the output. After each file has been processed, a form feed is printed at the end, which breaks up the output into paged sections. This is used mostly when the documentation headers are very long and need to be visually broken up.

Note that "strip" in this and the following two utilities does not imply *removal,* but copying of the relevant information. No change is made to any of the input files.

When all files on the command line have been processed, the script ends.

Examples

1. `$ stripc test?.c > test.filehdrs`

Strip the file comment block from all files that match the string "test" followed by any one character, then .c. This matches test1, testA, testb, and so on. All the comment blocks are put into the file test.filehdrs in the order that they were processed in the for loop.

```
2.  $ for DIR in src1 src2 src3
    > do
    >                stripc $DIR/*.c > /tmp/$DIR.hdrs
    > done
```

This loop goes through each of the three directories src1, src2, and src3. In each are source files that need to have their documentation headers extracted. Each directory is taken one at a time, and `stripc` is called with all the C source files from that directory. The output of all the documentation headers from the files in that directory are placed in a file in the /tmp directory. The /tmp files have the names /tmp/src1.hdrs, /tmp/src2.hdrs, and /tmp/src3.hdrs. Note that the number of files passed to `stripc` has a limitation of about 255 characters. After that, the command line overflows and the script bombs.

Explanation

Lines 4-8 do the error checking. If the number of parameters on the command line is zero, an error has occurred. There must be at least one file name when calling `stripc`.

The loop in lines 10-22 is a for loop that runs through each file name in the positional parameter list from the command line.

The first thing to check is the existence of the file, in lines 12-15. If the file does not exist, an error message to that effect is issued and the loop continues with the next file.

Lines 17-20 are the `awk` loop that does all the important work. The input file to `awk` is the file name that the for loop is currently processing.

In case you're not very familiar with `awk`, an `awk` program is called like this

```
awk program filename
```

where the program consists of a sequence of statements that have the form:

```
pattern { action }
```

The specified action is applied to text that matches the pattern. For the `awk` program to work correctly, you must enclose the entire program in single quotes.

In `stripc`, the pattern goes something like this, with the English first and the awk pattern code after:

```
from the beginning pattern of /*     to the ending pattern of */

/^\/\*/                               /^ \*\//
```

The way to interpret this is by remembering your `ed`, `sed`, and `grep` regular expressions. Regular expressions (RE) must be delimited (/ character), and `awk` accepts two expressions separated by a comma (,) to signify the beginning pattern and ending pattern to qualify input lines.

In the example, the beginning expression means "from the beginning of the line (^), followed by a real slash (/) character (which must be quoted to remove special meaning, thus \/), and a real asterisk (*), use all lines encountered until the ending expression." This picks up only the first occurrence of the pattern we are matching (that is, the first comment block) because the awk program exits when the terminating line is found. (The rest of the comment blocks are picked up in stripf along with the function name and arguments.)

For each line that matches this begin-end expression set, the action statements are executed. Lines 17, 18, and 19 have an if-then-else statement that does all the work. If $0 (which is the entire line) is *not* equal to a space and the close comment (*/), the entire line is printed. By forming the if statement this way, we print the first line and all subsequent lines until we get to the end of the comment field.

When the last line is encountered, the test is false, so the else part is executed. Because we know that this is the last line, we print it out for consistency of the comment block, then exit from awk. Note that by nesting these two commands together with curly braces ({ }), they both are taken as one compound statement.

After awk exits, a form feed is echoed to the screen and the next file is fetched. This continues until all files on the command line have been processed.

Name for stripf

stripf   Strip C function header documentation

Function

Extracts and prints the comment header, the function name with calling parameters, and the declaration of the parameter types for all functions in a C source file.

Synopsis

stripf file [...]

Sample Call

stripf lib1.c

Strips the documentation headers for all functions in the file lib1.c

Code for stripf

```
1   :
2   # @(#) stripf v1.0   Strip function header   Author: Russ Sage
3
4   for FILE in $@
5   do
6           sed -n -e '
7           /^L$/ {
```

```
 8              s/^L$/.bp/p
 9          : loop
10              n
11              /^{/b exit
12              p
13              b loop
14        : exit
15              i\
16  {}
17              b
18        }' $FILE
19  done
```

Environment Variable

FILE   Holds the file name for each file on the command line

Description

Why do we need `stripf`?

Assuming that our C code follows the documentation model presented earlier under `stripc`, we need to have a way to keep documentation current with changes in the code. We saw that when we keep documentation in the source files, it is more likely to be updated when the code is updated. A problem occurs when we need to have hardcopy of the documentation that is found within the code itself. How do we get it out of the files?

What does `stripf` do?

`Stripf` solves this problem. It scans through an entire file and prints all the documentation for every *function* that resides in the file (including the "main" if present.)

The input to `stripf` is file names passed on the command line. `Stripf` processes one file at a time and puts the output to the stdout. The output can be redirected, but input must be on the command line.

Additional modifications are made to the output to configure the data for an `nroff` environment, so the output files can be formatted using that utility. All form feeds are changed into an `nroff` command of .bp, for begin page. This `nroff` command ejects a page and increments the page count. Changing control-L keystrokes to this value may not be what you want, but you can always tailor the actions of the script to whatever you need it to do.

Examples

1. `$ stripf module1.c ¦ grep >"^\.bp$" ¦ wc -l`

Prints the number of function modules contained in the file module1.c by looking for each occurrence of the `nroff` new page command and counting them. We know that one of these is output for each function found. This line could be put into an `echo` statement that says "there are X modules in file $FILE."

```
2. $ for FILE in *.c ../*.c $HOME/src/*.c
   > do
   >            stripf $FILE
   > done >> /tmp/func.hdrs
```

The files to be expanded for this for loop include all files in the current directory that end in .c, all files in the parent directory with same suffix, and all files in my home directory under the src subdirectory. For each file, the function documentation is stripped and sent to the standard output. The whole loop is redirected with > >, so the output from every call to stripf is *appended* to the file in /tmp.

Explanation

The whole program is one big for loop in lines 4-19. The loop sets the variable FILE to each name that is on the command line. This script has no options and no error processing.

The UNIX sed command is called for each file name. The sed program reads all the input and outputs the changed text to the standard out.

The -n option is used in sed to suppress all output, which is exactly the opposite of the default action of printing everything. The reason we use this flag is because we want to tell sed when to print output. The -e option is used to tell sed that the next sequence of text between the single quotes is an expression to evaluate.

Remember that sed is a stream editor that reads one line, checks it against the expressions, then reads the next line and does it all over again. The first thing we search for is a control-L on a line by itself. If we do not find it, the next line is checked, and so on until a control-L is found. (Remember again that a real control-L must be entered in the code where we have ^L).

When the control-L is found, it activates the entire expression enclosed within the curly braces. The first action is to substitute the nroff begin page command as previously noted. The substitution is printed, which makes it the very first output. In line 9, a label called "loop" is declared. This results in no action occurring but does set up a jump point that is used later. (Sed's control structures are pretty primitive, but they get the job done.)

Line 8 uses the n command in sed to force the reading of the next line. We're done with the first line, the one with the control-L, so we can throw it away. In the case of looping, we see later that sed advances when we tell it and not on its own.

Remember the documentation model that we looked at earlier. This model includes a documentation header for the file as a whole, which is in the normal C style. The model is ended with a control-L. This first block is handled by stripc as described earlier. We don't want to use it here with stripf. Thus, we have now positioned ourselves past the file documentation header.

Following the control-L character is another set of one or more C comment lines that describe the function following them. Next comes the function name itself, the declaration of any parameters, and the opening character of the function itself, which is the left curly brace ({).

Line 11 looks for that brace. If it is found, execution branches to the flag marked exit (line 14). We can assume that we're done if the brace is found because this character should only occur as the beginning of a function module. When we find the curly brace, we have printed all the comment information and the function header via line 12, which we describe in a moment. What if a brace occurs in the comment field? No problem, because the search for the brace is anchored against the beginning of the line with the caret (^). This makes the expression mean "from the first character of the line." We only match the brace if it occurs as the very first character on the line.

Line 12 then assumes that we have not yet encountered the brace, so we need to print the line. The p statement prints the current line that sed is processing. This output goes to the screen.

Line 13 is an unconditional branch to the label called loop. Notice that the branch only altered the flow of execution and did not force the reading of another input record. This is something we have to be careful about in controlling the flow of execution in sed. We had just printed the current record, so now we have to trash that one and get the next one, which means going back to line 9. This print-next loop goes until the brace is found, which then forces execution to the exit label.

Line 14 is the exit label. When we get here, we know that the control-L has been found, the comment header has been printed, the function name and its parameter declarations have been printed, and the brace has been found. Notice that the brace has not been printed. We only branched when we found it.

Line 15 finishes off the output by inserting some text in the output stream. We cannot say "print this literally" so that it goes right into the text, as with echo. We have to play by the rules set up by sed. Any output has to be generated by normal ed-like commands. Inserting text with the "i" command does this for us. Note that we are also inserting the carriage return character (or line feed, depending on how much of a guru you are). This can be determined by the backslash character (\). The backslash takes away the special meaning of characters, and when used at the end of a line like this, means the special character that got embedded in the expression is the carriage return. In addition to the carriage return, we insert the pair of curly braces. This signifies the begin-end declaration of the function that we are processing. Because we are inserting the text, we do not have to tell sed to print it.

Line 17 is an unconditional branch statement by itself, which tells sed to branch to the top of the whole sed expression. When this occurs, we end up looking for another control-L and start the whole process over again. In this way, we can extract all the functions in one file, no matter how many there are.

Line 18 is the end of the sed expression and also contains the file name to be passed to sed. This is part of the regular sed syntax, but looks sort of out of place because of all the indenting going on. When all files have been processed, the outer loop terminates and the script is done.

Name: strips

strips   Strip shell documentation header

Function

Prints the beginning comment lines of a *shell script* file, as the "s" in the name suggests. The first line is ignored for compatibility with the C shell.

Synopsis

strips file [...]

Sample Call

strips *.sh

Strip comments out of all script files in current directory

Code for strips

```
1    :
2    # @(#) strips v1.0   Strip shell comment header    Author: Russ Sage
3
4    for FILE in $@
5    do
6         cat $FILE | (read LINE; echo $LINE
7         while read LINE
8         do
9              if [ "`echo $LINE| cut -c1`" = "#" ]
10                  then  echo "$LINE"
11                    else  exit
12                fi
13        done)
14   done
```

Environment Variables

FILE   Holds each file name from the command line

LINE   Holds each line of input text from the file being read

Description

Why do we need strips?

Just as we need documentation processing tools for C source code files, we also need this kind of tool for shell script files. The difference between stripping comments from C code and stripping them from shell script code is the way the comment fields are delimited in the source file. C source uses the /* */ pair, whereas shell scripts use # to separate the rest of the line as a comment.

It makes documentation so much easier when script files follow some form of standardized documentation. There really is no formal standard, but the closest one comes from the UNIX manual pages themselves. Standard fields are the script name, the way the script is called, what the script does, and maybe some notes on how it does it, other places to look for information, and what files the script uses. A sample format looks like this:

```
:
# NAME
#      strips      Strips shell comment fields
```

```
#
# SYNOPSIS
#      strips file [...]
#
# AUTHOR
#      Russ Sage    mm/dd/yy
#
# DESCRIPTION
#      This script strips the shell comment headers from script files.
#
# SEE ALSO
#      sh(1), cat(1)
```

Notice that the first line has the : statement, which is a null statement to the shell. It does nothing, but always returns a successful exit status, and is on line one because it signifies a Bourne shell script. If you run /bin/csh instead of /bin/sh, script files can get messed up. C shell looks for the # in the first column of the first line. If it is there, it thinks the file is a csh script. To tell csh that the script is for the Bourne shell, we can leave the line blank (which doesn't print too well and is liable to be deleted) or put in a statement that tells the C shell that it is a Bourne shell script while doing nothing under the Bourne shell.

What does strips do?

Strips reads a script file and prints all the comments from the beginning of the file that are contiguous (that is, it prints until a non-comment line is reached.) The first line is ignored but printed. When a line does not have a # in the first character position, strips stops reading that file.

The script file must have a comment structure similar to the one given in our preceding example. The # characters must start in column one, and each line must have a #. If you have a blank line anywhere in the starting comment block, strips prints only the first part of the block.

Examples

1. $ strips 'kind /bin /usr/bin'

The comment blocks are stripped from the text files that reside in the /bin and /usr /bin directories.

2. $ find / -name "*.sh" -print ¦ while read FILE
   > do
   > strips $FILE > /tmp/doc/$FILE
   > done

Find generates a list of all file names that end in strips. The output of strips goes into a doc directory in /tmp. The final output goes into a file name that is exactly the same as the original file, only the output is placed in /tmp, so nothing is accidentally removed.

Explanation

Lines 4 and 14 enclose the outer loop that feeds file names to the script. There is no error processing or checking. As long as the command line has files, the loop continues. You could, of course, check for the presence of arguments and the validity and existence of files. By this point, we think you have seen enough examples of error checking that you can add it where you wish. Thus we sometimes omit it in our code to save space and to highlight the essential function.

Line 6 `cat`s the file that is currently being processed. The output is going into a pipe to be read by another shell. The new shell receives a long command line (as signified by the nested parentheses in lines 6 and 13). The first read command reads the very first line. Because we are not going to check this line, we echo it back out, then drop into a continuous read loop. The assumption is that the first line starts with a colon, but if it starts with a #, it still is printed, so you won't lose any text.

Lines 7-13 are the inner while loop that reads lines of text from the standard input, which was the output from the `cat` command. When the text stops, so does the while loop.

Lines 9-12 are the decision-making lines. First, we echo the current input line and pipe it through the `cut` command. The first character is cut out, then the test command checks to see whether it is equal to the comment character. If it is, the line is echoed to standard output. If it is not the comment character, the end of the comment block must have been reached, so the inner loop exits. Control goes back to the outer (for) loop, which starts over and gets the next file name. When all files have been processed, `strips` exits.

Name: `ctags`

ctags   Make a source code tag file for easy vi access

Synopsis

ctags [file ...]

Sample Call

ctags proj*.c

  Make a tag file for all the project source code

Code for `ctags`

```
1    :
2    # @(#) ctags v1.0   Create a C source code tag file   Author: Russ Sage
3
4    awk -F'(' '/^[a-zA-Z_][a-zA-Z0-9_]*\(/ {
5         printf ("%s\t%s\t/^%s$/\n", $1, FILENAME, $0) }' $@ | sort -u +0 -1
```

Environment Variable

FILENAME `awk`
    variable name that contains the file name

Description

Why do we need `ctags`?

UNIX is designed to be a software development environment. It supports and encourages the modularity of program source code. Modularity is the concept of dividing up a project into separate files, breaking ideas up into routines, and compiling separate source code files into relocatables for later assembly into an executable.

This philosophy of software development can lead to problems, though. The major one is trying to get some sort of cohesiveness out of all the little pieces of the puzzle. Calls are made to routines that exist in other files, maybe even in other directories. What we need is a tool that allows us as humans to look at the software in a human way, that is, by content rather than physical location. The approach is something like reading a book versus reading a computer printout. The printout forces you to a sequential lookup while the book allows random access (and usually provides a table of contents and an index for finding specific items).

`Ctags` bridges this gap by creating a file with a specific format that the vi and ex editors recognize. This file contains "tags" that can be used from the editor to provide automatic access to any desired function without your having to know what file it resides in.

In effect, then, `ctags` provides you with an index into a group of C source files. When you combine it with the editor, you can quickly find any function with a name that you know, and you can look at the function body. It also means that you can easily copy and paste functions into whatever source file you're currently working on.

If the editor didn't have the tag capability, or we didn't build a tool taking advantage of it, we would have to `grep` for the function name in a collection of C source files (hoping we had the right files!), notice which file had the function we wanted, edit that file by hand (typing all the characters for the file name), then type characters for the search pattern. This is a lot of work and can be very time-consuming. By utilizing the tags feature with the file of tags extracted from the source code, all this manual work is eliminated.

This combining of capabilities illustrates something that can't be stressed too often: UNIX masters are ever alert to the opportunity to take advantage of the vast facilities already built into things like vi or ex. Often 90 to 95 percent of the capabilities that you need are already there, waiting for a relatively simple shell script to tie them together into a powerful new tool.

`Ctags` already exists as an executable in Berkeley (BSD) and the current AT&T System V. It originated in Berkeley but is now supported with System V. This illustrates the interaction between these two wellsprings of the UNIX world as they adopt worthwhile ideas from each other. This particular incarnation of `ctags` is an `awk` script that simulates the executable program from Berkeley, which means XENIX and earlier AT&T users can now benefit from it. Another advantage of the script version is that it can be modified easily to handle other C language features, something you can't do with an executable unless you have an expensive source code license.

What does ctags *do?*

Ctags looks through C source files passed on the command line and prints out a list of function names in each source file. Function names have a specific syntax and must be in this format, or awk does not recognize them as such. The rules are that the function name must start at the beginning of a line and be followed by legal characters and a left parenthesis. No blanks are allowed in the function name. A sample C program module submitted to ctags looks like this:

```
main()
{
}

func1(arg1,arg2)
int arg1,arg2;
{
}

func2(arg1,arg2)int arg1,arg2;
{
}
```

The printout from ctags is to stdout (the screen), so it must be redirected to be captured in a file. The input to ctags is any number of file names. Remember that if multiple files are input, the output is one continuous stream of data, ending up in one file. If you need an output file for each input file, a shell script that has a loop for each file could control ctags like this:

```
for F in *.c
do
        ctags $F > $F.tags
done
```

The actual output consists of three fields. The format is in this form:

```
tag     filename    search_pattern
```

The real output from the sample C program format given previously would be:

```
main    /usr/russ/src/program.c   /^main()$/
func1   /usr/russ/src/program.c   /^func1(arg1,arg2)$/
func2   /usr/russ/src/program.c   /^func2(arg1,arg2)$/
```

The first field is the tag name (which is the same as the function name). The second field is the pathname to the file containing the function. The third field is a search pattern used by the tags facility in the editor to access the function within the file (more on this later).

Assuming that you can generate a correct tag file, how do you interface the tag file with the editors so that you can look up the function you are interested in? The vi editor provides a number of ways to do this. The first way is to put the name of the tag file to be used in the .exrc file. (The .exrc file is sort of a .profile for the ex editor and also works with vi, which is not surprising because vi is built on ex. Because vi is the most popular UNIX editor, we use it for our examples here.) You could have your .exrc file look like this:

```
set tags=/usr/russ/mytags
```

Then when you reference a tag, this tag file is used. Another way is to set the tag file after you get into the editor. To see what your tag file is by default, type this when you are inside vi:

```
:set tags
```

This command prints out the tag file that it knows about. To alter the currently defined tag file, type the syntax that was in the example for the .exrc file:

```
:set tags=/usr/russ/mytags
```

Now that the editor knows the file in which to search for the tags that you reference, let's look at how to reference a tag (that is, a function name). The first way is to declare it on the command line when calling the editor. A sample syntax would be

```
$ vi -t tag
```

If you are already in vi, you can use this command to look for another tag:

```
:ta tag
```

The colon means that we are going into ex to perform this lookup. We tell ex to look for the specified string as a tag that resides in the currently defined tag file. When the tag is found in the tag file, vi edits the corresponding file name, which it gets from field 2. This is analogous to ":e filename." When the new file has been brought into the editor buffer, the last field of the tag file is used as a pattern search string. The syntax is exactly what you would type by hand. The cursor moves to the location in the file that matches the search string, which puts you at the function that you are interested in.

The Relationship Between ex and vi

As a brief digression, let's look at the two files, /bin/ex and /bin/vi. A little investigation reveals that these are actually the same file. We can verify this by looking at their inode numbers. Type a command like this:

```
$ ls -li 'path ex vi'
```

The output shows that the two numbers in the first column are the same.

```
510 -rwx--x--t   5 bin      bin        121412 Sep 19  1985 /bin/ex
510 -rwx--x--t   5 bin      bin        121412 Sep 19  1985 /bin/vi
```

This number is the inode. Because both files are the same, invoking either file name runs the same executable image. How does the file know how you are calling it? The program looks at the string argv[0] and sees what you used to call the file. The editor then sets up its interface to correspond with how you called it.

Notice that this program has five links. How do we find all the other names under which vi and ex can be called? We can use the UNIX ncheck command. Ncheck accepts an inode number and prints out all files that have the same inode number. Sample commands are

```
$ ncheck -i 510 /dev/root
```

or

```
$ ncheck -i 510
```

The first syntax tells ncheck to look for files with inode 510 in only the root file system. Ncheck is limited to looking in a single file system, which reinforces the fact that files cannot be linked across file systems because each file system starts at inode 2 and goes up sequentially. Each file system has an inode 510, which is unique to each file system. The output of the preceding command looks like this:

```
/dev/root:
510      /bin/edit
510      /bin/ex
510      /bin/vedit
510      /bin/vi
510      /bin/view
```

If no file system is given, as in the second example, all file systems mounted at the time are searched. This wouldn't do us very much good because the five links to vi must reside in the same file system. Otherwise the files would be linked across file system boundaries. We can tell already that no editor files reside in a /usr directory that resides in a second disk partition from the root file system.

Examples

1. `$ ctags *.c`

Generate a tag file for all the C source files in the current directory. The output goes to the screen in sorted order for each file. The file order is alphabetical because of the file name expansion. Of course, in most cases you will want to redirect the output of `ctags` to a file.

2. `$ ctags 'Find /usr/src -name "*.c" -print'`

This syntax uses command substitution to find all the file names ending in .c and place them on the command line. The problem is that if too many files are found, the command line for `ctags` may overflow and bomb the whole command. Depending on the overflow's severity, it may bomb your entire shell process.

3. `$ find /usr/src -name "*.c" -exec ctags {} \; > tags`

Find all the C source files under the tree segment /usr/src. For every file that qualifies, run the `ctags` program with that file. Using this notation prevents bombing of your command (as described previously) and also runs `ctags` for every file name. The entire output is put into the file named tags for later reference.

4.
```
$ find /usr/src -type f -print | sort |
> while read FILE
> do
>          ctags $FILE
> done >> tags
```

Taking advantage of multiple directories, find and sort all the files from the /usr/src directory and print their pathnames to the standard output. Then they are sorted and piped to a while loop. The while loop is used to handle an infinite number of files without overflowing any buffers. The output of the while loop is appended into one file, tags. This loop is bulky and slow, but gets the job done.

5. `$ find /usr/src -print | ctags`

The wrong way to use `ctags`. The output of the `find` command is pathnames. `Ctags` reads stdin because no files are on the command line. The data that `awk` reads is going to be pathnames from `find`, which don't have the correct fields to be matched for the function patterns. Nothing is matched.

A similar problem of this type would be

```
find /usr -print | wc -l
```

You might interpret this to mean "count how many lines are in all the files in /usr",

but it really says "how many file names are in the tree structure /usr." To count the
total number of lines in the files, the syntax is

```
find /usr -exec cat {} \; | wc -l
```

which says "find all the files in /usr, cat each one of them, then count how many
lines there are." To do this with ctags, the synta x would be

```
find /usr/src -name "*.c" -exec cat {} \; | ctags
```

Rather than the output looking like it did above

```
func1   /usr/russ/src/program.c   /^func1(arg1,arg2)$/
func2   /usr/russ/src/program.c   /^func2(arg1,arg2)$/
```

the output would look something like this:

```
func1           -               /^func1(arg1,arg2)$/
func2           -               /^func2(arg1,arg2)$/
```

Explanation

There are "-" characters for the file name because ctags is read from stdin. Awk
automatically sets its internal variable FILENAME to this because it knows no files
were on the command line.

The entire script is an awk program. The input to the awk script is $@, which
represents all positional parameters. Each parameter is assumed to be a C source
file name. If no files are passed on the command line, awk looks to the standard
input stream for data, but this creates an incorrect output, because the FILENAME
variable in awk is set to "-" as a default. Because awk requires file names, we need
to call ctags with file names and not pipe data to it through standard input, as
shown in the previous example.

Awk reads one line at a time from the data file and checks it against the
pattern matching string. For each line that matches, it performs the given program.
The first thing ctags does is change awk's default field separator from a blank to
the left parenthesis. By using this character as the field separator, the function
definition line is broken into two fields: the function name and the rest of the line.

The awk search pattern corresponds to the syntax for a C function name. It
can start with a character a-z, A-Z, or an underscore. The rest of the name can be
anything from a-z, A-Z, 0-9, to __. No spaces can be used between the name and
the parenthesis. The search starts from the beginning of the line (^), is followed by
the sequence of legal characters (a-z, A-Z, 0-9), then the left parenthesis.

When a line of that form matches, the output is generated by the printf
statement. The first field is a string supplied by $1. In this case, $1 is the function
name only, excluding the left parenthesis. A tab character is printed, then the next
string, which is the FILENAME variable from awk. This variable must have been
supplied from the command line, otherwise awk won't know what the file name is

where this function resides, and the tag file lacks the information needed to access the file containing the tagged function. Another tab is printed, then the search string is printed. The search string is $0, which represents the entire line that `awk` is working with. The line is preceded by a ^ and followed by a $.

The output is piped through `sort` so that all the tags end up in sorted order. The sort options tell `sort` to examine only the first field and to print only one occurrence of a line if there are multiple records.

Modifications to `ctags`

Now that we know what the generic format for the editor tag file is, can we use it for other useful purposes? We know that we can identify regular structures in C programs and create tags by which they can be accessed in the editor. C programs have structures of interest other than function names, for example, structure names. These can be handled by a modified version of `ctags`. The only thing we have to know is what the official syntax is for a data structure. The kind of data structure we would be interested in most is the kind that has the format like this:

```
struct name {
      int  val1;
      char val2;
};
```

All we have to do is make `awk` look for all occurrences of the struct definition. Then we can build a tag file with the tag as a structure name, the file would be the same, and the search string would find the structure definition rather than a function name. In fact, the combination of `awk`, tags, and editor could be used for any kind of information you might want to keep in a file with a specific format, such as addresses, notes, bibliographic references, and so on. You would just have to devise appropriate delimiters and use them consistently.

We hope we've made your program maintenance easier and given you ideas for other ways to automatically handle documentation. You can easily establish and maintain local documentation conventions using scripts similar to the ones we have presented here. One project you might want to try is interfacing our "strip" programs and others you write so that they can read a makefile (see `Make`(1)) and produce complete documentation on all source files involved in a given project.

5
Personal Management I: Time and Office Management

Time management

`at`	execute task at a specific time
`b`	background task subshell
`greet`	timely greeting from the terminal
`lastlog`	report last login time
`timelog`	logs sessions for accounting and statistics
`today`	print calendar with today highlighted

Office management

`jargon`	technical jargon generator
`phone`	telephone number database
`office`	office manager

Personal Management I: Time and Office Management

Introduction

We've learned a lot about files and about how to manage the file structure. It's time to look at how we can use UNIX to manage the many tasks that make up our workday and keep us in touch with what other people are doing. The term "personal management" implies that you need and want to create your own uniquely *personal* working environment and tools. What we do is give you a toolkit that you can configure to your needs. In fact, we present four separate toolkits in this and the following chapter, each dedicated to a particular aspect of personal management.

Time management tools help us schedule tasks to be done by the computer as well as manage our own personal time. *Office management* deals with storing and retrieving information as well as making a variety of UNIX functions accessible through an easy to use menu-driven interface.

For each of these areas we give an overview, then present the group of tools.

Time Management

Because the UNIX system has built-in time functions and a clock, it is already set up to keep track of time. Combining the time-keeping function with the ability to run automatically a group of commands means we can arrange it so that the computer performs many of our time-related chores. We also can use the computer to keep track of our own time.

The tools presented in this section are at, b, greet, lastlog, timelog, and today.

At gives us the ability to tell the machine to do something (display a message or perform some other command(s)) at a specific time. The task is put in the background so that we can continue with other things and is performed automatically at the time specified. The task can consist of any legal set of UNIX commands, so the facility is very flexible. We present just a few ideas on how to use it.

The second tool is b. It is a background task handler. Many times when a background process is spawned, we never know when it has finished. To find out, we need to manually look in the process table or find some other sign that the job has been completed. B runs the job, manages any I/O, then alerts us when the job is done.

Greet shows how to translate the internal time kept by the computer into categories more meaningful to people. It recognizes three parts of a day: morning, afternoon, and evening, and responds with an appropriate message. This is rather elementary, but it provides a good framework for approaching other time-related problems.

Next we present two tools that form the beginnings of a time-management system. In many kinds of work, we need to keep track of the amount of time we spend on a given project so that we can bill our client accordingly. Lastlog runs automatically when you log in. A database is built that records all your login times for later analysis and/or record-keeping.

A companion tool is timelog. This is a utility that performs time accounting. It can keep track of total time spent on any specific project. Then statistics can be generated that reflect when and how long each project has been worked on.

The last time-related tool is today. This is a utility that modifies the output of the UNIX cal command. It prints the regular calendar but with today's date displayed in inverse. This makes it stand out clearly so that it is easier to see. You can extend this tool to mark holidays or other special days.

Name: at

at   Execute a command or file at a specific time

Function

Places any command line in the background and executes it at the specified time.

Synopsis

at hr:min cmd [;cmd ...]

Sample Call

at 12:00 echo "time for lunch!"

At twelve o'clock, print the message on the terminal screen

Code for at

```
1   :
2   # @(#) at v1.0  Execute command line at specific time   Author: Russ Sage
3
4   if [ $# -lt 2 ]
```

```
5    then  echo "at: wrong arg count"            >&2
6          echo "usage: at hr:min cmd [;cmd ...]" >&2
7          exit 1
8    fi
9
10   ITS=$1; shift
11
12   while :
13   do
14          TIME=`date | cut -c12-16`
15
16          if [ "$ITS" = "$TIME" ]
17          then  eval $@
18                exit 0
19          else  sleep 35
20          fi
21   done &
```

Environment Variables

ITS   The time at which to execute specified commands
TIME   Current time on the system

Description

Why do we need at?

Throughout our workday, we perform many small tasks that need to be done at various intervals. Some things simply have to be done once in a while, whereas other things need to be done at a particular time each day. For example, you might want to have a file backup procedure run every night, log onto another system once a day, and check for mail, or check for usenet messages on a given topic every few days.

At provides a mechanism for performing time-related tasks. We can tell the system what we want to do and when we want to do it. The task remains asleep in the background until the designated time and gives us the ability to turn the computer into an alarm clock, secretary, appointment manager, and so on.

The concept is not new and already exists on Berkeley UNIX under the same name, at. It is also implemented in the latest releases of System V.

So why are we presenting our own version here? For one thing, many of you may have earlier versions of UNIX that lack this tool. Perhaps more important is that our objective is not to make existing at commands obsolete but to show how easy it is to monitor the time and implement time-related processing. By having our own at command, we can tailor it to our liking and modify it when necessary. The at command presented here is actually more flexible than the Berkeley at, though it does lack some of its features. It is more flexible because you can put actual commands into the at background task, whereas with the Berkeley at, you must use a shell script file name. The Berkeley method restricts you from calling executables directly on the command line. Our at does not. (Of course you can use shell scripts as well if you wish.)

What does at *do?*

The at command gives us the capability of bundling a collection of commands together and having them run at a later time. When they are executed, their output can either go to the screen or be redirected to another file.

The command line takes two parameters: the execution time and the command line to execute. The time is expressed in hour:minute format. The hour must be a two-digit string represented in military time because date uses it. By using the same standard as the date command, at can be greatly simplified. The executable phrase can be any command that would normally be entered on a shell command line. Pipes, multiple commands, and redirection can also be used. There is no restriction on what command can be executed. At can run a regular UNIX executable or a shell script of your own.

The output from at goes to stdout by default. Stdout in this case is the terminal screen. The Berkeley at does not have a default output, which makes it a little more difficult to capture output or to send output to the screen.

At always runs as a background task. It doesn't make much sense to have it run in foreground where it locks up the terminal until execution time. By staying in the background, at frees the resources but still works for you. By the way, note that when processes are put into the background from inside a script, the process id is not printed to the screen as it is when the processes are put into background from the keyboard.

Spawning many background processes can have a degrading effect on the system. Each background task is a shell while loop that runs very slowly. Many background tasks mean less CPU time for everyone else. The result is sluggish system performance. On large systems, this is probably not a problem unless the system is loaded down with lots of users, but you should use this utility judiciously.

Note that the hour:minute format is only for one complete day. This at routine is designed to be a daily routine and has no facility for running on a specific day or month, although you could easily extend it once you understand how the time information is read and used.

Examples

1. `$ at 11:45 echo ^G^G It's almost lunch time`

At fifteen minutes before twelve, ring the bell (control-G) twice and print the lunch message.

2. `$ at 10:45 "if [ -s $MAIL ]; then echo ^G You have mail; fi"`

At fifteen minutes before eleven, check to see whether my mail file exists and has at least one character in it, where $MAIL is /usr/spool/mail/russ. If my mail file does, ring the bell and tell me that I have mail.

3. `$ at 17:00 "c; date; banner ' time to' ' go home'"`

At five o'clock in the evening, clear the screen (using the c command described later in this book), print the date, and banner the message "time to go home" across the screen. By using quotes in the banner command line, we can force the output of a carriage return, which puts each set of words on a separate line. If any of these commands fail (such as c not being found), the whole background session is bombed.

Explanation

The first thing at does is to check whether it was called correctly. Lines 4-8 do the error checking. At least two parameters must be included: the time and a command. This would make the positional parameter count equal to 2. If the count is less than 2, an error has occurred. The error messages are forced to standard error by redirecting to file descriptor 2.

The shell variable ITS is initialized in line 10. It is set to the first positional parameter ($1), which is the hour:time. Once we have this value in a variable, we don't need it on the command line anymore. The shift command removes $1 from the command line and throws it into the bit bucket. The command line is then a combination of the calling command ($0) (that is, at itself) and the rest of the line ($@ or $*). The calling command is not evaluated as part of the rest of the line, so you don't have to worry about the argument $0.

Next at goes into a while-forever loop in lines 12-21. The command that makes it a forever loop is the : command. This : command is a built-in shell command that does nothing except always return a successful exit status, thus forcing the loop to continue. The shell command true is very similar and makes for more readable code. We use :, instead, to reduce the overhead of forking a process for each loop iteration. : is built into the shell itself. True, on the other hand, is an external command in bin just like ls and must be looked up in its path, executed, and have a value returned. This consumes much more CPU time.

For each iteration of the loop, the current time is checked against the preset time passed from the command line. The current time is extracted from the date command in line 14. Date normally prints in a format like this:

```
Mon Mar 31 06:54:25 PST 1986
```

Because this is a fixed string size, we can count the number of columns where the hour and minute reside. The hour:minute data is in columns 12 through 16. To get these characters, we run the date command, pipe it through cut, and chop out the desired columns. The whole output is assigned to a variable named TIME. Note that the seconds field is not used. The finest granularity in this routine is the minute.

Lines 16-20 perform the magic work for this command. If the command line time is equal to the current time (line 16), evaluate and execute the rest of the command line arguments (line 17), then exit with a successful status value of 0 (line 18). If it is not time, sleep for a while longer (line 19) and do it all over again.

The ampersand at the end of the loop in line 20 forces the entire while loop into the background. How can we be sure that the shell performs all of its commands in the background and not some of them in the foreground? We really can't. We must believe that the shell will do it. Because most of shell programming is done by experience and gut feelings, you have to try things to see how they work out. Once in a while the shell surprises you and does something totally different than what you were expecting.

Explorations

What would happen if you put an at job in the background, then logged off? The answer depends on which shell you are running. If you run the Bourne shell, entering a control-D to log off kills all your background tasks. The only way to keep background tasks alive after logging off is to use the nohup ("no hang up") command. Nohup keeps all hangup signals from reaching the process. By not receiving a hangup signal, the process thinks you are still logged on. The syntax for this would be:

```
nohup at 13:00 echo "back from lunch yet?"
```

If you are running the C shell, all background processes live on after you log off. This is because the C shell puts all its background tasks in a nohup state. This process is automatic and does not need to be explicitly stated.

You might be wondering why the command "eval $@" is used in line 17. This came about by trial and error. In the beginning stages of developing at, the command "$@" was used by itself. When used alone, this command means "execute all the positional parameters." Because that was the only command, the entire positional parameter line was executed, then problems began to appear. Using redirections and shell variables caused at to become very confused.

To illustrate, let's look at a couple of examples. If we run at with the command line

```
at 09:30 echo $HOME
```

everything seems to work. The value $HOME is expanded first, and echo prints the expanded form, /usr/russ. But if we run the command line

```
at 09:30 echo \$HOME
```

the variable is not expanded and echo actually prints $HOME rather than the value of the variable $HOME. We get around this easily by using the eval command to evaluate the command line again before it is executed. The essence of the problem is that the calling shell does not expand the value, so we force the executing shell to reparse the command line and evaluate all variables. The variables get expanded at that time so that the end result is still the same.

Modifications

One thing that you might want to look at some more is the time interface. As it is now, the only kind of time at accepts is military time for one day. A nice addition would be to make it accept conventional time, such as 8:30 a.m. or 8:30 p.m. It would also be nice to be able to say "in 10 minutes do such and such." The command might look something like this

```
at -n 10 echo "do in now plus 10 minutes"
```

where -n would be the now time and 10 would be added to it.

Another obvious area for modification is to allow at to keep track of periods of time longer than one day. This could be tomorrow, a specific day, or even a specific month. Doing a specific month might not be totally realistic because a script that would live in the background for a month would require massive amounts of CPU time as well as keep the process id count steadily increasing, probably giving people a distorted view of system activity. When the maximum process number is reached, it rolls around to low numbers again, so no serious damage would result. Whether fulfilling your purpose is worth these problems depends on whether you think your requirements produce unnecessary wear and tear on the system.

Name: b

b	Background task handler

Synopsis

b any__command__with__options__and__arguments

Sample Call

b cg f.c

Compile the source file in the background, where cg is a compiler command line presented in Chapter 10.

Code for b

```
1   :
2   # @(#) b v1.0    Background task handler    Author: Russ Sage
3
4   ($@; echo "^G\ndone\n${PS1}\c") &
```

Description

Why do we need b?

As you saw in the last section, the Bourne shell gives us the capability of running tasks in the background. The ampersand character (&) does this. What really happens when we put something into background? Another shell is forked, which has its own command line to execute. When all of its commands have been run, it dies. You can identify background tasks in the output of the ps command. They appear as shells running under your device but their owner, or parent process, is really init rather than your login shell (this holds true for nohupd shells only).

Non-nohup shells are owned by your login shell. Here is a sample background task ps listing. The command put into background was

```
while :;do date; done &
```

Ps shows my login shell (PID=32), my command line in background (PID=419), and the shell to do the while loop (PID=449).

```
UID    PID  PPID  C   STIME TTY  TIME COMMAND
root     0     0  0   Dec 31   ?  0:03 swapper
root     1     0  0   Dec 31   ?  0:02 /etc/init
russ    32     1  0 14:18:36 03  1:26 -shV
russ   419    32  0 15:30:31 03  0:02 -shV
russ   449   419  2 15:30:31 03  0:02 -shV
```

The ps listing that shows the background shell owned by the init process looks like the following. It was generated by the command "b ps -ef", where b is the utility to be explained in subsequent text. As you can see the last process, 471, is a shell in the background owned by process 1, which is init and not my login shell (PID=32).

```
UID    PID  PPID  C   STIME TTY  TIME COMMAND
root     0     0  1   Dec 31   ?  0:04 swapper
root     1     0  0   Dec 31   ?  0:02 /etc/init
russ    32     1  1 14:18:36 03  1:30 -shV
russ   472   471  5 15:46:46 03  0:12 ps -ef
russ   471     1  0 15:46:46 03  0:00 -shV
```

What does this all lead to? When we use background tasks, we have to put up with the "unniceties" of asynchronous process handling. What are these drawbacks?

First, we never know when the background tasks are done. The only way to tell when the tasks are complete is to check the result of some file or some work done by the task or to use ps and constantly watch for the process to die. Watching ps is not a very good idea because ps takes lots of CPU time and is very slow.

Another area that is messy is the prompt after output has gone to your screen from a background task. After output from the background task, your login shell is waiting for a command, but the prompt may be gone because it was moved off the screen due to some output. You can wait all day for a prompt, but one is never printed because it has already been printed. You just have to know that the shell is waiting for your command.

What we need is a tool that alerts us when the background task is complete and also patches up our screen after any output is finished. Can we tell whether a background task has done any printing or not? No, we have to hard code the screen patch into the code.

What does b do?

B is a mechanism that assists in performing background tasks. It runs our background tasks. When finished, it echoes the word "done" to the screen, then reprints the shell prompt.

This tool has no options or error checking. The background handler actually executes the command line we pass it and does the later processing. Note that to have your prompt put on the screen, you must export the PS1 variable from your current environment. This might not hold on all machines because each UNIX has its own implementation. In XENIX, the PS1 variable is not passed on, possibly because it is a shell that calls another shell in the background. If you say "sh" interactively, it does pass on the prompt. UNIX is so strange and beautiful!

Examples

1. `$ b ls -R ..`

Starting from the parent directory, list all files recursively and print them to the screen. Notice that you cannot pipe things to more effectively when using background tasks because the normal input device for background tasks is /dev/null. More blows up when put in background. This also makes sense because you might have two tasks, one in background and one in foreground, putting stuff on the screen. The background more would have to keep track of what the foreground command is putting on the screen.

2. `$ b echo hello > z`

File z contains not only "hello", but also the message "done" because the redirection to z happens at the outermost shell. The redirection for the subtask must be redirected in the parenthesis of the b script, which we cannot possibly do in this case.

3. `$ b sleep 5; echo hello`

We can't do this because the b script only takes the sleep command. The echo command is not put into background and executes right away.

4. `$ b "sleep 5; echo hello"`

We can't do this either because the two commands are sent through the b script as one command. Then sleep bombs because "5; echo hello" is not a valid reference to a time period for sleep.

Explanation

Notice that in line 4, the entire command structure is enclosed in parentheses, followed by an ampersand. The parentheses force the entire structure into a subshell, which then is put into background. By lumping all the commands into one shell, we are guaranteed that the "done" statement is printed after the last process is completed.

The command line is executed by using the $@. This means "put everything from the command line right here." Because the $@ is by itself (that is, not in an echo statement or something similar), the shell simply executes the commands from the original command line. Exactly what we want! Notice that there is no `eval` statement. Because what we're doing is similar to the "command line interpreter" type of input and execution, you would think `eval` would be necessary. From experience, we know this is not true. Putting in `eval` seems to make the execution of the whole thing go haywire. Even our old test using environment variables works, as seen in the following.

```
b echo $HOME
```

produces the output

```
/usr/russ
```

When the command has been executed, the bell is rung and a message is printed to alert the user that the operation is complete. Since the message affects the output on the screen, the primary prompt (PS1) is redisplayed. This makes the screen look normal in the sense of the shell prompt being there waiting for input.

Name: greet

greet   Timely greeting from the terminal

Function

Determines which part of the day it is and prints a greeting and a message to the terminal based on the time of day.

Synopsis

greet

Sample Call

greet   Calls greet, which determines time and prints message accordingly

Code for greet

```
1 :
2 # a(#) greet v1.0   Timely greeting from the terminal   Author: Russ Sage
3
4 if [ 'expr \'date +%H\' \< 12' = "1" ]
5   then  echo "\nGood morning.\nWhat is the best use of your time right now?"
6 elif [ 'expr \'date +%H\' \< 18' = "1" ]
7   then  echo "\nGood afternoon.\nRemember, only handle a piece of paper once
!"
8 else    echo "\nGood evening.\nPlan for tomorrow today."
9 fi
```

Description

Why do we need greet?

One of the nicest features of multiuser operating systems is that they have a well-designed concept of time. They usually include a real-time clock and some sort of software that manipulates it. But there is always room for more time-based software. Tools for time can be written either in C or in shell language.

How do we extract and isolate time using a shell script? Many ways are available, but the regular UNIX `date` command is probably the best way. From C, you have to handle programmatically the time conversions and time zones. `Date` does this for you.

Time granularity is also important. Should we be able to recognize the second, minute, hour, day, or week? It all depends on the application at hand. For our simple example, we are only considering the three parts to a day: morning, afternoon, and evening. We define these periods to be midnight to noon, noon to six o'clock, and six o'clock to midnight respectively.

What does greet do?

`Greet` is a utility that greets the user with different messages depending on the time throughout the day. The messages that are printed are not that important. They are used mostly as examples to show how commands can be executed. If you work alone and would like some automated inane conversation, they could be read randomly from appropriate files to provide a bit of automated chit-chat based on the time of day.

The real objective is to create a skeletal routine that can key on time parameters. By expanding on the time concept, you can create other utilities that know when they are run (in whatever sort of time periods are appropriate) and can behave differently according to the time.

`Greet` does not require any input on the command line. No error checking is done, so there are no usage statements in the code. The output can be redirected to another file, or piped into another process.

Examples

```
1. $ if greet | fgrep 'morn' > /dev/null
   >    then morning_routine
   > fi
```

Execute `greet`. Pipe the stdout of greet to the stdin of `fgrep`. Look for the string "morn" in the data. Redirect all the output to the bit bucket so that it won't trash the screen. If the exit status of `fgrep` is zero (it found the string), execute the file morning__routine.

```
2. $ at 10:30 greet; at 13:50 greet
```

You could put this in your .profile. Two `at` processes would live in the background of your machine until their run time and when executed would greet you on your terminal. This might actually create a minor nuisance. The messages could arrive when you are in the editor, which messes up the output, but it does not actually alter your editor file.

Explanation

The entire program is one large if-then-else statement in lines 4-9. The logic in pseudocode goes like this:

```
if it is morning
  then echo morning statement
else if it is noon
  then echo noon statement
else echo evening statement
```

The actual code is fairly complex, so take a deep breath and we'll proceed.

Line 4 checks to see whether the current time is less than 12 o'clock. If it is, the `expr` clause prints a "1" to standard output. Because the grave accent (') characters that enclose the clause catch the standard output, the 1 character becomes part of the test statement, which is indicated by square brackets ([ ]). `Test` then checks whether the `expr` output is equal to a literal 1 character. If they are the same, the morning message is output in line 5.

Let's look more closely at the expansion of the `expr` statement. First, it is in grave accents. This means it is executed before the test statement. Then the output is placed in the test statement for `test` to operate on. But inside the `expr` statement is another set of grave accents that are executed before the `expr` statement. This precedence of execution is being handled by interpreter code inside the shell.

The inner grave accent characters are retained in the initial parsing of the line because they are quoted with backslashes. The `date` command runs first with its output as only the current hour, due to the use of the format %H. `Expr` then uses this hour value to see whether it is less than 12. If so, expr prints the value 1. If the hour is equal to or greater than 12, the return value is 0. This evaluation of 1=true and 0=false is the same notation used in C.

However, we remarked earlier that in the world of shell programming, 1=false and 0=true. This is because the if statement test value is really the exit status from the previously executed command. Zero stands for good execution, so 0 is used to trigger the true test and execute the then statement. To convert the return status of 1 (from find, the hour was less than 12) into a zero (to trigger the then statement), we use the `test` command. The return status of 1 is equal to the constant 1, so the test command returns a 0, which represents truth. Whew!

If nested grave accents were not used, the only way to pass this type of information down would be by using shell variables. Using nested command substitution gives us more flexibility and ease of use in programming. The deeper the nesting occurs, the deeper the quoting of the grave accents occurs. The backslash quote nesting order is none with the outermost command, one with the second innermost command, and five for the third innermost command. The fourth level is probably seven or nine (I haven't tried that yet), but there probably isn't much need for nesting that deep.

If the test in line 4 is false, line 6 is executed. This is the else from the first if, and is another if itself. For these special cases, the shell syntax changes. The "else" becomes an "elif".

The second if uses the test command the same way that the first one did. The hour checked here is 18, which represents 6 o'clock in the evening. If the second test also fails, the last statement in line 8 is executed. This else does not use the test command because after the first two checks, we can assume that the only time period left is after 18:00 hours.

Name: lastlog

lastlog   Report last login time

Function

This tool records and displays the day and time of your last login session.

Synopsis

lastlog [-l]

Sample Call

lastlog   Prints the date of the last time you logged in

Code for lastlog

```
1   :
2   # @(#) lastlog v1.0   Report last login time   Author: Russ Sage
3
4   if [ $# -gt 1 ]
5     then  echo "lastlog: arg error"  >&2
6           echo "usage: lastlog [-l]" >&2
7           exit 1
8   fi
9
10  if [ "$#" -eq "1" ]
11    then  if [ "$1" = "-l" ]
12            then  date >> $HOME/.lastlog
13                  lastlog
14            else  echo "lastlog: unrecognized option $1" >&2
15                  echo "usage: lastlog [-l]"              >&2
16                  exit 1
17          fi
18    else  echo "Time of last login : `tail -2 $HOME/.lastlog |
19          (read FIRST; echo $FIRST)`"
20  fi
```

Environment Variables

FIRST   Holds the first of two input lines
HOME   Holds the directory name of your home in the system tree

Description

Why do we need lastlog?

One advantage of working on a UNIX system is that a record is made automatically of your starting time for each session—your login time. This information might be useful to have around for a couple of reasons. First, you can remember when you were actually on the system last and check to see whether anyone has logged in on your account while you were gone. As we see in Chapter 9, there are a number of ways that someone can "borrow" your account without asking. For that reason, many commercial systems tell you when you logged on last (or when it thinks you logged on last).

Another possible reason would be to calculate at the end of the session how long you have been on the system. You could use this as accounting information for yourself or a computing center. A little later, we introduce a tool to help with such accounting.

The tool we design must have a way to record new times and display the last time we logged in. It is important that the program can be invoked in a way that does not update the database file but continually prints the last login time.

What does lastlog do?

Lastlog is a program that records your login time every time you log in. Then this time is stored in a data file in your home directory, namely $HOME/.lastlog. The reason the lastlog file is named with a dot first is to keep it an invisible file to the ls command. Keeping "utility" files out of the default listing gives them a bit of security from prying eyes and keeps them out of your way when you're looking for other things.

To provide this last login date for us, when invoked with no option, lastlog prints the lastlog date by getting the entry from .lastlog.

To make a new entry into .lastlog, lastlog needs to be invoked with the -l option, which logs the new time into the .lastlog file, then calls itself to print that new value out to the screen. A wee bit of recursion.

For lastlog to work automatically, you should execute it from your .profile at login time. If set up this way, it puts the earliest date into .lastlog. For an example, see the .profile in the first chapter.

Explanation

Lines 4-8 do the error checking. If you call lastlog with more than one argument, you cause an error. A message is printed to standard error and lastlog exits with an error status of 1.

Lines 10-20 are an if-then-else statement that figures out whether this call is for recording new times or printing old times.

In line 10, if the number of positional parameters is equal to one, we know the parameter must be either the -l option or an error condition. The next if statement in line 11 checks the first positional parameter to see whether it is the -l option. If it is, the current date is appended to the $HOME/.lastlog file and lastlog is called again with no arguments to print the previous login date. (We see how it does that in a moment.) If the argument was not -l, lines 14-16 do the error handling.

If the number of positional parameters is zero, the else statement in line 18 is executed. No option means that we want to find the last time we logged in on the machine and print it. This seems very straightforward, but then who said machines are straightforward?

If you remember the sequence, we first log a new time, then we want to find the previous time we logged in. In the .lastlog file, this means our current login time is at the very end of the file and our previous login time is the line right before it. This means we have to get the second line from the bottom of the file. Hmm.

As can be seen in line 18, the easy part is getting the last two lines. The tail command does a nice job of this. What we need is to have a way we can read just the first line, and throw the second one away, which is done in line 19. We pipe the output of tail into a subshell (determined by the parenthesis) that reads the first line, then echoes it. What about the second line? It never is touched and goes away into the bit bucket. Another approach might be to pipe the output of `tail` to "head -1".

Because this command has no other options, we won't give any further examples. However, let's look at our other time-logging tool now.

Name: `timelog`

timelog   Time accounting and statistics

Function

A menu interface for monitoring and maintaining time log files.

Synopsis

timelog

Sample Call

timelog   Prints the main menu from which choices are entered

Code for `timelog`

```
1    :
2    # @(#) timelog v1.0   Time accounting and statistics   Author: Russ Sage
3
4    PROJ=""
5
6    while :
7    do
8            set 'date'
9            echo "
10
11   $1, $2 $3                   $4
12
13           Time Logger
14           -----------             Project:  $PROJ
15    s) Select a project file
16    c) Create a new project file
```

```
17      l) List current project files
18      v) View the project file
19      n) Turn billing on
20      f) Turn billing off
21      r) Report statistics
22
23      enter response (s,c,l,v,n,f,r,<cr>): \c"
24
25          read RSP
26
27          case $RSP in
28          "")  break;;
29          s)   echo "\nEnter project name (<cr> for exit): \c"
30               read PROJ2
31               if [ "$PROJ2" = "" ]
32                 then continue
33               fi
34               if [ ! -s $PROJ2.time ]
35                 then echo "you must specify a valid project file"
36                       continue
37                fi
38               PROJ="$PROJ2";;
39          c)   echo "\nEnter the new project name (<cr> to exit): \c"
40               read PROJ2
41               if [ "$PROJ2" = "" ]
42                 then   continue
43               fi
44               if [ -f "$PROJ2.time" ]
45                 then   echo "\n  ** $PROJ2 already exists  **"
46                       continue
47               fi
48               PROJ="$PROJ2"
49               echo "\nProject file created: $PROJ"
50               echo "Project file created: 'date'\nOFF: begin" > $PROJ.time;;
51          l)   echo "\nCurrent project files:\n"
52               ls -l *.time 2>/dev/null || echo "no project files" |
53                 sed "s/\.time//";;
54          v)   if [ "$PROJ" = "" ]
55                 then echo "you must select a project file first"
56                       continue
57               fi
58               echo "\n:--------------------------"
59               more $PROJ.time
60               echo ":--------------------------";;
61          n)   if [ "$PROJ" = "" ]
62                 then echo "you must select a project file first"
63                       continue
```

```
64                    fi
65                    if [ "'tail -1 $PROJ.time|cut -d: -f1'" != "OFF" ]
66                      then  echo "logging was not turned off"
67                            continue
68                    fi
69                    echo "\nBilling turned on for project file: $PROJ"
70                    echo "ON: 'date'" >> $PROJ.time;;
71          f)   if [ "$PROJ" = "" ]
72                      then echo "you must select a project file first"
73                            continue
74                    fi
75                    if [ "'tail -1 $PROJ.time|cut -d: -f1'" != "ON" ]
76                      then  echo "logging was not turned on"
77                            continue
78                    fi
79                    echo "\nBilling turned off for project file: $PROJ"
80                    echo "OFF: 'date'" >> $PROJ.time;;
81        r)  while :
82            do
83                        echo "
84        Statistics
85        ----------              Project: $PROJ
86    a)  Accumulative time totals
87    n)  All times on
88    f)  All times off
89
90    enter response (a,n,f,<cr>): \c"
91
92                    read RSP
93
94                    case $RSP in
95                    "")  break;;
96                    a)   awk '/Total:/ { PRINT $0 }' $PROJ.TIME;;
97                    n)   awk '/ON/ { print $0 }'      $PROJ.time;;
98                    f)   awk '/OFF/ { print $0 }'     $PROJ.time;;
99                    *)   echo "\n  ** Wrong command, try again  **";;
100                   esac
101           done;;
102      *) echo "\n  ** Wrong command, try again  **";;
103      esac
104 done
```

Environment Variables

PROJ	Holds the current project name
PROJ2	Holds the temporary project name typed by user
RSP	Holds the command response for the menu choice

Description

Why do we need timelog?

Time is a valuable commodity. There is never enough of it and once used up, it can never again be reused. We want to make sure we get compensated properly for our time. We can and should make tools to help us manage and record our time.

The kinds of things we need to consider are which projects we are working on, when do we work on them (that is, start and stop), and what other information we need keep track of.

Just about all of these functions are handled in timelog. We have written quite a lot of code here, but we note that the facility isn't really complete. Enough of timelog exists to get you up and running on a time management system. You have to provide your own code for producing reports based on the time statistics.

What does timelog do?

Timelog addresses itself to the most important areas surrounding time recording and management. Note that the number of accounts that can be created, viewed, and managed is limited only by available file storage space.

Timelog is a totally menu-driven interface. Menu systems in UNIX are somewhat new and have their advantages and disadvantages. Some advantages are that all the work done to the data is programmatic, not manual. Each function also is visible and easy to select. You don't have to memorize options and file names, just press one key to perform an action.

The disadvantages are that menus run more slowly than on a manual interface (that is, simply typing and executing commands directly). This is a very valid point, but we also have to remember that programs must be easy to use, easy to modify, and do lots of small things associated with one idea or area of function. Wasting computer time is often better than wasting human time! Another disadvantage is that to get to a specific function, you must go through a couple of levels.

For example, to print a report you must call timelog, select the statistics menu, then select the report you want. This is three levels compared to having a utility where you would say "report report_file", just one command.

For single-function utilities, having one command with a few flavors is very efficient. This is the approach taken with most shell scripts. But when you have many, many small tasks to perform on a couple of objects, menus are handy.

Some systems provide both a menu-driven and a command-driven interface. This pleases more people and avoids most of the disadvantages mentioned previously. Of course, some inevitable processing overhead occurs with this approach, and a lot more coding must be done.

The initial menu, as seen below, is displayed on invocation of timelog.

```
Thu, Jun 19                      21:32:12


        Time Logger
        -----------              Project:
    s) Select a project file
```

```
c) Create a new project file
l) List current project files
v) View the project file
n) Turn billing on
f) Turn billing off
r) Report statistics

enter response (s,c,l,v,n,f,r,<cr>):
```

The top left shows the day of week and the date. At top right, the time is shown. This is the real time and is updated with every display of the menu. The name of the menu is "Time Logger." "Report statistics" produces a submenu.

The line that says "Project:" shows that the current project name is null. To work on a project, you must first create a project file, or if one already exists, select a project file. All actions carried out after that point are done to the current project file.

The first selection is s for select a project file. When chosen, the message is displayed:

```
Enter project name (<cr> for exit):
```

You can enter any text string for the project name, or if you do not want to be in this option, pressing the return key exits gracefully. If you cannot remember project names, you can use the l option explained later. When the name of an existing project file is input, the current project name (which is printed at the upper right of each menu) is set to that file.

The next option is c for create a project file. As noted, this must be the first thing you do when starting with `timelog`, but after that you usually select existing files. When you choose c, the following prompt is printed:

```
Enter the new project name (<cr> to exit):
```

Input here is the same as for selecting a project. To exit, press a carriage return. When a name is input, the current project name is changed, the project file is created, the time is stamped, and the file is loaded with initial information.

The next option is l for list project file names. Because each project is a file, the regular `ls` type listing is displayed. Watch out, though. The output is not straight out of `ls`. The names have been changed to protect the innocent.

Each project file is stored on disk under the format "project.time". The project part is different for every file and is the name typed from the create option. All files have the suffix .time. When the list option is printed, the .time has been stripped so that the file names are just the projects, which is what you type for the select option. It works out, but you must remember that if you want to look at the time files manually, the names are not the same. If no project files exist, a message stating so is displayed.

The next option is v for view the project file. The file that is going to be viewed is the current project name. This name is displayed on the menu to the right of the "Project:" line. If no name appears, you must either create a new project or select an existing project. The project file is displayed by the UNIX `more` command.

The next option is n for turn on billing. This means to begin recording a new session for the project. The project name is checked to see whether a project file has been selected. If not, a message is displayed to do so. The project file is then checked to see whether the previous action was to turn the file off. If yes, the time logger can be turned on. You cannot turn the time on twice. You have to turn it off, then on, etc.

The next option is f for turning off billing on a project file. The current project name is checked for null and displays a message if true. Then it checks to see whether the file was previously turned on. If it was, an off billing record is appended to the project file.

The last option is r for reports and statistics. When chosen, a submenu is displayed as follows:

```
Statistics
----------              Project:
a)   Accumulative time totals
n)   All times on
f)   All times off


enter response (a,n,f,<cr>):
```

As mentioned previously, this menu is not really implemented. Some stub commands allow the menu to be functional, but this area is where you can customize the reports to your own specifications. Notice that the project name is also displayed on this menu. The name is then available for any functions residing in this menu.

Examples

1. `c,l,v`

This is the first set of commands when running from scratch. The c is the menu choice for create a project file. The l command lists all project file names, and v views the initial data that is in the project file.

2. `n,n`

This sequence shows the error checking inside the program. First turn on billing for the current project file, then turn on billing again. `Timelog` recognizes this and states that you must turn billing off before you can turn it on again.

3. `s,junk`

This sequence also shows error checking. Try to select a new project file name. The name is junk (which you should not have). `Timelog` tests to see whether the junk time log file exists. If not, the error message states that you should select a valid project file.

Explanation

This script has a lot of code, but the concepts aren't particularly complicated.

Line 4 initializes the variable PROJ to null. PROJ is the variable that holds the project name displayed on the menu. We want to make sure this variable is set to null in the beginning.

Lines 6-104 are a huge while-forever loop that implements the whole program. Because it is a forever loop, we can exit it by either **break**ing out of it (typing the usual interrupt characters) or going out through the exit command.

Line 8 sets the positional parameters to the output of the **date** command. By doing so, we can then reference each piece easily without having to cut it up—the shell parses them for us. We can reference the data as $1, $2, and so on.

Lines 9-23 actually print the main menu. The top line references the data from the date command. $1, $2, and $3 are the day, month, and date. $4 is the time. Before **echo** prints the lines of text, the variables are expanded so that they appear in the menu. If the PROJ variable is null, nothing is printed for the name of the current project. If PROJ has a value, it appears in the menu. The \c at the end of the huge **echo** statement forces the cursor to stay at the end of the prompt on the same line so that we are ready for user input.

After the menu is printed, the response is read in RSP in line 25. Then comes a huge case statement (lines 27-103), which contains a branch for each command.

In line 28, the response is checked to see whether it was only a carriage return, indicating that the user wants to exit. If so, the while loop is exited via the shell **break** command and the program ends.

Sometimes the carriage return is a more desirable method of exit than the shell **exit** command. Eventually the shell command gets down to the exit and _exit routines at the C interface. Making the exit call in C sometimes has unexpected side effects, whereas letting the code go out the normal bottom of a program does not have the same results. We once ran into this sort of problem when we were using escape sequences to alter the coloring on a color monitor. When the code exited normally the colors weren't reset. However, when the exit system call was made, certain escape sequences were being printed that reset areas of the monitor. Very strange!

Lines 29-38 handle the project selection function. The project name is prompted for and read into PROJ2. PROJ2 is used to hold the value temporarily. If the input was a carriage return, the continue statement forces the next iteration of the outer while loop. This allows the user to abort this function, if it was entered by accident, yet still remain in `timelog`. If the input wasn't null, the project file is checked to see whether it exists and has some data. If the file does not exist, the user is told to specify a valid project name. If the name is a valid file, PROJ is set to PROJ2. Only after the script knows for sure that the user's input is valid is it assigned to the current project name. This prevents the current project selection being lost due to user error. Now PROJ is printed on the menu screens.

The create command is handled in lines 39-50. Again the name is prompted for and checked for null. If a name was typed, it is checked to see whether the file already exists. We don't want to re-create and wipe out an already established file. The file is created in line 50. The initial time stamp for the file being created and the initial message indicating billing is off are echoed into the file name.

The list option is in lines 51-53. A banner is printed, then the `ls` command is used to generate the list. If there are no files of the type we are looking for, `ls` returns a status other than 0, which triggers the `||` statement. In effect, this shell trick gives us a built-in if-then that can use the results of the preceding command. If the `ls` command fails (that is, doesn't find any matching files), its error message is tossed into the bit bucket and the echo statement is executed. The `echo` command prints that there are no files, so you know.

Any `ls` output is filtered through `sed` to strip away the .time file name extensions. To save space and keep things simpler for the user, we only want to see and type project names, not file names. However, we want to maintain file names internally with a special format so that we can process them more easily and maintain unique names.

The view command is in lines 54-60. The current project file is checked to see whether a name has been selected. If not, the main menu is printed again. Otherwise, a line of dashes is printed, the project file is printed using `more`, and another line of dashes is printed to frame the output. You may wonder why the `echo` statement has the : character as the first character. This is a kludge because if you try to echo a hyphen (-) as the first character, echo `thinks` it's an empty option and doesn't print it to the screen. You just have to have some nonblank character other than a dash in that first position. Turning the billing on is handled in lines 61-70. The current project name is checked to see whether it has been selected. If so, the project file is checked to see whether it has been turned off. We do this by using `tail` to cut off the last line of the file, then pipe that string to `cut` where we change the delimiter character to a : and slice out the first field. If this field is the characters OFF, everything is okay. Then line 69 echoes a message to the screen for the user's information and line 70 puts the ON string in the project file followed by the current date. This marks the file as being turned on. Billing is started now. If billing was already on, we tell the user it is already on and exit the selection.

Lines 71-80 handle turning the billing off. It is almost identical to the code that turns the billing on except that wherever the word "on" was, the word "off" is now.

Lines 81-101 handle the reports and statistics submenu. As you can see, a menu screen is laid out the same way: while loop, print menu, read response, case on command, etc. The r command is like the main menu, only shrunk to fit inside a case statement. You also can see that lines 93-96 do not have very much processing in them. This is where you have to do some work.

Line 102 does the error handling for any wrong inputs. An error message is printed and the case statement exits to the next iteration of the while loop and it all starts over again.

Modifications

The main possibility is to add actual processing of time information. One approach is to ask for an hourly billing rate at the time a project file is created (assuming you work on this basis). The rate could be stored as the first item in the project file. The next two lines could be reserved for "billing for current session" and "cumulative billing," respectively. When billing is turned off on a project, the current system time and the beginning time for billing could be parsed and converted to minutes (for ease of arithmetic) using `expr` (or perhaps `awk`). This total would be multiplied by the rate stored in the file and the result would be stored in the current session record and *added* to the cumulative total record.

Name: today

today   Print calendar with today's date highlighted

Function

Modifies the output of the `cal` utility to print today's date in reverse video.

Synopsis

today

Sample Call

today   Prints this month's calendar with today's date highlighted

Code for today

```
1    :
2    # @(#) today v1.0    Calendar with today highlighted    Author: Russ Sage
3
4    SYSV=n
5
6    set `date`
7
8    if [ "$SYSV" = "y" ]
9      then RVR=`tput smso`
10          BLNK=`tput blink`
11          NORM=`tput rmso`
12          cal ${2} ${6} | sed "s/${3}/${RVR}${BLNK}${3}${NORM}/g" -e "s/^/
/"
13      else RVR="^[[7m"    # termcap so
14          NORM="^[[0m"    # termcap se
15          cal ${2} ${6} | sed -e "s/ ${3}/ ${RVR}${3}${NORM}/" -e "s/^/  /"
16   fi
```

Environment Variables

RVR   The reverse video control character for your terminal

| BLNK | The blinking video control character for your terminal if it has one |
| NORM | The control character to return your terminal to normal mode |

Description

Why do we need today?

It is always nice to have tools that present us with information about our environment. The kind of information that we are looking for here is a modified calendar printout. The normal cal command prints the days of the month but does not tell you which day is today. How do we know? We have to run date to find out the day. A rather trivial problem, but our solution could lead to some fancier graphics that may add truly useful information to the calendar.

To do this kind of modification, we need to postprocess the output of the cal command. Because all terminals do not have the same capabilities, this routine may need to be adapted to your machine.

What does today do?

Today is a tail-end processor for the cal command to make its output more informative and graphically pleasing. The modification to cal is dependent on which system you are running. If you are on a UNIX System V, Release 2 or later, you have the terminfo utility. Terminfo is a replacement for termcap and comes with some utilities that return the terminfo values. Terminfo provides an easy way to get the terminal's characteristics. If your computer is not running on System V, you have to do a little research on your particular terminal type and manually put these values in your program.

The whole business with termcap and terminfo illustrates evolution at work in the UNIX world. UNIX has from its earliest days striven to be device-independent. The first step is the use of device files and drivers. The next step was termcap, which provided a uniform way for accessing information about terminals. The latest stage is terminfo, which provides this information in a way that can be better accessed functionally by programs.

Because there is no easy way to tell from within the script which system your computer is running, a variable is used. This variable can be changed with the editor and forces today to run under one system or the other. Some ways to check on the system could be uname, the existence of a particular shell program in /bin, or some file on the system that contains the release number. The default setting of today is *not* to run as System V. This forces the code into the manually updated section.

How do you get this information manually? Each terminal has its own specific functionality. All terminals are characterized in generic terms by the termcap file. In termcap, each feature is given a name and what the hardware-specific code is for that function. That way vi, for example, can look into termcap and figure out how to drive the terminal we are on. Termcap is very cryptic and magical. There is not very much documentation on this area, so it involves a lot of trial and error.

The variables we are interested in are "so" for stand out (inverse mode), "se" for end stand out (normal mode), and blink if your terminal has it. Termcap doesn't seem to indicate how to do blinking, so you probably will have to find documentation for the terminal in question. For System V, Release 2, the tput command returns the appropriate value.

The default entries in today are for an ANSI terminal, specifically the console for XENIX. These codes were manually looked up in /etc/termcap and put into the script. If yours are different, you must look them up. Notice that in /etc /termcap, an ESCAPE character is represented as \E. This does not work in today and you must change it to a real ESCAPE. Because ESCAPE is the character to exit input mode in vi, you must use the control-V command in vi to enter control characters. A control-V prints the ^ character and an ESCAPE prints a [. The actual command to go into standout in our default thus appears in vi as ^[[7m. This command includes the ^[for the real ESCAPE you typed, then the usual [7m for changing modes.

Now that the terminal characteristics are taken care of, the object of today is to highlight the current day on the calendar as reverse video and leave the rest of the output in normal video. The way this is done is to pipe the output of cal into sed. Sed then finds the number in the output and substitutes the special graphics escape characters. Because your terminal uses the special characters to change modes, you do not see them printed to the screen.

This program has no options or special inputs. It prints out the calendar with today highlighted.

Explanation

Line 4 initializes the SYSV variable to "n". This forces the code to go through a specific area where manually obtained terminal control codes have been hard coded. If you are running on the latest system V, you want this variable to be "y".

Line 6 forces the positional parameters to be set to the output of the date command. We refer to these values later.

Lines 8-17 are the rest of the program. It is one if-then-else statement. Lines 9-12 handle the system V tput method, whereas lines 13-15 handle the manual method.

In both cases, the shell variables are assigned escape sequences. These values are used later. They both call the cal command using the month and the year from the date output. This calendar image is piped through sed, which looks for the specific day "today", also obtained from the date command. When the day is found, sed replaces the day digits with the reverse-video sequence, the blinking sequence if you have it, the day characters, then the normal sequence. The last sed command substitutes some blanks at the beginning of the line to center it on the screen.

Office Management

Much work time is spent keeping track of important information, such as appointments, addresses, phone numbers, schedules, project billing, and so on. Most of this information can be kept in the UNIX system in the form of simple structured text files and can be manipulated with appropriate tools. Automating these areas can free more time for us to get our "real" work done.

Although powerful commercial programs for keeping track of such information are found in the MS-DOS world, these programs are not as widespread in the UNIX world. Often you don't need large standalone programs to do these things with UNIX anyway. UNIX provides a good middle ground between easy-to-use but inflexible commercial programs and programming in powerful but hard-to-use traditional programming languages. The shell plus the rich assortment of built-in UNIX commands provides a powerful, flexible, and *relatively* easy-to-use compromise. In this section, we present a wide variety of personal management tools that you can customize to suit your needs.

We start with something just for fun. It's a program called jargon, a technical word generator that builds fanciful phrases which can be used to impress people with how much you know or start you off on a profitable second career as an advertising copywriter. The words combine to form hundreds of evocative phrases.

Next, we look at phone. Phone is a menu-driven tool that maintains a database of phone numbers and related information. It brings together all the various aspects of database maintenance and query lookup.

The last tool is called office. It is a menu-driven utility that gives us single keystroke access to all the office functions. The areas addressed are mail, news, calendar functions, phone numbers, and automatic reminders.

Name: jargon

jargon   Technical jargon generator

Function

Computerized version of the old table lookup technical jargon generator.

Synopsis

jargon

Sample Call

jargon   Enter the code 125 in response to the prompt, output is Total
  125   Monitored Concept

Code for jargon

```
1    :
2    # @(#) jargon v1.0   Technical jargon generator   Author: Russ Sage
3
4    echo "\n\t\tThe Jargon Generator"
5    while :
6    do
7            echo "\nEnter a 3 digit number (000-999), ?, or <cr>: \c"
8            read NUM
9
10           case $NUM in
11           "")  exit;;
12           \?)  cat <<EOF
13
```

```
14  0. Integrated          0. Management          0. Options
15  1. Total               1. Organizational      1. Flexibility
16  2. Systematized        2. Monitored           2. Capability
17  3. Parallel            3. Reciprocal          3. Mobility
18  4. Functional          4. Digital             4. Programming
19  5. Responsive          5. Logistical          5. Concept
20  6. Optional            6. Transitional        6. Time-Phase
21  7. Synchronized        7. Incremental         7. Projection
22  8. Compatible          8. Operational         8. Hardware
23  9. Balanced            9. Third-Generation    9. Contingency
24  EOF
25          continue;;
26      ???) expr "$NUM" : "^[0-9][0-9][0-9]$" > /dev/null ||
27          { echo "\nNot a valid number, try again"; continue; };;
28      *)  echo "\nInvalid input, try again"
29          continue;;
30      esac
31
32      N1='echo $NUM|cut -c1'
33      N2='echo $NUM|cut -c2'
34      N3='echo $NUM|cut -c3'
35      SEN=""
36
37      case $N1 in
38      0)  SEN="${SEN}Integrated ";;
39      1)  SEN="${SEN}Total ";;
40      2)  SEN="${SEN}Systematized ";;
41      3)  SEN="${SEN}Parallel ";;
42      4)  SEN="${SEN}Functional ";;
43      5)  SEN="${SEN}Responsive ";;
44      6)  SEN="${SEN}Optional ";;
45      7)  SEN="${SEN}Synchronized ";;
46      8)  SEN="${SEN}Compatible ";;
47      9)  SEN="${SEN}Balanced ";;
48      esac
49
50      case $N2 in
51      0)  SEN="${SEN}Management ";;
52      1)  SEN="${SEN}Organizational ";;
53      2)  SEN="${SEN}Monitored ";;
54      3)  SEN="${SEN}Reciprocal ";;
55      4)  SEN="${SEN}Digital ";;
56      5)  SEN="${SEN}Logistical ";;
57      6)  SEN="${SEN}Transitional ";;
58      7)  SEN="${SEN}Incremental ";;
59      8)  SEN="${SEN}Operational ";;
60      9)  SEN="${SEN}Third-Generation ";;
```

```
61          esac
62
63          case $N3 in
64          0)  SEN="${SEN}Options";;
65          1)  SEN="${SEN}Flexibility";;
66          2)  SEN="${SEN}Capability";;
67          3)  SEN="${SEN}Mobility";;
68          4)  SEN="${SEN}Programming";;
69          5)  SEN="${SEN}Concept";;
70          6)  SEN="${SEN}Time-Phase";;
71          7)  SEN="${SEN}Projection";;
72          8)  SEN="${SEN}Hardware";;
73          9)  SEN="${SEN}Contingency";;
74          esac
75
76          echo "\n\"$SEN\""
77  done
```

Environment Variables

N1	The first digit in the number
N2	The second digit in the number
N3	The third digit in the number
NUM	Input from the user at the keyboard
SEN	The sentence using looked-up words

Description

Why do we need jargon?

In this high-speed, high-tech world of ours, we are under great pressure to produce results. Unfortunately, the high-speed part of high tech refers to the execution of programs, not their creation. When we've only completed about a third of the program and it's time to go to market, how can we make our products seem to do more than they really do? We need to produce bits of flurf on demand. Flurf consists of phrases that look and sound impressive. Upon close examination, we can even see the phrase is made of genuine English words, the meanings of which we can look up in the dictionary. The phrase as a whole is pretty meaningless, but if we're lucky the reader won't notice this!

One easy way to get this kind of thing is to have a table of interchangeable words that can be used to create "mix and match" sentences. If you have BSD you can also run jargon as a companion to fortune, which simulates a randomly opened fortune cookie. The wisdom of the ages can be yours!

What does jargon do?

Jargon is a tool to generate a phrase made of technical words. It does so by creating a phrase that is a combination of three words. The first two words are adjectives used to describe the last word, a noun. Each word is taken from a column of ten possible words. That's what gives jargon its special creative ability. It can combine a word in one column with any of the words in the other columns to create many useful phrases. If you want to see the whole table of words, enter a ?. A sample table is printed below:

```
        The Jargon Generator


Enter a 3 digit number (000-999), ?, or <cr>: ?

0. Integrated       0. Management        0. Options
1. Total            1. Organizational    1. Flexibility
2. Systematized     2. Monitored         2. Capability
3. Parallel         3. Reciprocal        3. Mobility
4. Functional       4. Digital           4. Programming
5. Responsive       5. Logistical        5. Concept
6. Optional         6. Transitional      6. Time-Phase
7. Synchronized     7. Incremental       7. Projection
8. Compatible       8. Operational       8. Hardware
9. Balanced         9. Third-Generation  9. Contingency
```

There are three possible inputs. You can enter a three-digit number, a ? to print the table, or a carriage return to exit the program. The three-digit string is checked to see whether it is a valid number. If everything is okay, the number input is split into its three constituent digits. Each digit is used as a lookup key into the ten words to obtain its portion of the sentence. All the words are put together in a sentence to make a jargon phrase. Then you are prompted for the next set of inputs.

If you enter a ?, the table of words is displayed as shown in the previous example, and you are prompted again. If only a carriage return is entered, the loop that issued the prompts is exited and the program terminates.

The only error checking is done internally within the program. Jargon is set up like a menu-driven program, only there is no menu. It is a loop that keeps running until only the carriage return is pressed.

Examples

1. `$ jargon`
   `898`

This reveals that my PC is 898, or Compatible Third-Generation Hardware.

2. `$ jargon`
   `187`

Like, wow, this is a Total Operational Projection.

Explanation

Line 4 prints the banner when you first run the program. It echoes a carriage return, two tabs, and the message.

Lines 5-77 are one big while-forever loop. There is only one exit point, which is inside the case statement in the loop. Line 7 prints the prompt and line 8 reads the input into the NUM variable.

Lines 10-30 are the case statement that checks the input from the keyboard. If only a carriage return is entered, line 11 sees the input as null. The action is to exit the program. This is the legal exit point.

An inputted question mark matches line 12. Notice that the question mark is quoted. This is because the ? character is special to the shell. It is used to represent any single character in file name generation. To make it a normal character, we must quote it to take away the special meaning.

In lines 12-24, the `cat` command is being fed the text right from the script. This kind of file is sometimes called a "here document." The here document feature is activated by the < < sequence. The word that follows is the begin-end marker, in this case, EOF. After the text has been concatenated to the screen, line 25 continues the next iteration of the outer while loop.

As an aside, to see how the shell handles here documents, look in /tmp while the script is running. There is a file named "shXXXX", where XXXX is the process id of the shell that created the file. The entire here document is placed in this tmp file. Then the shell redirects its input from that tmp file. Very simply executed.

Line 26 matches all input entries that have three characters. These characters could be letters and/or numbers. The shell does not know at this point. To verify that input is in fact all digits, we must use `expr` to do some more pattern matching. The `expr` statement says "check the string NUM against the sequence 'beginning-of-line digit digit digit end-of-line.'" If the match is successful, `expr` returns a successful exit status and the code falls through. Because `expr` returns the number of characters matched, the output must be thrown away to the bit bucket in /dev/null.

If the match failed, the ¦¦ statement is activated (we saw this kind of control structure earlier), which prints an error message and forces the next loop of the while statement. This syntax does essentially the same thing as an if-then-else statement. Because a list can follow ¦¦, more than one command can be put inside the simple list delimiters { }. Be careful. If the simple list delimiters are not used, the `continue` statement is executed after the error message *and* when the `expr` command is executed successfully. This could lead you to do a bit of debugging until you figure out what was happening.

This same number check could have been done by the case pattern match. The syntax would have been the same except for the anchor characters ^ and $. The case pattern would look like this:

```
[0-9][0-9][0-9])   statement;;
```

I used the `expr` statement to show how expr can be used for this type of checking.

Any other input is caught in line 28 by the wildcard matching character *. An error message is printed and the `continue` forces the next iteration of the while loop, which asks for the next value of input.

Note how the shell looks at strings. The `test` command actually does the string value comparisons. Even though test(1) has its own manual page, it is a built-in function of the shell. If the `test` command is used with the =, != syntax, the two arguments are treated as strings. But if the test command uses -lt, -eq, it is comparing the two argument strings as numbers and does numerical processing on them. These two different modes cannot be mixed, that is, do not compare strings with a numerical operator as in str1 -eq str2.

In lines 32-34, each digit is cut out of the number and placed in its own variable name. Then the variables are used as an index to a case statement that contains the magic words. Line 35 initializes the sentence variable SEN. (Before we start getting letters from you grammatical purists: Yes, we know that what we're generating is a phrase, not a true sentence, because no verb is included.) We start out with a null sentence and add one word to it at a time.

Lines 37-48 are the first case statement. The Case statement looks at the value of N1 and appends the word at that value to the sentence. We actually don't need to include the value of SEN in what we are assigning here because there's nothing to append to yet. However, this makes the code more flexible if we decide to pre-generate more of the sentence by some other means first. Similar case statements handle the next two digits.

The final sentence is printed in line 76 after all the words are looked up. You could say the whole thing is a feat of 754, or Synchronized Logistical Programming.

Modifications

It might be fun to play with this a bit. You could get a random number based on the current system time (using extraction and `expr`) and base the lookup on this number rather than a user-supplied number. You also could use each digit of the random number to control selection of a word from a separate jargon database, perhaps by having one file for each of the three word positions and setting a loop to the random value to read each word. Words would be read and discarded from the file until the word corresponding to the random digit is read. Lots of other possibilities are available. If you aren't careful, you might find yourself writing a game!

Name: phone

phone   Telephone number database

Function

A menu-driven tool that maintains a telephone number database.

Synopsis

phone

Sample Call

phone   Call the phone database
s   Take the search option
russ   Find the number for russ

Code for phone

```
1    :
2    # @(#) phone v1.0   Maintain telephone database   Author: Russ Sage
3
4    if [ $# -gt 0 ]
5      then  echo "phone: argument error" >&2
6            echo "usage: phone"           >&2
7            exit 1
8    fi
9
10   BASE="$HOME/.phone.list"
11
12   while :
13   do
14          echo "
15
16   phonebase = $BASE
17
18          PHONE MENU
19          ----------
20     add name to list
21     delete name from list
22     edit list
23     search for name in list
24     view complete list
25     <cr> - exit program
26
27   Press a,d,e,s,v or <cr>: \c"
28   read RSP
29
30          case $RSP in
31          "")     exit 0
32                  ;;
33          a|A)    echo "\nEnter name to add (<cr> to exit): \c"
34                  read NAME
35                  if [ "$NAME" = "" ]
36                    then  continue
37                  fi
38                  echo "Enter description of person: \c"
39                  read DESC
40                  echo "Enter number to add: \c"
41                  read NUM
42                  echo "$NAME\t$DESC\t\t\t$NUM" >> $BASE
43                  sort -t" " +1 -1.3b -o $BASE $BASE
44                  ;;
45          d|D)    echo "\nEnter name to delete (<cr> to exit): \c"
```

```
46                  read NAME
47                  if [ "$NAME" = "" ]
48                    then continue
49                  fi
50                  sed -e "/$NAME/d" $BASE > $BASE.new
51                  mv $BASE.new $BASE
52                  ;;
53          e|E)    vi $BASE
54                  ;;
55          s|S)    echo "\nEnter name to search: \c"
56                  read NAME
57                  echo "\n------------------------------------------------
-"
58                  grep -y "$NAME" $BASE
59                  echo "----------------------------------------------------"
60                  ;;
61          v|V)    echo "\n\tPhone List\n\t----------" &
62                  more $BASE
63                  echo "\nhit <cr>\c"
64                  read RSP
65                  ;;
66          *)      echo "Not a valid command"
67                  ;;
68          esac
69    done
```

Environment Variables

BASE	The actual name of the phone database file
DESC	The description to enter into the database
NAME	The name to enter into the database
NUM	The phone number to enter into the database
RSP	The response from the user

Description

Why do we need phone?

Phones are a very important item in our business day. We use them for calling prospects, ordering products, and many other things. Think about it. If almost every desk in the United States has a phone, there are millions of phone numbers. How do you keep track of all of yours?

What we need is "yadb", or yet another database. This database should handle data input, retrieval, modification, and deletion. We now have quite a bit of experience in implementing menu-driven programs, and it makes sense to use a menu here.

What does phone do?

Phone is a general-purpose utility for using and maintaining a telephone database. Completely menu-driven, phone contains all the necessary functions associated with database maintenance: adding, deleting, viewing, editing, and searching.

The actual file that is the database resides in your home directory, $HOME /.phone.list. Phone uses your home directory so that the same executable works for everybody. No matter where phone resides or who runs it from anywhere in the whole system, you always get your phone file because it is keyed to your home directory via the shell's built-in HOME variable.

There is only one main menu. It is displayed on the screen and the prompt appears at the bottom. Most options prompt for further information. The menu looks like this:

```
phonebase = /usr/russ/.phone.list


        PHONE MENU
        ----------
    add name to list
    delete name from list
    edit list
    search for name in list
    view complete list
    <cr> - exit program

Press a,d,e,s,v or <cr>:
```

The top line of the menu prints the name of the phone database that you are using. If this is not your file, you know right away that an error has been made. The options are chosen by typing the first character of the word. If only a carriage return is pressed, the program exits.

Examples

1. ```
   $ phone
   a
   russ sage
   unix master
   123-4567
   ```

This is the sequence used to add a person to the database. Call up the menu, take the add option, type the name, the description, and the number when you are prompted to do so.

2. ```
   $ phone
   v
   ```

Look at (view) all entries in your database.

Explanation

Lines 4-8 do some error checking. If you call phone with any arguments, an error message is printed and the program exits. Because phone is menu-driven, it doesn't use option arguments.

Line 10 initializes the BASE variable to the phone database file. This assignment is done through the HOME variable to get your home location.

Lines 12-69 are one big while-forever loop. The overall structure is similar to that of the other menu-driven tools we have presented. The menu is printed via the `echo` statement. Again, the actual menu text is *not* indented like the rest of the program because the echo statement is taking the text as literal data, including spacing.

Line 28 reads the input response and lines 30-68 are the case statement that checks the value of the response. If the input was null, the program exits.

If the input was an *a,* the add option is taken. (Actually each option is checked for both upper- and lowercase for flexibility.) The add code asks for the name, description, and number of the entry. If you accidentally get into the add option, use the escape feature by typing a carriage return in response to the name question. No exits are available once you enter a name. You either have to put the bad entry in or type a break character to get out of the whole utility. The description can be any length, but it won't look nice if it is too long. After all the fields have been input, the complete line is echoed into the end of the database. Note that tabs are added to provide fielding. Then the database is sorted back into itself, placing the new entry into its alphabetical sequence.

If the input is a *d,* it is matched in line 45. The name to delete is prompted for. If only a carriage return is input, the continue statement puts us back into the while loop, and the main menu is printed again. `Sed` is used to delete the entry, so the input must be in a form that matches the exact entry in the file. The result of the deletion is put in a temporary file, then moved back onto the real database, thus updating the deletion in line 51. One area of modification would be to show the user what is going to be deleted, then ask whether this is okay. If so, that data is permanently removed. As it stands now, you really don't know what is going to be removed. You have to enter the name exactly. After all, this is intended to be a relatively quick and dirty approach. You could even use vi directly to do searches and deletions.

The edit option in line 53 does only one thing, namely run the vi editor on the phone database. By using vi, you then can manually patch the database file to your specifications. Frequently, the input data is misaligned with everything else because of its length. All the data is in free form and can be moved around anywhere on the line.

When vi edits your file, all vi commands are active. This even includes escaping to a shell and doing normal stuff. Just remember to kill that shell or else you are surprised at the end of the day when you log off. To exit vi and return to `phone`, use the usual methods. These include ZZ, :x, and :wq.

The search option in line 55 prompts for the name to be searched for, reads the name, prints a banner before and after the data, and uses `grep` to find the actual entry. The `grep` command in line 58 uses the -y command to cause case insensitivity. This means that you can enter either upper- or lowercase to match an item. If nothing matches, no output goes to the screen.

The view option starts on line 61. A banner is printed first in the background for speed. The background issue is really just an experiment to see whether asynchronous events print on the screen synchronously. They do in this case. The file is printed with the `more` command. While `more` is paging through the file, all `more` commands are accessible. (Our `m` script in Chapter 4 illustrated some things you can do with `more`.)

In line 63, a message is displayed that tells the user to press the carriage return. Line 64 does a read. This sequence holds the printed data file on the screen so that it doesn't scroll off. If we did not have these statements, the main menu would print right away and we would lose the top of the screen.

Line 66 does the error checking on the menu as a whole. If you input data that does not match any of the first patterns, they are matched by the *. The error message is printed and control falls out of the case statement, to the bottom of the while, and starts printing the main menu at the top.

Name: office

office   Office Manager

Function

Provides easy access to many of the office management utilities that we have already presented.

Synopsis

office

Sample Call

office   Check my mailbox, and tell me whether it is empty
m

Code for office

```
1    :
2    # a(#) office v1.0   Office Manager   Author: Russ Sage
3
4    if [ $# -gt 0 ]
5      then  echo "office: argument error" >&2
6            echo "usage: office"          >&2
7            exit 1
8    fi
9
10   while :
11   do
12         c
13         set 'date'
14         echo "
15 $1, $2 $3                    $4
16
17         Office Menu
18         -----------
19         Mail
20         News
```

```
21          Calendar
22          Phone
23          Automatic Reminders
24          Shell Command
25          <cr> to exit
26
27  press m,n,c,p,a,s or <cr> : \c"
28
29          read CMD
30
31          case $CMD in
32          "")     exit;;
33          m¦M)    if [ -s /usr/spool/mail/$LOGNAME ]
34                  then  echo
35                        ll /usr/spool/mail/$LOGNAME
36                        echo "\nWould you like to see it (y/n): \c"
37                        read CMD
38                        if [ "$CMD" = "y" ]
39                           then echo
40                                mail
41                        fi
42                  else  echo "\nNo mail today"
43                  fi
44                  echo "\nhit <cr>\c"
45                  read CMD;;
46          n¦N)    PWD=`pwd`
47                  cd /usr/news
48                  echo "\nThe following files are news items in /usr/news:\n"
49                  lc
50                  echo "\nEnter filename or <cr> to exit: \c"
51                  read NAME
52                  while [ "$NAME" != "" ]
53                  do
54                          if [ -s $NAME ]
55                            then  echo "\n------------------------------------"
56                                  cat $NAME
57                                  echo "------------------------------------"
58                            else  echo "$NAME is not a news file"
59                          fi
60                          echo "\nEnter filename or <cr> to exit: \c"
61                          read NAME
62                  done
63                  cd $PWD;;
64          c¦C)    echo "\n"
65                  today
66                  if [ -s $HOME/calendar ]
67                     then  echo "Calendar file:\n`ll $HOME/calendar`"
```

```
68                          echo "\nCalendar notifications:"
69                          PWD=`pwd`
70                          cd $HOME
71                          calendar
72                          cd $PWD
73                          echo "\nCheck your mail for calendar notifications"
74                  else  echo "\nYou do not have a calendar file at $HOME"
75              fi
76              echo "\nhit <cr>\c"
77              read CMD;;
78      p|P)    phone;;
79      a|A)    greet
80              $HB/at 11:45 echo ^GLunch in 15 minutes
81              $HB/at 16:45 echo ^GShift change in 15 minutes
82
83              echo "\nYou will receive notices at 11:45 & 4:45"
84              echo "\nWould you like to leave some reminders (y/n): \c"
85              read CMD
86              if [ "$CMD" = "y" ]
87                then  echo "\nThe syntax is: at HR:MN executable_phrase"
88                      echo "The time now : `date '+%T'`"
89                      echo "\n\ncmd (<cr> to exit): \c"
90                      read CMD
91                      while [ "$CMD" != "" ]
92                      do
93                              eval $CMD
94                              echo "cmd (<cr> to exit): \c"
95                              read CMD
96                      done
97                fi;;
98      s|S)    echo "\nenter command: \c"
99              read CMD
100             eval $CMD
101             echo "\nhit <cr>\c"
102             read CMD;;
103     *)      echo "\nInvalid command"
104             echo "\nhit <cr>\c"
105             read CMD;;
106     esac
107 done
```

Environment Variables

CMD	Holds various commands at different levels
HOME	Another exported variable picked up from the environment
LOGNAME	Shell environment variable that was previously exported
NAME	Holds the name of the news file

Description

Why do we need office?

Many tools in UNIX can perform useful office-related functions. Because of the way UNIX is designed, these tools are separate and standalone. To know about them requires looking through the manuals until you find all the tools, learning about each one individually, then remembering to go through all of them every day. What a hassle.

In addition, we've just added a number of powerful commands to our UNIX office, including several separate menu-driven utilities. How can we integrate them?

What we need is one mechanism by which we can access all business-related functions. If we used a menu, we could get at each function with only one keystroke.

What does office do?

Office is an attempt to bring the most commonly used office functions together into one menu-driven package. By doing so, office simplifies these functions because you don't need to know where these utilities reside or their calling interface. If you have a clerical assistant without any real degree of UNIX expertise, you can let him or her perform many of the functions for you. You can add new functions and layers of menus as needed.

The office has integral needs as well as unique add-ons. This utility attempts to maintain both the basic needs and the fancy stuff. The basic needs addressed are mail, news, calendar appointments, and a telephone number database. The add-on features include an "at" based reminder system and the ability to run outside shell commands while still inside the office. With all these features, everything is in one place for easy access and maintenance.

The main menu has all the functions accessible. It looks like this:

```
Fri, Jun 20                16:18:23


         Office Menu
         -----------
         Mail
         News
         Calendar
         Phone
         Automatic Reminders
         Shell Command
         <cr> to exit


press m,n,c,p,a,s or <cr> :
```

The day and date at the top left are from the UNIX date command. Each time the main menu is displayed, a new time is printed. This gives you an indication as to when you started and how long you have been on.

The first option is mail. It checks your mail file for a size greater than zero. If it is zero (or nonexistent), the message "no mail today" is printed. If you have mail, the mailbox file information is listed in long form from the `ls` command and you are prompted as to whether you want to read your mail. If you say yes, the regular UNIX `mail` command is run.

The second option is news. News files are stored in one directory where each news item is an independent file. All the news items are stored in the special directory of /usr/news. Office lists all the news files, then asks whether you would like to see one. If so, enter the name of the file, and it is printed by the `more` command. We are assuming that you have implemented usenet or some facility that provides news.

The third option is calendar. Because a calendar has many dimensions, this option has different dimensions. First, a complete calendar of the current month is printed with today's date highlighted, using the `today` tool presented earlier. Next, the system calendar utility is addressed. If you have a file named calendar in your home directory, the `calendar` utility (executed by `cron` to look at everyone's home directory) looks at your calendar entries. If any entries are for today or tomorrow, calendar mails them to you.

`Office` takes a little different approach. First, your calendar file is checked for existence and a size greater than zero. If the file exists, a long listing is done on the calendar file so that you can see the actual file and the information pertaining to it. Then the calendar function is executed. When run like this, it prints to stdout any qualifying calendar entries. The calendar run by `cron` only communicates by mail. If your calendar file does not exist, a message is printed stating so.

The next option is phone. To handle the phone database, the `phone` utility presented in the preceding section is used. Because no preprocessing or postprocessing is done around `phone`, you can reread that section to refresh your memory on how the facility works.

The fifth option is automatic reminders. This option is meant to help keep you on track at critical times during the day. It starts by greeting you, à la `greet`. Next two `at` scripts are put into background. They fire off at 11:45 to announce lunch and 4:45 to announce the end of another day. If you want to put some of your own scripts into background, answer yes to the next question. The `at` syntax is printed for reminders, the current time is printed for those close calls, and the command line accepts your `at` entry. Nice and easy to use! (If your system has a built-in `at` facility and you've implemented our version of `at` under a different name or with a different path, be sure to change the code accordingly.)

Because of the way the `at` commands that you type are executed, you could enter any command, not just an `at` command. A loop is set up to accept as many commands as you want. To drop out of the loop, enter only a carriage return.

The last option is to execute any command desired outside of `office`, yet still remain in the office. You could even run a shell outside the office (by doing an `sh`), then control-D out of it to get back into the office. Just about anything is possible.

To exit office, press only the carriage return. This breaks out of the infinite loop and returns to your previous shell.

Example

```
$ office
s
sh
$
```

Run office and select the shell option. Then run a shell command called sh, which is the shell. When this runs, you fork a new shell and get a shell prompt. When done with this shell, type ^d to kill it and you go back to the office main menu.

Explanation

Lines 4-8 do error checking. If you call office with any options at all, you create an error condition.

Lines 10-107 are one huge while loop. The structure is similar to the previous menu-driven tools. Line 12 clears the screen with the c command (presented in Chapter 7). If you don't want to read ahead and implement that command yet, you can omit the line for now, or, if you have BSD, use the clear command. Line 13 sets the positional parameters to the output of the date command.

Lines 14-27 print the actual menu, and line 29 reads the input command. Lines 31-106 are the case statement that recognizes the command and performs the associated actions.

Line 32 exits office if the input is only a carriage return. Lines 33-45 handle the mail command. First, the mail file is checked with test to see whether the file has a size greater than zero bytes. If so, a blank line is echoed and the mail file is printed, using the long form of ls. Then you are asked whether you would like to see the mail. If you enter "y", the mail command is called. Any other input makes the program fall through and go back to the main menu.

Lines 46-63 handle the news command. First the PWD variable is set to our current working directory. We do this so that when we cd to somewhere, we can cd back to where we began when we are done processing. We then cd to /usr/news. This is the directory where the news files are kept. On the Berkeley system, a /usr /msgs directory is available. This directory is very similar and can be used instead of /usr/news if you wish. The files in /usr/news are listed in column form (line 49), and you are asked if you would like to see any of these files. If you enter a carriage return, test sees this as a null and drops out of the while statement.

The while loop keeps on running until NAME is null (line 52). The name input is checked to see whether it exists. If it does, it is printed by the cat command, bordered by dashed lines. If it does not exist, a message is printed saying that the name is not a new file. Then you are asked for another file name. You continue in the loop until you press only a carriage return. When you drop out of the loop in line 62, the cd command is executed to change directory back to where you were when you started. This cd has no effect after office is run. You have to tell your login shell to cd. Another script running from a spawned shell cannot cd for you.

Lines 64-77 perform the calendar functions. First, two blank lines are printed. Why two? Because echo normally puts a newline at the end of whatever string it is

185

printing and the string it is printing is another newline. Then the today program is run in line 65. Today prints the visual image of a monthly calendar. Line 66 checks to see whether you have a calendar file in your home directory. If you do, it is listed in the ls long form in line 67. A header message "Calendar Notifications" is printed.

Line 69 captures the current working directory in the variable PWD. We then cd to $HOME so that we are in the same directory as the calendar file. Line 71 calls the UNIX calendar command. Calendar looks in the calendar file and prints any messages that are matched. We cd back to our original directory to keep everything in order. Line 73 echoes the message to check your mail for calendar notices. As described previously, the calendar command works both ways.

The else statement in line 74 tells you if you do not have a calendar file. At the bottom of the if statement in lines 76 and 77 is the message to press a carriage return, then the read statement. The read is a blocked read, which means that it stops and waits for any input. This is the opposite of an unblocked read, or the more commonly known polling technique of reading. Polling can be achieved by C programs but getting polling running under the shell might take a little more work. To learn more about polling, see the chapter on terminal devices.

Line 78 handles the phone command. It calls the phone utility that we saw earlier, then falls through to the bottom of the while loop. The main menu is printed and it all starts over.

Lines 79-97 handle the automatic reminders. First the greet program is run. Greet was described earlier in this chapter. Then in lines 80 and 81, two at scripts are placed in the background to be executed later in the day. In line 84, you are asked whether you want to leave reminders. If you answer with y, lines 87-96 are executed. If you don't input y, there is no else statement to execute, so control falls through to the main menu. You can see that this facility is intended to be used once a day.

Lines 87-89 print some information you need in order to leave reminders to yourself. The at syntax is shown, the current date is shown with only the time format, then the prompt for your command is printed. Line 90 reads your command. Line 91 says "although the input was not only a carriage return, do this loop." So the while loop continues until you press only the carriage return. Line 93 tries to execute the command that you should have typed.. The eval command is used to expand any variables that might not have been expanded earlier. Line 94 asks for the next command and line 95 reads it. Because the read is at the bottom of the loop, the while statement tests the new keyboard input.

Lines 98-102 handle the shell escape code. This piece of code is almost identical to the loop in reminders. We prompt for the command, read it into a variable, then eval the variable. If you want a shell escape, make sh your command and it spawns a shell. Lines 101 and 102 stop the main menu from appearing by waiting for you to press a carriage return.

Lines 103-105 do the error checking. Any commands not matched fall through to here. An error message is printed and the "hit <cr>" prompt is made.

6

Personal Management II: User Awareness and Personal Security

User awareness

`activ`	display terminal activity
`info`	display password info on a user
`uchk`	check processes of another user
`watch`	watch for specific logins
`whox`	who with expanded options

Personal security

`acme`	display accounting information
`inuse`	disable terminal
`lock`	lock and unlock files

Personal Management II: User Awareness and Personal Security

Introduction

We have now developed a number of tools to help us manage personal information more effectively. However, we do not work in a vacuum. We each work with a number of people and usually share the system with other users. For several reasons, it's important to be aware of what other people are doing on the system. First, we may need to find ways to schedule processor-intensive work for times when the load on the system is low. Learning the typical usage patterns of the system can help us schedule such work and cooperate with other users to mutual benefit.

We might also want to know whether someone is in their office so that we can talk to them or whether someone is very busy and would not appreciate being interrupted.

Finally, there is the matter of security, which we deal with at greater length in following chapters. Basic security starts with awareness of what other people are doing—and perhaps shouldn't be doing.

Therefore, we will present two groups of tools here. *User awareness* tools help us keep track of what other people are doing and thus make communication easier. *Personal security* is important for protecting our account and data and getting information about our actions.

The first group of tools we look at here involve "user awareness." These tools are `activ`, `info`, `uchk`, `watch`, and `whox`.

`Activ` provides a modified form of the `who` command that displays each user's name, terminal line, and the length of time since the person has typed something on their keyboard. From this information, we can tell who is around, whether they appear to be actively working, and if they are using dedicated lines, where they are.

The next tool is `info`. It provides the capability to get password information about a specific list of people. With this utility, you get general information on these people and see where their home directories are located.

Another informative tool is `uchk`. This routine is useful for seeing what a specific user is doing at the current time. From this information, you can tell whether they are idle on the system or are doing something important and should not be interrupted.

The next tool is `watch`. It is a "daemon"-like program that sits in the background of the machine and constantly watches for the login of specific people. When a person that you want logs in, a message is sent to your terminal to inform you that they are now on the system. This way, you can continue your work without having to constantly stop what you are doing.

The last utility in this section is `whox`. `Whox` provides comprehensive information dealing with all the users who are logged on the machine. You can get "who"-type information that is sorted in different ways, display terminal information, or even send mail to each user.

User Awareness

Name: `activ`

activ   Display terminal activity

Function

Shows all logged-in user names, their terminal device number, and when they used their keyboard last.

Synopsis

activ

Sample Call

activ   Prints out the activity of users on their terminals

Code for `activ`

```
1    :
2    # a(#) activ v1.0   Display terminal activity    Author: Russ Sage
3
4    if [ $# -gt 0 ]
5      then  echo "activ: argument error" >&2
6            echo "usage: activ"          >&2
7            exit 1
```

```
8   fi
9
10  who -u | cut -c1-17,38-42
```

Description

Why do we need activ?

Computers were originally used exclusively for running self-contained information processing tasks. The advent of multiuser systems made at least rudimentary communication between users possible. Communication is now an increasingly important aspect of our computer work.

UNIX provides `mail` and `write` for batch and interactive dialog respectively. With a telephone, we can't tell whether someone is available until we've placed a call and perhaps talked to one or more other people. Because the UNIX system continually records information about the activities of users, it would be useful to be able to use this information to find out who is available and get a general idea of what they are doing. We can then decide how and when we want to communicate with them.

`Activ` can tell us how long it has been since someone has typed on his or her keyboard. If you have dedicated lines into your machine, you can also get a good idea whether the person is in the office or not.

What does activ do?

`Activ` prints activity information for each user on the system. The printout contains the user name, the terminal they are logged onto, and the time of last activity on their keyboard. If the keyboard has been used in the last minute, a dot is shown for that terminal. If the terminal has not been used for 24 hours, the string "old" is printed. Otherwise, the time that the terminal was last used is printed in minutes and seconds. Here is a sample printout:

```
root      tty01   01:23
sage      tty05   .
batch     tty12   old
nuucp     tty16   .
```

The important question is, how does the system know when someone types on their keyboard? Because terminal devices are files, we can glean information about a terminal by looking at the status of the file associated with it. In this case, the information we are looking for is when the keyboard was used last.

The functionality we are looking for is already implemented in the system. It is an option of the `who` command, -u. This option exists only on AT&T UNIX System V, however, so `activ`, at least in its present form, can only be implemented on that system. Activ takes the printout from "who -u" and cuts out some data that is not relevant to our purpose.

Through trial and error, then verification from source code, I discovered that the value used in "who-u" is the "modification" time of the device file, supplied by the stat(2) system call. The `stat` manual page provides a complete table of the system calls that update the file times. Table 6-1 defines each file time:

Table 6-1
File Times Defined

Inode Times	System calls that update times
Access time	creat, mknod, pipe, utime, read
Modify time	creat, mknod, pipe, utime, write
Create time	creat, mknod, pipe, utime, write, chmod, chown, link

Let's take a side trip for a moment and talk about what these inode times mean and how they can be modified. One interesting note: UNIX gives you as a normal user the capability of making the access and modify time for a file any value you wish. This is both good and bad. It allows flexibility in dealing with the inode information, but it also allows for covering tracks in a security-related breach. Take `login` for instance: Someone could put a new login on top of the old one and change the two file times back to the original value. Then anyone who does an `ls` on /bin/login is not able to tell that the file was altered.

However, UNIX has a third time, called "creat" (create). The system does not let you alter this time through normal commands. The `utime`(2) system call provides for changing only access and modification time. The `touch`(1) command also can change access and modify times but not creat. `Touch` is built on only the system call. It can do no more than what the call provides. The `fsdb`(1) (file system debugger) command is the only way that you can override the protections against changing the creat time. But even `fsdb` doesn't hand over the creat time. You have to step outside the boundaries of security enforcement that `fsdb` supports. How to do this is presented in subsequent chapters.

In the case of the login overwrite described previously, you could look at the creat time and see when the file was created, which should be very close to the current date. If someone used `fsdb` to patch the creat time, however, you could never be sure that the file was changed.

How does all this relate to finding out whether a user has done something at their terminal recently? The modification date is changed by a write(2) call. Therefore, it stands to reason that a write to the terminal would occur when the driver reads a character, then echoes it back to the screen. As long as someone types on the keyboard, the modify time is updated continually as characters are echoed. When characters stop coming from the keyboard, the writing to the terminal file stops. The formula to determine when there was activity on the terminal last is

```
last_activity = time(NULL) - mod_time.
```

which is coded inside of the `who`(1) command. Note that passing NULL to the time command returns the time right now.

This command has no options. If you use an option, an error message is printed.

Explanation

Lines 4-8 do the error checking. If the number of arguments on the command line is greater than zero, a message is printed to standard error and the program exits with a failure status.

Line 10 is the command that produces the printout. The `who` command is called with the -u option to get the basic data. Then this printout is piped to the `cut` command, which displays columns 1-17 and 38-42. This prints only the three fields as shown in our previous example.

Name: info

info   Display password information on a user

Function

Prints the comment field information from the /etc/passwd file for the specified users.

Synopsis

info login__name [login__name ...]

Sample Call

info russ   Print the information that is stored on russ

Code for info

```
1   :
2   # @(#) info v1.0  Display password info on a user  Author: Russ Sage
3
4   for NAME in $@
5   do
6          USER=`grep "^${NAME}:" /etc/passwd`
7          echo "$NAME:\t`echo ${USER}|cut -d: -f6`\t`echo ${USER}|cut -d:
    -f5`"
8   done
```

Environment Variables

NAME   Each name on the command line
USER   Complete /etc/passwd entry for the name

Description

Why do we need info?

UNIX uses configuration files to hold most information about users and other system information. Some of the most common configuration files are /etc/group,

/etc/passwd, and /etc/inittab. To get information about people, we need to look into these files.

Berkeley has the `finger` command that gets information on users from their home directory and the passwd file. Not too many programs in System V do this kind of lookup, so we need to develop one.

What does `info` do?

`Info` is a script that gets the home directory information and comment information on users from the /etc/passwd file. The output is in the form of:

```
name:    home dir    comments
```

If your installation utilizes this comment field, the information can be handy. A "manual" way to do a lookup on users in the password file is to type:

```
grep login_name /etc/passwd
```

This prints the whole line with all the fields of data. `Info` takes this raw data and cuts out the user's home directory and the comment field.

Multiple login names may be passed on the command line. Each name is taken in sequence from the command line.

Example

```
$ for NAME in 'cat /etc/passwd | cut -d: -f1'
> do
>         NAMELIST="$NAMELIST $NAME"
> done; info $NAMELIST
```

For every user name in the password file, add the name to a name list. Then this list is passed on the command line to `info`, which prints all the data. Essentially the command is "Give me information on all users of the system."

Explanation

Lines 4-8 are the for loop that processes all the names passed on the command line. For each name that is passed, lines 6 and 7 are executed.

Line 6 sets the variable USER to the output of the `grep` command as captured by the grave accents. `Grep` looks for the name, starting from the beginning of the line (denoted as ^) and followed by the colon (:) character. This specification forces the pattern matching to look only in the first field of the password file.

In line 7, we echo our output line with some subexecutions buried inside it. We could have obtained items of information separately, assigned each to a variable, then created a format using the values of the variables. However, capturing the information into a command line is faster, and the code is more compact, if not as readable. We also can use the formatting characters with echo to format our printout.

First, the name is echoed just as it is from the command line. Next, a tab is echoed (\t). Following the first tab is field six from the password file. Because we don't have that data yet, we have to cut it out of the USER value we already have from the previous line. To do so, we echo the entire line and cut out the sixth field using : delimiters. After that field, we echo another tab, then the fifth field of the password file. We get this field in the same way as we did the sixth field, by echoing and cutting.

This technique is slow because of all the processes involved but is about the quickest way to do it in shell language. Awk would be cleaner and maybe faster, but our implementation shows the flexibility of the shell language. Shell language can do nearly everything but is not always the best choice. That's why in some cases, you find us using C as we progress through the book.

Name: uchk

uchk   Check processes of another user

Function

Displays all the processes for each user name on the command line.

Synopsis

uchk [-a] login_name [...]

Sample Call

uchk -a   Print all the processes that the administrators are running

Code for uchk

```
1   :
2   # @(#) uchk v1.0   Check processes of another user   Author: Russ Sage
3
4   trap "rm /tmp/ps$$ 2> /dev/null"  0 1 2 3 15
5
6   if [ $# -eq 0 ]
7     then  echo "uchk: argument error"                >&2
8           echo "usage: uchk [-a] login_name [ ... ]" >&2
9           exit 1
10  fi
11
12  if [ "`echo $1 | cut -c1`" = "-" -a "$1" != "-a" ]
13    then  echo "uchk: invalid argument $1"            >&2
14          echo "usage: uchk [-a] login_name [ ... ]" >&2
```

195

```
15          exit 1
16  fi
17
18  ADMIN="administrators names go here"
19  if [ "$1" = "-a" ]
20  then   shift
21         set $ADMIN $@
22  fi
23
24  ps -ef > /tmp/ps$$
25  for NAME
26  do
27         echo
28         fgrep "$NAME" /tmp/ps$$
29  done
```

Environment Variables

ADMIN   A string of names that are the administrators at your installation
NAME   Holds each name that is read from the command line

Description

Why do we need uchk?

Because UNIX is a multiuser system, many tasks are happening concurrently. The only way to monitor these tasks is with the ps command. Ps is a very special command in that it has to go into memory (/dev/mem) and traverse the linked list of process structures. This is heavy stuff, so it's not easy to make your own command to customize printing of this kind of information, plus memory is protected and can only be accessed by the root user.

Thus, we either settle for the options that ps gives us or modify the output of the command. Uchk tends to fall in the latter category. What I wanted was a process status list by user name, not the mixed up display that is given with the "everyone" option. Although what I wanted doesn't correspond to any of the regular ps options, I found I could modify the output to get what I wanted.

What does uchk do?

Uchk is a tool that generates, analyzes, and reports on the processes that each specified user is running. You can check as many people as you want at one time. All processes for each person are printed together.

To do this, uchk must work with temp files. UNIX is set up to handle temp files gracefully. Shells allow using the process id to create unique file names for each and every run. After the utility has run, the temp files are cleaned up by the use of the trap command in the shell. The trap removes the file if someone interrupts the script part way or when the program is finished. This is a nice feature that eliminates stray files from accumulating in the system.

If uchk is called with no arguments or if an invalid option is used, an error message is printed and execution stops.

Uchk has a variable, ADMIN, that defines all administrators for your system. Edit the string assigned to ADMIN to include the administrator names that you want to check. The names must be separated by blanks. This allows you to check the processes of your administrators by specifying a -a on the command line. Any other names on the command line are included. Of course, you could set up other groups of people this way. Keeping an eye on the administrators might help you evaluate how they handle security as well as help you identify administrative tasks that tend to be processor intensive.

Example

```
$ uchk -a russ uucp
```

Display the processes for all the administrators, myself, and uucp in that order. All error messages are to standard error and all process listings are to stdout.

Explanation

Line 4 is the trap statement. The string between the double quotes contains the commands that are to be executed when the trap is activated. In this case, we remove the temp file and redirect any output to the null device. Error messages are output when rm tries to remove a nonexistent file. Because we don't know what files may be present at the time the trap is "sprung," we want to dispose of error output. The trap statement is activated by program exit (signal 0), hangup (signal 1), interrupt (signal 2), quit (signal 3), or software termination (signal 15).

Lines 6-10 check to see whether no arguments were passed. If you call uchk by itself, the error message is printed and uchk exits.

Lines 12-16 check to see whether there are any minus options and whether they are not -a, the only legal option. The script does this by using the test command to compare two different cases. The first test is to cut out character one of the first positional parameter and see whether it is a "-". The next test is to see whether the first positional parameter is not -a. Since these two are connected with an AND operator, they both must be true to qualify for a true condition. If they are both true, the error message is printed and uchk exits.

Why do we have to have a compound test like this? The problem is that we have no way of assuming that the first positional parameter is or is not an option. It may be an option or it may be a name to be searched for. Thus, we have to ask: "Is it an option, and, if it is, is it a valid option?"

Line 18 initializes the ADMIN variable to the following string. This is the line that you should modify for your particular system. All you have to do is use vi and put in the string the names of your administrators delimited with blanks. We use the ADMIN variable later to manipulate the command line arguments.

Lines 19-22 check to see whether the -a option was passed on the command line. If so, this option is shifted off the command line to get rid of it. Line 21 uses the set command to put the ADMIN string into the positional parameters. Set inserts ADMIN, starting from the first positional parameter, and pushes all the real parameters back. This sets up the for loop with more names to be to run through.

Line 24 does the ps command for everyone. This command uses the full option to print lots of data. This output is placed in a temp file that uses the process id number in the name. This one image is the source for the rest of the printouts. It probably is a little behind real time, but it makes the script run much faster than making multiple ps calls.

Lines 25-29 do the for loop, which runs from $1 to $x, where x is the last positional parameter. For each name, it prints a blank line to space the listing (line 27), then fgreps (for speed) out of the temp file all the processes belonging to that user. By grepping for each user name, all the processes for that user are printed at one time. When all the names passed on the command line have been examined, the loop terminates, the script terminates, and the trap statement is run, which removes the temporary file.

Name: watch

watch   Watch for specific logins

Function

Watches who is on the system and announces the login of specific people.

Synopsis

watch [-k] [login__name ...]

Sample Call

watch   Watch the system for all the names in the internal LIST

Code for watch

```
1    :
2    # a(#) watch v1.0   Watch for specific logins   Author: Russ Sage
3
4    if [ "'echo $1 | cut -c1'" = "-" -a "$1" != "-k" ]
5      then  echo "watch: invalid argument $1"          >&2
6            echo "usage: watch [-k] [login_name ...]" >&2
7            echo "           -k  kill background process"
8            exit 1
9    fi
10
11   if [ "$1" = "-k" ]
12     then  if [ -s $HOME/.watch ]
13             then  echo "killed 'cat $HOME/.watch'"
14                   kill 'cat $HOME/.watch'
15                   rm $HOME/.watch
16                   exit 0
17            fi
18   fi
19
```

```
20   echo $$ > $HOME/.watch
21
22   LIST="root sys bin administrator1 administrator2 $*"
23
24   while :
25   do
26           for NAME in 'who | cut -d" " -f1'
27           do
28                   for PERSON in $LIST
29                   do
30                           if [ "$NAME" = "$PERSON" ]
31                           then   echo ONLINE: $NAME
32                           fi
33                   done
34           done
35           sleep 10
36   done &
```

Environment Variables

HOME   The path to your home directory
LIST   A blank delimited list of system user names
NAME   Holds the names of currently logged in users
PERSON   A single name from the list of names in LIST

Description

Why do we need watch?

During one day, many people log on and off big systems. Sometimes the only way you can contact people is through a machine. We need a tool that tells us automatically when certain people are on line.

What does watch do?

Watch is meant to be a background task that constantly monitors who is logged in. When a person or persons that you have previously identified logs in, a message displayed on your screen indicates that they are on line.

The number of names that you can watch for has no limit. The total number of names is the concatenation of the command line and the list of system users, that is, root and its admin cohorts. In watch, the list of system names is *always* included. The reasoning is that these are important people and you always want to be aware of their comings and goings. This differs from uchk in that the latter requires the -a option to include the system name list.

Although we've set up watch from the point of view of a user who wants to keep track of administrators and other users, there is no reason why an administrator might have a list of "problem users" or suspected security violators and use watch to give an alert for those logins.

Whomever we watch for, we have one problem to deal with. After an identified person logs in, the on-line message keeps printing to the screen no matter what you are doing, which is not very desirable. The only way to stop the message's printing is to kill `watch`, which is made easy by placing its process id in the file $HOME /.watch. Then this id can be used with the `kill` statement to stop execution of the script. To make it as easy as possible to get rid of `watch`, the kill capability is provided as the -k option within the script.

Examples

1. `$ LIST="root bin" watch daemon`

If LIST were not initialized within `watch` itself, we could initialize it at the shell command level, then call `watch`. The list of users to watch would be root, bin, and daemon in that order because `watch` adds names passed on its own command line to those found in LIST. This alternative would be more flexible than our exiting partly hard coded `watch` but would require more remembering and typing on your part.

2.
```
echo "Watch (y/n): \c"
read ANS
if [ "$ANS" = "y" ]
  then watch
fi
```

This is a piece of code that could go in your .profile. When you log in, you automatically are prompted to run `watch`. If you enter "y", `watch` is put in the background to run in default mode (looking for the LIST of names). If any character other than a y is entered, `watch` is not executed.

Explanation

Lines 4-9 do the error checking on the command-line options. The first positional parameter is checked to see whether it has a dash in it and is not the one valid option, "-k". If this is true, the error message is printed and the script exits.

Lines 11-16 check to see whether the first positional parameter is -k. If it is, the user wants to kill the already running `watch` process. In this case, a message is printed stating the process id that is being killed, and execution continues. In line 12, we check to see whether the .watch file already exists in the home directory. If it doesn't, the previous incarnation of `watch` presumably has been killed already, and we don't want to attempt to do it again, so execution falls into the remainder of the script and the regular `watch` processing takes place as though the "-k" hadn't been used.

If the .watch file is present, the `kill` command is used in line 13 to kill the `watch` background process. Remember that when the -k option is used, we assume that `watch` was invoked at an earlier time, so the file $HOME/.watch has the process id of `watch` itself. Line 14 removes the temporary `watch` file and line 15 exits the program. `Watch` is now no longer running in the background.

Line 18 is executed if the -k option was not used or if the .watch file is not present. (The latter might happen if the user tries to kill the process, having forgotten that it already had been killed.) If the -k was not used, we can assume that `watch` is being invoked to sit in the background and do its job. To set this up, the current process echoes its process id into the watch file. This file remains in your home directory until it is removed manually or changed by running **watch** again.

In line 22, the LIST variable is initialized. This variable is a string of names separated by spaces. You need to manually edit LIST before it will run on your system. Just remove its current contents and put in the names of the administrators for your system. If any additional names are included on the command line, they are appended to the LIST variable by the parameter expansion $*. This makes LIST a master list of all the names that will be watched for.

Lines 24-36 perform the constantly monitoring watch loop. At the beginning of each iteration, a list of user names is created from the **who** command and fed to the for loop in line 24. The for loop uses command substitution to generate a word list made of the first field of the **who** command. For each name that is logged on, they are checked with the list of predetermined names we are watching for. Note that the outer while loop is put into background by itself. This means that you do not have to type it from the keyboard.

Lines 29-33 drive the innermost loop, which runs through the list of names on our master list and compares them to the names from **who**. If a name from **who**s list of logged-on people is the same as a person in the list we are looking for, we echo to the screen a message that this person is logged on.

After all the names have been checked, **watch** goes to sleep for 10 seconds (line 35). When it wakes up, the next iteration of the while-forever loop is performed. All the logged-in names are checked against the list again. This continues until you kill **watch**. As stated previously, watch can be killed easily by using the -k option or can be killed manually by typing "kill 'cat $HOME/.watch'".

Modifications

Watch is doing quite a bit of processing and tying up some CPU time. You might experiment with increasing the **sleep** interval so that watch runs less frequently. Most people are on the system for at least a minute, so you might try sleep(60). Do you still catch most of the people that you are looking for?

Name: whox

whox   Who with expanded options

Function

Provides many extras to the output of **who** and allows using the **who** data for other applications.

Synopsis

whox [-f] [-n] [-m] [-p] [-t] [-w] [-x]

where
   -f fingers each logged on user
   -n sorts who by name

-m mail to each user

-p displays password information on users

-t sort who by time (default)

-w show writeability of logged-on terminal devices

-x extra home directory and gcos information

Sample Call

whox -w

Show the file permissions (read- and writeability) for each terminal device logged on

Code for whox

```
1   :
2   # @(#) whox v1.0   Who with expanded options   Author: Russ Sage
3
4   XTRA="no"
5   SORT="sort -b +2"
6   DISPLAY="norm"
7
8   CUT1="cut -d' ' -f1"
9   CUT5="cut -d: -f5"
10  CUT6="cut -d: -f6"
11
12  for ARG in $@
13  do
14          case $ARG in
15          -f)     DISPLAY="finger"
16                  COMMAND="finger \$NAME; echo";;
17          -n)     SORT="sort";;
18          -m)     DISPLAY="mail";;
19          -p)     DISPLAY="pass"
20                  COMMAND="grep \"^\$NAME:\" /etc/passwd";;
21          -t)     SORT="sort -b +2";;
22          -w)     DISPLAY="write";;
23          -x)     XTRA="yes";;
24          *)      echo "whox: invalid option $ARG"
25                  echo "usage: whox [-f] [-n] [-m] [-p] [-t] [-w] [-x]"
26                  echo "              -f  finger users"
27                  echo "              -n  sort by name"
28                  echo "              -m  mail to each user"
29                  echo "              -p  password info on users"
30                  echo "              -t  sort by time (default)"
31                  echo "              -w  show writeability of devices"
32                  echo "              -x  extra home dir and gcos info"
```

```
33                    exit 1;;
34         esac
35   done
36
37   if [ "$XTRA" = "yes" ]
38     then   EXTRA="| while read LINE; do \
39            NAME=\'echo \$LINE | cut -d' ' -f1\';\
40            ENTRY=\'grep \"^\$NAME:\" /etc/passwd\';\
41            echo \"\$LINE\t\'echo \$ENTRY|\$CUT6\'\t\'echo \$ENTRY|\$CUT5\'
\";done"
42     else   EXTRA=""
43   fi
44
45   case $DISPLAY in
46   norm)          eval "who | $SORT $EXTRA";;
47   finger|pass)   for NAME in 'who | $SORT | cut -d' ' -f1'
48                  do
49                        eval $COMMAND
50                  done;;
51   mail)          who | cut -d' ' -f1 | while read NAME
52                  do
53                        echo "mail to $NAME (y/n): \c"
54                        KB='line < /dev/tty'
55                        if [ "$KB" = "y" ]
56                           then  mail $NAME < /dev/tty
57                        fi
58                  done;;
59   write)         ls -il 'who | sed "s/...........\(.......\).*/\/dev\/\1
/"';;
60   esac
```

Environment Variables

ARG	Command line arguments
COMMAND	The command to be executed when who is used for a name list
CUT1	Holds the syntax to cut field one from a string
CUT5	Holds the syntax to cut field five from a string
CUT6	Holds the syntax to cut field six from a string
DISPLAY	Determines which display mode to use
ENTRY	The password file entry for a specific user
EXTRA	This variable contains an entire shell loop stored as a string
KB	The input from keyboard obtained while in a loop
NAME	Holds one name at a time from the list of all login names
SORT	Holds the type of sorting to take place
XTRA	Flag to determine whether the extra option should be activated

Description

Why do we need whox?

As has been discussed in other places in this book, UNIX tends to supply just the rudiments of functionality in any given area of interest. This is not to say that UNIX is bad. Indeed, it does a lot more than most other operating systems. But much of the time, we want to do something more than what is supplied by the basic system.

Getting information on who is using the machine can be used for a number of purposes. The basic information is provided by who, but it may not be in the form you want for a given purpose. In any case, all who does is give you the snapshot of who is logged in. We need some way to automatically access this list of logged-in names and use it for monitoring, communications, or other purposes.

What does whox *do?*

Whox is a tool that expands the functionality of the who command. It not only can reorder the who listing to suit your needs, it can also "finger" each person logged in, send mail to each logged-in user, look up password information on all logged-in users, and show the inode information on the terminal device files associated with each logged-in user.

The default action of whox is to print the normal who output in order of login time from the earliest to the latest. The -x option adds to this list the information from the home directory and comment field that is obtained from the password file. If this -x option sounds familiar, it should, because it is the same as the info command presented previously.

Whox has four different display modes. The first is the format of the regular who output. Whox allows you to sort it two different ways. The -n option sorts by name and the -t option (which is not required because it is the default) sorts by time of login.

The second mode of display consists of the finger and pass modes, invoked by the -f and -p options. The main difference from the first mode is that instead of printing the who output, who is used to generate a list of user names that are used for other purposes. What we do is finger each person or print the password entry of each user. The command that is executed is stored in a variable, so we can have a generic loop that uses variables for specific syntax. (Finger is available on Berkeley UNIX and on some, but not all, other implementations. See the manual for details on what is displayed.)

The third mode is the mail mode, where you have the opportunity to send mail to each person who is logged on. You are asked whether this is what you want to do. Nothing is forced on you. The -m option selects this mode.

The last mode is the write mode of display. The write mode (-w option) lists the terminal device file information for each terminal device logged on. This information is useful when you want to use the UNIX write command. By looking at the permission bits on the device file for a user, you can tell whether you are able to write text to his or her screen. Some users who don't want to be interrupted shut off write access to their terminal by doing a "mesg n". The matter of write permission applies to sending any kind of text to another file, not just using the write command. It also protects against something like this: "echo hello > /dev/tty00".

The way arguments are processed on the command line introduces some strange behavior with this utility. Each argument is checked in order and sets flags internally. If you put an option at the end of the list that modifies the same flag set in one of the earlier options, you get the response of the last option. (In other words, some options are mutually exclusive. The best way to learn about this is to read the source code carefully and do some experimenting with different combinations of options.)

For example, say we want to finger each person. We use the -f option. The -f option sets the display mode to finger mode. If we put the -w option right after -f, as in "whox -f -x", the display is set to write mode. The `whox` command would really respond as if you never used -f. This is really no big problem unless you don't know what each of the options do. By randomly mixing them in one command, you might get some confused printouts.

Examples

1. `$ sh -x whox -x`

Run a shell in debug mode, feeding it `whox` as script data, passing the -x option to the `whox` utility. Debug mode shows variable assignment and command calls. (We saw this earlier.)

2. `$ whox -n -x`

Print the `who` output sorted by name and put extra data into the printout.

Explanation

Lines 4-10 do variable initialization. The XTRA variable is set to no. XTRA is used to build the command line when the -x option is used. By setting XTRA to no, we have the default action of not getting extra information.

The default sort action is to sort on login times. This is specified by sorting on the column after 2 (+2) and ignoring leading blanks (-b) in line 5. This sort syntax is the same when set later with the -t option. The -t option is redundant, but it allows for better documentation of a command line if used. The -n option also changes the sort syntax to look at the first column, which is the list of names.

Line 6 initializes the display to normal, which is printing the normal `who` output. As other options are matched, the variable DISPLAY is changed accordingly.

Lines 8, 9, and 10 initialize some variables to cut commands, which reduces the amount of typing in later commands. When some command lines are long, you can put text into variables and substitute them when needed. The CUT1 variable looks like it should work but does not work on my system. Why it does not work is explained later. Just remember that this line is never used in the program. We're leaving it now so that we can talk about it later. You can remove it later if you wish.

Lines 12-35 process the command line arguments. A for loop sets ARG to each parameter in succession and does a case statement on the value of the ARG.

If the option is -f, line 15 changes the DISPLAY variable to the finger mode. It also sets COMMAND to the finger command that is executed in the loop below. The reason we need to have a command variable is because the loop that executes it is a generic loop used for two different things. To make the same loop handle two different tasks, we put the tasks into a variable and execute the variable. This saves considerably on total code, although it takes a little getting used to. Notice in line 16, that the $ is quoted in the assignment statement. This is necessary because we want COMMAND to contain the string $NAME and not the value that NAME has when the assignment is made. NAME is expanded in the loop as it is executing.

Line 17 handles the -n option. The only action needed is to change the way the who output is sorted to reflect name order. Because the name is column one of the who output, and sort sorts on column one as a default, sort with no options is used.

Line 18 handles the -m option for mailing. The thing we have to do is change the display to the mail mode. All the code in the mail loop is set to go and does not need any other variables initialized.

Lines 19 and 20 handle the -p option. The password option changes the display to pass mode and sets up the command that we are running while in the generic loop. In this case, we are using grep to get the password entry from the /etc/passwd file. Notice that in line 20, we are embedding double quotes. To do so, we need to quote the inside double quotes with backslash quotes. Remember that backslash is used to remove special meaning of special shell characters.

Line 21 handles the -t option. As mentioned previously, the -t option is not really required in this program. Because it is the default, action steps were taken in the beginning of the program to perform the same initializations. The sort syntax is exactly the same as it is in line 5.

Line 22 handles the -w option for displaying the writeability of terminal files. The only thing we need to do is change the display mode.

Line 23 handles the -x option. Because the extra information needs some heavy initialization, all we do is set the XTRA flag to show that we want to do the extra initialization later.

Line 24 is the catchall for error processing. The * matches anything that did not get matched earlier. The error message and usage statement are printed and whox exits.

Lines 37-43 set up variables used in the extra information option. Line 37 checks to see whether the XTRA variable is set to yes, which can only occur when the command line had a -x. If it is yes, the EXTRA variable is set to a lot of things that we look at later. Otherwise, EXTRA is set to null so that it disappears in the actual execution stage.

The EXTRA variable is very important here and actually performs a little magic. What we are going to do is put some code into the variable that is needed to process the -x data. Because the extra information that we want here takes some processing to get, we have a portable chunk of code that we put into a variable. Wherever the variable goes, so does the code. It is like a macro, only the code actually takes space in the running program.

Lines 38-41 are put inside the EXTRA variable. This is accomplished by double quoting the entire four lines. Any special characters that need to be part of the data in the variable have to be quoted with the backslash. In line 38, EXTRA gets a pipe character and the beginning of a while loop. The end of line 38 has a backslash to tell the shell that assignment is to continue past the end of line marker (which is the carriage return, or newline).

Line 39 sets up the variable NAME to be assigned a field that is cut from the data read into the while loop. Remember that this entire statement is being placed inside of the EXTRA variable. When I mentioned previously that the CUT1 line had problems, this is one of the spots to which I referred. When I tried to use CUT1 in this statement instead of having the cut command typed right in, the shell would not parse the statement correctly. The single quotes to mark the delimiter character to cut were not being parsed out. The net result is that `cut` thought the delimiter character was a `'` character, then blew up because the second `'` character was not a valid description of a list for the -f option. The -f string came later but `cut` never saw it because it blew up first. When I replaced the CUT1 variable with the actual `cut` command the problem disappeared.

Let's take a look at how I debugged this section. I used a shell with the -x option so that I could trace what happened. As we can see, when CUT1 is being initialized the single quotes are still in the statement, but when the actual `cut` command is executed the single quotes go away in the extra expansion. To generate this list of data, I made the following call: sh -x whox -x. Here's what I saw:

```
XTRA=no
SORT=sort -b +2
DISPLAY=norm
CUT1=cut -d' ' -f1                 ←The single quotes still there. Major problem.
CUT5=cut -d: -f5
CUT6=cut -d: -f6
XTRA=yes
+ who
+ read LINE
+ sort -b +2
+ echo russ console Jun 20 14:11
+ cut -d  -f1                      ←Now running correctly. Quotes are gone.
```

This printout is condensed. Still it shows that when `cut` ran, it did not have the single quotes. When CUT1 ran, it did have single quotes. I could not figure out how to get rid of the quotes, so I just put the literal command back in place. Maybe some budding young master out there can figure this one out.

In any case, you can see the usefulness of the debugging technique.

The actual loop that is being assigned looks like this in normal indented shell code:

```
| while read LINE
do
        NAME='echo $LINE | cut -d' ' -f1'
        ENTRY='grep "^$NAME:" /etc/passwd'
        echo "$LINE\t\'echo $ENTRY|$CUT6\'\t\'echo $ENTRY|$CUT5\'\"
done
```

To get this kind of loop into a variable means we have to quote all the special characters in this code.

Lines 45-60 are a case statement that performs the different display modes.

Line 46 does the normal display mode of the `who` command. Because the normal mode has the possibility of using EXTRA, we need to `eval` the entire command line so that variables are expanded to their true value at run time. Notice that `eval` has quotes around the whole command line. This is necessary so that the entire line is one piece to eval. Without the quotes, `eval` won't work. The EXTRA variable is left out of the evaluation.

Lines 47-50 handle the finger and pass display modes. Both of these modes use this same loop. A for loop is used to set NAME to the value of the first field of every line from the `who` command. For each name that is cut from `who`, the COMMAND variable (which was set in the argument-parsing case statement) is `eval`d. This reparses and executes the commands in COMMAND. For finger mode, COMMAND is the `finger` command, whereas pass mode has the `grep` command in COMMAND.

Lines 51-58 are similar to the finger mode. The loop, too, needs names from the `who` statement, but instead of using the for statement, we use the direct piping method. `Who` is piped to the `cut` command (CUT1 would not work here either), which pipes to a while read loop. Notice that no sorting is happening here. The default order of `who` is by terminal device number. I don't think it makes much difference how the output is arranged, though.

For each name, a prompt is printed that asks whether you want to mail to that person. The response read in line 54 has to be done using the UNIX `line` command. Why? Because the whole loop is using the read statement to read names. Read only reads from standard input, which is tied up in a pipe. To get input from the keyboard, we must use `line` to get in from the generic /dev/tty file. This is a common way to read data from the keyboard while in a redirected loop.

Line 55 checks to see whether the input is a y. If so, the UNIX `mail` command is called, again redirecting input from the /dev/tty device (that is, the lines of mail we have just typed.) In this case, we are actually redirecting the standard input for the subshell execution of the `mail` command. Without redirecting, `mail` reads from /dev/null, which bombs the entire `whox` loop.

Line 59 handles the write display mode. The object here is to use one `ls` command and by using subexecution, glean the terminal device files from the `who` printout. These files are the second field of the `who` output. The `who` command runs first, which pipes its output to `sed`.

`Sed` then uses the substitute command to take away everything except what was bounded by the \(\) characters. This bounded region is referenced as \1 in the latter part of the substitute command. By using the . character to match each character in the printout, we only need to count the columns that we wish to cut out. Also the device names in `who` do not have the /dev/ prefix, which we need. `Sed` inserts this in front of the text cut out of `who`. The end result is that `ls` has a list of full pathnames to all the device files for logged-on users. This is then output to the screen.

Personal Security

The other side of user awareness is the provision of a reasonable degree of security. Your need for security depends somewhat on the kind of work that you do and the sensitivity of the information that is under your control. But everyone wants privacy and the basic sense of security that comes from being reasonably certain that they cannot become a victim of a security breach. Just as you can do things to help make your home less attractive to burglars, so every user can do things to help maintain security and privacy for his or her work. Like police, system administrators usually can only deal with security breaches after the fact. You can use the tools we present in this section to help guard your files from unauthorized prying or damage.

Every computer system needs some sort of security. Security levels include physical protection (of CPU, disks, and terminals), file protection, process protection, and overall system well being. In a multiuser environment, it is even more important to stress security. Each user has the right to privacy and protection of his or her environment and files. No computer has 100 percent security. The environment is only as secure as you make it. A point also can be reached at which controls hamper the free exchange of ideas and make it hard for people to use the system flexibly or explore new aspects of it. Personally, I think that users should have the freedom to do what they want to as long as it is not harmful to the system or to other users. Much of the information in this book is evidence of that belief.

The kind of security that is discussed in this chapter deals with the personal side of being a UNIX user. I want my physical work location, my home directory, and any processes that I run on the system to be secure. For me to be totally comfortable, I need to know that no one is getting into my stuff (via the normal access methods or breaking in) or looking over my shoulder to watch what I am doing.

In this section, we look at the tools `acme`, `inuse`, and `lock`. `Acme` is a preprocessor to the UNIX `acctcom` command. `Acctcom` does a pretty good job of displaying accounting information, but certain options need to be specified all the time. `Acme` sets that up for us. Remember that accounting records are stored as a structure and not in text format, which is why we have `acctcom` do it for us.

The next tool, `inuse`, allows you to set your terminal as "in use" when you leave to go somewhere else. This effectively locks it and keeps anyone else from using it. Both C and shell programs are presented to implement the lock.

The last tool, `lock`, is used to lock and unlock file permissions and is really an easy interface for the `chmod` command.

Name: acme

acme   Display accounting information on me

Function

Generates the necessary options to display information about me that is stored in the accounting file.

Synopsis

acme [-l] [-u]

Sample Call

acme -u   Print all the accounting information on user $LOGNAME

Code for acme

```
1   :
2   # @(#) acme v1.0   Give accounting info on me   Author: Russ Sage
3
4   if [ "$1" != "-l" -a "$1" != "-u" ]
5     then  echo "usage: acme [-l] [-u]" >&2
6           echo "       -l for ttyline"   >&2
7           echo "       -u for user name" >&2
8           exit 0
9   fi
10
11  OPT=""
12  for ARG in $*
13  do
14          case $ARG in
15          -l)     OPT="$OPT -l 'basename \'tty\''";;
16          -u)     OPT="$OPT -u $LOGNAME";;
17          *)      OPT="$OPT $ARG";;
18          esac
19  done
20
21  echo "acctcom $OPT"
22  acctcom $OPT
```

Environment Variables

ARG   Each value present on the command line
LOGNAME   Environment variable that has my login name
OPT   A concatenated list of all options and their arguments

Description

Why do we need acme?

Most large UNIX systems run the supplied accounting software. The results of the accounting transactions are usually put in the file /usr/adm/pacct. The actual accounting is done by the kernel. Each time a process exits, the accounting software in the kernel writes one record. The trigger that turns this on and off is acct(2). User-level commands also interface with the system call (accton(1M)) and print out the accounting results (acctcom(1)).

Now that we know where the accounting records are and how they got there, we need to print the information. Acctcom can print tables of information, but you have to know what index to use. Lookup could be by terminal line number (good for when you have process id's changed by setuid), user name, group, time, etc. The lookup options I use most often are by tty line and user name. With these, you can get a basic listing of all the data concerning you. When you call acctcom with these options, you need to supply extra information, like your tty name and your user name. It would be nice if we could reduce the amount of typing and calculation required to get the information. This is where `acme` comes in.

What does `acme` do?

`Acme` is a front-end processor to the `acctcom`(1) command. It fetches the information that it needs to satisfy the option specified. All you do is give `acme` the short form of the option and everything else is done for you. If `acme` is called without any arguments, the `acctcom` program prints all records by default.

The `acctcom` command has many options. We really only use one or two, but we use them often. The two options that `acme` accepts are -l and -u. When -l is specified, `acme` gets your tty name and puts it in the command line. If -u is specified, `acme` gets your user name and puts it in the command line. Once in a while, some other option is used to add specific information or to change the format slightly. To allow for the use of other `acctcom` options, `acme` includes any extra valid `acctcom` options passed on the command line. This way, `acme` supports a base functionality, yet still gives you the capability of tailoring the command to your liking.

Before the actual `acctcom` command is executed, the expanded form of the command line is echoed so that you can see the command line that `acme` generated. Without being able to see it, things can get confusing because you don't know what the program is up to.

Examples

1. `$ acme`

Give me *all* accounting data. This is a sequential list of all commands run from boot-up time to the present. Happy reading!

2. `$ acme -u -b`

Print in backward order all accounting records for my user name. Backward order means from the most recent previous command back to my first command.

3. `$ acme -l`

Print all accounting records for the terminal line that I currently occupy. This could include background processes still in the system from previous users of my terminal line or even processes that have different user id numbers (because of any `setuid` programs I might run) that are run from the same terminal line.

Explanation

In lines 4-9, error checking is performed. If the first positional parameter is not a -l or a -u, it must be an error. A message is printed and the program exits.

In line 11, the OPT variable is initialized to null. This variable holds all the extra `acctcom` options and their arguments.

Lines 12-19 are a for loop that iterates on the positional parameters. Each argument is checked in a case statement against the valid options. If the option is -l (line 15), OPT is set up with whatever it already has in it, the -l option, and the terminal device name stripped from the UNIX `tty` command is added. `Tty` prints the /dev prefix, which we do not need. To get rid of this prefix, we just take the basename of the string.

If the -u option is specified, OPT is appended with the -u and our login name. If the argument is any other data, it is simply appended to OPT. By doing so, we can pass other `acctcom` options through the `acme` command line. Notice that no error checking is being performed on the command line arguments. You could introduce a bogus value that `acctcom` would choke on. But that is the price we have to pay for flexibility in the command line passing, unless we add a ton of code.

After all the options have been processed, line 21 echoes out the command line to be executed so that we know what we've asked for. In line 22, the real `acctcom` command is executed. The output conforms to the description of acctcom(1).

Name: `inuse`

inuse   Disable terminal

Function

Locks your terminal by placing it in constant use. If it is tampered with, you are notified.

Synopsis

inuse

Sample Call

inuse   Put terminal into constant use
mypasswd Type my password but do not echo it to the screen

Code for `inuse`

```
1    :
2    # @(#) inuse v1.0   Disable terminal and alert if used   Author: Russ Sage
3
4    trap "echo you\'re BUSTED!!; stty echo; kill $$" 2 15
5
6    PATH=/bin:/usr/bin
7    SECRET="secret"
8
9    stty -echo
10   echo "Lock string: \c"
11   read BUF1
12   echo
13
14   while :
15   do
16           BUF2=`line < /dev/tty`
17           if [ "$BUF2" = "$BUF1" ]
```

```
18          then  break
19          elif [ "$BUF2" = "$SECRET" ]
20          then  break
21          fi
22          echo "^G\c"
23    done
24    stty echo
```

Description

Why we need inuse?

The work day is always busy: people shuffling, more paper shuffling, errands to run, and on and on. When you leave your desk, what are you going to do with your logged-in terminal? It takes too long to log in and out every time you leave, but you don't want to leave your account open to the world. What you need is a program you can run while you're gone and keeps other people from using your account.

It isn't enough, of course, to have some process that keeps running in foreground and makes the terminal appear to be in use. We have to trap interrupts in case someone types the "interrupt" or "quit" keys on our keyboard. The only way to unlock the terminal should be by entering the initial password or some predetermined word that always unlocks it.

What does inuse do?

Inuse puts your terminal to work forever. This means the terminal does not respond to your requests, or anyone else's. When you are ready to unlock your terminal, enter the secret password or one that you make up.

When you first invoke inuse, you are asked for a password. The echo is turned off on the terminal so that the password does not go to the screen. To be sure that no one tries to redirect a datafile into inuse, all reads are done directly from the terminal device /dev/tty rather than through the standard in-file descriptor. This keeps people from trying to break into sessions by feeding to standard input a huge file of words.

After reading your password, inuse goes into an endless loop that reads the keyboard and compares the input to the two passwords. Each time that someone inputs something that is not correct, the bell is rung. When one of the valid passwords is typed, the program stops and the terminal is unlocked.

We offer two implementations of inuse: the shell script given above and a C program. They do the same thing in pretty much the same way. They show how similar the two approaches are, but their subtle differences are explained later. First the script is discussed, then the C program.

Explanation

Line 4 initializes the trap statement. Three commands are executed when the trap handler is activated.

The purpose of the trapping is to respond to any attempts to interrupt the script and break in. The first command echoes a warning that you're busted, the second command turns echoing back on so that anything typed subsequently is

213

visible on the screen, and the last command causes the script to commit suicide. As we see later, this suicide is actually a special kind of death. The reference to "itself" in the kill statement is done by using $$, which is the process id of the running shell. The handler is triggered by signals 2 and 15, which are interrupt and software termination. Note that the quit signal (signal 3) is not used. We explain the reason for this a little later.

Line 6 sets up the path that inuse can reference. This way, it can never be overtaken by someone slipping in a Trojan Horse. Line 7 initializes the secret password to the string "secret", which is not all that obscure. You can change the password to something else before you install it. In a shell script, you have to keep the file permissions with no read access. Otherwise, people are able to see the secret word.

Line 9 turns off the echo, line 10 prints the prompt, and line 11 reads the password you enter into BUF1.

Lines 14-23 are a forever-while loop that can only be exited by typing the correct password. Line 16 reads the keyboard for input. When a carriage return is pressed, line 17 checks the keyboard input to see whether it matches the user password. If this fails, BUF2 is checked against the secret password. If either of the passwords match, the break statement forces execution outside the while loop, which exits the program. If the input does not match either password, the bell character is printed in line 22 and the read statement starts over again.

If a password is typed correctly, the terminal echo is turned back on in line 24 and the script exits. If the script is interrupted, the trap statement is activated. This operation is discussed in more detail later.

More on Trapping

We need to look at the significance of the quit key. Quit is an interrupt like the interrupt key, but it also core dumps the running process. We left the quit key untrapped because it becomes our last resort for stopping the inuse script. When your terminal is locked, it echoes characters but does not react to them. People typing on your keyboard see this and try to break out of it by pressing the interrupt key (usually DEL). When they do so, the message "you're busted" is printed, echo is turned back on, and the script kills itself (signal 15). When the kill signal is received by the script, the signal is trapped, thc message is printed, and it is killed again. This sequence is performed over and over again as in a forever loop. Each time the trap kills and runs again, the stack is being used. If left running long enough, the entire run-time stack fills up with activation records and overflow, bombing the session.

If the quit key is pressed before the trap statement is activated, the script exits cleanly. But if quit is pressed after the trap statement has started, it core dumps the process and exits. This is kind of kludgy, but shell programming gets to be that way, and it alerts you that someone is messing around.

The actual key values of the interrupt and quit signals are displayed in stty(1). The key values can be reset for any key you want. My current settings are

```
speed 9600 baud; intr = DEL; quit = ^|; erase = ^h; kill = ^u; eof = ^d;
```

By typing "stty intr z", you can set the regular z character to interrupt your processes so that changing the interrupt keys and running a forever loop is another way to protect your sessions. Because you need to get back in, you have to remember what you did. By customizing the signals, you can do just about anything you want with your terminal. This approach is less secure than interrupt trapping, but may provide you with a modicum of security without causing core dumps.

Now we present a version in C.

Code for inuse (C)

```
1    char id[] = "@(#) inuse.c  v1.0   Disable terminal   Author: Russ Sage";
2
3    #include <fcntl.h>
4    #include <signal.h>
5    #include <sgtty.h>
6
7    #define SSIZ 7
8    #define BSIZ 512
9    #define BELL "\07"
10   #define LF   "\n"
11
12   main()
13   {
14           register int fd, sig, n;
15           char    secret[SSIZ];
16           char    buf1[BSIZ], buf2[BSIZ];
17           struct  sgttyb sav_tty, chg_tty;
18
19           secret[0] = 's';
20           secret[1] = 'e';
21           secret[2] = 'c';
22           secret[3] = 'r';
23           secret[4] = 'e';
24           secret[5] = 't';
25           secret[6] = '\n';
26
27           buf1[0] = buf2[0] = '\0';
28           if ((fd = open("/dev/tty",O_RDONLY)) == -1)
29                   exit(1);
30
31           for (sig = 2; sig <= 15; sig++)
32                   signal(sig, SIG_IGN);
33
34           if (gtty(0, &sav_tty))
35                   exit(2);
36           chg_tty = sav_tty;
37           chg_tty.sg_flags &= ~ECHO;
```

```
38            if (stty(0, &chg_tty))
39                    exit(3);
40
41            write(1,"Lock string: ",13);
42            read(fd, buf1, BSIZ
43            write(1, LF, 1);
44
45            for (;;) {
46                    n = read(fd, buf2, BSIZ
47                    buf2[n] = '\0';
48
49                    if (strcmp(buf2, buf1) == 0)
50                            break;
51                    if (strcmp(buf2, secret) == 0)
52                            break;
53                    write(1, BELL, 1);
54            }
55            stty(0, &sav_tty);
56            close(fd);
57   }
```

Description

Why do we need inuse (C)?

The C version of inuse operates almost identically to the shell version. The major difference is that scripts call section (1) commands while C programs call section (2) and (3) commands.

What does inuse (C) do?

The theory of operation is the same as in the shell version. Initialize the secret password (in this case, using a syntax so that the strings(1) command cannot look into the executable), trap the signals, read the user password, and go into a forever loop that reads the keyboard. As input is typed and the carriage return is pressed, the input is checked against the two known passwords. If they match one, the program resets the terminal and exits. If there is no match, the terminal beeps and reads the keyboard again.

Because traps are ignored, tying to interrupt the running program does not work. The only way to kill it is using the "kill -9" sequence. The signal 9 is the only one that cannot be trapped. If it could, there would be no way of stopping the process short of pulling the plug on the machine.

Explanation

Line 1 puts a documentation string into a character array. By having the text in the object module, the what(1) command picks the text up so that we can identify our programs.

Line 3 includes the fcntl.h file. This file has all the C definitions for opening, closing, reading, and writing files. Line 4 includes signal.h. We use this file for the

SIG__IGN definition, which is the label for signal__ignore. Line 5 includes sgtty.h, which we use for definitions relating to getting terminal information via ioctl(2).

Line 7 defines the size of the secret password. The size does not have to be exactly the same as the size of the password. The size is specified for programming convenience.

Line 8 defines the size of the buffer that is read from the keyboard each time. Although 512 characters is a lot to read, reading stops when a carriage return is pressed. Having a large buffer gives us room to spare.

Lines 9 and 10 define the control characters bell and line feed.

Line 14 defines some working variables. Notice that we use register int. It is a good practice to use register variables for speed. If you declare too many variables for the amount of registers on your machine, no error occurs. The remaining variables are treated as ordinary variables. The fd variable is for the file descriptor when we open /dev/tty, the sig is for running through all the signal values, and n is the number of characters read.

Line 15 defines the secret array. This character array holds our secret password, which is hard coded into the program. Line 16 defines two buffers that we read characters into. Buf1 is our user password and buf2 is the password attempt that is read in when we want to stop the program. Line 17 defines two working structures that hold ioctl information. We have two because one is the original and the other is one we want to change without affecting the original.

Lines 19-25 load the secret array with the password. We assign one character at a time because the assignments break up any strings in the object module, a security measure that keeps probing eyes from finding too much information.

Line 27 initializes the two buffers to zero length.

Lines 28 and 29 open the /dev/tty device. If the file descriptor that was returned is equal to -1, an error has occurred and the program exits.

Lines 31 and 32 trap the signals. The for loop runs sig through the numbers 2-15. For each number the signal system call is made to ignore those signal values.

Lines 34-39 modify the terminal interface to turn off the character echoing. Line 34 gets the terminal information in the sav__tty structure. The gtty call is just a front end to the ioctl(get__values). If the call fails, the program exits.

Line 36 assigns the data from the sav__tty structure to the chg__tty structure. Line 37 then reassigns the sg__flags element as the same value only notd with ECHO, which effectively says "turn echo off." Then lines 38 and 39 write the changed value back out to the terminal device. The stty call is just a front end for ioctl(set__values).

Line 41 writes the prompt to the screen. File descriptor 1 is standard output, and 13 is the length of the string. Line 42 reads /dev/tty for BSIZ characters. After the read, a line feed is written to the screen. This is necessary because without echoing, no lf is printed when you type the password. Therefore, we need to put it there ourselves.

Lines 45-54 are the forever loop that reads the keyboard. Line 46 reads the terminal for a guess at the password In this line, the response is put into buf2 instead of buf1. We index into buf2 the number of characters read (n). Because arrays are zero-indexed rather than one-indexed, n characters places us at the end of the text where we place a null to make the entire input a string. We do this because the read command does not do string handling. Stdio calls do. They are in section (3) rather than section (2) manuals. We need to make the characters read into a string so that they can be compared with the passwords.

Line 49 checks what you typed against the password you typed at the beginning. If the strings are identical, strcmp returns a zero, which indicates a match. The break command kicks out of the for loop and the program continues. Line 51 does the same check against the secret password. If it matches, you also break out of the loop.

If there is no match, line 53 writes a bell character to the terminal and control goes back to the read statement at the top of the for loop.

If the for loop is broken out of, control goes to line 55. The original terminal configuration is written back, which turns the echo feature on. Line 56 closes the /dev/tty file and the program exits normally.

You can see that the C program, although somewhat more complicated than the shell script, has a few advantages. It cannot be stopped or destroyed by anything short of a kill -9. The password in the executable is hidden from prying eyes. You get better security and a cleaner approach at the cost of having to use a lower level language and write more code.

Name: lock

lock   Lock and unlock files

Function

Changes the readability and writeability of files, simulating locking and unlocking.

Synopsis

lock [-u] file [...]

Sample Call

lock $HOME

> Turn off writing capability for me and read/write capability for group and others on my home directory

Code for lock

```
1   :
2   # @(#) lock v1.0   Lock and unlock files   Author: Russ Sage
3
4   if [ $# -eq 0 ]
5      then  echo "lock: incorrect argument count" >&2
6            echo "usage: lock [-u] file [...]"    >&2
7            exit 1
8   fi
9
```

```
10   if [ "'echo $1 | cut -c1'" = "-" -a "$1" != "-u" ]
11     then  echo "lock: invalid argument $1"   >&2
12           echo "usage: lock [-u] file [...]" >&2
13           exit 1
14   fi
15
16   MODE1="go-rw"
17   MODE2="u-w"
18
19   if [ "$1" = "-u" ]
20     then  shift
21           MODE1="go+r"
22           MODE2="u+w"
23   fi
24
25   chmod $MODE1 $@
26   chmod $MODE2 $@
```

Environment Variables

MODE1   The file permission modes associated with group and other access
MODE2   The file permission modes associated with owner

Description

Why do we need lock?

All files in the UNIX system have permission modes. These modes change according to the file's use. The three classifications of access—owner, group, and other—need to be set for each file. Usually text files have mode 644, and executables and directories have 755. Some systems provide different defaults.

If you want to restrict read or write permission, the chmod(1) command must be used. The new mode can either be an absolute octal number (for example, 777) or an expression indicating which classification of user can do what (for example, ugo+rwx). When you want to add and remove specific capabilities, using the expression is easier. Even so, we still would benefit from a tool that minimizes typing and remembering of file permission particulars.

What does lock do?

Lock is a tool that manages the file security permissions for all your files. It provides the necessary permission modes to keep people out and let people in to a limited degree. By having predetermined permission modes, our files remain more consistent in their security position.

The input to lock is file names. Any file name generation string is valid to use. There must be at least one file name. Directory file names are allowable.

The default action of lock is to lock file names. The -u option unlocks file names.

If any invalid file names are passed in, the chmod command has a problem and gives an error message.

Examples

1. `$ lock -u $HOME/src *.c`

Unlock my source directory and all C source files in the current directory. Unlocking allows read capability for everyone and write capability only for myself.

2. `$ lock $HOME/bin`

Lock my bin directory so that no one can read or write files into it. Even though my directory is not readable, anyone can still cd into it if the x bit is on. If they try an `ls`, each file generates an error message of the form "filename not found." No one can get inode information, like times and permissions, but anyone can see the names of all the files from the error message.

Explanation

Lines 4-8 error check for the argument count. If no arguments are passed, an error message is printed. There should be at least one file name.

Lines 10-14 check to see whether the first character of the first positional parameter is a minus sign and the first option is not the valid -u string. If these conditions are met, error messages are printed and the program exits.

Lines 16 and 17 initialize the default permission mode settings. MODE1 is set to disable group and other permissions for read and write. MODE2 is set to turn user (that's me) permissions off for writing. This way I can't accidentally write over the file. We need two variables like this because the two modes are so different. The only way to handle this is to call `chmod` twice with two different settings.

Lines 19-23 check to see whether the -u option was passed on the command line. If it was, it is shifted off the command line and the mode variables are initialized for unlocking files. Line 21 turns on readability for group and others. Line 22 turns on writeability for myself. Notice that there is no modification of the x, s, or t bits in `lock`. This is deliberate in that the x bit should only be on if the file can be executed. For directories, the x bit should only be on when you want other people to be able to change directory to it. We also never set writeability for group and others, but we turn it off when locking the files. This is a blanket security measure in case the file has permissions that we don't want left on for some reason.

In lines 25 and 26, the `chmod` command is executed. The $@ parameter is used to fill in multiple file names from the command line. Doing so allows you to call `lock` with many files.

From the last 6 chapters, you should have gained lots of ideas on how you can secure your personal environment, deal with other users, and be more productive in general during your workday. We're ready to move on to some farther reaches of the UNIX system and explore the inner workings of file systems, devices, and communications.

7
Devices and File Systems

Terminal devices
Keyboard processing
Termcap generation
Disk devices
File systems
Boot disk
Size parameters

c	fast clear screen
mntf	mount the floppy disk on the system tree
mntlook	look for all mountable file systems
umntsys	unmount all file systems except root
lrgf	create the largest file your system can handle

Devices and File Systems

Introduction

Beneath the familiar territory of file systems is the world of devices and device drivers. In this chapter, we explore some of the techniques needed to deal with terminals, disks, and file systems directly. The tool c illustrates terminal access in a fast screen-clearing operation. Three tools, mntf, mntlook, and umntsys deal with mounting and unmounting file systems. Finally, the tool lrgf allows you to test the limits of your file systems' capacity.

The Body of UNIX

Before diving in, let's review some elementary facts that we should keep in mind as we look at all the layers of complexity in the UNIX system. At the heart of the hardware is the CPU, which executes the instructions that control the machine and actually accomplishes the work. An operating system is necessary to manage the work done by the CPU and to provide an interface between it and the resources that it needs in order to do anything useful: memory, storage, and other peripheral devices, such as terminals and printers.

An operating system, particularly a highly developed one like UNIX, has tons of utilities and special features, but let's ignore these for now. At the heart of the operating system (in this case, UNIX) is the kernel. The kernel controls the processes and directs the work being done. It also bridges the gap between the hardware and the outside world. In this chapter, we focus on the basic relationships between kernel, processes, and hardware.

Eventually, the system must interface with external devices. Having a basic understanding of devices is essential to fully understand how UNIX communicates with the outside world.

Much of our time in the real world is spent getting data into and out of the machine, and that means dealing with many different types of devices, each with its "features" and idiosyncrasies.

Fortunately for us, UNIX was designed to make handling data and devices as easy as possible. Unfortunately for us, there is a seemingly irreducible body of lore that we have to master anyway. The overall layout of what a UNIX system looks like is shown in figure 7-1. We can see that, to the kernel, all external peripherals are referenced as device files. Each type of device has its own driver and specific architecture, but every one is referenced using the same methods. We see how to use different ways to access devices, and we determine which ways are most efficient.

Figure 7-1
UNIX Environment Model

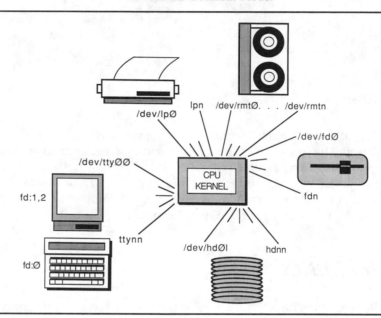

The way UNIX talks to peripherals is through "special files." The two types of special files are block and character. Both types have special uses and behaviors. Block (as in /dev/hd0) uses buffering and accesses large amounts of data on the hard disk. Character (as in /dev/tty00 or /dev/rfd0) does not use massive buffering but goes to the device with one character at a time. Even though these files get us to special places, they still maintain the same security mechanisms used by all the other files in the system.

The first area we look at is terminal devices and how we can manipulate them. Routines presented include a tool called c for fast screen clearing as well as example code for reading keystroke values and polling for single keystrokes. We also look at an example of a termcap file, which provides accessible definitions of terminal capabilities.

We then look at disk devices, like the hard disk and floppy disk. We see that there are different ways to view disk partitions using device files.

In addition to working with devices, we look at file systems on the hard disk. We all know that UNIX is heavily disk-dependent, and the more we know about file systems, the better off we are. To aid in the understanding of partitions and file systems, we present three tools. Lrgf tests the boundaries of file system parameters by making the largest file possible on your system. Mntf provides an easy way to mount and unmount floppy disks. Finally mntlook looks for unmounted file systems, a potential security risk.

Terminal Devices

The terminal device drivers are some of the most complicated of all the device drivers. This is because of the multiple layers of software that support the characteristics of interactive terminals. With a raw serial line, much support is needed to make a terminal easy to use. The different settings that a terminal can have are programmable through the stty(1) and ioctl(2) commands. Termio(7) also documents the different aspects of the terminal line disciplines.

Terminal I/O Line Disciplines

A line discipline is an agreed-on set of signals that allow the system to interpret lines of input correctly. There are four reasons for having a line discipline. The first is to support input processing of special characters, like erase and kill. Second, on the other end, we need to support output processing, such as inserting delay characters or changing the cr/lf sequence. The third reason is for supporting raw and "canonical" input modes. These two modes allow user programs to get data either one character at a time or one line at a time. The last reason for establishing line discipline is to make the configuration parameters changeable by the user.

The inside of the terminal subsystem is shown in figure 7-2. The diagram is divided into three sections: user space on the left, kernel space in the middle, and device space on the right. This illustration shows how data travels to and from the terminals and user programs.

When a process reads characters from the device, the data starts from the device driver buffer, called dbuf. From this buffer the data is moved to a receive buffer maintained by the kernel. The receive buffer is read by the kernel routine ttin( ) and the data is put into a clist structure called the raw queue. (The word "raw" means that no processing has been performed on the characters yet.) At the same time, the characters are also placed in the output queue, which lets the system echo characters as they are input.

The canon( ) routine then processes the raw queue into the canonical queue. ("Canonical" means applying the rules currently set by the system for processing special functions, such as the delete character, to a line of text.) This processing allows for transformation of the data before it gets to the user process. The last routine is ttread( ), which reads characters from the canonical buffer into the user process buffer in the data area of the process.

When characters are written from a user process to a terminal device, they follow much the same path in the reverse direction: from process space to device driver space. The major difference in the write routine is that the data goes through

Figure 7-2
Terminal Line Discipline Management

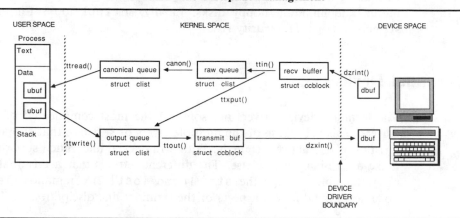

one less buffer. From the user process, characters are moved to a kernel output queue by ttwrite(), then moved to a transmit buffer by ttout(). From the transmit buffer, they go directly into the receiving device driver buffer via the device driver dzxint().

Determining Input Characters

There are times when we would like to see what characters the keyboard is producing. We could write a program to do this, but UNIX provides a built-in capability for this purpose.

The command is **od**, for "octal dump". The name is a vestige of ancient days of yore when octal was used extensively in debugging. Fortunately the output of **od** can be changed to character, hex, or decimal. The secret to using **od** to examine input and output is that **od** reads standard input by default if there are no files. A sample call

```
$ od -cx
test string<cr>
^d
^d
```

produces:

```
0000000    6574    7473    7320    7274    6e69    0a67
            t   e   s   t       s   t   r   i   n   g  \n
0000014
$
```

The call to od is done using no files on the command line and letting the output default to stdout. We use the option -cx to have the bytes interpreted as ASCII characters and the corresponding 16-bit words displayed in hexadecimal. As you type characters, they are echoed on the screen and od keeps them in its buffer. At the end of the line, press a carriage return, then a control-D. The control-D terminates the read that od is blocking on, which kicks out the printout with hex on top and character (ASCII) on bottom.

Note that the two characters printed for each hex word are the reverse of the two bytes that make up the word. For example, 6574 is interpreted as two characters, t and e, with the 65 being ASCII for e and the 74 the ASCII for t. To exit from od, type one more control-D to kill the blocked read. If you want to check more characters, keep typing. It works weirdly in that if you type enough characters, od kicks out the display on just a carriage return, but if you only type a few characters, it requires both a carriage return *and* a control-D to force the display.

One trick that we can now do is to change the canonical processing while reading in characters to od. This lets us see the effect of different line discipline settings. To do this, check out your current terminal settings. In System V, use "stty -a", whereas in Berkeley, you should use "stty everything". System V prints many more parameters than Berkeley does. Following is a sample from XENIX:

```
speed 9600 baud; line = 0;
intr = DEL; quit = ^|; erase = ^h;
kill = ^u; eof = ^d; eol = ^'
parenb -parodd cs7 -cstopb hupcl cread -clocal
-ignbrk brkint ignpar -parmrk -inpck istrip -inlcr -igncr icrnl -iuclc
ixon ixany -ixoff
isig icanon -xcase echo echoe echok -echonl -noflsh
opost -olcuc onlcr -ocrnl -onocr -onlret -ofill -ofdel ff1
```

After some head-scratching, we can see that the current flag for canonical is set to "icanon". That is, we can see that it is on because it isn't prefixed by a minus sign (though this is not a constant rule).

What kinds of things happen during canonical processing? The backspace is one important item. When you type a control-H, it enters the raw queue as a literal control-H. When canon( ) reads the control-H, it says "Change that to a backspace, a blank to overwrite the character, then another backspace." When it prints, you get character erasing on the screen. When canonical processing is off, you pass the control-H on through. Following is a display of how this works:

```
$ stty -icanon          turn canonical processing off
$ od -cx
test string^h^h^h^h^h^hcase<cr>
^d<cr><cr>...
```

```
0000000    6574    7473    7320    7274    6e69    0867    0808    0808
            t e s t    s t r i    n g \b \b    \b \b \b
0000020    6308    7361    0a65    0a04    0a0a    0a0a    0a0a    0a0a
            \b c    a s    e \n 004    \n \n    \n \n    \n \n    \n \n
```

After the word "string", you see a group of 08s, which is ASCII for control-H. These 08s show you that the literal control-Hs are indeed there in their "raw" form. Because control-H is no longer a special character, od sees it like any other character. A new problem is that because no special characters are recognized, we lose the ability to terminate the blocked read with an eof. When a control-D is entered, it is just another character. Then, we have to fill od's buffer until it is forced to do the dump. The control-D is the 004 character after the case \n.

Berkeley, by the way, uses the "cooked" and "raw" settings for stty to serve basically the same purpose as "canon" and "-canon".

Dynamic Interrupt Assignment

Notice in the previous stty -a printout that an "intr" and a "quit" occur. These are the two functions that interrupt your running processes. The strings intr and quit represent a specific functionality, not a particular keystroke. These functions can be equated to any key on the keyboard by telling stty to do so.

If we changed the "intr" to another character, the new character interrupts your processes. You can even set the interrupt key to a regular character. Here is how you do it:

```
$ stty intr x
$ this is a junk stringx
$
```

When you type an x at the end, it breaks off the line and you get a new prompt. To set the interrupt back to normal, type the old character. Assuming the old character was "delete", you would use:

```
$ stty intr DEL
```

What good is this? It shows how flexible stty is with the terminal interface, and it can be used as a personal security measure to foil people who might want to mess with your terminal. When you want to leave your terminal for a second, change the interrupt key to some other key and run a script that looks like this:

```
while :
do
:
done
```

The infinite loop runs constantly. If someone tries to interrupt the process using the delete key, nothing happens. When you come back, press the new interrupt key. It breaks the loop back to your prompt.

The "eof" is very important, too. Again, eof stands for "end of file," which happens to be a control-D. This explains why you log off UNIX with a control-D. When you send a control-D to your login shell, you are saying "Shell, this is the end of file marker for this session." Because the terminal is treated as a file, the control-D ends the file and the shell, which operates as a "while not EOF read command" loop, dies, which in turn sends a signal to `init`. `Init` spawns a `getty` on the terminal line, which prints the "login:" prompt to await the next user. If you change the eof character, you no longer log off the shell with a control-D. It displays on the screen just like any other character. Here is a sample session:

```
$ stty eof x
$ x
login:
```

The regular x character is now an end of file. When you type x, it is just like typing in control-D and you log off. This obviously would not be desirable, but it *does* show the great extent to which UNIX takes its flexibility in assigning characters to functions.

Terminal Device Files

Physical terminals are addressed through device files in the /dev directory. When you log in, you are assigned a specific tty number, such as tty01. This tty number is really a file, /dev/tty01. If you run the UNIX `tty` command, it prints the full pathname of the terminal device file you are running on.

The terminal device files look like regular files except that "ls -l" shows what are called major and minor device numbers, which are not part of regular files. The major number is an index into the cdevsw[] table that contains the address of the device driver used by the kernel for that type of device. The minor number is an identification for the particular physical device involved. These numbers appear in sequential order for the devices that use the same driver. Following is a typical list of terminal device files for XENIX:

```
crw--w--w-  1 russ   tricks   0,   0 Jun 22 02:34 /dev/console
crw--w--w-  1 russ   tricks   0,   1 Jun 22 00:41 /dev/tty02
crw--w--w-  1 root   tricks   0,   2 Jun 21 17:56 /dev/tty03
crw--w--w-  1 root   tricks   0,   3 Jun 21 05:47 /dev/tty04
crw-rw-rw-  1 root   root     0,   4 Feb 18 17:09 /dev/tty05
crw-rw-rw-  1 root   root     0,   5 Feb 18 17:09 /dev/tty06
crw-rw-rw-  2 root   root     5,   0 Jun 21 20:23 /dev/tty11
crw--w--w-  2 root   tricks   5,   8 Jun 22 02:20 /dev/tty12
crw-rw-rw-  2 root   root     5,128 Feb 18 17:09 /dev/tty13
crw-rw-rw-  2 root   root     5,136 Feb 18 17:09 /dev/tty14
```

We can see from the c in column one that these are character devices, and the permission bits show who has access to these files. The first column of numbers (0 or 5) is the major number. The minor numbers in the next column usually go in sequential order but not always, as seen here.

In addition to using the absolute tty number for your terminal, one device is used as a kind of "logical" or "generic" address for your terminal. It uses a different device driver, is called /dev/tty, and is used when the stdin and stdout are redirected to other files and the application needs to read from the keyboard or write to the screen. By accessing /dev/tty, a connection is made to the terminal itself. The choice to use tty rather than tty01 mainly depends on the problem at hand. If you need to have a program that is terminal-independent, use /dev/tty.

Terminal Permissions

Because the terminal device is a file, it has permission modes just like all the other files. The modes are protecting access to your terminal. If everybody has write access to your terminal (which would be notation rw--w--w-), they can write any-thing to your screen, and you would never know who did it. If you want to keep people out, just do a "chmod 600 'tty'", where the grave accents in the tty command fill in the pathname to your terminal file. An easier command to use is UNIX's mesg. "Mesg n" shuts off outside write access to your terminal. Your own processes still have access.

Terminal access permissions also have a security aspect that we describe in Chapter 9. For now, we note that whenever you open a file (whether for read or write), you get a file descriptor back. Then you can use this file descriptor in the ioctl system call. Obtaining that file descriptor is like getting a key to a person's terminal interface. Any ioctl alterations made to that file descriptor take effect immediately, and a security offender can read things being written or read at your terminal, or even trick your terminal into executing commands that confer unau-thorized privileges! The person who is running the terminal may never know what is happening or who is doing it.

Another example of this is write(1). It is used for online, real-time commu-nications or "chatting." It talks to the terminal by writing to the device file. Change the permission bits to off with "mesg n" and no one can write to you. That way you can "take the phone off the hook" when you don't want to be interrupted. Along the same lines, someone could do this

```
$ while :
> do
>        clear > /dev/tty00
> done &
```

which would create a background process that lives forever (until it's killed or you log off) that prints the clear screen character sequence to the person at tty00. As soon as that person types something to the screen, it is cleared. Most people won't know what is happening. If this happens to you, try turning your permission bits off. If the person doing it is root, no permissions stop him because root is not bound by file permissions. In that case, the administrator has a problem!

Another strange thing occurs if someone is writeing to your terminal, then you turn off permissions. Write still has access until it closes the device. On close, it doesn't have access to open the device again. What seems odd is that once you get access, you can't be bumped by permissions until you let go first.

Terminal Access Times

Another attribute of terminals that follows from their being files is the modify /access/change dates. Every file in the system has these three dates stored in its inode (as seconds) in a type *long*.

The dates could supply some interesting information. As described in the activ script in the last chapter, the modification date is the last time the person typed on their keyboard. The other dates mean something, but are not used that often.

Terminal Processing

As discussed previously, the default mode for the terminal driver is canonical, which is a line-based mode. When you type characters, the driver waits until you press a carriage return, then passes the whole line to the application. When you are not in canonical mode, each character is passed immediately to the application. A good example of this is vi. You type single keystrokes to move the cursor around, delete characters, etc., so vi obviously has to receive each character as it is typed.

How is this done from a program? The technique is an old one and is used often in UNIX, although it appears to not be well documented, one of those pieces of information that is absorbed through looking at a lot of code. We need to point out that this technique works best when done from a C program. Shell scripts get close by using stty, but the result is not the same. The following piece of code turns off canonical processing, then reads characters and prints them to the screen.

```
1    #include <termio.h>
2
3    struct termio  tsav, tchg;
4
5    main (argc, argv)
6    {
7            int c;
8
9            if (ioctl (0, TCGETA, &tsav) == -1) {
10                   perror("can't get original settings");
11                   exit(1);
12           }
13
14           tchg = tsav;
15
16           tchg.c_lflag &= ~(ICANON | ECHO);
17           tchg.c_cc[VMIN] = 1;
18           tchg.c_cc[VTIME] = 0;
```

```
19
20          if (ioctl (0, TCSETA, &tchg) == -1) {
21                  perror("can't initiate new settings");
22          }
23
24          while (1)
25          {
26                  c = getchar();
27
28                  if (c == 'x')
29                          break;
30
31                  putchar(c);
32          }
33
34          if (ioctl(0, TCSETA, &tsav) == -1) {
35                  perror("can't reset original settings");
36                  exit(3);
37          }
38  }
```

We have two "terminal" data structures, one that contains the original settings and another that we change and write out. The first `ioctl` call gets the terminal information. We then assign these values to the change structure (line 14). We make the modifications to the interface in lines 16-18. Line 16 turns off canonical processing and character echoing. Line 17 makes the minimum keystroke input one character. Line 18 says to wait 0 time units until the read goes back for more data. Essentially, this is a blocked read for one character.

The new information is put back to the terminal in line 20. At this point the terminal is changed. The while loop reads, checks, and prints. If you type only the x character, the loop breaks, the terminal is reset, and the program exits.

As we noted, the reading that is taking place is blocked. That is, the program waits for you to type a character. If you do not type, the program waits forever. How do we change the read from blocked to unblocked?

This is equivalent to saying: How do we poll the keyboard in UNIX? Polling is a very important technique for some kinds of applications. Polling works like this: "Take a look at the keyboard. If a character has been typed, get it and do some processing on it. Otherwise, keep doing whatever you were doing. After an interval determined by the code, check again." That way, if the user sits there, the program keeps on working instead of waiting until something is typed at the keyboard.

To make this work, we need to look at the terminal interface a little more. As stated earlier, a terminal is a file. That means it should respond to all the normal file primitives, like open, close, read, write, etc. We have seen also that terminals have line disciplines, such as the changeable `stty` settings. We saw that to get one key, you use the line disciplines. Now we see that to poll, you must use a technique relating to files, not `ioctl`.

The secret here is to open the terminal file, altering the mode in which it is opened. Then use the same code as in the preceding program to get one keystroke, and polling is achieved. See the following program.

```
1    #include <fcntl.h>
2    #include <termio.h>
3
4    struct termio  tsav, tchg;
5
6    main (argc, argv)
7    {
8            int c;
9
10           /* change the terminal based on file primitives */
11           close(0);
12           if (open("/dev/tty",O_RDWR|O_NDELAY) == -1) {
13                   perror("can't open tty");
14                   exit(1);
15           }
16
17           /* change the terminal based on line disciplines */
18           if (ioctl (0, TCGETA, &tsav) == -1) {
19                   perror("can't get original settings");
20                   exit(2);
21           }
22
23           tchg = tsav;
24
25           tchg.c_lflag &= ~(ICANON | ECHO);
26           tchg.c_cc[VMIN] = 1;
27           tchg.c_cc[VTIME] = 0;
28
29           if (ioctl (0, TCSETA, &tchg) == -1) {
30                   perror("can't initiate new settings");
31           }
32
33           while (1)
34           {
35                   putchar('.');
36                   c = getchar();
37
38                   if (c == 'x')
39                           break;
40
41                   putchar(c);
42           }
43
44           if (ioctl(0, TCSETA, &tsav) == -1) {
```

```
45              perror("can't reset original settings");
46              exit(3);
47          }
48  }
```

The main change is in lines 11-15. The close with file descriptor zero (which designates standard input) shuts down standard input. We then reopen the file /dev /tty. The file descriptor allocated is zero, so we redirected the standard input from a new device. The trick is that the open used a mode called NODELAY. This means when a read is performed on that file descriptor (standard input), it does not wait for input but looks to see whether any is there, then goes on.

In the forever loop, line 35 prints only a dot. When you run this program, a dot is printed to the screen as the program loops. If you wait, dots keep printing. As you type input, the characters are echoed between the dots. This shows that the program is working while you aren't doing anything.

Terminal Capabilities

Now that we understand some of the functionality of terminal interfaces, let's move to terminal capabilities. *Capabilities* describes the functions that the terminal hardware responds to. If we know this information, we can create a capabilities list and use it for the vi editor, for example. This is accomplished using a special data file with the `termcap` facility.

Most terminals that have been around a while already have a `termcap` entry. The file that holds all these entries is /etc/termcap. The `termcap` file and the vi editor originated with Berkeley. This combination is so effective that it has been merged into System V. With the latest System V Release 3, the `termcap` is no longer used and the AT&T `terminfo` facility replaces it. We used `terminfo` in connection with the `today` script in Chapter 5, but a detailed discussion of it is beyond the scope of this book. `Termcap` is still the standard for Berkeley, and it's still worth looking at in some detail.

Documentation on `termcap` exists, but don't expect it to tell you much. It gives the names and a one-line description of the supported functions, but not much information on how to figure out an entry from scratch. The best advice is to take an already existing entry and modify it.

As an example, we present a `termcap` entry for the Apple II computer. This description has been around for a while in different forms, but this entry is for the Apple II+ running the Videx UltraTerm card. Note that the capabilities offered through termcap are usually a `subset` of those actually available in the hardware. For example, the card in the Apple does some things that `termcap` won't do, such as custom bit patterns to change the attributes. The most we can do with video attributes through `termcap` is to turn inverse (reverse video) on and off.

On the other hand, some hardware doesn't implement all the functions provided for in termcap. For example, one function lacking in the Apple is a "scroll reverse" function. The hardware does not do it, so `termcap` shouldn't have that entry. Instead of scrolling down, the screen continues to show the text being printed on the top line.

To get an idea of how termcap relates general functionality to specific capabilities, we compare the Apple to the vt52 terminal. The two entries have many similar functions, but very different codes to achieve those functions. Following is a sample entry:

```
a2¦aii¦Apple II with UltraTerm :\
        :bl=^G:\
        :bs:\
        :cd=^K:\
        :ce=^]:\
        :cl=^L:\
        :cm=^^%r%+ %+ :\
        :co#80:\
        :cr=^M:\
        :do=^J:\
        :ho=^Y:\
        :kb=^H:\
        :kd=^J:\
        :kl=^H:\
        :kr=^\\:\
        :ku=^_:\
        :le=^H:\
        :li#24:\
        :nd=^\\:\
        :nl=^J:\
        :se=^O:\
        :so=^N:\
        :up=^_:
```

Table 7-1 is a list of termcap functions that cross reference the Apple II list with the vt52 list. If the function does not exist on one or the other, a blank is left.

Table 7-1
Termcap Definitions and Specific Terminal Values

f()	Apple II	vt52
bl—bell	^G	^G
bs—can backspace with ^H	true	true
cd—clear to end of display	^K	\EJ
ce—clear to end of line	^]	\EK
cl—clear entire screen	^L	\EH\EJ
cm—cursor motion	^^%r%+ %+	\EY%+ %+
co—number of columns in a line	#80	#80

Table 7-1 (cont.)

f()	Apple II	vt52
cr—carriage return	^M	^M
do—down one line	^J	^J
ho—home cursor (if no cm)	^Y	\EH
kb—sent by backspace key	^H	^H
kd—sent by down arrow key	^J	\EB
kl—sent by left arrow key	^H	\ED
kr—sent by right arrow key	^\\	\EC
ku—sent by up arrow key	^__	\EA
le—cursor left	^H	^H
li—number of lines per screen	#24	#24
nd—nondestructive space	^\\	\EC
nl—newline character	^J	^J
pt—has hardware tabs		true
se—end stand out mode (normal)	^O	
so—begin stand out mode (inverse)	^N	
sr—scroll reverse		\EI
ta—tab	^I	^I
up—up a line		^__

Probably the most interesting thing is that the vt52 and the Apple have their cursor motion coordinates reversed with respect to one another. The vt52 takes the x and y values in YX order, which is the default for `termcap`. The Apple takes them in XY, which requires the `termcap` entry to reverse them, hence the %r in the cm function.

Termcap enables you to hide most of the information about specific terminals (except capabilities that might be lacking or special ones not found in termcap). This means that you can write terminal-independent programs. That way you don't have to change all the specific references for each terminal, such as the escape sequences (the characters that signal to the terminal that the following character(s) should be interpreted as control codes): these are (\E) for the vt52 and the control (^) character for the Apple.

The best example is the way vi uses the `termcap` file. Vi starts to execute a specific function like moving the cursor, then says "What is the code for this function that we want to do?" It then looks up the appropriate sequence in the information supplied by `termcap`.

On the other hand, you sometimes want to optimize a function for speed by having it send codes directly to a specific terminal. In this case, you still can benefit from the existence of termcap files because you can look up the information you need in the appropriate termcap, then hard code that information into your program. This is what we do with the first of the actual tool programs for this chapter, c.

Name: c

c	Fast clear screen

Function

Prints the clear-screen sequence using fast C routines. Hard coded information must be changed to that appropriate for terminal to be used.

Synopsis

c

Sample Call

c	Clear the screen

Code for c

```
1    char id[] = "@(#) c v1.0   Fast clear screen   Author: Russ Sage";
2
3    #define FF "\014"
4
5    main()
6    {
7            if (write(1, FF, 1) == -1)
8                    write(2,"c: write error to stdout\n",25);
9    }
```

Description

Why we need c*?*

A command already exists on System V to clear the terminal screen, clear. It works by looking up your terminal type, then printing the clear screen character for that terminal. This is great but has one major drawback: It is very *slow*!

The function that we want to perform is clearing the screen as fast as possible. The fastest I/O in the system is a direct system call to read or write. We use this interface and also do some error checking as to the availability of the standard output.

What does c *do?*

C prints the screen clear character as fast as I/O can go on UNIX. By making a direct system call, we don't have to run extraneous software. Therefore, c is very fast. We grant that this same function could be put into a csh alias, so this program is most useful for System V people.

To find out what your terminal responds to, look up the cl entry in the termcap file. This is the value that you have to manually put into this program. If you are on a different terminal than the one for which it was written, this command does not work properly.

Explanation

We must first find out from `termcap` what the clear-screen code is. For the Apple, it is ^L, but for the vt52, it is \EH\EJ. Once you find out this code, insert it into the define in line 3 or make a string of it in line 7. The example code given uses the ^L to clear the screen.

The fastest way to get characters to a file is by a direct write statement. Because terminals are files, we can write directly to them by taking advantage of the predefined file descriptors 0, 1, and 2.

The `write` system call in line 7 puts the clear character to file descriptor 1, which is stdout. If the write fails (due to any number of problems), an error message is printed to file descriptor 2 or standard error. There is no checking to see if the write to standard error fails. If it gets that far, we probably won't care.

The program uses *no* `stdio` functionality. You should *never* mix system call I/O (that is, calls from (2), such as `read` or `write`) and standard I/O calls (that is, calls from (3), such as `getchar` and `printf`). The extra buffering that occurs in stdio functions does not have its timing coordinated with the system calls, so all the output is mixed together.

Another thing to keep in mind when deciding whether to use system calls is the advantage of having the smallest object code possible. Small code loads and runs faster. To keep all those unneeded `stdio` routines out of our object module, no reference is made in the source code to any `stdio` routines. However, your system might include them anyway. XENIX does, and along with `stdio` comes `malloc`, and everything else. You can look through the symbol table of your object module by using `nm`(1) or `nlist`(2). You see all the garbage that is added to your object module. It is not uncommon to get 6K worth of code for one `printf` statement! You might have to resort to coding directly in assembler to get what you want.

Explorations

When this program was created, the question arose: How can we test the failure of a write to stdout? This hadn't arisen before, but it seemed like a good thing to try. The solution was found in the `sh`(1) manual pages. The way to force the failure of the write statement to stdout is to close down the stdout file descriptor. This is accomplished easily by using the `exec` command that is internal to the shell:

```
$ exec >&-
```

It works by redirecting the standard output file descriptor 1 (notation >) to the file descriptor (&) of a closed device (-). This can be a useful addition to a thorough debugging of your application.

Disk Devices

Disk devices include floppy and hard disks. Each whole disk can be divided into one or more parts, with each part associated with a device file.

The major difference between disks and terminals is that disks are block devices and terminals are character devices. Instead of talking one character at a time, disks talk 512 or 1024 characters at a time. There is code that manages the blocking and buffering that makes block I/O possible.

Disk Partitioning

The parts, or areas of a disk, are known as partitions. A partition can hold a file system, which is generated with the mkfs(1) command, or it can hold raw data, as used with the cpio -o command.

In XENIX, the partition management is handled by a program called fdisk, which is similar conceptually to its namesake in the MS-DOS world. Other UNIX systems use different names. The AT&T 7300 UNIX PC uses iv, for "format", believe it or not. As mentioned previously, partitions usually hold one file system. Now with XENIX and the SCO XENIX, you can "divvy" up a partition into smaller pieces for more file systems. This is done because a DOS/XENIX machine has a limit of four disk partitions, and you might well want more file systems than there are available partitions. The AT&T 7300 UNIX PC manages disk partitions by having a list of the starting track numbers. You can create as many partitions as you want. Each set of these machine implementations has its advantages and disadvantages.

For most device names in the /dev directory, there are both block and character names. These names invoke different device drivers. Following is a sample list of the hard disk device interfaces.

```
brw-------  1 sysinfo  sysinfo  1,  0 Feb 18 17:07 /dev/hd00
brw-------  1 sysinfo  sysinfo  1, 15 Feb 18 16:59 /dev/hd01
brw-------  1 sysinfo  sysinfo  1, 23 Feb 18 16:59 /dev/hd02
brw-------  1 sysinfo  sysinfo  1, 31 Feb 18 16:59 /dev/hd03
brw-------  1 sysinfo  sysinfo  1, 39 Feb 18 16:59 /dev/hd04
brw-------  1 sysinfo  sysinfo  1, 47 Feb 18 17:07 /dev/hd0a
brw-------  1 sysinfo  sysinfo  1, 55 Feb 18 17:09 /dev/hd0d
crw-------  1 sysinfo  sysinfo  1,  0 Feb 18 16:59 /dev/rhd00
crw-------  1 sysinfo  sysinfo  1, 15 Feb 18 16:59 /dev/rhd01
crw-------  1 sysinfo  sysinfo  1, 23 Feb 18 16:59 /dev/rhd02
crw-------  1 sysinfo  sysinfo  1, 31 Feb 18 16:59 /dev/rhd03
crw-------  1 sysinfo  sysinfo  1, 39 Feb 18 16:59 /dev/rhd04
crw-------  1 sysinfo  sysinfo  1, 47 Feb 18 16:59 /dev/rhd0a
crw-------  1 sysinfo  sysinfo  1, 55 Feb 18 17:09 /dev/rhd0d
```

A file name with hd* indicates a block device, whereas rhd* indicates a "raw" character device. Not all character devices are raw block devices. Terminals, as we saw earlier in this chapter, are character devices. Table 7-2 shows the different characteristics of the two types of devices.

Table 7-2
Differences Between Block and Character Devices

Block Device	Character Device
/dev/hd0, /dev/fd0	/dev/rhd0, /dev/rfd0
kernel buffering, slow	no buffering, fast
data blocks skewed	data blocks contiguous
access through file system	access directly to disk
cpio -p	cpio -o, -i
mkfs, mount, df, du	tar
fsck, fsdb	

As you can see, there are many ways to look at devices.

Let's look at the device /dev/hd01 from the list given previously. If you want to address a physical partition on a disk as a block device, you can create a file system on it. All you would say to make a 5000K (or 5M) file system on a hard disk using our device name would be

```
# mkfs /dev/hd01 5000
```

Inside the partition (assuming it's at least 5000K) is a file system. The file system contains the superblock, free lists, etc., everything needed to keep track of files that reside there. Creating a file system does *not* mean that you can immediately access it, however: You must mount the file system first. The command for this would be

```
# mount /dev/hd01 /mount_pt
```

Files can be placed in the disk partition by using mv or cp, redirecting to that directory name, as in >/mount__pt/file.

To use a disk partition as raw storage rather than as a block device, use the device file that has the character device name which starts with r. For example, to use the same device as the one used in the previous example as a raw device, use the name /dev/rhd01. (You can see from the device list that this device is a character device, with its permissions in the first column starting with crw rather than brw). This device (and associated partition) now has no file system in it and is just an expanse of bytes. The limitation is that you can only back up 5M of data to that partition.

A sample command using the raw device is

```
$ find . -print | cpio -ocBv > /dev/rhd01
```

Examining Data

Once data is on the disk, it can be examined at a lower level than that used by `cat`, `more`, and so on. This is accomplished by using od(1) to dump the device file, as shown in the following example:

```
$ od -c /dev/hd01
```

If you dumped the *raw* device file (/dev/rhd01) it would look the same. The only difference is how that data is being accessed by the drivers. The format of what you see depends on whether it was backed up using `cpio`, `tar`, `mkfs`, or whatever. Some other ways to get data from a device name are

```
$ cat /dev/hd01
$ cat < /dev/hd01
$ tail /dev/fd0
```

If you dump a device file with a file system on it, the data would be seen as random blocks of 512 bytes. At one point, you would see the directory listings. In other words, the same device can be seen in two radically different ways: as a file system and as a collection of raw bits. Although reading a given device both ways can be educational, in most cases, you wouldn't want to *write* to the same device under both protocols because, for example, the raw device wouldn't know anything about the file system in the partition and would overwrite pieces of it.

Now that you know how the disk can be accessed, think back to Chapter 2 and the backup routines. The script `cpiobr` uses the raw disk device, /dev/rfd0, whereas `autobkp` uses the file system to copy files.

Most of these ways of playing with devices may seem quite esoteric and mainly for fun and education. However, fun often leads to some very productive work. You can only discover what the system can do by making the system do it. The hardware situation on the micro side is similar. A new box comes out and it takes years for software developers to find all the capabilities of the machine. UNIX is a software world that has been around in one form or another for over ten years, but people are still discovering new and amazing things that it can do.

Just because you normally have to choose one way or another to use a disk partition, you are not limited to making all the partitions on the same drive of the same type. The usual approach is to make all the possible partitions have file systems so that they can hold files. You can, however, combine file system and "raw" partitions any way you please. One possible scheme is to use one partition (fd01) as a raw device to back up files using "cpio -o". This takes up most of the disk, but some space is allocated to a second partition for a file system (fd02). The allocated space contains some help files and a text file that has the names of the files on the raw partition backup. Partitioning this way provides the best of both worlds. To get to the `cpio` data, you say "cpio -i < /dev/rfd01". To get the data on the second partition, you say "mount /dev/fd02 /mnt", then use `ls`, `file`, `grep`, and the other commands related to files in a file system. In this case, the file system partition serves to document the raw backup partition.

Boot Disk and Standalone Shell (SASH)

The installation of UNIX on a hard disk is usually assisted by a standalone shell (SASH). This sometimes runs on tape, but the easiest to use is floppy. The question is "How does the floppy boot into UNIX?"

Picture this: The floppy is one partition or maybe even divided into a root partition and a user partition. Either way, the floppy has a file system created from another system and placed on the disk. Block one of the file system is the boot record, which is placed on the media by the dd command. Dd copies bytes starting at the beginning of the device. The boot record contains code necessary to start UNIX from the disk.

Block two is the superblock, a kind of master directory to the file system, and has both the inodes pointing to information about each file and a list of available areas of free space. The root file system also has a floppy version of the kernel, which boots up and runs the shell just as its big brother, the hard disk kernel, does for the system as a whole. You can even mount the installation disk on another hard disk system and copy commands to it. The limiting factor is the size of the one installation disk. The largest PC floppy sizes are 1.2M (used in ATs), which is pretty large. You can almost fit the entire boot-up code that is needed to run multiple users from a floppy.

Once the floppy kernel boots, it has a complete file system with all the device files. It mounts the hard disk partition (assuming that it has been partitioned) and copies files to it in file system format. It would look like this:

```
# mount /dev/hd01 /mnt    ←issued from the floppy to mount the first partition of the hard disk
# copy /unix /mnt         ←copy hard disk kernal to hard disk partition
```

Updating the File System

We have described the superblock as the key record of information about the size and contents of the file system. A file system usually gets blown away because of a problem in the superblock. The sync(1) command writes the core image of the superblock to the disk, thereby updating it. This is something that should be done automatically and constantly to keep the disk image and the core image the same. System V has now implemented a program (update) that is run from one of the bootup /etc/rc files. It lives in the system and does a sync and sleep. The effect is that the disk file system information is kept current with recent changes in the actual file system. If you don't have this on your system, you can write a shell script with a loop, a synch call, and an appropriate length of sleep, and run it in the background to provide this safety feature.

Mounting File Systems

Let's look at what happens when a file system is mounted to the system tree. Figure 7-3 shows how the inodes of the two file systems come together.

Figure 7-3
Mounting of One File System onto Another

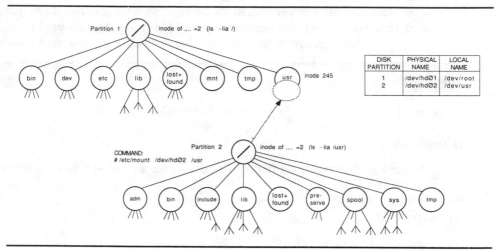

In the example shown in figure 7-3, the file system from partition 2 is going to be mounted on the root file system (partition 1) at directory /usr. However, remember that each file system has its own root directory. Each file system's inode count starts from 2, so inode numbers are duplicated between file systems. This is the reason that files cannot be linked across file systems.

One attribute of the root directory is that its inode number is 2. This can be verified on the root directory by doing an "ls -lid /". The directory /usr is just another file (specifically a directory) in the root file system. This directory can contain files and subordinate directories that are stored in partition 1. After the command "mount /dev/hd02 /usr", the root directory of partition 2 (inode 2) is placed under the inode of /usr (inode 245). If any files exist under /usr on partition 1, they stay there, but you don't have access to them. The only way to see them is to unmount the file system that was mounted over them. The magic of the mount command is that it makes the new partition seem like it belongs to the real root partition. In essence, it allows for an infinite file system.

The mechanism that allows this to happen is the mount table inside the kernel. When a file is referenced, its inode defines the path. If the mount table has an entry, the path diverts to the other disk partition/file system. To verify that the newly mounted file system is still unique, look at the inode of /usr from the point of view of the root directory ("ls -li /", inode 245), then look at it from the point of view of the other file system (ls -ldi /usr, inode 2).

How To Get More Information on File Systems

As described previously, a file system fits inside a disk partition. File systems are made by mkfs(1), maintained by fsck(1), patched using fsdb(1), and made accessible in the first place by mount(1). The /usr/include directory contains all the include files for use by the C programs that implement these commands. Thus, this is a good place to snoop around to find information on the file system because include files have global definitions used by file system routines. Bell Labs papers (in the programmer's guide) also describe some of the internal tables used by a file system.

Now we're ready to look at tools for automating file-system chores.

Name: mntf

mntf   Mount or unmount floppy disk

Function

Mounts and unmounts a floppy disk device on a directory as a read/write or read-only file system.

Synopsis

mntf [-d] [-h] [-1] [-r] [-s]

Options:
    -d dismount the floppy from the root file system

    -h use high-density drives rather than low

    -1 use the drive 1 mount point instead of drive 0 mount point

    -r mount the floppy as a read-only file system

    -s use System V device names

default: mount the floppy disk0, on the /mnt directory

Sample Call

mntf -d -1

    Dismount the floppy in drive 1

Code for mntf

```
1    :
2    # @(#) mntf v1.0   Mount floppies   Author: Russ Sage
3
4    CMD="/etc/mount"
5    DIR="/mnt"
6    DRIVE="0"
7    DENSITY="48ds9"
8    SYSTEM="xenix"
9
10   if [ $# -gt 0 ]
11      then  for ARG in $*
12            do
```

```
13              case $ARG in
14              -d)  CMD="/etc/umount"
15                   DIR="";;
16              -h)  DENSITY="96ds15";;
17              -1)  DRIVE="1"
18                   if [ -d /mnt1 ]
19                     then  DIR="/mnt1"
20                     else  echo "the directory /mnt1 does not exist" >&2
21                           echo "using the directory /mnt instead"    >&2
22                   fi;;
23              -r)  DIR="$DIR -r";;
24              -s)  SYSTEM="sysv";;
25              *)   echo "mntf: invalid argument $ARG"               >&2
26                   echo "usage: mntf [-d] [-h] [-1] [-r] [-s]" >&2
27                   echo "        -d  dismount"                   >&2
28                   echo "        -h  high density"               >&2
29                   echo "        -1  use drive 1"                >&2
30                   echo "        -r  read only"                  >&2
31                   echo "        -s  System V device"            >&2
32                   echo " default: mount XENIX drive 0 48 tpi to " >&2
33                   echo "          /mnt as a read/write filesystem" >&2
34                   exit 1;;
35              esac
36        done
37  fi
38
39  case $SYSTEM in
40  sysv)   $CMD /dev/fp${DRIVE}21 $DIR;;
41  xenix)  $CMD /dev/fd${DRIVE}${DENSITY}  $DIR;;
42  esac
```

Environment Variables

CMD	Main action command to be performed
DIR	Mount point directory
DENSITY	Density name as stated in the device name
DRIVE	Drive number, starting from zero
SYSTEM	Type of UNIX system device name

Description

Why do we need mntf?

On floppy-based machines, the floppy drive must be used frequently in daily operations. It is used as the source for installation and is the usual medium for backups.

The use of floppies under UNIX comes in two flavors. The first is raw sequential bytes, useful for tape and archival storage. The second is a block-by-block, file-oriented format. For the latter, the file system manages much of the overhead, but we have to implement some functions ourselves.

To use a floppy as a file system under UNIX, you need to prepare the disk and mount the floppy as a file system. When you are done, you have to unmount the floppy. This is different from DOS, where floppies can be put in and pulled out when you please as long as they're not being written to at the time.

Because using a floppy involves the reciprocal steps of mounting and dismounting, it would seem natural to use one command with appropriate options to mount and dismount the floppy. But UNIX didn't do it that way. Our `mntf` brings these two functions together in one command to make the interface more consistent. To make the functionality more independent, we wrote the program to be able to handle XENIX devices as well as the System V devices. (Berkeley (BSD) systems do not use floppies nearly as much, so we made no attempt to deal with them.)

What does `mntf` do?

This script provides all the functionality needed for mounting and unmounting floppy disks. It provides all the options allowed with the `mount` command, gives a central focus to the aspects of floppy file systems, and reduces the amount of keystrokes needed to get the job done.

The default action is to mount a low-density floppy in drive 0 to the directory /mnt. A number of options are available to change this to reflect your own needs. The -h option handles a high-density (1.2M) disk. On the PC-AT based machines, the first floppy drive is a 96 track-per-inch drive that stores 1.2 megabytes but can also read and write the low-density floppies. The second floppy is a low-density drive that stores with 48 tpi and has a capacity of 360 kilobytes.

The -1 (that's "one," not "el") option mounts the floppy in drive 1 rather than drive 0. The -r option mounts the file system as *read-only*. To *dismount* rather than mount the device, use the - d option. If the -s option is used, the device name is changed to reflect the System V microbased names rather than the XENIX-based names. This is a slight problem because the naming schemes are a little different. This script is built for the XENIX interface and provides the most functionality in that area.

Not all options are compatible with one another, and they are not cross-checked. For example, "mnt -d -r" tries to unmount a read-only file system, and the underlying UNIX `unmount` command rejects this with an error message. In the interest of simplicity, we have chosen not to check option compatibility but rather to let the underlying UNIX error messages inform the user of problems. If you want this script to be used by relatively inexperienced users, you might want to build in more error checking.

Examples

1. `$ mntf -s`

Mount the floppy as a read-write file system using the System V device file.

2. `$ mntf -h -1 -r`

Mount the high-density floppy, drive one, as a read-only file system using the XENIX device file format. This command should fail.

3. `$ mntf -d -h`

Dismount the file system from high-density drive 0, using the XENIX device file name.

Explanation

To make this script as straightforward as possible, the actual commands that are executed are put into strings. This allows more flexibility in the way the script can be coded. As the analysis of the command line is done, the command string is being built up and the result is executed at the bottom.

The strings initialized in lines 4-8 set up the defaults. CMD holds the UNIX command that eventually is executed: by default, `mount`. DIR is the directory where the device is to be mounted, with a default of /mnt. DRIVE is the drive number, with a default of 0, and is used to complete the correct device name. DENSITY is set by default to the low-density media for the PCs, 48 tpi, double-sided using 9 sectors per track (48ds9).

Line 10 checks to see whether the command line has any arguments. If the number of arguments is greater than zero, each argument is checked in sequence. If any of the arguments match the patterns in lines 13-35, the code at that point alters the makeup of the command line.

Line 14 handles the -d option, to dismount the floppy. CMD is changed from mount to umount. Then DIR is set to null because the `umount` command does not use a directory reference, only a device name. The DIR variable has to be part of the command line so that we can use one "boilerplate" command line for all variations. In this case, we set this variable to null, and it is removed during shell parsing.

Line 16 changes the density of the media that you are using. The way the different media types are referenced is by device file name. Each name references a device driver that talks to the appropriate hardware. The high-density drive can talk both and store both. If you use the high-density name on a low-density format, however, the drivers bomb because of read errors.

More on Construction of Device Names

To see how the device names apply, the following listing is an `ls` of the dev directory for an XT-based system, which has no high-density drive:

```
 32 brw-rw-rw-   3 bin    bin    2,  4 Jun 25 09:25 /dev/fd0
 32 brw-rw-rw-   3 bin    bin    2,  4 Jun 25 09:25 /dev/fd048
126 brw-rw-rw-   1 root   root   2, 12 Feb 18 17:09 /dev/fd048ds8
 32 brw-rw-rw-   3 bin    bin    2,  4 Jun 25 09:25 /dev/fd048ds9
125 brw-rw-rw-   1 root   root   2,  8 Feb 18 17:09 /dev/fd048ss8
127 brw-rw-rw-   1 root   root   2,  0 Feb 18 17:09 /dev/fd048ss9
131 brw-rw-rw-   3 root   root   2,  5 Feb 18 17:09 /dev/fd1
131 brw-rw-rw-   3 root   root   2,  5 Feb 18 17:09 /dev/fd148
```

```
129 brw-rw-rw-  1 root      root      2, 13 Feb 18 17:09 /dev/fd148ds8
131 brw-rw-rw-  3 root      root      2,  5 Feb 18 17:09 /dev/fd148ds9
128 brw-rw-rw-  1 root      root      2,  9 Feb 18 17:09 /dev/fd148ss8
130 brw-rw-rw-  1 root      root      2,  1 Feb 18 17:09 /dev/fd148ss9
```

The number on the far left is the inode number. We use this as a reference to determine unique file names. As we noted previously, several device names can refer to the same file under different colors, as it were, and you can see this in the list by noting that three devices have inode 32, for example. The number second from the left is the link count. Where it is greater than one, it also reveals that several devices are really the same file and so use the same inode. The next two numbers are the major and minor numbers. Major numbers are device drivers and the minor number is the unique number of a device driven by the same driver.

Most of these device names have a pattern. They consist of fd (for floppy disk) + 0 or 1 (the drive number) + 48 (the tracks-per-inch density) + ss or ds (single- or double-sided) + 8 or 9 (number of sectors).

We first see by the inodes that fd0 is linked to fd048 and fd048ds9. The most definitive (and hardest to type) is the fd048ds9. It spells out exactly which drive and media type that we are referencing. To make it easier, fd048ds9 is linked to increasingly easier names. All three file names are valid.

The next listing is from an AT-based system that has the high-density drive:

```
102 brw-rw-rw-  3 bin      bin      2,  7 Jun 17 14:28 /dev/fd0
 95 br--r--r--  2 bin      bin      2,  3 Jun  6 09:23 /dev/fd048
 93 br--r--r--  1 bin      bin      2,  2 Jun  6 09:23 /dev/fd048ds8
 95 br--r--r--  2 bin      bin      2,  3 Jun  6 09:23 /dev/fd048ds9
 92 br--r--r--  1 bin      bin      2,  0 Jun  6 09:23 /dev/fd048ss8
 94 br--r--r--  1 bin      bin      2,  1 Jun  6 09:23 /dev/fd048ss9
102 brw-rw-rw-  3 bin      bin      2,  7 Jun 17 14:28 /dev/fd096
102 brw-rw-rw-  3 bin      bin      2,  7 Jun 17 14:28 /dev/fd096ds15
 99 brw-rw-rw-  3 bin      bin      2, 11 Jun 26 19:34 /dev/fd1
 99 brw-rw-rw-  3 bin      bin      2, 11 Jun 26 19:34 /dev/fd148
 97 br--r--r--  1 bin      bin      2, 10 Jun  6 09:23 /dev/fd148ds8
 99 brw-rw-rw-  3 bin      bin      2, 11 Jun 26 19:34 /dev/fd148ds9
 96 br--r--r--  1 bin      bin      2,  8 Jun  6 09:23 /dev/fd148ss8
 98 br--r--r--  1 bin      bin      2,  9 Jun  6 09:23 /dev/fd148ss9
103 brw-rw-rw-  2 bin      bin      2, 15 Jun  6 09:23 /dev/fd196
103 brw-rw-rw-  2 bin      bin      2, 15 Jun  6 09:23 /dev/fd196ds15
```

If we look at the entries with inode 102, starting from the middle of the list, we can see the same progressive simplification of names until we get to the first entry, floppy drive 0, which is thus high density by default. To reference the first drive as low density, use fd048 rather than fd0. Because most floppy use is low density, this is the default in `mntf`.

Line 17 matches the -1 option and uses the drive 1 notation rather than drive

0. Lines 18-22 check to see whether the mount point (directory) for the second drive exists. If you are using two floppies at the same time, you cannot mount them both on the same directory. To solve this, `mntf` uses /mnt1 rather than /mnt to mount drive 1. If mnt1 does not exist, mnt is used as a default, which is okay if you are only using drive 1. Beware of mounting one floppy on top of another, however. You could get things very confused. If you are going to mount two floppies, make sure you have both the /mnt and /mnt1 directories.

Line 23 makes the mounted file system read-only if the -r option was used, which you do by appending the -r string to the directory name. It is not part of the directory, but when the shell processes the command, the space between the directory and the -r is enough for `mount` to pick it out as an option.

Line 24 matches the -s option and sets the SYSTEM variable to sysv. This makes the command use a different device file notation.

Lines 25-34 do the error checking. Any option other than the ones just checked is an error, so anything that matches the catchall case (*) must be invalid. In that case, the usage statement is printed and the program exits.

Lines 39-42 do all the work. The case statement acts on the value of SYSTEM. If the system is "sysv", line 40 is executed. Otherwise line 41, for XENIX, is executed. Note that the sysv line only has the drive number variable provided in our implementation of the script. If you are using System V, you can add a variable for density or other parameters if you need to.

Line 41 executes the XENIX version of the command. CMD, as we noted, contains either the mount or umount command. The /dev/fd makes the device file reference a floppy disk. DRIVE is 0 or 1. DENSITY is either high or low. If it is a mount command, DIR has a directory entry. If the command is umount, DIR is null.

Security Note

Normally only root can mount file systems. On a large mainframe, this makes sense. But on a small desktop machine, it may be too restrictive for the environment. To override this requirement, use the setuid capability. To allow any user to execute the mount and umount command, perform the following commands:

```
# chown root /etc/mount      ←make root the owner setuid and make executable for everybody
# chmod 4511 /etc/mount
# chown root /etc/umount      ←do the same for the other command
# chmod 4511 /etc/umount
```

This makes it easy for anybody to use the floppy, but it also opens a huge security hole in the system. If someone has a setuid trap door (see Chapter 9) on a floppy already, mounting the file system adds it to the main system and allows the user to become root on the entire system just from a floppy!

Name: `mntlook`

---

mntlook   Look for file systems on devices

Function

Looks through all the disk device files and finds all file systems, including those that are not mounted.

Synopsis

mntlook

Sample Call

mntlook /dev/hd*

Look for file systems on all hard disk devices

Code for mntlook

```
1    static char id[] = "@(#) mntlook v1.0   Look for mounts    Author: Russ
Sage";
2
3    #include <stdio.h>
4    #include <fcntl.h>
5    #include <sys/types.h>
6    #include <sys/param.h>
7    #include <sys/filsys.h>
8
9    #define BSIZ 512
10
11   main(argc,argv)
12   int argc;
13   char *argv[];
14   {
15           struct filsys sb;
16           int d, dev;
17           char buf[BSIZ];
18
19           for (d = 1; d < argc; d++)
20           {
21                   if (argv[d][0] == '-')
22                   {
23                           printf("mntlook: invalid argument %s\n", argv[d]);
24                           printf("usage: mntlook device [device ...]\n");
25                           continue;
26                   }
27                   if ((dev = open(argv[d],O_RDONLY)) < 0)
28                   {
29                           sprintf(buf, "cannot open %s",argv[d]);
30                           perror(buf);
31                           continue;
32                   }
33
```

```
34                  /* throw away first block */
35                  if (read(dev, &sb, sizeof(sb)) == -1)
36                  {
37                          perror("cannot read block 0");
38                          continue;
39                  }
40
41                  /* block 1 is the superblock */
42                  if (read(dev, &sb, sizeof(sb)) == -1)
43                  {
44                          perror("cannot read block 1");
45                          continue;
46                  }
47
48                  if (sb.s_magic == S_S3MAGIC)
49                  {
50                          printf("\nDEV: %s  --> VALID file system\n",argv
[d]);
51                          printf("filsys: %s\n",sb.s_fname);
52                          printf("pack  : %s\n",sb.s_fpack);
53                          printf("type  : %s byte block\n",
54                             (sb.s_type == S_B512) ? "512" : "1024");
55                          printf("magic : %lx\n",sb.s_magic);
56                  }
57
58                  close(dev);
59          }
60  }
```

Description

Why do we need mntlook?

File systems are the heartblood of UNIX. The entire system lives off a file system, and extensions of the system are handled by file systems.

Even though file systems are so important, UNIX does not provide any tools for locating file systems as such, or even tools that tell us what information resides in their superblocks.

What we need is an all-purpose file system tool. It needs to locate and identify superblocks that reside in device names. Note that opening a device usually requires root privileges.

What does mntlook do?

Mntlook is designed to look inside device files and search for the presence of a superblock. (We discussed superblocks briefly previously.) When a superblock is found, the file system name, the disk pack name, the block size used, and the identifying "magic number" are printed from the superblock itself.

The original purpose of this utility was to find sitting in a machine those file systems that were not mounted at the current time. But when the program opens and reads a device, it doesn't matter whether the device is mounted or not because the access is below the file system level. As a result, all file systems are found, whether or not they are mounted.

Let's review how file systems are connected to the physical media. A fixed number of peripherals are attached to each machine. To allow removable media, UNIX designed the concept of a mountable and unmountable file space. But the first step is putting the physical disk pack (or floppy) into the disk drive unit. Once inserted, references to specific device names can read and write to the physical media.

Mounting is a logical action that reads the superblock from the disk pack into memory where the kernel maintains its own version. Periodically the memory version is written back to disk to keep the two versions as close as possible. The program that does this in System V is `update`, which runs in the background from the bootup of the system.

To reference the physical media directly, commands like "od -c /dev/rfd0" dump the raw floppy device. One command that puts data to the device directly is "cp file /dev/fd0". The data begins from the first byte of the floppy. This is incompatible with `tar`, `cpio`, or a file system.

To reference a file system, the command "mount /dev/fd0 /mnt" is executed. From there on, all references to the device are through the directory /mnt. The main point is that a direct access to a device file is lower than a file system, so information about the superblock can be read directly out of the device.

The input to mntlook is device file names. No options can be passed on the command line. The device names can be either block or character. It makes no difference when the read occurs, as long as you have read permission. The program then reads the second block and checks for the "magic number" that defines a superblock. A superblock is just a C structure that is predefined by the system, in the file filsys.h as stated in the #include statements in our program. The magic number is a long integer that is a predetermined value. If the structure element being read from the disk contains this number, the rest of the structure is assumed to be valid data. There is only one superblock structure for each file system.

If the magic number is correct, the other file system information is printed. If the number is no good, nothing is displayed and the program loops for the next device file on the command line.

This script can serve a security function because it can identify file systems that someone has left in the machine without mounting them. As noted in Chapter 9, security offenders can read data from unmounted devices, so leaving a device or file system unmounted doesn't really protect it from unauthorized access.

Examples

1. `$ mntlook /dev/hd13`

Looks to see whether there is a superblock at the device name hd13. This name refers to drive 1, third partition. To see partitions in a XENIX environment, run `fdisk`. For System V environment, run `iv`.

2. `$ mntlook /dev/fd0*`

Looks for any floppy disk file systems with any of the densities in drive 0, again a XENIX example.

3.
```
$ for DEV in /dev/*[fh]d*
> do
>         echo "checking device: $DEV"
>         mntlook $DEV
> done
```

This loop goes through all the floppy and hard disk device names one at a time. Each name is printed to the screen. Then that device is checked for a file system.

Explanation

Lines 3-7 define the include files that this program uses. You should read through these include files because they not only help you understand this program but also show you important values related to the file system.

Line 9 defines the buffer size used. The buffer is used only for error messages, so it does not need to be very big.

Line 15 defines the superblock structure. The type is filesys (see the sys/types.h include file). The size of sb is 1024 bytes on my machine. If you aren't sure about yours, it can be verified by putting in the following statement:

```
printf ("the size is %d",sizeof(sb))
```

Line 16 defines a working variable, d, and the file descriptor, dev. Line 17 declares the buffer of size BSIZ.

Lines 19-59 are one big for loop. This loop is the whole remainder of the program. It loops on the number of arguments on the command line. The index starts with 1 because the first argument, argv[0], is the command name. The arguments that are expected are file names, so the loop uses each name sequentially.

Lines 21-26 check to see whether the current argument that we are looking at starts with the - character. If so, an option has been passed, which is an error, so an error message is printed and the continue statement forces the next iteration of the for loop. Thus the program rejects options but runs anyway if it finds file names.

Assuming a file name has been found, lines 27-32 open the device file name for read only. If this open call fails, we put a message into a buffer along with the name from the command line. This buffer is passed to the error routine (provided by the system), which uses our message as the first part of the error message, then supplies a system message that defines the error. The continue goes to the next iteration of the for loop.

Lines 35-39 read the first block from the file. For the root file system, the first block is a boot record. If this read fails, an error message is printed and the loop continues.

Lines 42-46 read the second block, which should be where the superblock is located, if there is one. With the information read into a structure, we can access each piece by its constituent name.

Line 48 checks to see whether the magic number in the structure equals the magic number defined in the header file. If these match, mntlook prints the name and a valid message, the file system name (if there is one), the pack name, the block size it uses, and the magic number in hexadecimal.

In lines 53-54, we have a somewhat cryptic structure: The printf statement uses a structure of an if-then-else type to figure out which string to print. After the first line is printed, a test is made and if it is passed, the value 512 is printed. If the test fails, the value 1024 is printed. This technique is described in B. W. Kernighan and D. M. Ritchie's *The C Programming Language* (Prentice-Hall, 1978).

Line 58 closes the device and the loop goes back to the top for another device name.

Size Parameters

Now that we've looked at the relationship between devices and file systems and at some of the parameters involved with disk formats, let's look at some of the nuts and bolts of these devices. Although much of this information may seem esoteric, it can become essential under some circumstances. For example, to install UNIX on a new system, you have to segment the disk and understand how UNIX is actually situated on the disk. If you write software that does any sort of low-level disk activity, you obviously need to know what you're doing. Administrators, because they have to add extra drives to the system, need to be able to determine how many file systems there should be (meaning how many disk partitions should be made), their sizes, and how set up the file systems inside these partitions. They also may have to write or modify device drivers. Finally, disks develop problems such as bad blocks that have to be isolated and dealt with.

Block Sizes

System V is the latest development of the AT&T branch of the UNIX family tree. This means that System V is the latest of the patches to the original UNIX. These patches are intended to make it a viable and stable commercial product. To increase its robustness, changes were made to the operations involving files and their block sizes.

Disk transfers are usually in 512-byte blocks. This is the size that the disk hardware deals with. To match this, UNIX originally used 512-byte blocks internally for the file system, which probably made the code easier to write and seemed like the right thing to do. But there is no denying that UNIX can be slow!

To speed it up, the internal code now uses 1024-byte blocks. The disk has to make two accesses of 512-byte blocks, but from then on the two reads are treated as though only one read of 1024 bytes is done. The only problem with this is that some utilities report in 512-byte notation and others use the 1024-byte notation, depending on when they were written. When the disk gets too close to its limits, you really need to know which notation you're dealing with.

To better understand the block size dilemma, Table 7-3 shows what utilities report which block sizes. This information is mostly from System V running on a VAX, another System V, and XENIX. These values may change on different machines, but the idea still stands.

You can see that most utilities display blocks in 512 bytes, but utilities that are related to file systems display in 1024 bytes. Because UNIX references disk space as

Table 7-3
Block Usage of Various UNIX Commands

512 bytes/blk	1024 bytes/blk
ls -s	fdisk (partition sizes)
sum	mkfs
cpio	fsck
df	
du	

blocks, it is important to be able to calculate the exact amount of space that is left on a file system. Not many things are worse than having a huge file in vi (which uses a /tmp file for intermediate editing), then not having enough room on disk to write the vi tmp file to the real file name. This can actually happen on a personal system with a limited (say 20M) total hard disk space.

Block Calculations

Another important area relating to physical drives and logical file systems is where a specific block is located on the hard disk. This block number is calculated from the cylinder, track, and sector numbers.

A time when block numbers become important is when a bad spot develops on the disk. The bad spot is labeled by the cylinder and head numbers. What you have to do is calculate which block the bad spot falls into and enter this block in the bad block table.

The converse of this is also critical. If fsck starts to report a bad block somewhere, how do we know which cylinder, head, sector, etc., this bad block is on? This backward calculation is difficult, if not impossible. First, a block is a multiple of four numbers. Going backward, it would be hard to know which numbers to use. Also, file systems may use base/offset type of information, so block 1 on the file system is really block 1382 on the disk as a whole. Which type of information is used in a given case is also difficult to determine.

The data in the following example is very machine-specific, but other machines may use a similar type of relationship. The data is for a XENIX/DOS machine using a 20-megabyte hard disk. First we look at the given values.
Drive specifics:

1 disk = 615 cylinders or 615 cylinders/disk

1 cyl = 4 heads (tracks) or 4 heads/cylinder

Industry standard:

1 track = 17 sectors or 17 sectors/track

1 sector = 512 bytes or 512 bytes/sector

1 K = 1024 bytes = $2^{\wedge}10$

1 M = 1024 kilobytes = $2^{\wedge}20$ = 1,048,576 bytes

The drive specifics change for each drive, but the industry standard sizes of sectors per track and bytes per sector stay the same. Table 7-4 shows some examples of drive sizes.

Table 7-4
Hard Disk Sizes and Their Configurations

Number of Cylinders	Number of Heads	Megabytes
981	3	25
697	5	30
981	5	42
925	7	55
1024	8	71

You can see that the number of cylinders and number of heads vary for each size drive. The way to calculate the maximum storage of the disk is to multiply all the numbers together. The following example calculates the total byte size of the preceding data.

$$\frac{615 \text{ cyl}}{1 \text{ dsk}} * \frac{4 \text{ trk}}{1 \text{ cyl}} * \frac{17 \text{ sec}}{1 \text{ trk}} * \frac{512 \text{ byt}}{1 \text{ sec}} = 21{,}411{,}840 \text{ bytes/disk}$$

$$\frac{21411840 \text{ byt}}{1 \text{ dsk}} * \frac{1 \text{ megabyte}}{1048576 \text{ byt}} = 20.4 \text{ megabytes/disk}$$

Note that if you describe the units correctly, all but two, one top and one bottom, cancel out, leaving the correct units for the answer. Thus, in the first calculation, the cylinders, tracks, and sectors on the top and bottom cancel out, leaving units in terms of bytes per disk. Because we're dealing with so many different units, this kind of calculation (sometimes called "dimensional analysis") assures us that we know what we're talking about.

The size goes down after formatting, deallocating bad blocks, and file system overhead. But this shows that the numbers fit together.

The one important thing to watch for is the mixing of the notation. Some people refer to the number of heads per cylinder, other people refer to the number of tracks per cylinder. When each of these terms is used, the other terms change, too. Here is a cross reference that shows which relationships hold:

cylinder track sector = physical sector

cylinder head byte = block

The two phrases are exactly the same. When you use cylinder/track/sector, the end result is a physical sector. When you use the cylinder/head/byte notation, the end result is a block number. The one thing to remember is that a *head* is the same as a *track*. If you remember this, all else falls in place.

Here are some general calculations that often arise when you deal with low-level disk activities. These examples deal mostly with the drive itself and do not deal so much with UNIX. After you understand the disk information, however, you will learn more easily how UNIX interfaces with other things at this level.

1. How many tracks are there per disk?

$$\text{Solution: } \frac{615 \text{ cyl}}{1 \text{ dsk}} * \frac{4 \text{ trk}}{1 \text{ cyl}} = 2460 \text{ trk/dsk}$$

2. How many bytes per track?

$$\text{Solution: } \frac{17 \text{ sec}}{1 \text{ trk}} * \frac{512 \text{ byt}}{1 \text{ sec}} = 8704 \text{ byt/trk}$$

3. How many tracks in 1 megabyte?

$$\text{Solution: } \frac{2460 \text{ trk}}{1 \text{ dsk}} * \frac{1 \text{ dsk}}{20 \text{ mb}} = 123 \text{ trk/mb}$$

4. How many cylinders in 1 megabyte?

$$\text{Solution: } \frac{1 \text{ cyl}}{4 \text{ trk}} * \frac{2460 \text{ trk}}{20 \text{ mb}} = 30 \text{ cyl/mb}$$

$$\text{or } \frac{615 \text{ cyl}}{1 \text{ dsk}} * \frac{1 \text{ dsk}}{2460 \text{ trk}} * \frac{123 \text{ trk}}{1 \text{ mb}} = 30 \text{ cyl/mb}$$

5. Given cylinder 47, track 2, sector 4, what is the physical sector number?

Solution:

The first thing we notice is that the question asks for sectors. The units given are cyl, track, sector. How do we translate? We know that heads are the same as tracks, so 4 heads can be used rather than 4 tracks:

$$47 \text{ cyl} * \frac{4 \text{ trk}}{1 \text{ cyl}} * \frac{17 \text{ sec}}{1 \text{ trk}} + 2 \text{ trk} * \frac{17 \text{ sec}}{1 \text{ trk}} + 4 \text{ sec}$$

$$3196 \text{ sec} \qquad + \qquad 34 \text{ sec} + 4 \text{ sec}$$

$$= \text{sector } 3234$$

File Sizes

Most of the time that we spend on UNIX systems, we act as though resources are effectively infinite: For example, we don't worry about creating a file that is "too big," a not uncommon occurrence on floppy-based PCs. If we are in charge of maintaining and administering a UNIX system, however, we have to be prepared to deal with situations that run up against various limits in the system. It's always better to explore these things in nonemergency situations, so let's look at the limits on file size and what they mean.

Certain parameters are "locked" into the kernel when it is generated. One of these values is the maximum file size. This parameter gives the largest number of blocks that a file can handle. This is built into the UNIX method for using the inodes. There is a series of pointers in which the first 10 pointers in the inode point to data blocks, the next pointer points to another table, the next to a table that points to a table, and so on.

There is another run-time file size limit that each user has, and that is the ulimit number. The ulimit is set when you log in, and represents the number of 512-byte blocks that you can write to any given file. The shell has a `ulimit` command, which when typed with no arguments, prints this number. The same command also allows you to decrease your ulimit size. Only root can *increase* ulimit sizes.

One side effect of decreasing your ulimit is that you cannot increase it back to the login value. The ulimit lasts for the duration of your shell, so to reset the value to the login limit, you have to log off, then log back on again.

Another interesting thing is that if you set your own ulimit to 0, you cannot create any files! The maximum allowable file size is zero, so no files can be created. This would seem reasonable enough, but there are other contexts where a zero-length file *can* exist. Again, you have to log off and log on again to reset to your normal ulimit.

As mentioned previously, only root can increase the ulimit value. The procedure for doing this is pretty straightforward. First the ulimit value must be increased with the `ulimit` command, then a shell is executed. This new shell has the new ulimit value. If we want the system to come up with a shell with a higher ulimit, we could set up a program in the inittab (system initialization table) to do this automatically.

The following sample program achieves this ulimit change and execs a shell with the new ulimit. Remember that this program must be run with root uid.

```
1    #include <sys/ulimit.h>
2    #include <stdio.h>
3
4    main()
5    {
6            long v1, v2, v3, newlimit = 5120;
7
8            v1 = (long)ulimit(UL_GFILLIM, 0L);
9            v2 = (long)ulimit(UL_SFILLIM,newlimit);
10           v3 = (long)ulimit(UL_GFILLIM, 0L);
```

```
11
12          printf("v1: %ld      v2: %ld    ulim: %ld\n",v1,v2,v3);
13          setuid(getuid());
14          execl("/bin/sh","ulimit sh",0);
15  }
```

The ulimit value is a return value from the ulimit system call. The first call to ulimit in line 8 gets the original default value. The variable v1 holds this value. The call in line 9 sets the new ulimit to newlimit. If the call was unsuccessful, the return value in v2 is -1, and we see that in the printout from line 12. If the call was successful, the return value is the new ulimit size, which we also see. Then the call in line 10 gets the ulimit value. It is the new value or the old value depending on whether the attempt to change the ulimit was successful.

Line 13 sets the uid of the current process to the uid of the person who is running the process. This only works if the person running the shell has a lower uid than the process itself. The purpose is to allow ordinary users to run the program by giving them temporary root identity. (Don't leave the source on the system where someone could turn it into a "trap door" and recompile it—we look at this kind of security hole in Chapter 9.)

Line 14 execs a shell. The argv line of that shell is "ulimit sh". This argv string is printed if we do a "ps - ef". The shell has the new ulimit.

The ability to change the ulimit gives us the ability to find out what the largest possible file size is. Creating one or more of these maximum-size files is useful for testing purposes, such as finding out how much a floppy disk holds without overflowing or what happens when the system runs out of free data blocks. We want to find out how gracefully the system responds under these conditions.

Name: umntsys

umntsys

Function

Unmounts all the currently mounted file systems.

Synopsis

umntsys

Sample Call

umntsys   Umount all currently mounted file systems

Code for umntsys

```
1  :
2  # @(#)umntsys v1.0   Unmount all file systems   Author: Russ Sage
3
```

```
4    if [ "$#" -gt 0 ]
5      then   echo "umntsys: too many arguments"  >&2
6             echo "usage: umntsys"               >&2
7             exit 1
8    fi
9
10   /etc/mount | sed -n -e '/^\/ /d' -e 's/^.* on \(.*\) read.*/umount \1/p
     ' | sh -
```

Description

Why do we need umntsys?

There are times when you as administrator want to run the system as though it were in single-user mode. For example, you might want to change or install hard disks, and you don't want anyone accessing the device while you're working with it. You might also want the system to run in a minimal configuration so that you can isolate a problem. Because doing a shutdown and reboot is a fairly lengthy procedure, it would be good to have a way to keep the machine running but switch to single-user mode, then quickly restart multiuser mode to minimize inconvenience to users. To do this, we have to understand the concept of and use "run levels."

A run level in UNIX is a state or configuration that the machine can be in. It is really a number that defines which things go on or off and whether the system is in single or multiuser mode. The definition of what occurs at each run level is in /etc /inittab. Usually the run level changes involve going from multiuser mode (for example, level 6) to single-user mode (level S).

One side effect of going from multiuser mode to single-user mode is that all the extra file systems are unmounted. The only mounted file system is the root file system (referred to as /dev/root, /dev/hd0a, etc). This can never be unmounted. When brought back to multiuser mode, the file systems are usually remounted from the /etc/rc file.

We can simulate single-user mode by killing all the processes in the system and unmounting all the file systems. Umntsys is provided for the latter purpose.

What does umntsys *do?*

Umntsys is a series of pipelines that eventually ends up unmounting all the currently mounted file systems. The root file system is recognized as special, so no attempt is made to unmount it. Attempts to unmount file systems that aren't already mounted are also avoided.

Explanation

The first thing umntsys does is check that no arguments were passed. Because there are no options, the command line should be empty. If the number of arguments is greater than zero, that is an error, so an error message is printed to standard error and the program exits.

All the work is done in line 10. This statement is like a whisper of magic. It starts by executing the normal mount command with no arguments. Mount's default behavior produces a table of information that has all the directories and device names of the mounted file systems. A sample table looks like this:

```
/on /dev/hd0a read/write on Mon Jan 06 09:53:03 1986
/tmp on /dev/hd01 read/write on Mon Jan 06 09:53:03 1986
/usr on /dev/hd02 read/write on Mon Jan 06 09:53:03 1986
/u1 on /dev/hd03 read/write on Mon Jan 06 09:53:03 1986
/u2 on /dev/hd04 read/write on Mon Jan 06 09:53:03 1986
/u3 on /dev/hd05 read/write on Mon Jan 06 09:53:03 1986
/mnt on /dev/fd01 read/write on Mon Jan 06 09:54:41 1986
```

When a file system is mounted, both the device and directory names are needed. When they are unmounted, only the device name is used. We have to cut the device names out of the mount table and put them into the umount command. This is done with sed.

Sed is going to run with the -n option, which suppresses the default output, so nothing prints until you tell it to print. We can use this to our advantage by filtering out lines we don't want. The first editing done to the mount table is to get rid of the root file system entry because we won't want to try to unmount it. Because the directory that is the root file system is "/", we can key on that string. The expression says "From the beginning of the line, look for a forward slash (quoted because it is a special character) and a space. When the slash is found, delete it." This pattern matches the root entry only.

The next editing expression performs more magic. It uses the facility of grouping regular expressions and referring to them later by number, which you have seen used in some of our earlier scripts. The syntax is (regular cxpr) to group the characters and \n to refer to them. The trick is to single out only the device name and group it, which the sed substitute command does. The first expression says "From the beginning of the line, match any character followed by any number of the same, a blank, and the word 'on'". "Group the next characters up to a blank, the word 'read', and all the characters after that." What all this does is isolate the device name and in effect, put it in a temporary variable so that it can be referred to later.

The second part of the substitution creates a new line to replace the whole line. This line consists of the word "umount", a blank, then the grouped expression number 1, which is the temporary variable holding the device name. This turned the whole mount table (except entry for root) into a series of umount commands with the device name arguments. The final output looks like this:

```
umount /dev/hd0a
umount /dev/hd01
umount /dev/hd02
umount /dev/hd03
```

```
umount /dev/hd04
umount /dev/hd05
umount /dev/fd01
```

These commands are now piped to another shell! ("sh -"). The "-" tells the shell to read its commands from the stdin, which in this case is our piped unmount commands. This unmounts all the file systems.

Name: lrgf

lrgf   Creates the largest file possible

Function

Keeps writing to a file until the file size boundary is encountered.

Synopsis

lrgf

Sample Call

lrgf   Find file size boundary

Code for lrgf

```
1    char id[] = "@(#) lrgf v1.0   Create the largest file   Author: Russ
Sage ";
2
3    #include <errno.h>
4    #include <fcntl.h>
5    #include <stdio.h>
6    #include <sys/ulimit.h>
7
8    #define FSIZ 512
9    #define BSIZ 1024
10
11   long ulimit();
12   char buf[BSIZ];
13
14   main()
15   {
16           register int n, fd, bcnt;
17           char file[FSIZ];
18
19           for (bcnt=0; bcnt<BSIZ; bcnt++)
20                   buf[bcnt]='x';
21
22           printf("\nMax file size: %ld bytes\n\n",ulimit(UL_GFILLIM,0L)*
512);
23
```

```
24          printf("filename to write to: ");
25          scanf("%s",file);
26          printf("\n");
27
28          if ((fd=open(file,O_RDWR|O_CREAT|O_TRUNC, 0644)) < 0)
29          {
30                  perror("\nopen");
31                  exit(1);
32          }
33
34          for (bcnt=0; ;bcnt++)
35          {
36                  if ((n=write(fd, buf, BSIZ)) < 0)
37                  {
38                          perror("\nwrite");
39                          break;
40                  }
41                  printf("block count: %d    bytes written: %d\r",bcnt,n);
42          }
43          printf("\nend of program\n");
44  }
```

Description

Why do we need lrgf?

As described previously, we need to know what happens when UNIX hits limits, not only file size limits, but all kinds of limits. Some of the more familiar limits are the number of processes that you can run, the number of total processes in the system, the number of files that you are allowed to have open, the number of free blocks, the number of inodes, the number of directories deep that still work, and so on.

What we need is a general program that creates a file which is the largest possible. We can then use this file for testing various file-related limits.

What does lrgf do?

Lrgf is a program that creates a file of the maximum file size. It does this by writing to a file until the write command fails. This signifies that the file will accept no more data and is at the boundary.

When invoked, lrgf prints out a message stating the total number of bytes that you can put in a file. This value is calculated from the ulimit value, so it is specific to you and the shell you are currently working with.

Next you are prompted for the file name. This name can be anywhere that you have write permission on the system. One way to test the hard disk is to write one of these big files into each disk partition, then test the individual file systems. As the program runs, you see a message string that is constantly being updated. The printout has the number of total blocks written and the number of bytes that were written for each attempt to write. Each time lrgf writes to the file, it writes 1024 bytes. Depending on what your ulimit value is, the number of bytes written at the very end of the file may not be a full 1K. The printout is constantly being printed on the same line, refreshing the screen over the old value. This is accomplished by printing only a carriage return rather than a newline each time.

When the program cannot write any more data, a final block count message is printed. This reflects the total number of blocks written to that file.

Examples

1. ```
$ lrgf
/dev/rfd0
```

Enter the device name in response to the prompt for the file name to write to. Doing this makes lrgf continually write to the floppy drive in raw mode, thus checking the device driver to see whether it recognizes the end of the floppy device. This is important to know for the cpio command, which relies on the device driver to tell it when to stop and prompt for the next medium.

2. ```
$ lrgf
/usr/tmp/lrg
```

This makes a file on the /usr file system. Most XENIX systems put /usr on a separate file system from the root file system. By making the file on /usr/tmp, we can check the situation on this frequently used file system.

3. ```
$ lrgf
/tmp/lrg
```

This takes space on the root file system (if you don't have /tmp on a file system of its own). It won't take many of these files to consume all the free blocks on the root file system.

4. ```
$ lrgf
/mnt/lrg
```

This make the file on the floppy disk, assuming that the floppy has a file system on it, and has been mounted to the /mnt directory.

5. ```
$ F=0
$ while :
> do
>   echo -r "--> Making file $F <--"
>   ./lrgf <<-!
> $F
>   !
>   echo
>   F='expr $F + 1'
> done
```

This loop runs lrgf an infinite number of times. The counter is variable F. F must be set to zero first, so the shell treats it as a number instead of a string. First the message is printed telling which file name is being created. The first file name is 0. Lrgf is run using the input from the "here document" (that is, the script itself). The $F is the input to the question asked about the file name. The F variable is
```

incremented and lrgf is called again. The file names are 0, 1, 2, and so on. This continues until there is no more free space. This is not something you want to do a lot, but for testing provides a nice tool to consume free space. If you want to see what your system does when it runs out of free blocks, try it.

Explanation

Lines 3-6 include any necessary header files. These files have definitions and labels necessary to the program.

Lines 8 and 9 define the buffer sizes for file names and the buffer that is written to disk. BSIZ can be adjusted if the program runs too slowly. You might want to increase BSIZ to 4096 so that not as many writes have to be performed.

Line 11 defines the return value from the ulimit system call as a long integer. Line 12 allocates the buffer that is to be written. This buffer is outside the main part of the program because of the size limitation inside functions. In the main program block, the largest automatic array you can have is equal to the size of your stack. You can get around this by declaring the buffer as a static variable in main. We choose to move it outside the main and not have to declare it static.

Line 16 declares some working variables. Notice that they are put into registers. This makes for faster execution and smaller code.

Line 17 allocates the buffer that you type the file name into.

Lines 19 and 20 initialize the write buffer with the character "x" so that when the file is created, we can see characters in it.

Line 22 prints the ulimit size for your process. Notice that the ulimit call returns the number of blocks, so we have to multiply that number by 512. The result is the total number of bytes the file can be.

Lines 24-26 prompt for the file name, read it, and fix up the screen. Lines 28-32 open the file name to get a file descriptor. The file is opened as read-write, creating it if necessary and truncating it if it already exists. If the open fails, an error message is printed and the program exits.

Lines 34-42 perform the writing. The for loop is infinite because the middle of the statement has no check value. The bcnt variable keeps getting incremented as the writes occur.

Line 36 does the write to the file. If it fails, an error message is printed, and the break statement breaks out of the for loop. Line 41 prints the number of writes that have occurred and the number of bytes written. Notice that this print statement contains a carriage return (\r) and not a newline. This allows the cursor to stay on the same line and write over the old number. The screen doesn't scroll, so it is easy on the eyes. The loop continues until the write system call fails and the break statement kicks out of it. When this happens, execution continues to line 43, which prints "end of program". An ls -l of the file that was written shows how many bytes the max file size is, which should match the number that the program told you in the first line.

This chapter has presented just a handful of the possible explorations into the inner workings of UNIX file systems and devices. Some of the things we have shown may not apply to your version of UNIX or to your hardware configuration, or may be different on your system. The principles hold, however, and you can use them as a launch pad for your own investigations.

8
UNIX Communications

Physical connectivity
Micros to UNIX
UNIX to micros
Modem usage and data capturing
UNIX-to-UNIX public access areas
Network security
Uucp debugging

`cuchk`	check for a free cu line
`talk`	talk to another system
`uust`	uucp status and housekeeping
`uutrans`	transfer a file tree from UNIX to UNIX

UNIX
Communications

Introduction

In this chapter, we look at the communication facilities of UNIX. Although communications in the MS-DOS world usually are limited to a "black box" (software packages and fairly standard modems), UNIX communications is more complex. UNIX offers several levels of communication including file transfers, remote login, remote mail, and extensive message systems that can link hundreds of UNIX systems.

However, most UNIX systems don't have conveniently packaged, menu-driven communications facilities. Rather, they have complex system commands and many files to maintain. Usually, more details of modem configuration and use have to be mastered as well. We offer both theoretical background and practical suggestions, plus tools to help you master this aspect of UNIX and get communications working on your own system. We cover not only direct communication between machines, but also with remote terminals and modems.

First, we cover physical connections, which is the first step in setting up a communications link. We look at the model of an RS-232-C connection and how to wire a direct connection.

The next area we look at is calling UNIX from a micro. We talk about what kinds of protocols are available and which are best to use.

The next area we cover is how to use a modem from a UNIX system to call other systems, like bulletin boards and non-UNIX systems. You can learn how to find all the modem connections on a system, lock onto the serial port, and command the modem. When calling another system, you can capture all the data that comes across your screen and keep it in a file for future use. The scripts in this section (cuchk and talk) monitor the communication line for availability and establish the connection with the modem.

The last area we look at is UNIX-to-UNIX communications with uucp. We see how and where to transfer files between systems, how security files govern the uucp environment, and ways to debug the uucp file transfer mechanism. The scripts presented here are uust for uucp housekeeping chores and uutrans for copying a directory tree structure from one system to another.

Physical Connectivity

Most machines running UNIX have one or more serial ports. These ports are the eyes and ears that let the system communicate with the outside world. They can be used with any RS-232-C device and for communication or controlling. In this section, we look at how to wire an RS-232-C connection to support UNIX-to-UNIX, terminal-to-UNIX, and modem-to-UNIX connections.

Let's start by looking at the basic RS-232-C model in figure 8-1. This model shows how two machines and/or terminals can communicate with each other, either with modems over telephone lines or via a direct (hardwired) connection. Although we mostly talk in the following discussion in terms of telephone connections, the same basic principles apply to direct connections, except that the data communication equipment (DCE) devices aren't needed.

Figure 8-1
Standard RS-232-C Connection Model

On each end is terminating equipment, which is called DTE (data terminating equipment). A DTE can be a terminal, such as a VT-100, or a CPU for a micro, mini, or mainframe.

Each DTE must use a DCE device, commonly known as a modem, to modulate and demodulate the signals that pass over the phone lines. Each DTE uses pin number 2 to transmit data and pin number 3 to receive data. Because the pin 2 transmission on each machine is received on pin 3 of the other machine, a crossover occurs through the phone lines between the DCEs.

The wiring and signal handling between a DTE and a DCE are what the RS-232-C standard is all about. A hardware protocol allows the DTE to use the DCE to send and receive data with another DTE.

The cable that physically connects the DTE and DCE is called a "straight through" cable. It allows the DTE to send commands (or pin signals) to the DCE and the DCE to send commands back to the DTE. The connection from one DCE to the DCE of the other machine occurs over the regular telephone lines.

The reason that the DCEs are needed is because the DTEs are digital and the phone lines are analog. The only way to send digital information over analog lines is to encode the digital information into an analog signal, send that signal over the phone lines, then decode the analog signal back into digital information.

Connecting without DCEs

If your machines are so close together (within 50 feet) that you don't need a modem, you can use a "null modem" cable in place of the DCE. The null modem cable simulates the same protocol as a DCE, but does not require the modem to be present for communications. The main thing the null modem connection does is force the crossover between the transmit signals and the receive signals. Figure 8-2 shows the general architecture for a non-DCE connection.

Figure 8-2
Null Modem Configuration

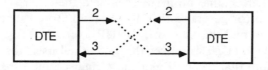

To make a connection that simulates a DCE without using a DCE requires some manipulation of the signals. This manipulation is also standardized in the null-modem cable. Let's look at this cable as shown schematically in figure 8-3 and see how it simulates the DCE signals.

Figure 8-3
RS-232-C Null Modem Cabling

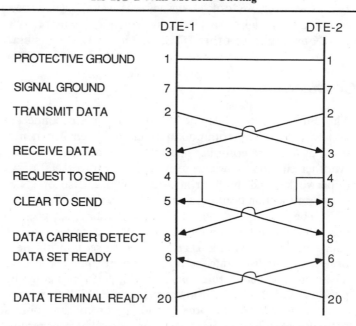

Lines 1 and 7 are used for chassis and signal ground, respectively. Lines 2 and 3 are crossed so that when one side talks, the other listens. Both sides can talk at the same time, called full-duplex operation, if we use different sets of wires.

To simulate the control signals, lines 4, 5, and 8 are connected as in figure 8-3. Every time DTE-1 raises (puts a signal on) the Request to Send line, it gets back a Clear to Send, which indicates the other side is ready for data. Then by forcing the Data Carrier Detect line high, it signals the other side that data is coming. This orderly "hardware handshaking" ensures that no data is sent until the other side is ready.

Lines 6 and 20 are connected to supply the last of the null modem control signals. As long as the DTE is awake (Data Terminal Ready, line 20), the other side thinks you are a modem that is still awake (Data Set Ready, line 6). With 6 and 20 wired the way they are, every time you pull your cable out of your machine, or flip to another channel on a switcher box, the other side loses your awake signal and hangs up (or generates the HUP signal). To create a cable that does not hang up when you pull the plug (or NOHUP), wire the DTR output into the DSR input on the same DTE. This makes the system tell itself that the modem is always ready.

Note that this null modem wiring scheme is recommended, but no hard and fast standard exists, so don't expect every null modem to be the same. Each installation usually tailors its null modems for the specific environment or action that it wants, like having a nohup versus a hup connection.

Now that we know the two different ways to connect machines, we can look at the ways that communication takes place and what types of cabling we should use.

Micro or Terminal to UNIX

In this section, we look at the various ways that microcomputers and standalone terminals can talk to a UNIX system. Our assumption is that one DTE is non-UNIX and calls the other DTE, which is a UNIX system.

Direct Connection

The simplest setup has the terminal or micro connected directly to the UNIX system. This is very common in development environments where a UNIX system is used as a cross compiler and the resultant code is downloaded to the micro. Another situation is where terminals are on workers' desks and are used to handle paperwork, send mail, print documents, and so on. See figure 8-4 for a typical direct connection configuration.

The typical scenario for a terminal connection goes something like this: A user uses a terminal, for example, a DEC VT100, to log into a UNIX system on a direct connection. The terminal DTE needs to be set up with the correct internal configuration, including baud rate, start and stop bits, number of data bits, and parity (if any). These are common settings on terminals, performed either by flipping dip (dual in-line package) switches or by using terminal "SETUP" firmware.

A micro, on the other hand, needs to run some sort of communications software to drive the hardware correctly. These programs usually have menus or

Figure 8-4
Direct Connection for Terminals and Micros to UNIX

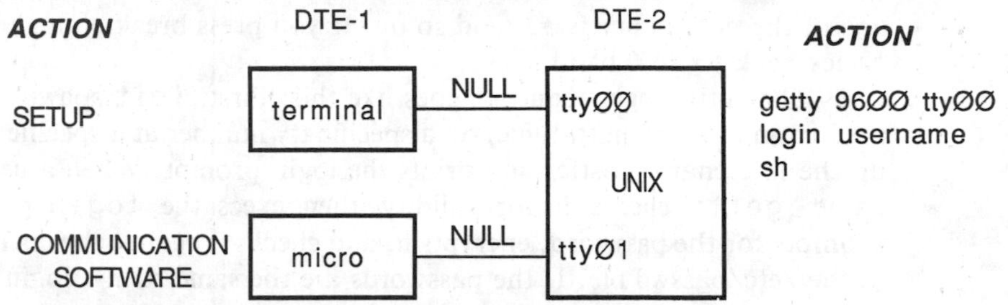

some other way to specify the parameters, which are the same as for terminals. Indeed, software packages are available that provide complete or almost complete emulations of popular terminals such as the VT-100. The communications software that you use is not set up specifically for UNIX but for the RS-232-C signal handling, which usually is not dependent on whether the connection is direct or through a modem.

The cabling between direct connections from terminals (and micros) and a UNIX system must be a null modem. When there is no DCE, a null modem cable is used.

The UNIX DTE is configured to have a `getty` (which originally meant "get teletype") running on a specific port and looking for someone trying to log in. This `getty` program (explained in `init`(M) and `getty`(M)) prints the "login:" prompt and reads the line for character input.

For direct connections, the `getty` process can be run at 9600 baud, so users can take advantage of this speed, which is considerably faster than the 1200, or sometimes 2400 baud, usable over ordinary phone lines. Depending on how the `gettydefs` file is set up, you usually can force the `getty` speed to go to another rate by pressing the break key. Break is not a character but a signal on the line that lasts for a certain length of time. The UNIX device drivers recognize this signal and act accordingly. The actual method by which the `getty` goes through the different baud rates is beyond the scope of this book. The important thing to know is that if the `getty` is running at 9600 baud and you are using a terminal set for 1200 baud, you need to roll getty out of 9600 baud and through all the intermediate baud rates until it gets to 1200 baud. Keep pressing the break key until `getty` is at the speed you need. The following data is from XENIX System V gettydefs, which shows how one baud rate is linked to the next.

```
5# B9600 PARENB CS7 OPOST ONLCR # B9600 SANE IXANY #Login: #1
4# B4800 PARENB CS7 OPOST ONLCR # B4800 SANE IXANY #Login: #5
3# B2400 PARENB CS7 OPOST ONLCR # B2400 SANE IXANY #Login: #4
2# B1200 CS8 OPOST ONLCR # B1200 SANE IXANY #Login: #3
1# B300 CS7 OPOST ONLCR # B300 SANE IXANY #Login: #2
```

In the preceding case, specifying #5 in the inittab (or ttys file for XENIX and System III users) spawns a `getty` that runs at 9600 baud. If you press break, the next in line is number 1 (as indicated at the end of the #5 line). If you press break again, the next in line is #2, and so on. If you press break enough times, the getty cycles back to 9600 baud.

The entire login sequence goes like this: First, `init` spawns a `getty` (initiated from the /etc/inittab file) on a specific tty number at a specific speed. This sets up the line characteristics and prints the login prompt. When a user types a login name, `getty` checks it for validity, then execs the `login` program. `Login` prompts for the password, encrypts it, and checks it against the encrypted password in the /etc/passwd file. If the passwords are the same string, login execs a `shell` that prints the shell prompt and reads your commands from the terminal. The actual shell run is determined from the passwd file, given by the entry for that login name. The following entry is for my login name:

```
russ:j9egLecqEpXLg:201:51:Russ Sage:/usr/russ:/bin/shV
```

The shell run in this case is a system V shell, one of the new shells from AT&T.

Remote Connection

The flip side of direct connection is the remote connection via a modem line, shown in figure 8-5. The setup for the terminal or micro configuration is almost exactly the same except for the baud rate at which the terminal runs. This needs to be 1200 baud for most modems.

Figure 8-5
Remote Connection for Terminals and Micros to UNIX

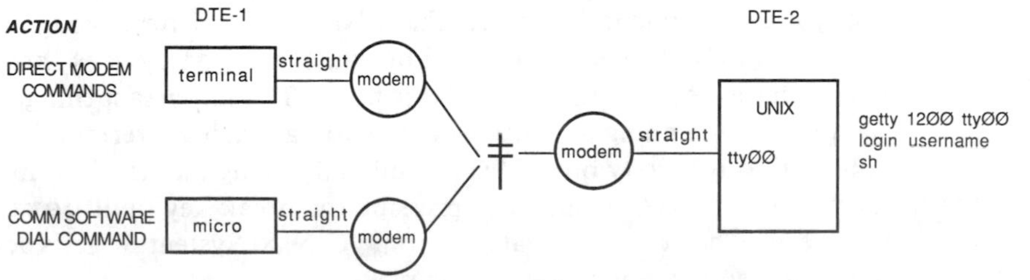

The terminal (when set up for 1200 baud) talks directly to the modem. This involves modem commands to dial, hang up, and so on. The micro, running communications software, usually has a dial command that generates a command to the modem. The cabling between the terminal/micro and the modem should be a straight cable. The modem also has a telephone cable that goes into the phone system.

As far as UNIX is concerned, the login sequence is exactly the same as previously described, except the initial `getty` speed usually is 1200 baud to match the modem speed. If it is not, use break to roll the `getty` around to 1200 baud.

Once all configuration has been completed, how do the terminal and micro communicate with the UNIX system? When logged in, the termcap database is used to handle screen management. See the previous chapter on how to generate a termcap entry if you don't have one already. Terminals (because they are usually just hardware) are not very flexible or user friendly. They don't have much capability beyond logging in and running some programs. The micro, on the other hand, has great flexibility and can add much to the user interface of a UNIX system.

Communications programs usually have a RAM buffer that you can use to capture data and put it on a disk. By using this buffer, you may not need to use any special UNIX commands to transfer files. You can give the command to turn your data capture on, then display the file to the screen (by using a command such as `cat` or listing the file in an editor), unless the file is too big for the buffer.

Program files or other files that require 100 percent transmission accuracy have to be transferred explicitly using error-checking protocols, however, because phone lines or even direct connections can have "noise," and one wrong character can make a program useless. Some protocols supported in the micro world have been ported to UNIX machines, such as `xmodem` and the `kermit` program.

Of the two protocols, xmodem is the most widely used in the micro world and is supported by nearly all bulletin board systems. Kermit is very common in the UNIX world, is growing in popularity in the micro world, and is available for nearly every model of micro for little more than the cost of the disk.

Using these protocols, a micro can send and receive files from a UNIX system without your having to worry about data errors. To learn more about these protocols, ask administrators of your UNIX system and other micro users that have these same needs.

UNIX to Micros

The opposite situation from that described previously is calling from a UNIX system to a non-UNIX system, be it a micro or mainframe. To do this requires knowledge of how to get the serial port, command the modem to dial a number, then log onto the destination system. A model of this situation is shown in figure 8-6.

The DTE-1, or UNIX system, uses a straight cable to the modem. No `getty` should be running on the serial line, which is tty00 in our example. The `getty` program is only for logging into the system, not calling out. The `cu` program controls the serial port on the UNIX machine. The non-UNIX system has some sort of login sequence. If you are calling a micro that is running bulletin board software, the non-UNIX system usually asks for your name, city, etc., and a password. (You normally can login as a new user and establish a password, but this varies with the policy of the bulletin board). If the other system is a mainframe, its login sequence must to be known in advance.

As mentioned previously, the main program that UNIX provides for calling out is `cu(1)`, for "call unix." In practice, as in our example, the other system

Figure 8-6
UNIX Calling to a Non-UNIX System

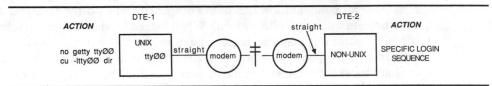

doesn't have to be UNIX, so the program perhaps would be better described as "connect onto a UNIX port."

The cu program opens the serial port and puts a "lock file" into the /usr /spool/uucp directory. This lock file simply indicates by its presence that the port is in use and prevents other users from accessing it. You have this exclusive access until you quit cu and relinquish the port to someone else.

When cu is called, two processes are started: a reader (which reads the serial port) and a writer (which writes to the serial port). When you type characters to the cu program, it checks them for any special characters that it must react to. Usually cu responds right away to special cu command characters. Otherwise, the characters are passed on through the serial port to whatever is on the other side. In addition to passing characters back and forth, cu provides many functions that a micro communications package would supply.

Finding Modems on a System

If you are on a large mainframe, you need to find out which ports on your system are connected to a modem and outside line. If you are the administrator, you need to know how to configure these lines yourself.

The first place to start is /usr/lib/uucp/L-devices. This is the main file that defines which ports are used and how they are used. Following is an example printout showing the ports:

```
ACU    cul0    cua0    1200
DIR    tty00   0       300
DIR    tty00   0       1200
DIR    tty00   0       2400
DIR    tty00   0       4800
DIR    tty00   0       9600
```

In L-devices, each port is defined as either a direct connection (DIR) or a special device known as an automatic call unit (ACU). We talk about call units later. For now, we only need to look at the DIR entries. Cu uses the direct entries and uucp uses the ACU entries. This makes especially easy the identification of each serial port as to how it is referenced, at what baud rate it runs, and if we can call out on it.

The L-devices data shows, for example, that the tty00 serial port is used as a direct callout line. The baud rates that you are allowed to call out with are 300 through 9600. This is the entire spectrum of baud rates normally used, with the higher rates used for direct connection to other machines rather than a modem.

What about modem lines that come *in* to the machine? A way to find these is to look in the /etc directory. The two files dialin and dialup define which tty lines go through the login secondary password sequence for remote users. These tty lines are only for dialing into the system and usually cannot be used for dialing out.

Using and Configuring the Line

Now that we know which line to call out on, we need a call command. The latest System V updates to cu give it more calling power than earlier versions. We usually don't need this much power, so our command lines are a little more primitive and should run on just about every cu around.

The basic options we have are to select the line number (that is, the tty device), the speed at which to operate, and whether to connect directly to the device for manual dialing or have it dial the number automatically. The easiest way is to have cu dial the number, but if this is not available, you should connect directly to the modem. The following example connects directly to the device and manually commands the modem to dial a number. The modem, in this case, is a Hayes 1200 Smartmodem, a very common configuration. If you have a modem that isn't "Hayes compatible," you have to look up the equivalent control sequences in your documentation.

```
$ cu -ltty00 dir          # get the terminal line direct, 1200 baud
Connected                 # cu acknowledges
ATdt555-1212              # Attention modem, dial using touch
                          # tone the following number
CONNECT                   # modem acknowledges connection
<cr>                      # send carriage return to destination system
Welcome to Micro BBS      # get initial banner from micro
     .
     .
carry on a session with remote system
     .
     .
exit                      # log off micro system, OR
+++                       # optional if you don't want to log off,
                          # escape out of modem connect
OK                        # modem response of escape
AThO                      # tell modem to hang up the phone
OK                        # modem response
~.                        # terminate cu connection
```

To tell cu to dial automatically, use a different syntax on the command line. We use the ACU, or automatic call unit, to generate the call. The actual dial command is generated by the program /usr/lib/uucp/dial. A sample call looks like this:

```
$ cu -acua0 555-1212
```

Changing Baud Rates

Smartmodems can operate at 300 and 1200 baud. By default, the cu program connects to the serial port at 1200 baud. If you connect by default, verify the baud by escaping from the cu connection and using stty to display the baud rate

```
~!stty < /dev/tty00
```

which should print the regular stty settings for serial port /dev/tty00. The baud rate should be 1200. Smartmodems kick down to 300 baud automatically when answering the phone. When calling out, you have two different ways that you can kick the modem down to 300 baud.

The first way is to force cu to open the line at 300 baud by putting the 300 in the cu command line. Note that when you use an alternate speed (anything other than 1200 baud), the entry for that baud rate *must* be in the L-devices file *and* on the cu command line, as in the following example:

```
$ cu -ltty00 -s300 dir
```

The second method is trickier but ultimately provides more flexibility. We can call cu with the default value of 1200, then escape from cu and call the stty program to force the baud rate of the serial port to 300 baud. This must be done after you cu onto the line. The baud rate change only lasts until you close the line (that is, exit cu), at which time the port is reinitialized. An example session follows:

```
$ cu -ltty00 dir              # grab the line at 1200 baud
Connected                     # cu acknowledges
~!stty 300 < /dev/tty00       # escape out of cu and force
                              # the tty line to 300 baud
```

Note that this method does *not* require an entry in L-devices for 300 baud because we are manipulating the serial port outside the domain of cu.

As a side note, escaping from cu is just like escaping from any other UNIX command. You can escape to run a specific command, like

```
~!echo "you can run any command here"
```

or you can escape to a shell and work like you always do.

```
~!sh
```

Remember, however, that you are still cud to the serial port and the phone is still connected to the remote system until you manually log off or hang up the phone, or the remote system times out and hangs up the phone.

Capturing Data

Now, we can find a modem, connect to the serial line, and dial another system. If we are calling a bulletin board, we might want to capture files for later reference. The cu program does not provide this function. As we have noted, micros usually do this with a RAM buffer that is saved to disk when it fills up, but UNIX does not operate this way.

The easiest way I have found to capture data from another system under UNIX is to pipe all the output to a terminal through the UNIX tee command. Any input from your keyboard is not captured, but all stdout is captured in the tee file. Here is how it looks:

```
cu -ltty00 dir | tee capture_file
```

One of the consequences of capturing incoming information this way is that all the carriage returns printed from the remote system are captured in the tee file. You see these as "^M" at the end of every line in the file. To get rid of all the carriage returns easily, try this ed sequence:

```
ed capture_file
1,$s/^M//g
w
q
```

For every line in the whole file (1,$), replace a carriage return (^M) with nothing (//). Do this for any number of carriage returns on a single line (g for globally on a line). You can get the control-M into the substitution string either by entering a backslash (\) and a real carriage return keystroke or, in vi, use the control-V prefix to allow entering of control characters. After editing, write the file and quit ed.

Of course, you can put the whole thing into a shell script for convenience.

Tools for Communications Lines

The two utilities that we present here are involved with acquisition and access of the serial port. You are notified immediately when the line is free and can take control of it with very few keystrokes.

Name: cuchk

cuchk   Cu check—check for a free cu line

279

Function

Polls the process status table looking for cu processes. When the processes go away, a message is displayed on your screen and the program terminates.

Synopsis

cuchk   Tell me when cu is free to use

Sample Call

cuchk

Code for cuchk

```
1    :
2    # a(#) cuchk v1.0   Check for a free cu line   Author: Russ Sage
3
4    if [ "$#" -gt "0" ]
5      then  echo "cuchk: too many arguments" >&2
6            echo "usage: cuchk"                >&2
7            exit 1
8    fi
9
10   while :
11   do
12           ps -e | fgrep cu > /dev/null  \
13                 && sleep 5              \
14                 || { echo "\ncu is free"; exit; }
15   done &
```

Description

Why do we need cuchk?

Most UNIX systems seem to be short on serial ports. When there is only one output port for six or seven people, it becomes a very valuable item. Experience seems to show that if you don't get a port right away, you have to wait for it again and again, and you don't know how long the current user is going to stay on a particular port. Instead of wasting time checking repeatedly for a free port, why not let the machine tell you when the port is free?

What does cuchk do?

Cuchk, when invoked, lives in the background of the machine. It is powered by a forever loop to keep it running. It watches the system by looking through all the processes that are running. If it sees a cu process (which may or may not be the port we want), it sleeps for 5 seconds and looks again. If there are no cu processes running on the machine, it prints the message "cu is free" and dies by itself. This way we do not have to manually keep track of cuchk, it can run by itself and go away by itself. This makes sense because the whole purpose of the utility would be defeated if it, itself, had to be checked periodically!

Explanation

Lines 4-8 do the error checking. Because `cuchk` responds to no options, the command line should have zero parameters. Any more than zero parameters is too many, and this is an error.

Lines 10-15 do the forever-while loop. Notice that the ampersand in line 15 automatically puts `cuchk` into the background because there's no reason why you would want it to be in foreground.

Line 12 does a "ps -e", which gives the status for all significant user processes and pipes that data through `fgrep`. `Fgrep` then looks for any occurrence of "cu". We hope that this only matches the cu processes we are looking for. It could, however, match something totally unexpected, like "picuser" or some similar made up name. The output from `fgrep` is redirected to /dev/null to get rid of it. All we really want is the exit status of `fgrep`, which tells us if it found an occurrence or not.

At the end of line 12 is a backslash character, which tells the shell that the next physical line is really part of the same program line and to include it as part of line 12 instead of executing it by itself. Breaking up long physical lines into lines with backslashes allows us to have nicely indented, more readable source code.

Line 13 is executed if the `fgrep` is successful (that is, if it gives a return status of zero). This means that an entry with "cu" was found, thus `cu` is in use and is not available at this time. The process then sleeps for 5 seconds. When it wakes up, execution continues at line 10, repeating the forever loop, and the process checking continues.

If `fgrep` did not find "cu" (returned an exit status of nonzero), line 14 is executed, which prints the message that `cu` is free and exits. We thus know immediately when the `cu` line is open, so we can grab it as soon as possible.

Name: `talk`

talk   Talk to the serial port

Function

Executes the command line to set up the serial port to talk to another system.

Synopsis

talk [-bBAUD] [-l] [-tTTY] [-u]

Options:
   -b set a new baud rate
   -l log all incoming data
   -t use another tty port
   -u use UNIX baud rate of 9600

Sample Call

talk -6300 -t01 -l

   Talk to serial port tty01 at 300 baud and log the output to a text file

Code for `talk`

```
1    :
2    # @(#) talk v1.0    Talk to the serial port    Author: Russ Sage
3
4    BAUD="1200"
5    TTY="tty11"
6    PIPE=""
7
8    for ARG in $@
9    do
10           case $ARG in
11           -b*) BAUD="'echo $ARG|cut -c3-'";;
12           -l)  echo "logging in /tmp/talk.$$"
13                PIPE="| tee /tmp/talk.$$";;
14           -t*) TTY="tty'echo $ARG|cut -c3-'";;
15           -u)  BAUD="9600";;
16           *)   echo "talk: invalid argument $ARG"            >&2
17                echo "usage: talk [-bBAUD] [-l] [-tTTY] [-u]" >&2
18                echo "        -b   baud rate"                  >&2
19                echo "        -l   log the output"             >&2
20                echo "        -t   use another tty"            >&2
21                echo "        -u   9600 baud to UNIX"          >&2
22                exit 1;;
23           esac
24   done
25
26   eval cu -s$BAUD -l$TTY dir $PIPE
```

Environment Variables

ARG	Argument from the command line
BAUD	Baud rate to pass to cu
PIPE	Contains the string which creates the data capture pipe
TTY	The tty port number to use

Description

Why do we need `talk`?

Logging into a remote system expands the horizon of your computing capabilities. With UNIX becoming more and more prevalent in the micro world, dial-up UNIX systems soon will be everywhere. In addition, you can call lots of micro bulletin board systems from your UNIX system.

What we need is a good interface to control the modem line and make it easier to use. We need to capture data if possible, alter baud rates, and change terminal ports if necessary. All this is done by `talk`.

What does talk *do?*

Talk generates a cu command line based on a default configuration. This configuration is 1200 baud, connected to the terminal line /dev/tty11 (SCO XENIX serial port 1) with no data capturing. All default parameters can be modified in the source file, and the tty line has to be set up for your specific system.

If you want to alter the baud rate, use -b option with the speed you want (assuming it's a standard speed supported by cu). For example, "talk -b2400" would set a speed of 2400 baud. The speed specified is passed on down to the cu command to directly alter your connection.

Note: This speed must be defined in L-devices file.

If you want to capture all the data printed to your screen, turn on the logging option with -l. The capture file is /tmp/talk.$$, where $$ is the unique process id of your currently running shell. This file name is printed when the option is invoked so that you see it on your screen. The unique file name means that you won't inadvertently lose log files from previous sessions (or at least, you have only a very small chance of doing so.)

If you have an optional serial port with a modem or you want to connect to any line you please, use the -t option. Pass the tty number along with the -t, which is then passed down to the cu command. This is a very useful option if you have lots of different cu lines.

If you do not use your serial line for modem use, but have a direct connection to another UNIX system, the -u option sets your baud rate to 9600 baud immediately. Note that this could also be achieved by saying -b9600, but the -u option is easier to type and remember.

Examples

1. $ talk -l -t12

Connect with the secondary serial port and capture all the data that comes across the screen.

2. $ talk -u

Connect with the primary serial port using 9600 baud. Do not set up data capture.

3. $ talk -b2400 -t04 -u

Watch out! First BAUD is set to 2400, but -u came later, which reset BAUD to 9600. Terminal tty04 is used.

4. $ talk -u -l -b4800

Watch out again! First the line is set up as a direct connect at 9600 baud. Then the logging is turned on. Last, BAUD is reset to 4800 from 9600. If the getty you are cuing to is really 9600 baud, you have to kick it down, if possible, by hitting ~ %b to generate the break signal.

Explanation

Lines 4-6 set up the default action of talk. This is totally configurable by editing the source file. The nice part is that if this is the configuration you use most, all you have to do is type "talk", with no options.

Line 4 initializes BAUD to 1200, for the default modem speed. Line 5 initializes TTY to tty11, which is the first serial port in hardware. This is usually tty00, but SCO XENIX has a virtual console where tty02-tty10 are separate screens accessed from the one console device. If this isn't true of your system, put in the correct TTY here. Line 6 initializes PIPE to null because the pipe is used for data logging, and the default is to not capture data.

Lines 8-24 are a for loop that runs through all the command line arguments. Lines 10-23 use a case statement keyed to the option to perform the desired functions.

Line 11 checks to see whether the option starts with a -b, followed by anything else. If so, the characters following the -b are cut out and put into the BAUD variable. Notice that this requires you to type "-b2400" and does not allow "-b 2400".

Line 12 checks to see whether you want logging turned on. If so, the log file is echoed to the screen, and the PIPE variable is set to pipe stdout to the UNIX `tee` program. `Tee` is a general purpose pipe splitter that can be used to send a copy of the data stream to a particular destination without affecting the main pipeline. In this case, we use it to send a copy of the data that is coming through the serial port to the screen and to our log file in /tmp/talk/.$$. (If you think of a water pipe with a T-shaped joint, you can visualize what is going on.)

Line 14 checks to see whether the option started with a -t. If so, the tty number is cut out. Any tty value can be passed here, but remember that the tty number must also be in the /usr/lib/uucp/L-devices file. This is how `cu` knows that this tty device is a legal port.

Line 15 checks to see whether you are going to a direct-connect UNIX system. If so, the baud rate is automatically set to 9600 baud for fast terminal throughput.

Lines 16-22 do the error checking. If any option passed on the command line did not match any of the first case patterns, it is caught here, the error messages are printed, and the script exits.

Line 26 is the magic line. Because all the shell variables have been set to their appropriate values, we can use them on the command line to substitute in the necessary values. First, the `eval` command is used. This expands any variable names that have been put as values into our variables.

In this case, we construct a complete `cu` command line: The speed is in BAUD, the line is in TTY, and the connection is direct. If we are not logging, PIPE is null, which gets thrown away by shell parsing. However, if PIPE has our command for piping to the log file, `eval` makes this effective by actually doing the pipe we told it to.

UNIX to UNIX

Now let's look at full UNIX to UNIX communications. This is one area where UNIX has been ahead of its time. The `uucp` system allows multiple machines to be linked to create what is in some respects a virtual environment that lets you work on any machine. The basic functionality of the network includes remote login (`cu`(1)), remote command execution (uux(1)), electronic mail (mail(1)), file transfer (uucp(1), uucico(1)), and system node recognition (uname(1) and uuname(1)).

Before we look at implementation of UNIX-to-UNIX communications, let's consider some of the ways that UNIX machines can be connected physically in a work environment.

Connecting UNIX Machines

In work environments, machine configurations are constantly being changed for testing purposes, hardware changes, office moves, and so on. Planning the configuration of your machine(s) so as to maximize flexibility can help avoid chaos and frustration.

Your needs affect how you connect different UNIX machines. If a port contender is involved, you need to deal with it. Some lines may be direct-connect, others may be direct-connect through a port contender, others may be through modem dial-ups. One step toward being able to deal with all these possibilities is to find some way to graphically represent the configurations.

The first type of connection is the direct connection (see figure 8-7). On the left is the calling system, on the right the system being called into. The calling system is using the serial port for output, so no getty should be on the port. The initiating command is "cu -ltty00 -s9600 dir", which connects to serial line tty00 at a very high baud rate. Direct connections can support this speed. The cable itself should be wired as a null modem (described earlier in this chapter). The processes involved on the called system are a getty running at 9600 baud on the incoming tty. When the user types in a login name, getty execs login, which asks for the password, and if it is correct, execs a shell.

Figure 8-7
Direct Connection from One UNIX to Another

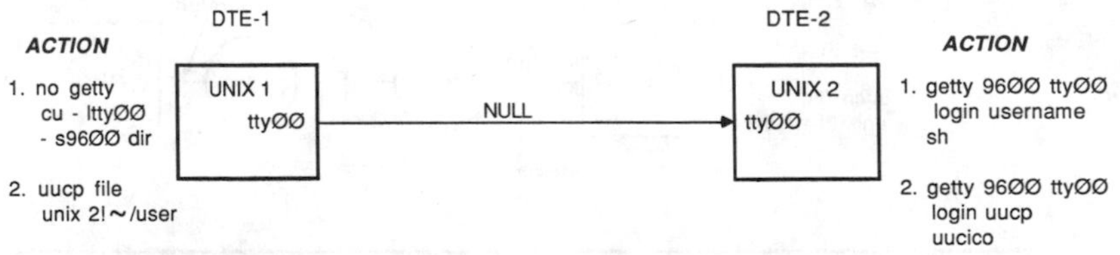

ACTION	DTE-1			DTE-2	ACTION
1. no getty cu - ltty0Ø - s96ØØ dir	UNIX 1 tty0Ø	NULL	UNIX 2 tty0Ø		1. getty 96ØØ tty0Ø login username sh
2. uucp file unix 2! ~/user					2. getty 96ØØ tty0Ø login uucp uucico

What happens with uucp is similar. The uucp command generates a uucico process that initiates a call to the system shown on the right. The login sequence is the same except that instead of getting a shell at the end of the sequence, another uucico process is run that communicates with the calling process.

The next configuration is a direct connection through a port selector, shown in figure 8-8. Again the cable from DTE-1 to the port selector should be a null modem.

A port selector takes any number of input lines and switches among a smaller number of fixed input lines to the computer. This way, all the terminals can be hooked up without having an input line that would often be idle because it's dedicated to a specific person. The login sequence is exactly the same as for the direct connect, except for any extra keystrokes it takes to get through the selector. Usually a carriage return activates the line to get the login prompt.

Figure 8-8
Direct Connection through a Port Selector

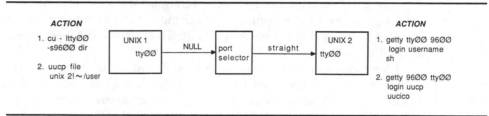

The last configuration, in figure 8-9, is a remote connection of two UNIX systems. Each DTE is connected to its modem by a straight cable. DTE-1 calls DTE-2 either by hand using `cu` or by `uucp` using `uucico` and a dialer program. The biggest difference is that the connection is at 1200 baud. This means that either DTE-2 runs a 1200-baud `getty`, or maybe a 9600 getty that would require you to kick the baud rate down. To kick baud down in `cu` requires a ~ %b for a break, or, in `uucp`, the BREAK string can be placed in the L.sys file to send it to the called system.

Figure 8-9
Remote Connection of Two UNIX Systems

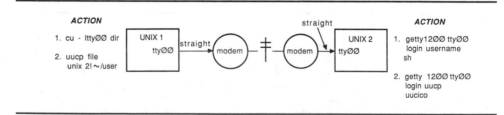

Transfer Areas

When you transfer files between machines, `uucp` adopts certain protocols and standards, and one of these has to do with where files can come from and where they can go to. To minimize chaos and to provide a measure of security, protected and public directories are created to hold queued jobs and transferred files.

The directory with the most action is /usr/spool/uucp. It contains LOGFILE, which when used in the command "tail -f LOGFILE", provides a run-time window into transfer operations. All uucp and mail transactions go into this directory. A transaction usually consists of a control file (C.*) and the data file (D.*). When one machine is used as the central node, its uucp directory can fill up with a very large number of files. Regular maintenance and constant monitoring of the lock files (LCK* and STST*) is required to be sure that everything is running all right.

The next directory of interest is /usr/spool/uucppublic, commonly known as PUBDIR (a shell variable). It contains directories named after each user to store files in transit from one machine to another. Most directories have all permissions granted so copying files to other people is possible. I find it helpful to create a shell environment variable that contains the path prefix to my directory in /usr/spool /uucppublic, that is, P=/usr/spool/uucppublic/russ. Then I can reference files by typing $P/*. This reduces typing substantially and makes it easier to move files in and out of the directory.

PUBDIR is supported in the syntax of uucp. In this example, the notation used is uucp syntax.

```
$ uucp * remote!~/user
```

This command copies every file in the current directory to the system "remote", then ~/ expands to the prefix /usr/spool/uucppublic. If the user is not a directory, the files copied are named user instead of being copied under the directory name user. You need to create the directory yourself, then chmod 777 on it so that copies can be made to it. Just for reference, ^user expands in uucp to $HOME /user and ^/user exapnds in uucp to $PUBDIR/user.

Another way to type the command using the shell variables is

```
$ uucp * remote!$P
```

This copies all the files to my PUBDIR directory. If I have a login on that system, I could type

```
$ ls -al $P
```

or

```
$ cd $P
$ ls -al
```

to see all the files that have been copied.

One thing that you must watch for is the destructive "uuclean" type of scripts. These programs usually get run by cron or some other background program. They go to all the uucp-related areas of the system, find files that have not been referenced in a certain length of time, and remove them. This can be disastrous if you are using PUBDIR as a temporary holding area. Here's what one of these "cleanup" operations might look like:

```
PATH=/usr/bin:/bin
export PATH
cd /usr/spool/uucp
find C. D. TM. X. XTMP -type f -mtime +7 -exec rm {} \;
cd /usr/spool/uucppublic
find . -type f -mtime +7 -exec rm {} \;
```

If you have these cleanup scripts running on your system, there are a few things you can do to keep files from being swept away inadvertently. The first thing is to constantly touch all the files so that they are not matched by a find statement that is looking for old files. This can be accomplished by doing:

```
$ find $P -exec touch {} \;
```

Touch updates the access- and modify-time of the file. The { } means to put in the literal name that matched the find statement. You would want to put this in a scheduled process that runs more often than the cleanup program does!

Another strategy is to analyze the clean program (or script). Does it run by root? If not, a "chmod 000 $P" might keep it from looking inside my directory for names. If it runs under root, of course, permissions do not stop it. At what time does it run? Can I get it to pass me without looking at my files? What is the starting directory of the clean script? By looking into these areas, we can gather much information about what the script does and how we might take action so that it doesn't wipe us out.

The easiest thing to do (assuming that you are authorized to do so) might seem to be simply removing the cleanup program. This, however, is not conducive to keeping free space open and the directories clean. Too, if you want to disable cleaning of certain directories that are very important to you, you have to take responsibility for their maintenance.

Network Security

The uucppublic directory, as we saw, contains files that are in transit between systems. Usually all the subdirectories in uucppublic have permission modes rwxrwxrwx. This immediately creates a security problem because anyone can create, destroy, or alter files in the directories.

This same permission scheme needs to be followed for any directory that is a source or destination of uucp files. Uucp wants all intermediate directories to have read or write permission for everyone. If uucp is using a directory for source files, read permission needs to be granted. Likewise, write permission is needed for destination directories. If you want to uucp files directly into your home directory, you have to open your directory to write access from the world at large.

Wide open write access allows files to be delivered directly to your doorstep, but you don't know what you are opening your doors to. If you are security conscious, you won't like the idea of anyone being able to write anything into your space. One solution is to unlock your home directory but lock all your subdirectories except the ones for uucp. The major hassle with this is setting all the permission modes so that every file is covered properly.

A simpler solution is to keep your uucp directories out of your home directory tree. This isolates you from the security problem but means you have to manually copy files after their receipt to the directory where you want them to actually live.

Restriction Files

When a remote system logs into a central system via uucp, several files on the central system define what capabilities the remote system has. These configuration files reside in /usr/lib/uucp.

The first file of interest is L.cmds. It contains the names of all the commands on the central system that can be executed from remote systems. If the remote system is sending a command via uux, it is only executed if the command name is in L.cmds.

The next file, USERFILE, defines which directories on the central system the remote system may access. You can restrict transfers to one directory or allow access to any file on the system. The default entry for USERFILE is

```
uucp, /
```

which allows the uucp user (default uucico process user name) to copy files into and out of anywhere from / on down, which is the whole system. This opens up security holes like this

```
uucp central!/etc/passwd /tmp
```

which retrieves the password file from another system. With this file, user names without passwords could be found and people could break into your system. A more stringent USERFILE would be

```
uucp /usr/spool/uucppublic /tmp
```

which would restrict file transfers to these directories only. This would foil the previous attempt to transfer the passwd file.

The last file, L.sys, is probably the most important file in uucp from a security point of view. It contains the node names, phone numbers, login names, and passwords for all remote systems known to the central system. If any of this information were made available to the public, someone could perform a uucp transfer with one of the remote systems and pretend to be the central system. The new HoneyDanber uucp system in System V takes steps to keep remote systems from intercepting mail and data transmissions by pretending to be other remote systems. Chapter 9 looks in more detail at security aspects of uucp and communications in general.

In the following example, an L.sys file is given in which two different kinds of systems are defined: direct-connect type systems and dial-up remote systems.

```
remote Any ACU 1200 5551212 ogin:--ogin: uucp word: uucp
selector Any ACU 1200 5551213 \d--CLASS--CLASS A ogin:--ogin: uucp word:
uucp
direct Any tty00 9600 tty00 ogin:-@-ogin: uucp word: uucp
```

The entry for system "remote" shows that it is a dial-up line, can be called "any time", is accessed through an ACU (automatic call unit) at 1200 baud and at the number 5551212. The login sequence is defined as the uucp login name and uucp password. The "ogin" is not a typographical error: Uucp uses "ogin: " to distinguish its login prompt from the regular UNIX login. Pattern matching "ogin:" is more reliable than using "Login:" or "login:".

The "Any" can be replaced with specific times if 24-hour access is not to be allowed. Note that the "ACU" entry matches the ACU entry in the L-devices file, (as described previously). In the following L-devices entry, the names cua0 and cul0 are linked to the device attached to the modem, in this case /dev/tty00:

```
ACU    cul0   cua0   1200
```

The link can be verified by typing "ls -li /dev/tty* /dev/cul* /dev/cua*".

The "selector" system entry in our L.sys file is also a dialup, only it goes through the port contender. The extra information that starts with the "\d" is required to talk to the port contender. The L.sys fields are arranged in "expect send expect send ..." order. When we first connect to the port selector, nothing is printed to our line. This is just the way it works. The selector requires a <cr> to become active, but uucp's first field is expect. How do we expect nothing and send carriage return? By telling uucp to expect an impossible character, like a control-D (\d). Uucp never gets it, so he times out and sends a carriage return (-).

If the word CLASS comes back when we send the CR, we send the character "A", which is the class for system identification specified in the entry. When that connects, we look for "ogin:" for the login prompt. If we don't find it, we send carriage returns. This may be required because the initial getty on system A could be at 9600 baud. We would have to send either carriage returns or breaks to kick it down to our 1200-baud session.

The last system entry, "direct", does not use an ACU and phone number. It is going to go right to the terminal line tty00 at 9600 baud to get the login sequence. There is no port selector to go through, just a direct line. The line it uses in the L-devices file is

```
DIR    tty00   0   9600
```

Debugging Communications

For those occasions when uucp is not working properly, some debugging tricks are available. The sequence for debugging usually goes in a circle: Try to transfer a file, determine location of problem, perform a fix, do another transfer. The areas covered here deal with locating the problem and forcing another transfer.

If after checking and double checking all the configuration files, the file transfer refuses to take place, run /usr/lib/uucico by hand with some debug flags activated. This shows exactly what handshaking is going on. The command line for debug mode is

```
/usr/lib/uucp/uucico -r1 -x9 -ssystem_name
```

where r1 tells uucico to start in master mode calling system_name, and x9 specifies the level of debugging messages. If you want less detail from uucico, reduce the level of debugging to x4 or so. The range of debug output is from x1 to x9.

The typical sequence for this command would go: First, queue some files to go to another system. By queuing the files, you avoid automatically starting uucico. After the files are queued and ready to go, run the debug mode and watch the protocol take place. It would look like this:

```
$ uucp -r *.c remote!~/src
$ /usr/lib/uucp/uucico -r1 -x4 -sremote
```

If you only need to activate the uucp transfer normally, the easiest way is to use the mail command. Mail some text to a user on another system and immediately the uucp machine goes into action. The following sequence forces the machine to call "remote" and run rmail(1) on the other system to mail file "dummy" to "user":

```
$ mail remote!user < dummy
```

A command explicitly invokes /usr/lib/uucp/uucico: the uusub(1M) command, which resides in /usr/lib/uucp. It is called with the name of the system with which you want to connect. Most systems have it. If you don't have it, use uucico. If you do have it, you have yet another way to run uucico. The syntax looks like this:

```
$ /usr/lib/uucp/uusub -c system
```

Now that we know how all these commands can be used manually, we can show you some tools that automate much of your uucp work.

Name: uust

uust   Uucp status and housekeeping

Function

Provides menu-driven access for many housekeeping functions associated with the uucp utility and file transfers.

291

Synopsis

uust

Menu Options:
c - connect to another system in debug mode

d - show files in your directory under PUBDIR

f - long list files in the spool directory

l - display the logfile dynamically

r - reconnect with another system

s - give user summary of transactions

u - unlock all tty lines (CAUTION: can destroy session)

w - display logfile for the last week

Sample Call

uust   List the LOGFILE dynamically to monitor uucp transactions
l

Code for uust

```
1   :
2   # @(#) uust v1.0   Uucp status utility   Author: Russ Sage
3
4   if [ $# -gt 0 ]
5     then  echo "uust: argument error" >&2
6           echo "usage: uust"          >&2
7           exit 1
8   fi
9
10  UUNODE='uuname -l'
11  echo "
12                  UUST MENU               system node: $UUNODE
13                  ---------
14      c - connect with another system in debug mode
15      d - show files in your directory under PUBDIR
16      f - long list files in the spool directory
17      l - display the logfile dynamically
18      r - reconnect with another system
19      s - give user summary of transactions
20      u - unlock the tty line
21      w - display logfile for the last week
22      <cr> - exit program
23
24  Press c,d,f,l,r,s,u,w,or <cr>: \c"
25  read CMD
26
```

```
27  case $CMD in
28  "")      exit 0;;
29  c)       echo "\nSystem name (<cr> to exit): \c"
30           read SYSTEM
31           if [ "$SYSTEM" = "" ]
32             then exit 0
33           fi
34           echo "\nrm /usr/spool/uucp/STST.$SYSTEM : \c"
35           rm /usr/spool/uucp/STST.$SYSTEM 2>/dev/null \
36                   && echo "" || echo "no STST files"
37           echo "\n/usr/lib/uucp/uucico -r1 -x4 -s$SYSTEM:"
38           /usr/lib/uucp/uucico -r1 -x4 -s$SYSTEM;;
39  d)       echo "\n/usr/spool/uucppublic/$LOGNAME:"
40           ls -l /usr/spool/uucppublic/$LOGNAME;;
41  f)       echo "\n/usr/spool/uucp:"
42           ls -l /usr/spool/uucp | more;;
43  l)       echo "\n/usr/spool/uucp/LOGFILE:"
44           tail -20f /usr/spool/uucp/LOGFILE;;
45  r)       echo "\nSystem name (<cr> to exit): \c"
46           read SYSTEM
47           if [ "$SYSTEM" = "" ]
48             then exit 0
49           fi
50           echo "\nrm /usr/spool/uucp/STST.$SYSTEM : \c"
51           rm /usr/spool/uucp/STST.$SYSTEM 2>/dev/null \
52                   && echo "" || echo "no STST files"
53           echo "uusub -c$SYSTEM:"
54           if [ -f /xenix ]
55             then /usr/bin/uusub -c$SYSTEM
56             else /usr/lib/uucp/uusub -c$SYSTEM
57           fi
58           tail -20f /usr/spool/uucp/LOGFILE;;
59  s)       echo "\nuulog -u$LOGNAME:"
60           uulog -un$LOGNAME | more;;
61  u)       echo \\nrm /usr/spool/uucp/LCK* :
62           rm /usr/spool/uucp/LCK* 2>/dev/null || echo "no lock files";;
63  w)       echo "\n/usr/spool/uucp/Log-WEEK:"
64           more /usr/spool/uucp/Log-WEEK;;
65  *)       echo "uust: invalid argument '$CMD'" >&2;;
66  esac
```

Environment Variables

CMD	Contains the input command character from stdin
LOGNAME	Environment variable which contains your login name
SYSTEM	The uucp node name of the system you are sending to
UUNODE	The uucp node name of the local system

Description

Why do we need uust?

Many areas of UNIX are really subsystems in themselves. Uucp is one of them. It uses configuration files, spool files, lock files, and has a number of executables that make up the system. If you use uucp heavily, you do a lot of viewing of log files, cleaning up directories when uucp crashes, and monitoring the system in general. To do all this by hand requires that you remember the directories, files, commands, and options, and that you don't mind typing lots of characters. Uust reduces this overhead considerably and makes uucp almost pleasant to use.

What does uust *do?*

Uust is a menu-driven interface providing the main housekeeping functions needed for the uucp environment. You only need to type uust, then the desired options.

It's also quite possible that you will discover labor-saving functions that you didn't know about before.

The first thing that prints is the main menu:

```
            UUST MENU                      system node: russ
            ----------
   c - connect with another system in debug mode
   d - show files in your directory under PUBDIR
   f - long list files in the spool directory
   l - display the logfile dynamically
   r - reconnect with another system
   s - give user summary of transactions
   u - unlock the tty line
   w - display logfile for the last week
   <cr> - exit program

  Press c,d,f,l,r,s,u,w,or <cr>:
```

The first option is c, for connect the uucp line in debug mode. This generates the command line for running a uucico process by hand, as described in the previous section. Uust prompts you for the system name to connect to.

The next option, d, gives a long listing of files in your directory in $PUBDIR, or /usr/spool/uucppublic/$LOGNAME. If you do a lot of uucp transfers, many files can collect here. This gives you an easy way to see them.

The f option gives a long listing of all the files in the spool directory. The output is piped to more just in case there are lots of files. This directory is the heart of the uucp run-time system. Most everything is either in this directory or is related to it.

The l option is probably the most used in the whole utility. It shows the dynamic execution of uucp by watching the logfile. When first called, it prints the last 20 lines of the file, then keeps watching until it is killed. Total keystrokes to invoke this command from uust are 5: 4 for calling uust and 1 for the menu option. To type the command by hand requires 31 characters. That's a savings of time and hassle that really adds up!

The r option is really nice. Give it a system name and it forces a connection with that system through `uucp`. The method of doing this is different than that used in the c option, but works with System V. Note however that on most systems the command used here, `uusub`, requires root capability. `Uusub` returns execution back to your shell, but then makes the `uucp` call in the background. While this is happening, `uust` goes ahead and shows the dynamic tail of the logfile as described above. Then you can watch `uucp` go through all the motions of calling in, transferring files, and closing down.

The s option shows all of your `uucp` transactions by scanning the logfile for only your name. Usually there are many entries, so the output is piped to `more` for readability.

The next option, u, must be used with extreme caution. It removes the lock files that `uucp` sets up for itself. If `uucp` is running at the time, another person could `cu` onto the line and destroy everything. These lock files also exist when someone uses `cu` on a serial line. The reason why this option exists is because sometimes `uucp` or `cu` crashes. When it does, the lock files need to be removed so that everything can restart. This option should only be used for this purpose, or for planned experimenting to see what can happen.

The last option, w, is for displaying the logfile for the last week's worth of `uucp` transactions. This isn't the most exciting thing to do, but if you were looking for a specific transaction, you could use the string searching capabilities of `more` to look for it.

Example

```
$ uust
r
```

This tries to reconnect the `uucp` line. It could be used to poll another system or send/receive queued data. The first thing that it does is ask for the system name to call. Then it tries to remove any failure-indicating files and make the call.

Explanation

`Uust` is a one-pass utility: That is, it has no internal loops. You choose an option and when that option is over, the script is over. The main reason for doing it this way is because you have to break out of the `tail` command that is used by some of the menu options. However, the break key kills everything, even `uust`. It wouldn't make much sense to loop internally, as the loop would seldom be able to reiterate.

Lines 4-8 do the command-line error checking. If any arguments are passed, an error message is printed and the script exits.

Line 10 initializes the UUNODE variable with the current uucp name of the system you are on, as provided by a call to `uuname`.

Lines 11-24 print the main menu in one big echo statement. The system name, as found in the value of UUNODE, is printed for reference on the top right portion of the screen.

Line 25 reads the user selection, and lines 27-66 do the command check and execution. If you type only a carriage return, it is matched in line 28 and the program exits.

Lines 29-38 handle the c command (connect) in debug mode. The system name is prompted for and is checked to see whether it was null. If it is, the script exits. Otherwise, line 34 echoes that uust is trying to remove any STST files, which are created when a failure to call happens. You must remove any STST files before you call the system. If no STST files exist, the rm command fails, and the message "no STST files" is printed.

Lines 39-40 perform the d option. First, the banner of the directory that we are looking at is echoed for reference. Then the PUBDIR directory is listed in long form. Note that LOGNAME fits anyone who runs this program and does not hard code any value into the program.

The f option in lines 41-42 is handled in a similar way. The directory that we are printing is the spool directory.

The l command in lines 43-44 echoes the banner that the logfile is being displayed, then the "tail -f" command is used. The -f option says to keep displaying what is in the file so that as transactions are printed to the file, they are displayed on your screen. The user must press the break key to exit the script.

Lines 45-58 do the r command, which attempts to reconnect. First, the system name is prompted for and checked against a null. If a name was typed, we attempt to remove the STST files and give a message that tells whether it was successful. Next, the message that uusub is being run is printed. Line 54 checks to see whether the kernel file is XENIX. If it is, uusub is referenced in its new location in XENIX. Otherwise, it is referenced in the usual location of /usr/lib/uucp. After the uusub is executed, the dynamic tail of the logfile is displayed until the user presses the break key, after which the script exits.

Lines 59-60 perform the summary check. The command is uulog, and the LOGNAME of the running user is passed to it. See the uulog manual entry for more details.

The u option is in lines 61-62. The rm command to be run is echoed first to notify the user, then the command is executed to attempt to remove the lock files. If the remove command fails, an error message is printed indicating that there were no lock files.

Lines 63-64 run the w option to see the week-long activity of uucp. The file Log-WEEK is printed via the more command. The log week file is created by uucp to provide a concise summary of activity for the week.

Line 65 matches any commands that were not matched earlier. Such commands are errors, so a message is printed. When execution falls through, the program ends.

Name: uutrans

---

uutrans   UNIX-to-UNIX transfer of file trees

Function

Copies a complete file system hierarchy through uucp to another UNIX system and maintains the file tree structure.

Synopsis

uutrans

Sample Call

cd $HOME/backup
uutrans
remote
~russ

> Starting from my home directory backup subdir, run uutrans to transfer every file I have, sending the files to the system remote and placing them in my login directory (/usr/russ)

Code for uutrans

```
 1  :
 2  # @(#) uutrans v1.0   Transfer file trees via uucp    Author: Russ Sage
 3
 4  if [ $# -gt 0 ]
 5    then  echo "uutrans: argument count error" >&2
 6          echo "usage: uutrans"                 >&2
 7          exit 1
 8  fi
 9
10  SELF='uuname -l'
11
12  echo "source directory(<cr> to exit): \c"
13  read SOURCE
14  if [ "$SOURCE" = "" -o ! -d "$SOURCE" ]
15    then  exit 1
16  fi
17
18  echo "\ndestination system(<cr> for $SELF): \c"
19  read SYSTEM
20  echo "\ndestination directory(<cr> for ~/$LOGNAME): \c"
21  read DEST
22
23  : ${SYSTEM:="$SELF"}
24  : ${DEST:="~/$LOGNAME"}
25
26  echo "\nQUEUEING:"
27
```

```
28   find $SOURCE -type f -print | sort | while read FILE
29   do
30           echo $FILE
31           uucp -c -d -r $FILE $SYSTEM!$DEST/$FILE
32   done
```

Environment Variables

DEST	The destination for files to be copied to
FILE	The specific file to be copied
LOGNAME	Environment variable that holds the login name
SELF	Contains the node name of the current system
SOURCE	The source of all files to copy
SYSTEM	The system name to copy files to

Description

Why do we need uutrans?

Copying files from one system to another via uucp is a fairly easy task: Tell it which files should go where. But what if you need to copy a hierarchy of files? How do you guarantee that the files end up as a hierarchy on the destination system, instead of being shoved into the same directory? One sentence in the uucp documentation (not even in the manual pages) tells how to do this. If you never read it, your transfers have a high probability of failure.

What we need is a tool that transfers tree structures to other systems and still maintains their shape. We want to make it easy to do this so that we don't have to look up obscure information each time.

What does uutrans do?

Uutrans provides a flexible interface that guarantees that file hierarchies are copied properly. It knows which files to transfer, which system to put them on, and where on that system to put them.

When you run uutrans, the first prompt is for the source directory for the transfer. If you do not want to continue, press a carriage return to exit. Remember that the find command is used, so the path you give in response to the prompt is the prefix pathname for all files transferred. For example, if your current directory is $HOME and it is going to be the source, type ".". A sample pathname generated from find for the file /src/f.c would be ./src/f.c. If you input a name like /usr/russ, however, the resulting pathname would be /usr/russ/src/f.c. Thus, a little forethought is needed to avoid creating more directory levels than you want in the destination system.

The next prompt is for the destination system. If you want it to be your own system, press the carriage return. Doing this copies the files around on the same hard disk or other file systems.

The default for the destination directory prompt is PUBDIR. If you don't want this, give the exact pathname to the directory from which you want the hierarchy to start on the destination system. (Remember also that many systems restrict where you can copy files with uucp.) The way uutrans maintains the correct file tree is by specifying the absolute pathname on the destination system all the way down to the file name *for each file*. The only way this can be done is to have the pathname in a variable and use it on both source and destination paths when calling uucp.

When all the input has been entered, the find command is used to find all the files that are in the hierarchy. Each pathname is then piped to a loop that echoes the name and uucps it to the destination location.

To make the whole process faster and save space, the files are queued in the spool directory (that is, no attempt is made to call the remote system), and no files are copied to the spool directory. This saves time in copying large numbers of files and may even save your machine from bombing because copying lots of files eats up all the free space.

When all the files are queued, you need to manually connect uucp through either the c command or the r command in uust. All the directories on the destination system should be created automatically when the transfer occurs.

One area that is a little sticky is the ownership and permission of the files at the destination side. The usual sequence is to

1. Queue the files into uucp, using the uutrans tool.
2. Log off the source system.
3. Log on the destination system.
4. Run uust and reconnect the uucp link.

If you do this queue and transfer technique, you have total control over which files go and when they go. The one side effect is that the permissions of the files in the destination directory are set according to the shell umask of the process that starts the reconnection.

The major ramification is that if you do not have write permission on in your umask, a transfer directory is created, and no files can be placed into it, thus bombing out the uucp transfer. To solve this, change your umask to "000", which is the default of 777 for directories and 644 for regular files.

Examples

1. cd $P
    uutrans

    .
    remote
    <cr>

Change directory to PUBDIR. Transfer all the files from the current directory (.) to the remote system, putting them into the default directory of ~/$LOGNAME, which is my directory in PUBDIR.

2. uutrans
    /etc
    remote
    /tmp/etc

Transfer all files from /etc to the system remote, placing them into the directory /tmp/etc.

Explanation

Lines 4-8 check for error conditions. If any arguments are on the command line, an error is printed.

Line 10 initializes the variable SELF to the name of your system uucp node.

Line 12 prompts for the source directory and reads it into SOURCE. If the input is null or is not a directory, the program exits.

Lines 18-21 prompt for the destination system and the destination directory. The default is your own system and the PUBDIR directory for the location. These defaults make it easy to configure the transfer sights without having to type much data.

Lines 23 and 24 check to see whether the variables have been initialized. If SYSTEM was set to a carriage return, it is set to SELF. If the DEST directory was null, it is set to ~/$LOGNAME. These statements effectively enforce the default settings.

Line 26 prints the message that the files are being queued. Lines 28-32 do the actual magic. The find command starts from SOURCE and finds all the regular files. This list is passed to sort, so uucp transfers the files in sorted order. This makes it easier to trace which files have been transferred if any problems arise.

This sorted list is fed to a while loop that reads file names. Each name is echoed to the screen for reference, and the file is queued for the remote system. The options to uucp in line 31 are -r for queuing, -c for no copying the files to the spool directory, and -d to create the directories needed on the remote system.

The magic syntax that we use to maintain the tree structure is $SYSTEM!$DEST/$FILE. We need to copy files not only to a system and a directory, but we also need to define the pathname down to the file itself. This ensures that the files are pushed into the subdirectories. If the syntax was $SYSTEM!$DEST, all the files would end up in one directory and lose their hierarchical structure.

After all the files have been queued, they sit in the queue until the remote system calls, at which time, any files for that system are copied.

Configuration Solutions

Often times in the real world, we can accumulate a lot of not particularly compatible hardware around our UNIX system, including terminals, micros, and modems. How do we get them to work together? Now that we've looked at both the general hardware and software facilities for UNIX communications, we're ready to present some examples of working UNIX communications setups. We are going to look at a number of configurations that use various combinations of hardware. The problems change, but our general approach is consistent.

UNIX to Modem and Mainframe

The first problem that we look at is using a "personal" UNIX system, a modem, and a mainframe. We have a UNIX system in our office with one serial port, but we have both a modem and a direct-connect line to a larger system. How do we use the one serial port for both the modem and the mainframe? The solution is shown in figure 8-10.

Figure 8-10
Connecting a UNIX System to a Modem and a Mainframe

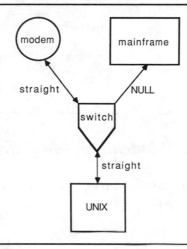

We need a switch box. The box has one input on one side and two inputs on the other side. We connect UNIX to the main connection, and that allows us to switch it to either the modem or mainframe. The different connections to this are

unix←→modem   calling out with cu, uucp, and in from remote terminal
unix→mainframe   calling out to mainframe as direct-connect terminal

UNIX and Terminal to a Modem

This is similar to the previous configuration except that all the hardware is local. We want to use the modem with both the terminal and UNIX. The configuration is shown in figure 8-11.

A UNIX port is connected to one side of the switch and the terminal is connected to the other side. Note that the terminal will *not* go into the UNIX system. All cables are straight. The possible configurations with this setup is

unix←→modem   calling in from remote terminal and out for cu, uucp
terminal→modem   for calling out only as dumb terminal

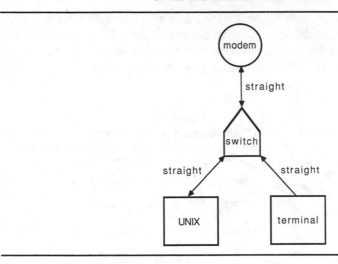

Figure 8-11
UNIX and Terminal to a Modem

UNIX to Terminal, Modem, and Mainframe

This situation is rather complex and requires two switch boxes. The architecture is shown in figure 8-12.

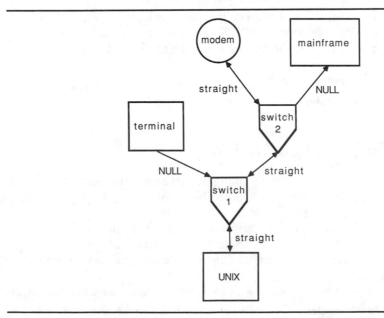

Figure 8-12
UNIX to Terminal, Modem, and Mainframe

We start from the UNIX system. It has a line that goes into switch box 1 as the master entry. It switches between the terminal and switch box 2. This allows UNIX either to receive the terminal for logging in (assuming a getty is running), receive the modem for logging in, or send out to the modem or mainframe (assuming no getty). Note that a null modem must be between the terminal and UNIX, but we can't have the null right next to UNIX because we need it to be straight for the modem.

Switch box 2 then switches between the modem and the mainframe. The line to the modem must be straight and the line to the mainframe must have a null. The possible settings are

unix ← terminal	call in to UNIX from terminal on getty line
unix ← →switch ← →modem	call out with cu, uucp and in from remote terminal
unix →switch →mainframe	call out using cu, uucp

UNIX System, Micro, and Modem

This configuration also requires two switch boxes. What we have is a machine running UNIX with two serial lines, a standalone micro, and a modem to share between the two. The UNIX machine also accepts logins from the standalone system, allowing the latter to emulate a terminal if we have the proper software. The solution is shown in figure 8-13.

The micro can go two ways: either a terminal to the UNIX system or a terminal to the modem for calling out. The UNIX system has one serial line that is enabled for login to the micro through switch box 1. The other serial line goes to switch box 2, which is connected to the modem. This line can go either out for calling or in for remote login through the modem. Switch box 2 switches the modem between the micro and the UNIX system. The combinations are

micro →switch →modem	calling out with commware
micro →switch →unix	login under terminal emulation
unix ←switch ←micro	login from direct connect terminal
unix ← →switch ← →modem	call out by cu, uucp, call in remote login
modem ←switch ←micro	call out modem from micro
modem ← →switch ← →unix	call in or out; requires change of getty for serial line and auto answer for modem

Alternate Solution

There's another possible solution to the preceding problem. It opens up a few more possibilities than the previous solution. The same basic problems are solved, yet the approach is very much different.

Figure 8-13
UNIX System, Micro, and a Modem

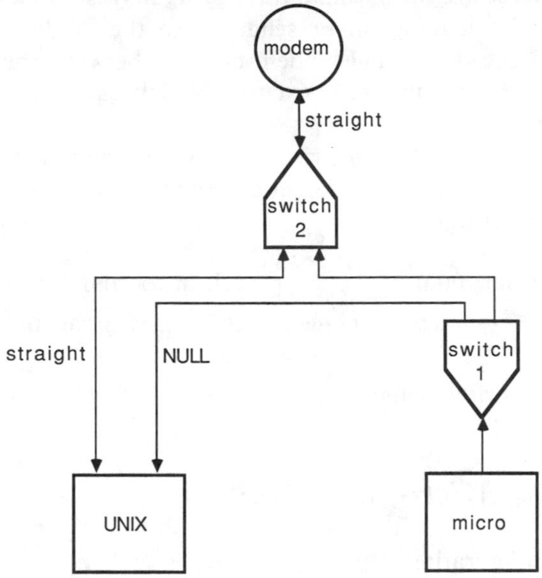

In this configuration, shown in figure 8-14, the switch boxes are moved to different junctions from those used in the preceding setup. The same, as well as some new, paths are available.

The micro and the UNIX system both go into switch box 1. This switch box then goes into switch box 2 as the main connection. The micro, UNIX system, switch box line, and modem line should all be straight cables. The only null modem line should be the one to the input line for the UNIX system.

Switch box 2 switches one of the CPUs between the modem and the second UNIX serial line. The modem line can go in or out, but the UNIX line only goes in because a `getty` is running on it. The possible combinations are

micro→switch→modem	call out through commware
micro→switch→unix	login under terminal emulation
unix←→switch←→modem	call in or out with cu and uucp
unix→switch→unix	first line as output goes into second line for login
modem←→switch←→CPU	CPU is dependent on switch 1
unix←switch←CPU	depending on switch 1, either CPU can login

Three UNIX Systems

The last configuration we look at is the connection of three UNIX systems. The configuration that prompted this solution was a 16-bit PC XENIX machine, a 32-bit

Figure 8-14
UNIX System, Micro, and Modem in Alternate Configuration

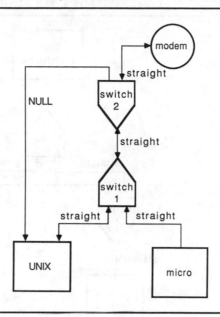

PC XENIX machine, and a VAX mainframe direct connection. To make such a connection, we need three two-way switch boxes.

The positions of the 32- and 16-bit machines are not crucial between micro1 and micro2. These machines would be in your office, and the mainframe is someplace else with a cable to your office. This assumes that the cable from the mainframe is already null at your connection. The only other null cable is between the two micro UNIX systems because they would log into each other as terminals. The rest of the cables are straight through. See figure 8-15.

Each micro goes into a switch box as the master connection. Those switch boxes (1 and 2) switch to each other and switch box 3.

Micro1 can switch between micro2 as a terminal/uucp interface and the mainframe as a remote terminal only. In this case, the mainframe line went through a port selector. Micro2 can switch between micro1 and the mainframe in the same fashion. Switch box 3 switches the mainframe between micro1 and micro2. The combinations are

micro1→switch→mainframe	login as remote terminal
micro1←→switch←→micro2	call in or out depending on getty
micro2←→switch←→micro1	call in or out depending on getty
micro2→switch→mainframe	login as remote terminal
mainframe←switch←micro1	login from remote terminal
mainframe←switch←micro2	login from remote terminal

Figure 8-15
Three UNIX Systems

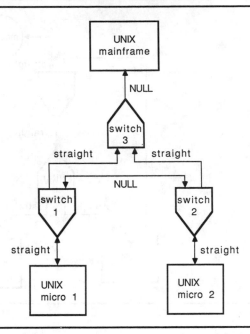

Although it is unlikely that any of the configurations we have looked at match your needs exactly, we have presented them so that you can see a variety of typical solutions that you can adapt to your needs. In the next chapter, we step back a bit from all these nuts and bolts and look at the larger issues involved in administering a system, particularly the issue of security.

9
Administration and Security

Administrator's duties and responsibilities
Maintaining security on the system
Typical security problems

```
access   show all free access logins
chkset   check the system for setuid/setgid files
suw      watch the sulog for violators
```

Administration and Security

Why Do You Need To Learn About Administration

Your career as a UNIX disciple (soon to be master!) can be described in fantasy terms as a quest for the three rings of power. The first ring is that of initiation into the workings of UNIX as a whole, and especially its heart, the file system. The first three chapters laid this groundwork and provided practical tools for system house-keeping. The second ring is that of managing your own work and personal environment: the subject of Chapters 4 through 6. Chapters 7 and 8 looked in more detail at two special aspects of practical work with the UNIX system: devices and communications.

Now we are ready to reach for the third ring of power: that of guardianship of the system itself, more prosaically known as system administration.

If you are currently a user who does some programming or you are a full-time systems programmer, you may wonder why you need to understand the viewpoint of a system administrator and master his or her essential tools. There are two good reasons: knowledge and necessity.

System administration requires an intimate knowledge of where everything is in the system and the relationship of a given process to the system as a whole. Programmers tend to pick up odds and ends of esoteric commands and tricks that they find useful, but they often have not taken the time to become familiar with UNIX as a whole. We would like to encourage you to make a more systematic study of UNIX so that you can find new treasure troves of knowledge. That's why throughout this book we created tools that not only do useful things but also aid in your exploration of the system itself.

Necessity makes its impact felt when you discover that you've just been given the job of system administrator, or the administrator has gone on vacation and the users are lined up at *your* desk waiting for help because you're the resident guru. Another possibility is that of becoming the proud owner of your own UNIX micro and having to set up and maintain the beast yourself. Look upon such administrative necessity as the opportunity to gain a comprehensive and thorough knowledge of UNIX that can serve you well in every aspect of your daily computer work.

Being a UNIX master is a matter of attitude as well as of technical knowledge. UNIX masters learn to pursue knowledge for its own sake while trying to meet the demands of necessity. UNIX masters not only play the game well, but they stay one step ahead.

A Few Observations from Someone Who Has Been There

The system administrator position is one that requires a wider perspective of the system than that needed by a user or even a programmer, and carries with it much responsibility. The ability of all the little UNIXettes to get their work done depends on the administrator's ability to keep the system running while anticipating and solving problems before they become disasters.

One of the most important issues of administration is security. The security issues presented here were collected as a result of working with administrators, being an administrator, and occasionally, having to work around uncooperative administrators.

In addition to security, some of the more global aspects of the administrator's job are presented. Few manuals or books tell how to be an administrator. It's mostly done by the seat of your pants. Your system configuration, users' needs, and priorities are all going to influence how you perform administrative tasks. We help by showing you tools and tricks, sharing stories about traps and pitfalls, and describing the kinds of approaches that have worked in the real world.

Administrative Duties

On most large computer systems, the administrators are very important people. They are responsible for keeping the computer system running 24 hours a day, making upgrades when necessary, assisting users with problems, and patrolling and enforcing security. Administration is really several different jobs in one. We are going to look at each of these areas in detail, then offer help and tools for mastering them.

Keeping the System Running

Keeping the system running is the number one priority. This involves more than avoiding full-fledged crashes though, as important as that obviously is. Keeping the system running requires preventative care, too. One of the best things you can do after finishing your first reading of this book is to go back through it and look from an administrative viewpoint at the ideas and tools it presents. Consider, for example, how properly implemented file backups and garbage collection (see Chapter 3) can help prevent crashes caused by overflow conditions, or if a crash occurs, allow you to get everyone's data restored as quickly and completely as possible.

310

Enhancing System Capabilities

As more and more people use the system, more resources are required, but you also can find ways to use existing resources more efficiently. You will find yourself looking for ways to fine-tune system performance, such as reorganization of inefficient file systems and automatic removal of "garbage" files, using tools presented in Chapter 3. There are seldom enough printers, disk drives, serial ports, networks, and so on, on a UNIX system, but more efficient use can accomplish the same thing up to a point as would adding resources.

Probably the most important resource is CPU time. Get 30 users on a system designed for 24 and you experience CPU shortage. The job of the administrator is to support the current resources as well as plan for future growth of the system. This requires that you know what the typical patterns of use of your system are, where the bottlenecks occur, how to allocate existing resources efficiently, and what the most cost-effective ways to upgrade the system might be. Some of the information you need can be obtained by a "static" survey of the file system using the tools we presented in Chapter 2. You can get a more dynamic picture of system use by frequently using the ps command to see what processes typically run at a given time, and (with Berkeley) using the w command, which gives statistics on system load and queuing.

Helping Users

The users of the system are definitely high priority. They need to have things done on the system so that they can get their own jobs done. The administrator must see that all reasonable (and some unreasonable) user requests are performed.

Meeting user needs can include mounting tapes and other file systems, backing up files, debugging communications lines, and making personal entries for users in privileged files like crontab and inittab. (These two files allow users to have greater flexibility in their environment and task scheduling but are too sensitive for direct user access.) It may sound like easy stuff, but it is the small things that are time-consuming.

Security: Being the Watchdog

The administrator is the one who enforces all security issues. Usually he or she is the only one who does this job. Users don't enforce security because they can't or don't know how. Violators of security can attack the system in many ways. They can consume the system resources by filling the process table or open file table, and allocating all free disk space and free inodes. They can mess with other users on the system or change the system time. They can corrupt data files or executables, and even forge mail. And those are often just the "abusive users" within your organization. Later we look at some of the things more serious security abusers, those who gain unauthorized root access, can do.

The best approach to security is to enforce what really needs to be enforced instead of trying to be a super cop. You especially have to be aware of the needs of systems programmers and other experienced "gurus" on your system. Ideally an administrator should work *with*, not against, the resident gurus and develop a good working relationship with them. Not all offenders have the same motivation. For example, a local guru might want to gain root access to be able to do some kinds of work without having to wait for you to get around to it. Someone else might be mad at a particular individual or the world in general and seek revenge by destroying files. Each situation needs individual evaluation. Remember that the line between administrators and system gurus is frequently a vague and shifting one. Security sometimes becomes a game where certain users try to see what they can get away with, whereas the administrators try to keep control of the system.

Five areas are involved with being a security watchdog.

1. Guarding against illegal logins, files, programs, and su's
2. Preserving the confidentiality of certain data
3. Watching over modem usage
4. Preventing illegal file transfers
5. Minimizing opportunities for break-ins

This is a lot of stuff to do! UNIX is so large and files can hide in so many places that it's almost a full time job just looking for intruders. It requires the administrator to work smarter rather than harder. To have a fighting chance, you have to put the system to work helping to defend itself. Later in this chapter, we present the scripts `access` and `suw` to help you guard against illegal logins, and `chkset` to deal with preserving confidential files. We also present a more detailed look at particular security problem areas.

Guarding Against Illegal Logins, Files, Programs and Su's

There are many ways to get unauthorized privileges in a UNIX system. The easiest is to have a root shell, which is one that runs as the specially privileged process that has the ability to read, delete, or modify *any* file in the system regardless of the permissions set for the file by its owner. A root shell can be obtained by learning the root password from a careless administrator, or by other means described later.

An unauthorized user, having gained root access, can create "trap door" programs that facilitate further illegal accesses. These programs allow the offender to run a shell with root privileges. We look at them in more detail later.

Trap doors can have many different faces. They can be executables, patches to system utilities, or patches to system files. The administrator needs to keep a constant watch for changes in the system that could conceal doors or other tampering. Later we present some tools and techniques that help you detect such infiltration.

Logins

Let's start with unauthorized logins. These can occur in many ways. The offender could have added his or her own login name to the password file and put in a private password. If the administrator is not familiar with the password file, or has not reviewed it recently, the unauthorized entry might be overlooked.

Another way unauthorized logins can occur is that someone could have acquired all the passwords by "patching" the login program with code that sends all passwords entered by users to a hidden file. We look at several types of patches later.

Of course, fancy stuff often isn't necessary. People have been known to leave passwords written on pieces of paper in unlocked desk drawers. To some people, using the height of secrecy is using a combination of their first and last name as a password. However the offender gets passwords, he or she can use different login names each time to avoid showing a suspicious usage pattern.

One area that opens up security holes in UNIX is "executable login names." These are names that run a program instead of simply giving you a shell, which is the normal way of starting a user's session on the system. They would appear like this:

```
date::100:50:Print the date:/bin:/bin/date
who::101:50:Print all logged on users:/bin:/bin/who
```

These can be run by anyone who has access to a terminal or modem port. Sometimes these are valid names, like date, who, and sync. Although it can be convenient for the administrator to have certain programs run on login, they frequently become holes through which someone trying to break in finds out a lot of information about the system.

Major holes appear when these login names execute shell scripts. Once an offender has obtained root privileges (even if only temporarily), an entry can be placed in the password file that runs a shell script at login (or an existing entry with a script could be modified). These scripts can be changed at any time to do what the unauthorized user wants them to do. For example, a sample entry in the password file could look like this:

```
break::102:50::/:/usr/bin/break
```

which would allow anyone to type the name "break" at a login prompt and have /usr/bin/break executed. When break is done, the login prompt comes back, and there is a new hole in the system. Why? Because the script "break" could contain commands to an editor that would edit the password file and add unauthorized entries. The reason this works is because getty (which prints the login prompt) is run by init, and the owner of that file is root. This privilege is passed on to the script because it is being run at login time, and routines that run at login usually need root access to perform necessary initializations. In this case, however, it allows the editor to read and write /etc/passwd. Thus, once the offender can get *one* write access to /etc/passwd (such as through a "trap door"), permanent access can be established, often through multiple entry points.

A few bugs also are floating around in old versions of UNIX that give away root capability. For example, if no uid (user ID) number is specified in a user's entry in the password file, the UID defaults to 0, or root. This is an easily overlooked hole. An example entry would look like this:

```
rt::::The Super User:/:/bin/sh
```

Here are some other problems that the administrator should watch for: If the first line in the password file is blank, a user can login as root with no password. Also check the "bin" entry in the password file, which usually runs system programs. If the bin entry has no password, as in the example above, someone could login as bin, and edit the crontab file to do a `chmod` (change permission mode) on the password file, gaining access to it. The bin user can also edit /etc/rc to change the password file. The rc file is used to configure the system at startup by running a series of programs automatically. All that is needed for the tampering to take effect is to wait for the administrator to reboot the system (because this is when the file is run). After rebooting, the person could login as a regular user, edit the password file, write it out, then be able to login as root anytime. These are only a few of the ways a person could achieve an unauthorized login. Unfortunately, more are being thought up every day.

Files and Programs

Another area of abuse involves unauthorized tampering with files and programs. The hardest step for someone who wants to break UNIX security is to become root that first time, but once this is achieved by any means, tampered files can be put anywhere in the system. Tampering can include placing "trap doors," patching `login` to enable it to steal passwords, reading and altering system accounting files, and so on. We show examples of these and other techniques later.

The major files that a root offender usually tampers with are /etc/passwd, /etc/*rc*, /usr/lib/crontab, and /usr/lib/uucp/L.sys. The key for identifying chinks in your armor as an administrator is to look for files that have the setuid bit (identified by an "s" in the permissions, visible with an "ls -l") on, and ownership of root. The purpose of the setuid bit is to allow a program to have temporary access to a more privileged status (such as root) while it is running. This is actually a very useful part of the UNIX system because it allows controlled access to many facilities that you would not want users to get at directly. Unfortunately, these programs can be tampered with so that they use their temporary root status to work some of the mischief we have been describing. A finite number of these files exist, and they can all be examined. The `chkset` script presented later automates the examination process for you. Knowing which files *could* be tampered with, however, doesn't tell you which ones *have* been tampered with or how. The hardest ones to find are the patched system files. Some of the commonly patched files are `login`, `su`, `passwd`, `ps`, `crypt`, and `mv`.

A sophisticated offender would cover up the file modification dates so that no one would suspect a switch. The only way to catch this tampering is to have a *checksum,* or record of the sum (number of bytes), of all the important files and store it offline or in encrypted form. By periodically checking the old sums with the new ones, the changed files are revealed.

Another thing to watch for as an administrator is the "hidden" file. Hidden files are part of the system and have their place: They make for less cluttered directory listings. The way to hide a file is to make the first character of the file name a dot (.). When using the `ls` command, you must specify -a for the dot files to be listed. Finding illegal files can be difficult if a file is buried down three or four directory levels and named inconspicuously. The solution is always to use the -a option with `ls` when you are looking for problems. Some commands print out dot files by default. `Ncheck` (1M) prints all files that have the setuid bit on. If a file is named strangely, it stands out right away. One of my favorites is the file "...". It looks rather strange, but it is a valid file name. You could even have a file name made of 14 dots, the maximum length of a file name.

Su's

The last area to watch for is illegal su's. Su is a facility that allows you to *substitute* another user ID for your own. If someone gets the root password, they can login on any terminal and use the `su` command with the root password. This is probably where offenders have the hardest time getting away with anything, however. First, all su transactions are recorded in a file called sulog. Unfortunately, this is no real hindrance if the offender can login as root because root can modify the log file to remove tell-tale entries. Further, if vi is invoked without a file name, nobody can see which file is being edited while the mischief is being done.

However, the alert system administrator can use the `ps` command. It prints out the `su` command line just as it does for all other processes, and it would be noticed right away that someone is su'd to root. Their parent process is under their login name and the su is owned by root: a dead giveaway. Last, the root password is needed. If someone already has the root password, why use su? The only reason to use su would be if it were patched to not log the transaction, and it changed the string that `ps` prints. We don't know if anyone has accomplished that yet.

Preserving Confidential Data

Even admitting that secrecy may be overdone, there are times when administrators need to protect important files from prying. This can be done in UNIX with special file permissions, special group access, encryption, or even by having the data on a disk pack that is only mounted when it is needed. However such data should not be left physically connected to the system if it isn't to be mounted, because an offender could mount it and gain access. The `mntlook` script presented later can scan all the devices and find such accessible but unmounted file systems.

The attitude should be "If you don't want anyone to see it, don't have it on line." And don't think that you have it so well hidden that no one can find it. If people have root access to your system, they could get a list of every file on that system within a matter of minutes. Then, while you aren't looking, they could uucp an interesting file to another system for later examination, put it on floppy, or even print it. Remember, when an unauthorized user gets into your system *there is no security!*

Controlling Modem Usage

Modems are one of the big holes in system security. Unless you have special hardware to prefilter callers, a UNIX system is always vulnerable through the modem ports.

Large mainframes can have any number of modems, both call-in and call-out. You might think that as long as login has the extra password for dial-up lines, everything is secure, but this is not true. There are programs that can try many combinations of likely login names and passwords, and it only takes *one* to get in!

Calling out to other systems with modems is another story. Usually a valid login wants to call out. But what if you have catchall logins at your site, such as "class", "education", "test", etc.? Someone could log in as one of these users and use the modem with no risk of being caught. The only way they can be caught is by the terminal line number if you have dedicated lines.

What if someone called into your system by modem, logged in as one of the previously mentioned catchalls, then called out to some faraway land? There would be no way to trace the call back to a specific user.

Preventing Illegal File Transfers

Illegal file transfers deal almost exclusively with uucp. On the Berkeley (BSD 4.1 and later) system, the networking commands also have similar problems. Here's an example: If someone runs a "door" script on a Berkeley system, the remote login command (rlogin) logs them in on another machine as root and never asks for root password. How is that for a blatant hole in the system? An unauthorized user can also use the remote copy (rcp) to copy the "door" program around to all the systems.

The main thing is to watch the log files. Then again, what if the offender removes all the questionable entries from the log files? You have no way of telling that it ever happened. Another area to watch for is offenders using systems that call and pretend to be a valid remote system. They can achieve that by changing the node name on their system to match that of one of your authorized "correspondents." It's very hard to catch a sophisticated offender, but we present some ideas that help.

Minimizing Opportunities for Break-Ins

This is where administrators often slack off. Point one is to *never* leave a terminal logged in as root unattended. Leaving a root access terminal unattended is like leaving a thousand keys to the company safe on your desk. All unauthorized users have to do is to have a "door" script ready and waiting. Once they can get their hands on your terminal, it only takes one command to give them infinite root capability. From then on, the system is no longer secure.

System administrators must examine their systems and look at them from an offender's point of view. Is there a time, anytime, when systems are vulnerable? What about in the middle of the night when backups are running? Can anyone get to the consoles? What about when someone comes into your office for help. If you leave for a second, could they do the chmod command, then trash the screen with something else so that you couldn't tell what had been done? These are the risks you have to think about.

Typical Security Problems

Having looked at the general duties of system and administrators and, in particular, the main areas of system security, we are ready to look in more detail at how security breaches can occur. Each method of tampering with the system has different advantages and disadvantages from the point of view of the offender, and leaves a different kind of evidence in its wake. By being aware of these characteristics, the administrator has a better chance of detecting security breaches and discouraging would-be offenders.

Trap Doors

We've already mentioned that people who can gain a root access to the system, if only briefly, can create programs that provide them with regular root access. Remember that the first thing that someone interested in breaching the security of a UNIX system wants to do is to find a way to become root. As we've noted, a breach of physical security or a poorly secured root password can give the offender the opportunity to run a process as root, which gives access to files (such as standard UNIX executables) that aren't modifiable by an ordinary user and allows people to make themselves "trap doors."

The key to the whole affair is in how the ownership and privileges associated with a file are stored in a UNIX system. In addition to the familiar user/group /others permissions that are set by the chmod command, there are two highest order bits called the setuid (set user id) and setgid (set group id) bits.

Normally a process run by a given user has only the access privileges that belong to that user. However, many system commands must access files that we would not want to allow a user to access except under very restricted circumstances. A perfect example is the passwd command, which allows a user to change his or her password. Obviously, this command must have write access to the /etc/passwd file, something only root normally has.

This is handled by the executable file for the passwd command having its setuid bit set to the file's owner, which for regular system commands, is root (a uid of 0). This means that *while the command's process is running,* the user has root privileges! When the command terminates, so does the root access ... unless the command has been tampered with in some way, or a special setuid program has been installed by an offender. Enter the trap door.

A trap door is usually a file owned by root but tampered with by an unauthorized user who has gained write access to it through some means, normally by gaining a temporary root access. The critical element to be understood about the trap door is that it is just another process, a clone of an ordinary user shell with one significant exception: It has a different user id number, usually 0, the id of root. Because the user id is stored in the process itself, it can be tampered with.

The actual passing through the door into root happens when the "door" program is run. The magic used here is the setuid bit. When this bit is on, the program sets (or changes) the user id of the process to that of the owner of the file (which happens to be root). While the uid is temporarily root, the program turns itself into a shell (usually by doing an `exec` system call). This shell is then on the other side of the door, in the realm of root, with all privileges pertaining thereto.

As we noted in the section on su's, the more sophisticated offenders can do several things to conceal their penetration of the system. One thing that can be done is have the "door" program do nothing unless it is called with an obscure option like -z. It is unlikely that a trap door prints a helpful syntax message if you call it without the right option.

Another trick is to have the door change its command line (which can be displayed by the full process status command ("ps -ef")) to something innocuous that is usually run by root (such as a `getty`).

A reasonably sophisticated offender is unlikely to leave the source code for a door on the system, so the administrator is left looking at an executable. The debugger (`adb`) can be used to disassemble the object code, but unless you have an insanely intimate acquaintance with UNIX internals, it would be very hard to figure out what is going on. The more sophisticated doors also avoid having recognizable strings in the executable. You can, however, use the `strings` command (if available on your system) to search for any strings that might be there.

Log Files

One of the easiest traps to walk into while playing with root is to generate an entry that is put into a log file. Administrators thus need to watch log files for entries that could indicate ongoing skulduggery. Later we show you a tool that automatically watches one of these logs, the sulog, that contains "substitute user" transactions. Another log file to check frequently is the one used by the `uucp` program because that program can be used for unauthorized file transfers. Many offenders try to check the log files and remove suspicious entries generated by their intrusion. There are ways administrators can deal with this. None are 100 percent effective, but they catch some offenders and by making offenders work harder, may discourage intrusions.

In addition to the regular log files that UNIX supports, some administrators make their own log files, then patch key commands to put data into these new log files when they are run. This can help defeat careless intruders. One administrator of our acquaintance made a log file for the `cu` command and called it /tmp/... /.culog. Quite a clever hiding trick, but he had an entry in /usr/lib/crontab to periodically print the file. A dead giveaway: A better disguise was necessary. Also note that your "hidden" log file names can be obtained by using `strings` to look through the executable image of the command.

If you have a user you suspect is doing something unauthorized, you might be able to set up a special logging system that would go into high gear when that user gets on the system. The `watch` program from Chapter 6 could be modified to call a special logger program when a user on the suspect list logs in. The logger program could do repeated `ps` (process status) commands and/or "snapshots" of the regular log files (especially the accounting files) and send the results to a concealed log file. The idea is that suspicious processes could be detected before the offender has a chance to go in and change the log files. (You should probably avoid using `at` with this program and use a periodic `sleep` instead. Otherwise, the offender might recognize the function of the entry in the crontab file.) Once you have the output from a suspicious user session, you could `grep` for the appropriate names or write a tool to do that for you.

Accounting Files

Probably the most important log file is accounting. The accounting file has a record for each and every process that runs in the system. The exact structure is in /usr /include/sys/acct.h. One of the fields in this structure records the processes that have superuser capability.

When someone goes through the root door, the shell they are running and all the processes that they spawn are owned by root. The accounting file includes the terminal number from which the process was run, so you can look for root processes run from terminals that shouldn't be used by people authorized for root access.

If you have regular dial-up lines, all such entries may not represent the same user. Other logins may have the same tty number but different uids. However, you can know who should have access to some dedicated lines.

When processes have a user id different than that of the person running them, the accounting files can be very revealing. Look for processes that were owned by a given user but had superuser capability. These can be valid entries, like `lpr` because any system program run with the setuid bit on shows up. The ones that we are looking for are shells with the accounting su flag set. This is a dead giveaway that a trap door was executed. Examine the acct.h include file to see the definitions. By using the ASU bit to check the field, we can isolate the one flag area that exposes superuser privilege. The best way to see this structure is to write a C program to print all the elements of the structure. The following printout shows some key accounting fields:

cmd	f	uid	tty	btime
more	0	russ	0	Sat Jul 5 01:25:59 1986
ls	0	russ	0	Sat Jul 5 01:31:12 1986

ps	0	russ	0	Sat	Jul	5	01:31:59	1986	
id	0	russ	0	Sat	Jul	5	01:34:00	1986	
pwd	0	russ	0	Sat	Jul	5	01:34:12	1986	
sh	1%	russ	0	Sat	Jul	5	01:33:51	1986	←effective root shell
sync	0	russ	0	Sat	Jul	5	01:34:21	1986	
df	0	russ	0	Sat	Jul	5	01:34:27	1986	
id	0	root	0	Sat	Jul	5	01:34:37	1986	
sh	2#	root	0	Sat	Jul	5	01:34:33	1986	←real uid root shell notice 2# for su bit, AND owner change to root

Note that effective uid shells mask a bit in the same flag as the superuser flag, but their processes are owned by the regular user. Whether or not all systems use the value of 1 to flag effective uid shells is uncertain. It seems that Berkeley does but System V does not.

Su

As we've noted earlier, the normal way UNIX provides a user to become root is by su. As seen previously, we can distill su to the `exec` system call. The would be su has to know the root password, the transaction is logged in /usr/adm/sulog, and a ps gives away the fact that a root shell is being run. This is not the most subtle technique either.

Root Terminal Access

Remember what we said about *never* leaving a terminal where you are running as root? While you're gone, someone can use the terminal to do the `chmod` command to set the userid bit. The well prepared offender has a door program already compiled, owned by root, and waiting to have the permissions changed. Are consoles left logged in as root during the night while backups are being performed? In this case, the early bird might leave the administrator holding the worm!

More on the `bin` User

We've already mentioned a "hole" in some systems that allows the "bin" user to immediately get root access. "Bin" has some further ramifications: If unauthorized users can log in as bin (the owner of most distribution executables), they are almost guaranteed to become root. First, in some releases all the executables in /bin and /usr/bin are owned by bin. This means offenders can overwrite or patch executables with their own version that could do something special, like "chmod 4755 door," then replace itself with the original version of the executable.

Another way bin can easily get to be root is by modifying /etc/rc, which is the "run command" file. It gets run every time the machine boots into multiuser mode. By editing it to "chmod 777 /etc/passwd", the offender can change the password file as a regular user after the machine has booted.

The last way bin can get in is through /usr/lib/crontab. This path has changed for the latest System V release. It is now in /usr/spool/cron/crontabs/xxx, where xxx is a crontab file for each user. The old way, /usr/lib/crontab, sometimes is owned by bin. Someone can edit the file and put in commands like this:

```
* * * * *      chmod 777 /etc/passwd
* * * * *      chmod 4755 /tmp/door
* * * * *      /bin/su root -c "chmod 777 /etc/passwd"
```

The reason this works is because `cron` is executed by `init`. Because init is one of the first processes run, it is owned by root. Thus any command executed by `cron` has root privilege. The asterisks tell cron to execute at the next possible moment. Cron runs a process that changes the permissions of the specified file. Offenders can change the password file (which is a little more dangerous) or just activate a trap door. If the first two do not work, they change the ownership to root by brute force by doing a su, then passing the command to the su shell. You should check crontab and /etc/rc frequently!

Write Capability to Special Files

This one is a little farfetched. It presumes that a regular user has write permission to an executable or a special file. If they can write to an executable, say ls, they can put in some code that installs a trap door, then replaces itself with the real utility. This works best when a user with root capability runs the command because it then runs as a privileged process. Hiding code in this way in a program and having an unsuspecting user run it is called the "Trojan Horse." It looks harmless but hidden inside is something that launches an attack on the system security. As we noted previously, periodically checking sums on standard executables is one antidote to Trojan Horses.

If offenders gain read or write capability for device files, they can read those files for the superblock/file system and gain access to any file. They would need to traverse the file system for the file they want, patch it, and write it back out to the device file. People who do this and slip up can crash the whole system.

If the device file is mem or kmem, users can scan memory directly for process or kernel information. The old technique of monitoring the clists for the incoming password of a user logging on can be used. This still requires much knowledge about where the information is in memory and how to get at it, so this is likely to be used only by the sophisticated offender.

Reboot System

On some systems, rebooting the machine can allow the console to come up with a root shell. This may occur in single-user mode, or on a micro that is running as the console for a mainframe. The obvious solution is to restrict physical access to the console.

Take Advantage of $PATH

Others can take advantage if a user has his $HOME/bin in front of the system /bin and /usr/bin in his PATH variable. By placing a doctored routine in the innocent user's home directory, they can have that routine executed rather than the real one because the system executes the first file matching the command name that it encounters along the user's defined path list. An example of this would be the ls command.

When the command executes, it runs with the same capability as the person running it. The ultimate is to get root to run it because offenders can execute any command as though they were the root user. The routine can install a root trap door or even trap doors to become other regular uids. It could remove itself so that the next time that command was executed, the real one would be executed. As administrator, examining your own workspace for suspicious files (particularly executables) is a must.

False Tape Release

We haven't heard of anyone doing this, but it's worth guarding against. An industrious offender would first make patches to the system, put these patches on a tape and mail it to you, the administrator. You would probably assume that it is a valid update to the system and install it. Your system now has the offender's "fix" installed. Administrators might want to check new releases with their vendor before installing them.

Crypt Database

Although we can't guarantee that some intelligence "spook shop" hasn't figured out how to crack it, UNIX password encryption with the DES algorithm is believed to be quite secure. (The mechanics of DES are beyond the scope of this book.) One thing that adds to this security is two randomly generated characters called "salt" that are stored in the /etc/passwd file for each entry. The salt is used to determine which of 4,096 variations of the DES algorithm are used to encrypt a given password. An offender could grab a password, use its salt, and encrypt a list of known passwords. If the result matches the sample password, they've cracked that account.

The offender would have to have access to some pretty sensitive techniques to pull this off. One general precaution the administrator can take is to watch for excessive use of the `crypt` command (if it is on your system). This command is purposely designed to use lots of CPU time: not enough to inconvenience the occasional, legitimate user, but enough to discourage automated cracking attempts.

Decoy

Decoy only works on dedicated lines. When UNIX is waiting for somebody to login, it prints the login string in /etc/gettydefs. The user enters his login name and password and gets on the system.

A decoy program takes advantage of this. What it does is simulate the login screen. When the user types his or her name and password, the program prints out a "login incorrect" message, then runs the real login program. The user thinks he or she made a mistake and does it again, this time successfully. The logname and password can be stashed somewhere for later examination. An administrator's best defense against this is educating the users, perhaps with regular mail or bulletins reminding them that if they think they typed the password correctly and still got the "incorrect" message, they should immediately change their password and report the incident to the administrator. There are going to be cases where the user indeed made an error, but a rash of such incidents should be viewed with grave suspicion.

Mount Command

The mount command was created to allow multiple disk drives to be connected to the system. Back in minicomputer days, the only kind of disk drives were the big ones, with large packs that fit inside. They were usually in the machine room and only administrators mounted them.

Today many systems have floppy disks. They are much more personal than large disk packs and much smaller. This reduction in size influences the perceived importance of the object itself. It seems now that each person can handle their disks and it's not necessary to have the administrator do it. This scenario leads us to the following kind of shenanigans.

The usual action taken on small systems to allow users to handle their own floppies is to set the user id bit on /etc/mount. That way when mount is run, its uid is forced to root and it can mount the floppy disk. The umount command needs to be fixed the same way.

Someone can take advantage of the runability of mount to become superuser. Usually in offices with small systems, one machine is open for an unauthorized person to play with. What they do is become root on your system, make a trap door, and place it on the floppy disk. The owner is root and the permission is 4755. Then they unmount the floppy and go to the protected system.

At this point, they can merely log on as a regular user, with no special permissions required, and mount the floppy that has the trap door. When the floppy is mounted, the floppy file system is integrated into the hard disk file system and the two systems become one. This means that the root trap door just became one with the hard disk file system.

When they run the trap door that is on the floppy, it makes them just like one that was on the hard disk. The key to prevention is to control the use of `mount` on your system. `Mount` should be a restricted command, or if it must be made available to certain users, it should not allow the mounting of setuid files.

Standalone Shell (SASH)

On UNIX systems that install with floppy disks, a boot disk usually boots from the floppy drive. This disk is meant to be used for preparing the hard disk and copying all the UNIX files from floppy to hard disk, but it is more than that.

The bootable floppy is really a compact, transportable version of UNIX. Instead of living on the hard disk, the kernel is adapted to live on a floppy disk. When you boot it, you get a shell and environment just like the hard disk has. This is where the name standalone shell or SASH came from.

The floppy root file system even looks just like the hard disk file system. In fact, you can mount the bootable disk, and copy utilities from the hard disk to the floppy disk. The two critical commands needed are mount and umount. The limitation is the size of the floppy. Not much fits.

The scenario by which an unauthorized user could use a SASH to get into a system with root privileges would go something like this. First, they would power down or reset the protected system. Next, they would boot up the SASH and mount the hard disk root file system to a mount point on their floppy file system. The commands would be:

```
# /etc/mount /dev/fp001 /mnt    ←for System V
# /etc/mount /dev/hd0a  /mnt    ←for XENIX
```

This gives them access to the hard disk by referencing it as /mnt/*. All they have to do to edit the /etc/passwd file on the hard disk is go down the directory tree. A typical command string might be

```
# /mnt/bin/vi /mnt/etc/passwd
# sync
```

At this point, the hard disk is changed and put back to bed. The offender can halt the standalone UNIX and reboot from the hard disk. They can use the new login created from the SASH. How often people might try this, we don't know. Small systems are more vulnerable but also have fewer users (and potential abusers). In many cases, the bottom line of "logical security" becomes "physical security." Most people who have mainframes or even minis are constantly aware that they have a tangible asset which must be guarded, but micros look so "friendly" and commonplace that people tend to forget that the information they contain may be just as desirable or valuable under some circumstances as that found on a big machine.

Source Code Patches

By far, source code patches are the most powerful, if not the easiest way, someone can penetrate a system. By implanting their own code in just the right places, unauthorized users can get all the secret information they can handle. However, code patches can be useful to the administrator, too. An administrator might want to make a patch to the login program to see who and how many times people try to log on the machine. Another possibility is to patch "suid" and other restricted programs to log their sessions to a secret log file.

Kernel

Another place to watch for unauthorized patching is the kernel libraries. Patched object modules can be easily placed unnoticed into libraries. All other libraries are game too. Additional clever fixes to the kernel might be found in the `chmod` and `chown` system calls. When these system calls are made, they check to see whether you have a uid of 0. If not, you are not granted the request. By disabling the check, any normal user could change the ownership of a file to root and also change the mode to have the setuid bit on, which would effectively eliminate the security barrier.

Passwd

The `passwd` program is the gatekeeper of the UNIX system. Just as many an ancient city fell because the enemy bribed the gatekeeper, an otherwise well secured UNIX system can be blown wide open if someone patches this program. Because users use `passwd` to change their passwords, a patched version can write the new password that the user types for the change to a secret file belonging to the offender. This could yield every newly created password on the system. The password within `passwd` is only a character array, so it is easy to manage the data.

Crypt

A possible patch to `crypt` (the file-encryption program) would be to stash away the file name and crypt key every time the program is used. This way you can monitor who runs the command, which file they used, and what key is used to get into the file.

The nasty thing about these last two cases is that someone can subvert the system's security measures. If you believe you have attractive, sensitive data on your system, as administrator you better check these programs frequently (with checksums or compares) for tampering.

Su

Because su provides root access to ordinary users who have the root password, it's
another potential security hole.

The general flow of su is as follows:

```
get info on user: uid, gid, password, tty, ...
if the password is null or the uid is zero
   then go past the password questions

prompt for the password
if the encrypted version of what was just typed
       doesn't match the password string from /etc/passwd file
then    log an unsuccessful su attempt
        print sorry
        exit
passed:
   log a successful su attempt
   make the system calls to force uid and gid
   set up the environment if requested
   log a message to the console if this a root shell and
     you are not on the system console
   fixes up argv to show su in a ps command
   execs a shell
```

A patched version would require only minor changes in the above sequence.
Instead of encrypting the password right away, su could be checked for the offender's "secret" password.

If this password is entered, the password check and logging would be skipped,
so the illegal access would not be logged. The unauthorized user would cause all
other su passwords to be logged in a "secret" file, so he or she gradually obtains all
the interesting ones for possible use. The user would get his or her su if the
password is valid, and the offender gets the password.

Login

An unauthorized user can attack `login` using methods similar to those used for
`passwd`. The administrator can do more than guard this program from abuse,
however. On the theory that the best defense is a good offense, the administrator
can do his or her own patch of `login` and use it as an intrusion-warning system.
Each time someone logs in or tries to log in, a record of the name and password
used can be updated. This can alert you to any brute force hackers trying to guess at
passwords.

Because of the way that `login` was written, only one patch is needed. Both
the user password and the dialup password checking algorithm call the same sub-
routine. Unfortunately, we can't show it here, since unauthorized users could use it
to collect passwords for their own purposes. Further, if you set up your own
security log file for login attempts, you have to try to make sure offenders can't read

it and save themselves the trouble. One thing you might do, although it would add overhead, is to `crypt` the passwords in the log file under your own secret key so that even if someone reads the file, they won't be able to use the information.

Venial Sins

The cases that follow are lesser but still potentially troublesome security problems. They do not involve ways to become root but are ways to fool the system and get away with it.

System Mode

This technique is unlikely to be encountered unless you run into someone who is very familiar with the low-level operation of whatever processor your machine uses. It goes to the heart of the hardware environment and slips one over on the operating system. Nevertheless, administrators need to be aware that such things are possible.

In many CPUs, the Motorola 68000 for example, there is a Processor Status Register commonly known as the PSW, although the actual name varies with the processor used. The PSW has a bit that determines whether the machine is in "supervisor" mode or user mode. The mode is important to multiuser hardware because all user programs run in user mode, which segments and protects memory from "collisions" between processes.

The kernel, on the other hand, runs in supervisor mode, which means that the memory protection is not enforced and the CPU may alter the contents of any memory location in the whole machine. The kernel requires this content alteration because the kernel maintains a swapping mechanism for moving a process in and out of protected memory when it is executed.

If security offenders can get a program to run under system mode, they gain the ability to change all memory in the system.

The results could range from sheer destruction, such as storing zeros in every memory location, to the ability to read any sort of data in memory, including passwords and otherwise highly restricted information.

To access system mode, the offender needs the capability of generating and installing a new kernel. The method used depends on whether they have the kernel source code. The details given here pertain to the 68000 but could be similar with other processors.

System Call

The first method is to create a "custom" system call. The system calls are in the source files os/sys?.c. There are about 60 system calls and each has a specific number. This number is dictated by the sysent table, which is a table of addresses of the entry points into the system calls. Code would be provided to add the new call. When the kernel is recompiled and installed, the system call could be made from any program in the system. Once activated, the call would run the machine in system mode.

Fortunately, it isn't easy for an "ordinary" user to recompile and reinstall your kernel. This technique probably requires an "inside job." Keeping your source off the system would help, but if you need to have system programmers modify the source regularly, all you can do is try to restrict access (and pick reliable people)!

Pseudo Device

The second method could be used by offenders who don't have source, but do have all the libraries that make up the kernel. The approach here is a little bit different, but gives the same result.

The same idea of system mode applies: The goal is to have the PSW in the CPU set to privileged ("supervisor" or "system mode") access. Instead of using the kernel proper, this method uses an outside driver that is linked with the kernel. The way this is done is by creating a pseudo device. A pseudo device is like a real one, but the name does not lead to a physical peripheral. The device is accessed with all the same primitives (open, close, read, write), but it accesses a logical area, not a physical one.

To define a pseudo device, the master device file must be modified. In the master file (named /etc/master or /usr/sys/conf/master) is a table of all the device driver names associated with each primitive. When a pseudo device is created, a new entry is put in the device driver table. The table names the routines that support the primitives.

Privileged mode is achieved by opening the pseudo device. The open system call passes control to the device driver, which is the code that was added. When the code runs, the machine is already in system mode because when the "open" call was made, it was "trapped" by the system and handed over to a handler that runs in system mode. Then the device driver can do what it wants.

Impersonate a Remote uucp *Node*

If login is like the fortress gate, uucp is like an abandoned escape tunnel that enemies might use to get into the palace. A whole new set of security holes arise when intermachine communications come in.

With uucp, unauthorized users can get in by impersonating a remote uucp node. This is very easy to do. They can look in the /usr/lib/uucp/L.sys file on your system and find where the remote systems are by looking up logins to other machines. Then they look in /etc/passwd for logins that run uucico programs rather than a regular shell. If they find out the associated passwords, they might try some likely ones or use one of the patching methods discussed previously for intercepting passwords.

Then they could change the node name of their system to the node name of the remote system to impersonate. They can login under "uucp" or the special login name for the remote machine. Uucp gives their node name (which is the forged name) to your system.

They can transfer mail, files, etc., from your system to their machine. If you have anything in the queue waiting for the legitimate remote machine, they get it right then and there. You might get suspicious when one of your legitimate remote system's operators calls and asks you why they haven't gotten any mail or other routine transactions from you for weeks! However, a sneaky offender could remail a copy of the purloined files back to you and use the forwarding facility to send them on to the legitimate remote machine.

Falsification of Mail

This is pretty well known, but we include it for the sake of completeness. However, it doesn't seem to work in all versions of UNIX. It works on System V but not on XENIX System III or Berkeley 4.2. What is done is to change the user's LOGNAME environment variable. Because `mail` uses this to identify you when you send mail, the mail header is changed. This would usually just be a nuisance, but you should make people aware of it so that they think twice about messages that don't seem to be characteristic of their alleged sender.

Hide Filenames While in Vi

Doing occasional `ps` commands is a useful security practice, being more or less equivalent to walking a beat once in a while to see whether anything suspicious is going on. One thing to note, however, is that people using vi to do unauthorized things can cover their tracks by fixing the name of the file they are editing so that it doesn't appear in the `ps` listing. The simplest way that they can do this is call vi without a file name. This starts vi with a null file. Then they can issue the ex command to edit the file they want: :e filename. This keeps the file out of the ps listing because it is not part of vi's argv vector. The argv array is set when vi is called, not after it is running.

The other way is to use a disguise. They can move the file they want to edit to a dummy name like tmp, then use the tmp name when calling vi. This sets the argv array to the name tmp. That's what appears in `ps`.

Name: access

access

Function

Searches the password file for all logins that don't have passwords.

Synopsis

access

Sample Call

access   List all logins that don't have passwords

Code for access

```
1   :
2   # a(#) access v1.0   Show all free access logins   Author: Russ Sage
3
4   if [ "$#" -gt 0 ]
5     then  echo "access: too many arguments"  >&2
6           echo "usage: access"               >&2
7           exit 1
8   fi
9
10  grep '^[^:]*::' /etc/passwd || echo "All logins protected"
```

Description

Why do we need access?

We mentioned that login entries in the password file can be security holes if they have no associated password, that is, the password field is empty. The problem is that on large systems, the password file can get really big. To try and scan it manually for logins that lack passwords would be painstaking, and you would be prone to make errors. Why not let the system do the work for you?

What does access do?

Access uses the grep command with a search pattern that describes a login entry which has no password. When one is found, it is printed on stdout. If no entries are found that qualify, the message "All logins protected" is printed.

Explanation

The first thing access does (in lines 4-8) is check to see whether it was called correctly. Because there are no options, the command line should have nothing on it. If the number of arguments on the command line is greater than zero, the error message is printed to standard error and the script is exited.

  The statement in line 10 searches the password file. Grep is used because we are using an expression in the command. If we were using a fixed string, fgrep would be a better choice because it is faster. The search expression means: Find from the beginning of the line noncolon characters and continue until two contiguous colons are found. If you look in /etc/passwd, you can see that the first field is a name (from beginning of the line to the first colon). The password then falls between the first colon and the second colon. If there is no password, the first colon is immediately followed by the second colon, which matches our search pattern. The search is performed on the file /etc/passwd. If grep was successful for even one entry, the return status is zero. If grep did not match anything, the return status is one, triggering the last part of line 10 and echoing the message that all logins are protected.

Name: chkset

chkset

Function

Displays all files that have the setuid/setgid permission bit on.

Synopsis

chkset [-l] [dir ...]

Sample Call

chkset -l   Search from the root directory (/) because no directory is specified.
Display files that have either the uid or the gid bit set on, using the
"ls -ld" format. Output is sorted by file name

Code for chkset

```
1    :
2    # @(#) chkset v1.0   Check for set bits on   Author: Russ Sage
3
4    FORM="-print"
5    SORT="sort"
6
7    if [ "`echo $1 | cut -c1`" = "-" ]
8      then  case $1 in
9            -l)     shift
10                   FORM="-exec ls -ld {} ;"
11                   SORT="sort +7";;
12           *)      echo "usage: chkset [-l][file/dir ...]" >&2
13                   exit 1;;
14           esac
15   fi
16
17   if [ "$#" -gt 0 ]
18     then  SRC="$*"
19     else  SRC="/"
20   fi
21
22   find $SRC \( -perm -4000 -o -perm -2000 \) $FORM | $SORT
```

Environment Variables

FORM   Holds command and options for listing
SORT   Holds command and options for sorting output
SRC   Holds source directory to start searching from

Description

Why do we need chkset?

We have described the security problems that can arise when executable files have the uid bit set on such that they run a shell with root or other high-level privileges. The gid (group id) bit can be set for the same purpose. Therefore, the system administrator must constantly seek out and examine all the files in the system that have these bits on to see whether they are being used for unauthorized purposes.

Not all the violating shells are owned by root. One user could be running a shell that is owned by another user who has a higher privilege. This effectively gives the user running the shell all capabilities of the owner of the file.

Setuid/setgid shells can be easy or difficult to find, depending on the person who installed them. The easy ones to find are those that:

- Have unusual names (some offenders like to flaunt their achievements)
- Have strings in the executable file that can be read
- Are placed in an uncommon or obvious directory
- Have no restrictions on who runs them

The tricky ones have names that sound like regular UNIX commands, file sizes that match the other files around them, hidden strings that can't be easily read, and perhaps a special option that triggers the shell or even a special password that is needed to get the shell. The toughest ones are real UNIX commands that have been worked over to provide root shells, then reinstalled in place of the original ones. The only sure way to identify this last type is to run byte-for-byte comparisons between your distribution copies of the UNIX commands and the versions currently residing on your system.

Of course, you have to find all the set-bit files before you can examine them. A couple of commands in UNIX do this: One is find(1) and the other is ncheck(1M). Find looks up files to our exact specification and can be used to find files with a given set of permissions, including set bits. Ncheck prints a mixture of special files and setuid files. This is a very large list and takes a lot of time to read and identify the files we are interested in. Thus, it is useful to create a script that provides all the information we need, but only that information. Chkset uses find and looks only for set bit files, so its output has just the information we are looking for and is immediately usable.

What does chkset do?

Chkset has two different operating modes, one for scanning the entire system and the other for scanning specified directory trees. This is a nice feature because scanning every file in the whole system is very time-consuming. With many large disk drives, it might take as much as an hour to check everything on the system. Chkset is also a real CPU hog because of all the processes it generates. By providing directory names, you can single out certain areas of the system tree to examine. Note however that because chkset uses find, it does not scan just the directory you specified but *all* subordinate directories. Note also that `chkset` finds *all* files with the uid or gid bits set, not just those owned by root.

The output of `chkset` can also be specified in two ways. If no option is used, the output is from "find ... -print", which gives the full pathnames of the files found. The pathnames are then sorted.

If the -l option is used, the "ls -ld" command is used to format the output, which in this case consists of the long listing information. This includes the full permissions, number of links, owner, size, and file name. This output is also sorted by file name.

Which format you want to use depends on circumstances: If you want to check a large part of the system and get a list of suspect files, the default (no option) listing is more compact and, as we see later, uses considerably less CPU time. If you want to home in on a particular directory and look at files in detail, the -l option provides more information and saves having to do `ls` commands manually on the files you are interested in.

Note that this command can be run by anyone, not just the administrator who has root privileges. If it is run by a normal user, however, the `find` command within `chkset` is limited to files for which the user has read permission. You could thus suggest to your more privileged users that they run `chkset` as part of their personal security precautions. If `chkset` is run by root of course, none of the file permissions hold and all files can be examined.

Example

```
# chkset /bin /usr/bin /lib /usr/lib
```

This forces the searching of the directories specified. In directories like /usr/lib, all subordinate directories are searched, which is a more thorough security check.

Explanation

The first thing `chkset` does is to initialize two variables, FORM and SORT. FORM contains the command used to generate the output from `find`, whereas SORT holds the command that determines what is sorted in the output.

In line 7, the first positional parameter is checked to see whether it is an option. If it is, the case statement (lines 8-14) checks to see whether the option is "-l". If it is, the command for listing the output is set (this is discussed later). The command for the `sort` is set for sorting on the owner field. The option is shifted away because any further arguments should be directories, and we want to be able to access them with "$#" later. If the option was not "-l", it is invalid, the error message is issued (line 12), and the script exits.

If more than zero arguments are left when we get to line 17, they are looped through to make sure they're all directories. If they are not directories, an error message is printed to standard error and the script exits.

If there are parameters (that is, directories), line 18 sets SRC to hold all of the directories. If there are no parameters, SRC is set to "/" instead, that is, to the root directory, to provide the default starting point.

The workhorse of this script is the `find` statement. `Find` allows multiple starting directories in its calling sequence, which accommodates any of the directories we read from the command line and store in SRC.

After telling find where to start, we tell it what to look for. In this case we are interested in all files that have either the setuid or setgid bit on. We tell find this by specifying the permissions to look for. The string -perm -4000 says to find all files that have the permission with setuid on and any other bits on. You can think of it as a kind of wildcard, 4???. We look for both the setuid (-4000) and setgid (-2000), so the two permission strings are joined with an -o for "or." (A more complete explanation of permission modes in symbolic and octal form can be found under chmod(1).)

The next task is to add the string in FORM to the command line. If the -l option was not used, the string in FORM is "- print", which causes find to print the pathnames of the files found. If -l *was* used, the string contains "-exec ls -ld { } ;" The -exec is a very versatile option to find that allows any commands which follow it to be applied to each file in the output. The commands in this case do the listing in long format (-l) with just the names given for directories (-d). This is where the most consumption of CPU resources occurs because the - l option requires a stat call. Because each file requires an ls, for each file ls is loaded into memory and executed and the file inode is accessed on the disk, which makes for a lot of overhead.

Then the entire stream of data is sent through sort. The field that we want to sort on is actually the eighth field (you can verify this by doing an "ls -l" and examining the output.) However, sort *skips over* the number of fields specified, with a default starting point of field 1, so using +7 skips to the eighth field, which is the file name.

An Alternative Approach

Another method, albeit a slow one, could be used to find the permission patterns that we are interested in. It is basically the statement we have now except that instead of looking for the permission modes by number, we look for them by character string. This requires that we use grep. The alternative command looks like this:

```
# find $* -exec ls -ld {} \; | grep "^[^ ]*s[^ ]*"
```

It works a little differently from the one we are using. It finds every file from the specified directories and does an "ls - ld" on each. Then the entire list of data is piped to the grep command. Grep uses the following pattern to match these types of files: From beginning of the line, find a nonblank character repeated, then an "s" character, followed by a nonblank character repeated. This pattern matches all permission modes that contain an s, whether they are a uid set bit or gid set bit. There is no concern whether the mode has r, w, x, or -. By making sure that there are no blanks, we force the pattern match to the permission field only. This is important when the s is followed by nonblanks because then the s can occur either in the owner portion of the permissions or in the group portion of the permissions and nowhere else.

This method has little to recommend it because it involves so much processing. However, if we had hit on this method first, we may not have realized that using find with "-perm" strings is a better way. The flip side of the incredible versatility of UNIX is that there are so many different ways to accomplish a task and many of them may produce equally good results, but at differing costs in terms of speed and CPU usage. Before using a general-purpose facility such as grep to solve a problem, consider whether another command has a built-in pattern matching option. Chances are the latter is optimized and much faster than using grep. On the other hand, sometimes you need a quick solution to an infrequently encountered problem and don't care all that much about efficiency.

Name: suw

suw

Function

Scans the sulog and prints the names of all users who have illegally su'd (substituted user) to root.

Synopsis

suw [-m] [sulog]

Sample Call

suw   Run in default mode, check /usr/adm/sulog, and print violating entries to stdout

Code for suw

```
1    static char id[]="@(#)suw v1.0    Author: Russ Sage";
2
3    #include <stdio.h>
4
5    #define FALSE 0
6    #define TRUE  1
7    #define MATCH 0
8    #define BSIZ  80
9
10   main(argc,argv)
11   int   argc;
12   char *argv][;
13   {
14        register int  alert, c, mail, n;
15        FILE    *fp1, *fp2;
16        char    *p, *uname, line[BSIZ], tmp[BSIZ],
17                *log = "/usr/adm/sulog";
```

```
18
19          static char   *legal[] = {"sage-root\n","root-root\n",NULL};
20          static char   *adm[]   = {"sage",NULL};
21
22
23      mail = FALSE;
24
25      if (argc > 1 && argv[1][0] == '-')
26              switch (argv[1][1])
27              {
28                  case 'm':
29                      mail = TRUE;
30                      --argc;
31                      ++argv;
32                      break;
33                  default:
34                      fprintf(stderr,"suw: invalid argument %s\n",argv[1])
35                      fprintf(stderr,"usage: suw [-m] [sulog]\n");
36                      exit(1);
37              }
38
39      if (argc == 2)
40              log = *++argv;
41
42      if ((fp1 = fopen(log,"r")) == NULL)
43      {
44              fprintf(stderr,"suw: error opening %s\n",log);
45              fprintf(stderr,"usage: suw [-m] [sulog]\n");
46              exit(1);
47      }
48
49      sprintf(tmp,"/tmp/suw%d",getpid());
50      if ((fp2 = fopen(tmp,"w+")) == NULL)
51      {
52              fprintf(stderr,"suw: error opening %s\n",tmp);
53              fprintf(stderr,"usage: suw [-m] [sulog]\n");
54              exit(1);
55      }
56
57      while (fgets(line,sizeof(line),fp1) != NULL)
58      {
59              p = line + 15;
60              if (*p == '+')
61              {
62                      p = p + 2;
63                      while (*p != ' ') p++;
64                      p++;
```

```
65                        uname = p;
66                        while (*p && *p++ != '-')
67                                continue;
68
69                        if (strcmp (p,"root\n") == MATCH)
70                        {
71                                alert = TRUE;
72                                for (n=0; legal[n] != NULL; n++)
73                                        if (strcmp (uname,legal[n]) == MATCH)
74                                        {
75                                                alert = FALSE;
76                                                break;
77                                        }
78                                if (alert)
79                                        fprintf(fp2,"Illegal --> %s",line);
80                        }
81                }
82        }
83
84        if (mail)
85        {
86                fclose(fp2);
87                for (n=0; adm[n] != NULL; n++)
88                {
89                        sprintf(line,"cat %s | mail %s",tmp,adm[n]);
90                        system(line);
91                }
92        }
93        else
94        {
95                rewind(fp2);
96                while ((c = getc(fp2)) != EOF)
97                        putc(c, stdout);
98                fclose(fp2);
99        }
100
101        fclose(fp1);
102        unlink(tmp);
103 }
```

Description

Why do we need suw?

You recall that the su command, which allows users to change their identities (and permissions), can be a source of security problems. The system keeps a log of all su transactions, called the sulog. Although more sophisticated offenders might be able to cover their tracks, the sulog is a good place to watch for potential security

337

breaches. Many amateur offenders can be caught this way. Naturally, we want to automate this process so that the system does the checking and alerts us when something suspicious is found. In addition, this program demonstrates techniques that can be used to monitor other log files.

What does suw *do?*

Suw reads and analyzes su log files. Each successful su to root found there is checked against a list of valid root users. If the user is not a valid root user, the specific entry is printed so that the administrator is alerted.

By default, the violating entries are printed to stdout. The default file is /usr /adm/sulog. If the -m option is used, the violating entries are mailed to a list of predetermined administrators. If a different log file is to be examined, like /usr /adm/Osulog, the name can be passed on the command line.

Examples

1. `# suw -m`

Check /usr/adm/sulog and mail the violating entries to the administrators defined in the program.

2. `# suw /usr/adm/Osulog`

Check the file /usr/adm/Osulog and print violating entries to stdout.

Explanation

In the beginning of the program, all the variables and lists are defined and initialized. Two flags are defined in line 14, alert and mail. They have the value of either TRUE or FALSE. Two files are used in this program, the sulog of your choice and a temporary file. Because we are going to use some of the stdio (standard I/O) routines, we are using file pointers, fp1 and fp2 rather than file descriptors. Two buffers are used, one for reading the sulog data into and the other for holding the temporary file name. The logfile name is initially sulog. If there is an overriding file name, log is reset to that name.

Next, the predetermined lists of legal root users and administrators are initialized. In this example, the two valid root users are sage (sage-root) and root (root-root). To configure this for your system, put in the names of the people you want to allow to su to root. The administrator list should also have the appropriate names put in. In this example, the administrator list has one name in it, sage. This means that sage is the only one to receive mail if the mail option is specified.

The default state for mailing is set in line 23 to FALSE, or no mail. This is done so that after the command line is parsed, the mail variable is correctly configured.

Next, error checking is performed. The first check looks somewhat bizarre but is really straightforward. Argc returns the number of arguments in the command line, whereas argv points to an array containing the arguments themselves, each of which is itself an array of characters. If the command line has any arguments at all (argc > 1) and the first character of the first argument (argv[1][0]) is a dash, a check is made to see whether it is a valid option. A case statement is used to check on the second character of the first argument (argv[1] [1]).

If the argument is the m character, the mail flag is set to TRUE, the number of arguments (argc) is decremented, and the base pointer to the array of arguments (argv) is incremented. This serves the same function as the shifting of arguments in shell scripts. Remember that argv is really an array of pointers, and arrays are treated just like strings with a base pointer and offset. So argv[0] == argv, and argv[1] == ++argv. If the option is not an m, the error messages are printed to stdout and the program exits.

In line 39, the arg count is checked to see whether there is another argument. Remember that argv is always one behind argc because the actual command name is the first argument in the array. Therefore, to get the second argument, we need to go to the next position (*++argv). If there is an argument, it should be a log file and log is set to that string.

Next, we try to open the files used in the program. First, the log file is opened for reading. If it doesn't work (returns a null), an error message is printed and the program exits. Then the temporary file name is generated in line 49, appending the process id to ensure a unique file name. The file is opened for reading and writing. If this operation fails, error messages are printed and execution stops.

We get to the main loop in lines 57-103. The control of the main loop is determined by whether all the data has been read from the log file. If no more bytes can be read, fgets (line 57) returns a null, which terminates the while loop. When a line of data is read from the log file, that data is put into the array called line. We use a character pointer to traverse along the line and check for a violating entry.

Examine an entry in your sulog file so that you can see where the fields are. First, the pointer is set to 15 characters from the beginning of the line. This is the position of the flag that determines whether or not the su was successful. If it was successful, the pointer is incremented by two to skip the blank and place the pointer on the terminal name. This name is of variable length, so we key on the blank at the end of the name. A while loop is used in lines 63-64 to make the pointer skip over all nonblanks. Then it is incremented one more time to skip the blank between the terminal name and the user name string.

At this point, the pointer is on the last field of the line. The variable uname is set to point here so that we can use it later in a string comparison. The next while loop (lines 66-67) goes through the string until it gets to the dash character. The while loop is true as long as we are not pointing to the end of the string (that is, pointing at a null, *p == '\0'), and we are not yet at the dash. Because the loop uses p++, when we get to the null, the loop stops with p pointing to the next character.

The check is made to see whether the person su'd to was root. If it is a match, the alert flag is set and we should check to see whether this person is a legal root user. A for loop (lines 72-77) runs through all names in the array containing the legal users until we get to the last entry, which is null. The user name string, which was set up previously, is checked against each entry in the legal name array. If they match, we can assume that the su was okay, and we turn off the alert and stop comparing names. If the alert flag is still true at the time the loop is done, the name is not in the legal array and there is a possible offender. The complete entry is written to the temp file and control is passed back to the beginning of the loop for another read.

When all the data has been read, the while loop terminates. In line 84, the mail flag is checked to see whether it is true. If it is, the temp file is closed (so the `cat` command works), and another for loop (lines 87-91) is executed. It loops through all the administrators and stops when it gets to the null at the end of the array. A mail command is constructed for each of the designated administrators and is sent to UNIX by a system call (line 90). The technique for mailing the temp file is to `cat` the file and pipe the data into the mail command.

If the mail flag is off, the temp file should be printed to stdout instead of being mailed. To make this as fast as possible, the temp file (which is still opened) is rewound (reset to the beginning) and looped through character by character. Notice that this loop is the heart of the `cat` command, as described on page 153 of *The C Programming Language* by B.W. Kernighan and D. M. Ritchie. After the file has been printed, the temp file is closed. Finally the log file is closed and the temp file is removed.

10
Miscellaneous Tricks

Conversion tricks for shell programming
Shell tricks for programming flexibility
Vi and ed tricks
Bugs, features, and explorations

Miscellaneous Tricks

Introduction

This book is the culmination of years of collecting and developing useful UNIX tools. A number of things didn't fit in any of the other chapters but are too good to leave out. These range from full-length scripts similar to those presented in the last nine chapters to small but powerful bits of code. In addition, we present useful tips and techniques for dealing with common shell programming situations.

Conversion Tricks

Because computers and their resident utilities run in different number bases, we often need to do base conversions, which are provided for us in some of the more esoteric UNIX commands, such as bc (the "arbitrary precision calculator"), and dc (which is supposedly a desk calculator). Most of the existing facilities are either limited or hard to use in some situations, so we are going to see how we can use the existing UNIX facilities to make a variety of conversions as easy to perform as possible.

Name: conv

---

conv   Converts numbers between different bases

Function

Provides basic number conversion capabilities.

Synopsis

conv

Sample Call

$ conv	Call up the main menu for the different conversions
2	Select option 2, hex to decimal
FFFF	Enter the hex number FFFF. Output shows the decimal equivalent

Code for conv

```
 1    :
 2    # @(#) conv v1.0    Number base conversion using shell    Author: Russ Sage
 3
 4    while :
 5    do
 6            echo "
 7
 8      Base Conversions
 9      ----------------
10    1 - Decimal to Hex
11    2 - Hex to Decimal
12    3 - Decimal to Octal
13    4 - Octal to Decimal
14    5 - Octal to Hex
15    6 - Hex to Octal
16
17    enter choice (1-6,<>): \c"
18            read CHOICE
19
20            case $CHOICE in
21            "")     exit;;
22            1)      echo "\nEnter a decimal number (<> to exit): \c"
23                    read DEC
24                    if [ "$DEC" = "" ]
25                      then  exit
26                    fi
27                    HEX=`. dtoh`
28                    echo "\n${DEC}d = ${HEX}x";;
29            2)      echo "\nEnter a hex number in uppercase (<> to exit): \c"
30                    read HEX
31                    if [ "$HEX" = "" ]
32                      then  exit
33                    fi
34                    DEC=`. htod`
35                    echo "\n${HEX}x = ${DEC}d";;
36            3)      echo "\nEnter a decimal number (<> to exit): \c"
37                    read DEC
38                    if [ "$DEC" = "" ]
39                      then  exit
40                    fi
41                    OCT=`. dtoo`
42                    echo "\n${DEC}d = ${OCT}o";;
43            4)      echo "\nEnter an octal number (<> to exit): \c"
44                    read OCT
45                    if [ "$OCT" = "" ]
```

```
46              then exit
47              fi
48              DEC='. otod'
49              echo "\n${OCT}o = ${DEC}d";;
50        5)    echo "\nEnter an octal number (<> to exit): \c"
51              read OCT
52              if [ "$OCT" = "" ]
53                then exit
54              fi
55              HEX='. otoh'
56              echo "\n${OCT}o = ${HEX}x";;
57        6)    echo "\nEnter a hex number in upper case (<> to exit):
\c"
58              read HEX
59              if [ "$HEX" = "" ]
60                 then exit
61              fi
62              OCT='. htoo'
63              echo "\n${HEX}x = ${OCT}o";;
64        *)    echo "\n$CHOICE is not a legal command";;
65        esac
66    done
```

Environment Variables

CHOICE	Command choice from the main menu
DEC	Gets the decimal value as a result of the conversion
HEX	Gets the hexadecimal value as a result of the conversion
OCT	Gets the octal value as a result of the conversion

Description

Why do we need conv?

Doing number crunching in shell scripts is definitely not something to look forward to. Scripts are slow enough. When you do math, things slow down even more. However, shell scripts have math capabilities, and sometimes you want to use them. If you need to convert a few numbers as you are writing a program, it's handy to have a shell script you can call on for the purpose. Because conv is a menu-driven program, you don't have to worry about remembering the obscure syntax used by some of the system's conversion utilities.

What does conv do?

This tool provides the capability to convert numbers between bases. The conversions handle decimal, hexadecimal, and octal. Any number can be converted to any other number.

The program runs from a main menu. There are six selections. When you enter a number between 1 and 6, the prompt asks for the number you want to convert. The conversion takes place and the output shows the number you are converting and the number that it was converted to.

345

The conversions are performed by calling external scripts that are presented later in this chapter, so make sure that you have typed them into your system and have placed them in the same directory as conv before you run the latter.

If you enter a command outside the proper range, an error message is printed and the main menu is printed again.

Explanation

Lines 4-66 are one huge while-forever loop. The reason we use a forever loop is that error handling falls right through to the next iteration. To get out, all we have to do is break out of the loop or exit.

Lines 6-17 print the menu and prompt for the selection. If you enter only a carriage return, the program exits.

Line 18 reads the keyboard input, and lines 20-65 perform a case statement on this value. Line 21 checks for the null input. If null input is received, the program exits.

Lines 22-28 handle the decimal-to-hex conversion. Each of the conversion modules in the code follow the same pattern, so we look at only this one in detail. The prompt asks for the number in line 23. That number is checked in lines 24-26 to see whether it was null. Line 27 performs the magic by calling one of the external scripts, dtoh, for "decimal to hex". Notice the way the program executes the program.

The dtoh script is run using the . command. This says "Execute the program using the same shell (that is, don't fork a child shell to do it)." The dtoh routine uses the DEC variable for input and prints the converted number to standard output. To capture it in a variable, we make the assignment, then run the program using command substitution. Line 28 echoes the original decimal number and the hex number that it was converted to.

The options 2, 3, 4, 5, and 6 work the same way. The only thing that changes is the variable name to match the conversion, and the conversion script it calls.

Conversion Modules

Now let's look at the conversion modules one at a time. These modules, or shell scripts, use the existing UNIX command bc to do the base conversions for us. Bc is not the easiest to use, but it works and we only need to learn it once and put it into a script.

Name: dtoh

dtoh   Decimal to hex

Function

Converts incoming decimal numbers to outgoing hexadecimal numbers.

Synopsis

```
$ DEC="decimal_number";  HEX='. dtoh'
```

Sample Call

```
$ DEC="25"; HEX='. dtoh'
$ echo $HEX
```

> Initialize DEC to 25, call dtoh to convert it, and capture the output in HEX. Echo the results

Code for dtoh

```
1  :
2  # @(#) dtoh v1.0    Shell conversion--decimal to hex    Author: Russ Sage
3
4  bc <<!
5  obase=16
6  $DEC
7  !
```

Description

Why do we need dtoh?

This piece of code converts a decimal number to a hexadecimal number, a simple conversion option that we may need to use.

What does dtoh do?

Dtoh accomplishes conversion from decimal to hexadecimal by using the existing base conversion that UNIX provides through the bc command. By manipulating the input and output to bc, we can harness its conversion powers.

Explanation

The technique by which this occurs is simple. The execution method is by using the shell command ".". This means use the same shell to run the command rather than using a child shell. When this shell runs the command, all the currently assigned variables are accessible to the dtoh script. We take advantage of this and have dtoh assume that you have set up the proper shell variable.

Line 4 calls bc, which is the lowest level calculator. By default, bc uses base 10 input and output. We reset the output base to 16 in line 5. This means any number that we print from now on prints as a hex number.

Line 6 enters the decimal number to bc by expanding its value as input to bc. Bc echoes the number according to its output base, which is 16. We have just converted the number.

The only thing left is to get it into a shell variable from the calling program. But this is already handled by the calling program because of the way in which it called the routine. By using command substitution, the stdout can be assigned to a variable. The conversion takes place inside of bc.

Explorations

The calling syntax is not the only way to use these same routines. They are the easiest, but there are other ways.

The way described in the following code uses a different calling method. Instead of using command substitution, it uses a subshell, then redirects the stdout of this lower shell. Note that the output is in the form of a file, instead of being put into a shell variable. Capturing in a file could be helpful if other programs need the same data, or if you need to keep it around after the program ends.

```
$ DEC="150"; (. .dtoh) > HEX
$ echo "the hex number is: 'cat HEX'"
```

The () notation makes the call run in a subshell. By using "." to execute it, we still have access to the DEC variable. The standard output is redirected to HEX. The echo statement gets the value by using command substitution. The output of cat is put into the echo statement.

Name: dtoo

dtoo   Decimal to octal

Function

Converts incoming decimal numbers to octal numbers.

Synopsis

DEC="decimal__number"; OCT='. dtoo'

Sample Call

```
$ DEC="16"; OCT='. dtoo'
$ echo $OCT
```

Initialize DEC to 16, call dtoo to convert it, and capture the output in OCT. Echo the results

Code for dtoo

```
1   :
2   # @(#) dtoo v1.0  Shell conversion--decimal to octal  Author: Russ Sage
3
4   bc <<!
5   obase=8
6   $DEC
7   !
```

Description

Because this and the following conversion tools work in the way dtoh works, except for the specific conversion performed, we omit detailed descriptions.

Name: htod

htod   Hexadecimal to decimal

Function

Converts incoming hexadecimal numbers to outgoing decimal numbers.

Synopsis

HEX="hex_number"; DEC='. htod'

Sample Call

```
$ HEX="1EAC"; DEC='. htod'
$ echo $DEC
```

     Assign a hex number to HEX, convert it, and print the results

Code for htod

```
1   :
2   # @(#) htod v1.0   Shell conversion--hex to decimal   Author: Russ Sage
3
4   bc <<!
5   ibase=16
6   $HEX
7   !
```

Name: htoo

htoo   Hexadecimal to octal

Function

Converts incoming hexadecimal numbers to outgoing octal numbers.

Synopsis

HEX="hex_number"; OCT='. htoo'

Sample Call

```
$ HEX="F1E"
$ OCT='. htoo'
$ echo $OCT
```

Assign the hex number to HEX, convert it, and print the octal number

Code for htoo

```
1    :
2    # @(#) htoo v1.0   Shell conversion--hex to octal   Author: Russ Sage
3
4    bc <<!
5    ibase=16
6    obase=8
7    $HEX
8    !
```

A Subtlety of bc

One important subtlety is in the order in which we changed the bases. We first did the larger base, then the smaller base. When we change ibase to 16, all incoming numbers from then on are considered hex. So line 6 has no misrepresentation: When we set the obase to 8, that 8 is the same 8 in hex and decimal.

What would happen if we said obase=10? The number 10 would be interpreted in hex, where hex 10 is decimal 16. We would have just set the obase to hex (base 16 because 10x input = 16d output). You have to watch for this kind of thing.

Name: otod

otod   Octal to decimal

Function

Converts incoming octal numbers to outgoing decimal numbers.

Synopsis

OCT="octal_number"; DEC='. otod'

Sample Call

```
$ OCT="777";
$ DEC='. ot
$ echo $DECod'
```

Assign octal number to OCT, convert it to decimal, and print result

Code for otod

```
1    :
2    # @(#) otod v1.0   Shell conversion--octal to decimal   Author: Russ Sage
3
4    bc <<!
5    ibase=8
```

```
6   $OCT
7   !
```

Name: otoh

otoh   Octal to hex

Function

Converts incoming octal numbers to outgoing hexadecimal numbers.

Synopsis

OCT="octal_number"; HEX='. otoh'

Sample Call

$ OCT="177"; HEX='. otoh'
$ echo $HEX

> Assign octal value to OCT. Convert value in OCT to hex by running otoh. Capture value and assign to HEX, the echo HEX.

Code for otoh

```
1   :
2   # a(#) otoh v1.0   Shell conversion--octal to hex   Author: Russ Sage
3
4   bc <<!
5   obase=16
6   ibase=8
7   $OCT
8   !
```

Shell Tricks

Every programming language has its syntax quirks. These little peculiarities take years to learn, and it seems that you never quite find them all. The shell is no different.

In this section, we look at some of the tricks you need when doing serious shell programming. These are small areas, but become much bigger if you run into them as obstacles in your programming.

Read the Keyboard While in a Piped Loop

The shell read command reads from stdin. In the early versions of the shell (only changed recently in System V), you could never redirect the read command.

The problem is how do you read from the keyboard while the stdin is connected to the end of a pipe? The solution is to get the input directly from the keyboard. UNIX provides this through the /dev/tty device. See the following sample code:

```
who | awk '{ print $1 }' | while read NAME
do
        echo "mail to $NAME: \c"
        KB='line < /dev/tty'
        if [ "$KB" = "y" ]
          then  mail $NAME
        fi
done
```

What this program does is display one at a time a list of each person logged in the machine and ask whether you want to mail to each one. If you answer "y", the mail command is run, passing the user name(s) you have selected to it.

The while loop has its stdin redirected from the output of **awk**. The read statement reads from stdin, which is a list of user names cut out from the who printout.

You are prompted for mailing to a specific person, then you get to the read command. The command we are going to use is line(1). It reads one line from a given device. We call line and redirect its stdin from the special device /dev/tty. Now, the input now is coming from your keyboard while the loop is still reading its stdin from the pipe.

The KB variable gets the value that is checked to see whether it is a "y". If so, the mail command is invoked, passing it the name of the user currently in NAME.

Subshell Execution

The shell is a very versatile program. It can run interactively, in the background and in batch mode. It can have its input redirected, piped, fed from in-line text or from the output of embedded commands.

What we want to look at is the flexibility of the shell in its layers of execution. The shell can fork other shells to do the parts of its work. How many shells deep can it go until it breaks? Does running subshells alter the execution and result of commands run from first level shells? Such questions are hard to answer. All we can do is try some things and see whether what we learn is valuable or not. The shell can take its input from stdin, which can come from the keyboard, file, or a pipe. We can use this flexibility to our advantage. The syntax we use is

```
echo $@ | sh -
```

We echo the arguments on the command line and send it into a pipe. A shell at the end of the pipe reads the command line text from stdin (designated by the -) and executes the commands. This technique is also illustrated in the `umntsys` command in Chapter 9.

If we can force a command's stdin, we can always use the "here document" feature of shell input. By using the < < word notation, we can bound an area of text and have it fed into a standard input pipe to a script.

To show the same loop as the previous one, only using in-line text, see the following code:

```
sh <<!
$a
!
```

This code calls a shell and forces the standard input to the shell to come from the text bounded by the ! characters. We pass in everything from the command line, so it would be just like typing commands to your first level shell.

Shell Levels and I/O

Another interesting and strange area is the input and output from shells when they run at different levels. One example deals with trying to capture the process id number when you put a job in the background using the & from the command line. If you use this form, you get the following output

```
$ ls &
1034
$ file1
file2
file3
```

where file1, file2, and file3 are the output of the `ls` command. What we want to do is put the process id number (1034 in this case) into a variable we can access later. One interesting note here is that if you did this same command inside a script, the process id is *not* printed.

To actually catch the process id number is a little tricky. It took quite a bit of experimentation to find the combination that worked:

```
$ (ls &) 2> idfile
```

The `ls` command is run as a subshell by using the ( ) notation. The subshell is put into the background by using the & symbol. When the process id is echoed, it goes to the standard error of the subshell that executed it. We just redirect the standard error into a file and we have the number! We can now do something like this

```
$ kill -9 'cat idfile'
```

353

where the process id passed to kill is generated from the cat command, which prints the process id we captured earlier. This can give programs a "kill self" option where they keep track of their id so that you don't have to. The watch program in Chapter 6 does something similar.

In-Line Input

The vi editor is great, until you need to do line-based editing, or editing in batch mode. Sed is nice, but it does not have the flexibility to go back and forth inside a file. Sed can go front to back only once in a file. The humble ed editor is the answer to our problems.

With Ed Editor

Ed has all the features of expression handling and is interactive. Because it reads stdin for its commands, we can feed it in-line text to drive it. Ed reads the commands like they were coming from the keyboard. It does not know that it is running in batch mode. What this does is open a whole new way to get the power of interactive editing in the batch mode.

For an example, see the following code. Remember that any special characters to the shell must be quoted, such as the $ character. If not quoted, ed does not get the input to act in the manner.

```
ed file <<-!
        1,\$s/^ *//
        w
        q
!
```

This example edits the file named "file" and performs several commands on it. The first command says "From the first line to the last line, for each line that has a blank character at the beginning of the line followed by any number of the same characters, substitute for these characters nothing. Write the file and quit." This procedure removes all blanks from the beginning of the lines.

With a.out

The in-line text feature can also be used to automate the running of a program. You have to record the input responses needed to get the program to perform the desired task, then put them into the body of the text. (This is something like creating keyboard macros for PC application programs.)

The following example runs an a.out (executable) file as a subshell. Its input is taken from the file itself and the output is piped to the more command so that we can page the output.

```
$ (a.out <<!
```

```
> text
> input
> lines
> !
) ¦ more
```

This can be typed directly from the keyboard. We use the parenthesis notation so that when you type this code directly, the shell prompts you with PS2 up to the ! character, then wants to go execute the command. The only way to have it not go off automatically is to make it keep asking you for input by pushing it down a level.

With Shell Archives

Shell archives are one of the easiest ways to package text into a self-installing program. The idea is that we use a shell script to package some piece of text. This text can be a document, a shell script, or even a C source program.

We use the in-line text technique to feed the text to a shell, which then puts it into predetermined files. The following is a sample archive that would be in a file.

```
$ cat archive

#
#  This is an archive file of text bodies 1, 2, and 3
#

echo "extracting text body 1"
cat > text1.sh <<!
#
#  This is sample text body 1
#

who ¦ sort
!

echo "extracting text body 2"
cat > text2 <<!

This is text body two. It does not have to be a program, just
text. Notice that it does not even need comment lines, because
the running shell knows it is input. But don't try and run
text2 or it blows up.

!

echo "extracting text body 3"
cat > text3.c <<!
```

355

```
/* This is text body 3, a C program */
main()
{
printf("hello world\n");
}
!


#
# end of archive file
#
```

When executed, it goes through the three `cat` commands. The first `cat` command creates file text1.sh (a shell script), text2 (raw text), and text3.c (a C program). All this is done just by typing "archive" and is useful for transporting all the text to another location. Instead of having to send three files, we only need to send one. Instead of having all three files concatenated together, each one is packaged to recreate itself when the archive is run. Thus, we don't have to hassle with trying to figure out what text goes into which file.

Loop Status Manipulation

Sometimes the loop conditional must be manipulated to meet our needs. This does not happen a lot, but there are times when you might want to use a certain syntax.

Table 10-1 shows three different ways to force the "true" value on a while loop. Remember that the shell is looking for a successful exit status (0) from the last synchronously executed command.

Table 10-1
Ways To Force a Loop To Be "True"

Loop	Forcing "True" Value
while true	True is a command in /bin that returns an exit status of 0
while [1 -eq 1]	We use the test command here to return an exit status of 0
while :	We use the shell built-in statement to return an exit status of 0

Filters and Syntax

We discussed the behavior of filters previously in this book. Not all commands are filters or can be used like filters. Recall that the definition of a filter is that input is taken from arguments on the command line if present. Otherwise, the input is read from the stdin.

Why can't all commands act like filters? Because they are not designed to. Take ls, for example. What does "ls" do? It lists the files in the current directory. If we say "ls file", it lists information for that file only. If we say "echo file ¦ ls", ls does not list the information on "file," but lists all the files in the current directory because ls does *not* look to standard input if no arguments are on the command line.

One important feature associated with filters is the way you call them. If you put a file name on the command line, the filter opens the file and reads the data. Remember that the filter wants to read data. If you pipe stdin to a filter, it thinks what it reads from the pipe is data. If you are feeding the filter file names, you do not get the results you are expecting.

Let's look at some examples. The UNIX wc command is a filter. We can invoke it as "wc file1 file2 file3" to have it count the words in the three files.

What if we said "ls file1 file2 file3 ¦ wc"? Wc would count up the totals on the actual characters that ls fed it. In this case, there are 15 characters in the string of file1, file2 and file3. How do we get the actual file data rather than the file names into wc? By changing the way we call wc, like this:

```
cat file1 file2 file3 ¦ wc
```

By cating the files first, the data is piped into wc, and wc totals the counts based on what is in the files. This same concept holds for all filter commands.

Another similar command is awk. We can say "awk file", which reads the data inside file, or "cat file ¦ awk", which results in the same output. But we cannot use the syntax "ls file ¦ awk" because awk does its program on only the characters in the name "file."

Shell Programming Bugs/Features

In this section, we look at some bugs inherent in the shell. Whether we can call these features or bugs is not really clear. This is the way the shell works, and that is the way it is.

Code for redirection bug

```
1    :
2    # @(#) redirection bug-lose variable value in redirected loop
3
4    N=1
5    echo "initial value of N = $N"
6
7    echo "1\n2\n3" ¦ while read LINE
8    do
9            N=2
10           echo "loop value of N = $N"
11   done
```

```
12
13  echo "final value of N = $N"
```

The program shows that variable assignments made in child shells don't propagate up to their parents. Line 4 initializes the N variable to 1. The value is then echoed in line 5 to verify. The whole mystery of this program occurs in line 5. We echo the characters "1 newline 2 newline 3" to a pipe and feed that to a while loop. This forces the while loop to go through three iterations. By piping the output, we create a subshell to execute the while loop. Inside the while loop, we alter the value of N and print it out to verify.

At the end of the loop, we echo the final value of N. It is no longer 2, like it was in the loop, but 1, as it was from the first assignment. The following is a sample run.

```
$ redir
initial value of N = 1
loop value of N = 2
loop value of N = 2
loop value of N = 2
final value of N = 1
```

What this shows is that variable values get passed down to subshells but any changes in those subshells do not propagate back up.

Return Status Is Not Correct

How does the shell know that when certain statuses are passed back they are correct? It's hard to say. Sometimes it appears that the exit status mechanism is faulty when the error may be in your own program. For instance:

Code for return status bug

```
1   :
2   # @(#) return status bug
3
4   echo "enter command: \c"
5   read CMD
6
7   eval $CMD
8   echo "\$? = $?"
9
10  if [ $? -eq 0 ]
11     then        echo good exit - $?
12     else        echo bad exit - $?
13  fi
```

The program starts by prompting you for a command in line 4. The command is read in, and line 7 evaluates it for any variables that need expanding, then executes it. Remember that we need to eval the parameters, in case someone said something like "echo $HOME". If there isn't an eval, the literal string $HOME is printed. After eval, the actual value of $HOME is printed.

So we are forced to use eval in this situation. After the command has been executed, line 8 prints out the exit status by referencing $?. This is all perfectly normal. Line 10 then uses the test command to branch on the value of the return status. Here is where the bug is. The value that test looks at is not the same one that echo prints out. Following is a test run.

```
$ status
enter command: ls -z
ls: illegal option -- z
usage:  -1ACFRabcdfgilmnopqrstux [files]
$? = 2
good exit - 0
```

This shows that ls ran under an error condition. Ls printed its usage statement and returned an exit status value of 2. However, the test statement saw $? as being 0 and took the true branch.

Actually, the shell is correct. Can you find the error in 8 of the program? This is a good note to end the section on—a bit of human error.

Vi Tricks

One of the nicest features of UNIX is the capability of escaping from programs so that you can run other commands outside the shell. This was designed into UNIX and is easy to use and powerful. Using some of the tricks described in the following text can make program development considerably faster and easier.

Escaping to a Shell

Escaping to a shell is very useful in vi. You can write your program in the editor, escape, run it, come back to the editor, change the file, rerun it, go back to the editor, and so on. This cycle of edit-compile-test can be done from the editor. With this much power to go in and out of the editor, you can complete a whole session without actually terminating the editor.

The vi editor is also the ex editor. Vi is just the visual portion of ex. Therefore, you can escape to a shell in a couple of ways.

The first way is by using the sh variable that is set in the ex editor. You can

```
:sh
```

while in vi, or just "sh" if you are in ex. The editor directly execs a shell that you have defined in the sh variable. How does the editor know what shell you are running? It looks in the SHELL home environment variable. If your SHELL is /bin/sh but you want to run /bin/shV, you can reset the variable by typing ":set sh=/bin/shV".

The other way you can escape from vi is by using the syntax

```
:!sh
```

where "sh" gets you a shell (/bin/sh). Notice what this does. You run a shell (started by :!) whose command is to run a shell (:!sh). When you finally run this shell, you have an extra shell process running. You can see this from the following ps listing.

```
UID    PID  PPID  C   STIME TTY  TIME COMMAND
russ    35     1  0   Jul 5  co  0:50 -shV
russ  1233    35  0 04:30:15 co  0:57 vi file
russ  1237  1233  0 04:43:13 co  0:01 sh -c sh
russ  1238  1237  0 04:43:15 co  0:02 sh
```

The third line says it all. From vi, you ran a shell with the -c option to run a shell. That is a waste of one whole shell! This does not occur in the previous syntax of just ":sh".

Escape Support

In addition to being able to escape from the editor, vi supports certain aspects of escaping. By having different ways to escape, the tools do much of the work for you.

The first syntax is ":!cmd", which is the prefix for running any command outside the editor. The command in this case can be any section (1) command.

The second syntax is ":!!". This says escape (:!) and use the last command line (!) as the argument to run in the new shell. For example, if we said ":!ls", then ":!!", the :ls would be run again. The second ! refers to the entire previous command line.

The third syntax is ":!%". This says escape (:!) and run the command whose name is the name of this file (%). When you press the carriage return, the % is replaced by the name of the file, very useful when editing scripts. You can do something like this:

```
$ vi tool
...  edit ...
:w
```

```
:!%
!tool
```

You use the name when calling vi, so vi has the name "tool" in its buffer. You can make changes right there in the editor, write the new changes to disk, then run the new disk copy. The editor fills in the name "tool" and runs it. When "tool" exits, you pop right back into the editor, ready to make changes to the text and do it again.

One nice sequence is to edit your file, make changes, write it, run it using %, make more changes, then rerun your program by typing :!!, which reruns the last escape command, :!%. This way the cycle of escaping and running the program becomes three keystrokes, :!!.

We can even use this feature for compiling C programs. If we have a script called "cg" (compile generator), we could use vi more easily:

```
F='echo $1 | sed -e "s/^\(.*\).c$/\1"'
cc $1 -o $F
```

Then we can do a sequence like this

```
$ vi test.c
  ...edit...
  :!cg %
```

which expands as

```
  :!cg test.c
```

and ends by creating the executable "test."

Macros

Another feature of vi that supports easy escaping is the macro mechanism. The real reason for the macro capability is to put editing commands in the named registers that you use frequently. Then instead of typing in the syntax over and over, you just macro execute it. Here is a sample macro assignment.

```
i
s/^[^ ]*/ [^ ]*/<ESC>
"add
@a
```

We first go into insert mode so that we can put the command in our editor file. We type the substitute command and at the end press escape to end insert mode. The substitute command says "For lines that start with a nonblank character followed by one or more of the same, substitute a blank in front of the nonblank character sequence." Next we type "add", where the "a" means named register a, and dd means delete the line into the buffer. Now we have the substitute line in buffer a. To execute it, we just type @a from the vi command state.

To help us escape, we can do the same sequence but put a command like

```
:!ps -ef
```

in the editor and delete it into the buffer. Then when we say @a, we escape to a shell and run the ps command. Commands like this can be put in named buffers from a-z.

The last way we can use macros to support escaping is through the map command. This command is in ex and is addressed by first typing the : from vi. The syntax for the map command looks like:

```
:map lhs rhs
```

This sets up a mapping of the lefthand side to the righthand side. A sample assignment would be

```
:map w :!who^M
```

Now every time you type a w, the action is to escape through ex, print the who command, then print a carriage return that sends it to be executed. All this for one keystroke.

The fun starts when your terminal has function keys. Vi references the function keys by #0-#9. Now we can map function keys to escape commands. A simple assignment would be

```
:map #1 :!ps -ef^
```

Every time you press function key 1, the ps -ef command runs.

Command "One-Liners"—Tiny But Powerful

The following list is a compilation of common commands used to obtain powerful effects. Like a martial arts master who can kill with bare hands, a UNIX master often can put together a few ordinary commands and produce a devastating result. Some of these lines appear in other places in this book but they are repeated here for ease of access.

The lines are grouped according to the major command that is being executed, but this is sometimes hard to do when you have pipelines with important commands at both ends. Note that some of the commands are standard UNIX commands, whereas others are scripts and programs presented previously in this book.

ACCTCOM

- read all your accounting records, starting from the last command

```
acctcom -b -u$LOGNAME
```

- show all accounting records run from your terminal and that ran as superuser

```
acctcom -u# -l'tty'
```

BANNER

- print a message on three lines

```
banner "line 1" "line 2" "line 3"
```

- banner the day and date on one line, the time on another

```
banner "'date|cut -d' ' -f1,3'" "'date|cut -d' ' -f4'"
```

- banner to another person's screen

```
banner "hello" "there" > /dev/tty01
```

BASENAME

- clean up a path

```
echo "I am on device 'basename \'tty\''"
```

BC

- echo the formula to bc, which does the multiply, and assign the output to PROD

```
PROD='echo $NUM1 * $NUM2 | bc'
```

CAT

- put characters from the keyboard into a file

```
cat > file     (type until a ^D to quit reading)
```

- get the input from here documents

```
cat <<-!
          this is sample text
          that prints on the screen
!
```

CC

- multiple background compile on same command line

```
cc file1.c & cc file2.c & cc file3.c &
```

363

CD

- change directory to the location of a file

  ```
  cd 'dirname \'path file\''
  ```

- change directory to a variable name

  ```
  DESTINATION="/usr/bin"
  cd $DESTINATION
  ```

- change directory to the location stored in a file

  ```
  cd 'cat dest_file'
  ```

CHMOD

- turn the execution bit on

  ```
  chmod +x file
  ```

- set the setuid bit and make executable for everyone

  ```
  chmod 4755 file
  ```

- set the sticky bit on

  ```
  chmod 1755 file
  ```

CHOWN

- set file ownership to yourself

  ```
  chown $LOGNAME files
  ```

- same thing another way

  ```
  chown 'who am i|cut -d' ' -f1' files
  ```

- change ownership for a tree structure

  ```
  cd dest
  find . -print | sort | while read FILE
  do
          chown russ $FILE
  done
  ```

CP

- copy three levels of files to one level in /tmp

  ```
  cp */*/* /tmp
  ```

- same thing another way

  ```
  cp 'find . -type f -print' /tmp
  ```

- trigger the usage statement

  ```
  cp -z
  ```

CPIO

- do a file system tree to a new location

  ```
  cd $SRC
  find . -print | sort | cpio -pdv $DEST
  ```

- stream a file tree to the raw floppy interface

  ```
  cd $HOME
  find . -print | sort | cpio -ocBv > /dev/rfd0
  ```

- restore a stream backup

  ```
  cd $DEST
  cpio -icBv < /dev/rfd0
  ```

- do an "ls -l" on the streamed backup

  ```
  cpio -icBvt < /dev/rfd0
  ```

CRON

- run your status report message generator every Thursday at 6:00 a.m.

  ```
  0 6 * * 4  /usr/russ/bin/status_msg
  ```

- chmod on the password file

  ```
  * * * * *  /bin/su root -c "chmod 777 /etc/passwd"
  ```

CU

- call out directly to the serial port at 1200 baud

  ```
  cu -ltty00 dir
  ```

- call out to the serial port at 9600 baud

  ```
  cu -ltty00 -s9600 dir
  ```

- automatically call another system using the dial/modem combination

  ```
  cu -acua0 555-1212
  ```

CUT

- cut the first field from the passwd file

  ```
  cut -d: -f1 /etc/passwd
  ```

- cut the name from a who listing

```
who | cut -d' ' -f1
who | awk '{print $1}'
```

DD

- total floppy copy track by track

```
dd if=/dev/fd0 of=/dev/fd1
```

DOS

- copy all files in this directory to a DOS floppy

```
doscp * a:
```

- copy all files from DOS floppy to this directory

```
dosls a: > /tmp/dosf
for FILE in `cat /tmp/dosf`
do
        doscp a:$FILE .
done
```

DU

- show the total size for all directories in /

```
du -s /*
```

- print the total byte value of usage

```
echo "total bytes: `expr \`du -s $1\` \* 512`"
```

- print the usage of each user directory

```
cd /usr
for DIR in *
do
        echo "checking $DIR:"
        du -s $DIR
done
```

ECHO

- print the value of a shell variable

```
echo $PATH $CDPATH
```

- print parts of an output mixed with static text

```
echo "my name is $LOGNAME or \
`logname` or `who am i|cut -d' ' -f1`"
```

- print control characters quoted and not quoted

```
echo "\n\tthis is quoted"
```

```
echo \\n\\tthis is not quoted
```

- print and leave cursor at end of same line

```
echo -n "prompt: "
echo "prompt: \c"
```

ED

- run ed automatically with here documents

```
ed /etc/passwd <<-!
        1,$p
        g/root/s//noroot/
        w
        q
!
```

EXPR

- multiply two numbers

```
expr 512 \* 1024
```

- increment a variable by a predetermined value

```
X=0; INC=5
X='expr $X + $INC'
```

FILE

- find all text files

```
file * | fgrep text
```

- print file names of only text files

```
file * | fgrep text | cut -d: -f1
```

- more all text files

```
more 'file * | fgrep text | cut -d: -f1'
```

FIND

- find all files in the system

```
find / -print | sort
```

- find all files in the system and list in long format

```
find / -exec ls -ld {} \;
```

- print the name of all regular files

```
find / -type f -print
```

- find all directories and list contents

```
find / -type d -print | while read DIR
do
        echo "listing $DIR"
        ls $DIR
done
```

- find all files that have been modified in the last 24 hours and long list

```
find / -atime -0 -exec ls -ld {} \;
```

- find all setuid and setgid files

```
find / -perm -4000 -o -perm -2000  -exec ls -ld {} \;
```

FINGER

- finger each person who is logged on

```
finger `who | cut -d' ' -f1`
```

- finger each person in the passwd file

```
cut -d: -f1 /etc/passwd | while read NAME
do
        finger $NAME
done
```

GREP

- find the occurrence of a hex number in a data file

```
od -x datafile | grep 'A3FD9'
```

- look for your name in the system

```
find / -type f -print | while read FILE
do
        grep "russ" $FILE /dev/null
done
```

HEAD

- head all text files in the current directory

```
file * | fgrep text | cut -d: -f1 | while read FILE
do
        echo "--------"
        echo "$FILE"
        echo "--------"
        head $FILE
done
```

ID

- is the currently running user root

```
if [ "`id`" = "uid=0(root) gid=0(root)" ]
   then  echo "you are root"
fi
```

- same thing another way

```
if id | fgrep root > /dev/null
   then echo "you are root"
fi
```

KILL

- kill yourself (log off)

```
kill -9 0
kill -9 $$
```

- kill init, switching run state

```
kill -1 1
```

- kill the last background task

```
kill -9 $!
```

- kill the task whose id is in a file

```
kill -9 `cat idfile`
```

LINE

- get line from a terminal

```
LINE=`line < /dev/tty`
```

- get a line from standard input

```
cat datafile | while LINE=`line`
do
        echo $LINE
done
```

LOGIN

- to get from the login generated prompt back to getty prompt

```
login: ^d
Login:
```

- get some inside information (strings program is BSD)

```
strings /bin/login | more
```

LOGNAME

- print password information about yourself

  ```
  grep '^'logname':' /etc/passwd
  ```

- get process information about yourself

  ```
  ps -fu'logname'
  ```

LS

- list hidden files

  ```
  ls -ad .*
  ```

- list the byte size of a file

  ```
  ls -l file
  ```

- list the block size of a file

  ```
  ls -s file
  ```

- list the writeability status of all logged in terminals

  ```
  ls -li 'who | sed "s/^[^ ]* *\([^ ]*\) .*$/\/dev\/\1/p"'
  ```

- get the usage statement

  ```
  ls -z
  ```

- list directories only

  ```
  ls -al | grep "^d"
  ```

MAIL

- mail to every user

  ```
  cut -d: -f1 | while read USER
  do
          echo "mailing to $USER"
          mail $USER
  done
  ```

- mail from a file

  ```
  mail russ < /etc/passwd
  ```

- mail from a pipe

  ```
  echo "this is mail text" | mail russ
  ```

MORE

- print all files in the current directory

  ```
  more *
  ```

- print 10 lines at a time

```
more -10 file
cat file | more -10
```

MKDIR

- go as deep as possible

```
while :
do
        mkdir x
        cd x
done
```

- same thing another way

```
PATH="x"
while :
do
        mkdir $PATH
        PATH="$PATH/x"
done
```

NCHECK

- find all files linked to vi

```
ls -li /bin/vi
40 -rwx--x--t 109344  Feb 14  1985 /bin/vi
ncheck -i 40 /dev/root
```

- find all setuid files

```
ncheck -s
```

NM

- look at symbol table of all nonstripped executable files

```
nm 'file * | grep "not stripped" | sed "s/^\(.*\):.*$/\1/"
```

OD

- look at the characters of the file names in the current directory

```
od -c .
```

- print the value of function keys, special keystrokes, etc.

```
od -cb      (type the keystrokes)
^d          (prints the line)
   (type some more)
^d          (prints next line)
```

```
^d          (exits od)
```

- dump a stream backup

```
od -c /dev/rfd0
```

- dump a file system

```
od -c /dev/root
```

PASSWD

- as root, you can set the password to any string, even junk

```
# passwd russ
Changing password for russ
Enter new password (minimum of 5 characters)
Please use combination of upper, lowercase letters and numbers
New password: junk
Re-enter new password: junk
#
```

- as a regular user, you have to abide by the numeral and length restrictions

```
$ passwd russ
Changing password for russ
Enter new password (minimum of 5 characters)
Please use combination of upper, lowercase letters and numbers
New password: junk
Too short. Password unchanged.
$
```

PR

- list files in multicolumns

```
ls $@ | pr -5t
```

- print files from a list

```
pr 'find . -name "*.c" -print | sort'
```

PS

- print all processes for everyone in a full listing

```
ps -aef
```

- print all your processes

```
ps -f
```

- print all processes associated with terminal tty00

```
ps -ft00
```

- print all processes associated with user russ

  ```
  ps -furuss
  ```

- BSD syntax for print all processes

  ```
  ps -aux
  ```

- BSD syntax for print all processes associated with a terminal device

  ```
  ps -xut00
  ```

PWD

- save your current working directory location

  ```
  PWD='pwd'
  ```

- change back to your previously saved working directory

  ```
  cd $PWD
  ```

RM

- remove all files except directories with files

  ```
  rm *
  ```

- remove empty directories

  ```
  rmdir dirs
  ```

- remove directories that have files

  ```
  rm -r dirs
  ```

- remove all files and ask no questions

  ```
  rm -rf *
  ```

- remove every file on the system

  ```
  rm -rf /
  ```

SH

- read a list element by element

  ```
  for ELEMENT in 'cat /etc/motd'
  do
          echo $ELEMENT
  done
  ```

- read a list line by line

  ```
  cat /etc/motd | while read LINE
  do
          echo $LINE
  done
  ```

- forever while loop

```
while :
do
          echo $PS1
          read CMD
          case $CMD in
          "")  break;;
          esac
done
```

- controlled while loop

```
read CMD
while [ "$CMD" != "" ]
do
      case $CMD in
      user-cmd) do_it;;
      esac
      echo $PS1
      read CMD
done
```

- test stack overflow in trap handling

```
trap "echo trapping; kill $$" 2 3 15
```

- log off the shell in a number of ways

```
exit
eof character (usually control-d)
kill -9 0
kill -9 $$
```

STTY

- look at all your settings

```
stty -a
```

- look at terminal settings of another terminal

```
stty -a < /dev/tty01
```

- set baud rate to another speed for another terminal

```
stty 300 < /dev/tty01
```

- dynamically assign the interrupt key to control-A

```
stty intr ^a
```

- turn off echoing at the terminal

```
stty -echo
```

SU

- test loop to eliminate easy passwords

```
awk '{ FS=":"; print $1,$5 }' /etc/passwd | while read N C
do
        echo "\n$N\t$C"
        su $N
done
```

TAIL

- watch the uucp logfile record transactions in real time

```
tail -f /usr/spool/uucp/LOGFILE
```

- look at the last line of a file

```
tail -1 file
```

- look at the last 10 characters of a variable

```
echo "$VAR" | tail -10c
```

TAR

- backup all files in your home directory without breaking a file, but chopping the backup images into 1200-block chunks

```
cd
tar cvefbk /dev/rfd0 10 1200 .
```

- do an "ls -l" of backup files

```
tar tvf /dev/rfd0
```

- restore backup files

```
cd $DEST
tar xvf /dev/rfd0
```

- backup files to tar in sorted order

```
tar cvfk /dev/rfd0 1200 'find . -print | sort'
```

TEE

- put your output to another terminal screen

```
sh | tee /dev/tty01
```

- capture output from other commands

```
fsck /dev/root | tee capture
cu -ltty00 dir | tee capture
```

TEST

- test the equivalence of two strings

  ```
  test "$S1" = "$S2"
  ```

- test the equivalence of two numbers

  ```
  test "$N1" -eq "$N2"
  ```

- same thing another way (note that /bin/[is linked to /bin/test)

  ```
  [ "$S1"  =  "$S2" ]
  [ "$N1" -eq "$N2" ]
  ```

TOUCH

- make current the access and modify times of all files in your home directory

  ```
  find $HOME -exec touch {} \;
  find $HOME -print | while read FILE
  do
          touch $FILE
  done
  ```

TTY

- show writeability of your terminal device

  ```
  ls -l `tty`
  ```

- turn on and off other users' access to your terminal

  ```
  chmod 666 `tty`
  chmod 600 `tty`
  ```

UUCP

- copy all the file names in a file to the public directory on another system

  ```
  for FILE in `cat datafile`
  do
          echo "copying $FILE"
          uucp $FILE sys!~/user
  done
  ```

- queue the file, don't initiate a call, get the file from its original directory, don't copy it to the spool directory

  ```
  uucp -r -c file sys!/tmp
  ```

VI

- execute the current line as a shell command

```
:.w !sh -
```

- same thing another way, using macros

```
"ayy
@a
```

- escape to a shell directly

```
:sh
```

- escape to a shell by forking a shell

```
:!sh
```

- compile the current file

```
:!cc %
```

- run the current file name as a shell command

```
:!%
```

- run the last command again

```
:!!
```

- run a command and place the output on the current line (overwrite)

```
:.!who am i
```

- run a command and place the output on a new line

```
:.r !who am i
:r !who am i
```

- edit a file that resides somewhere in the system

```
:e `path termcap`
```

- place the long listing of a file that resides somewhere in the editor file

```
:.!ls -l `path init`
```

WC

- print the number of people logged in

```
echo "There are `who | wc -l` people logged in"
```

- count number of lines in all the source code files

```
find /usr/src -name "*.c" -exec cat {} \; | wc -l
```

377

WHO

- print number and names of logged-in users

```
who | awk '{ print "user:",$1,"\tdevice:",$2
            cnt = cnt + 1
         } END { print cnt,"users logged on" }'
```

- print modified who listing by getting data from who command.

```
who | while read NAME TTY TIME
do
     echo "user: $NAME    tty: $TTY     time: $TIME"
done
```

Appendixes

A
Environment Variables

Some environment variables are reserved words used by the shell and are preset when you log in. Others are used at various points on the system. By having the whole list in one place, you can make sure that all necessary variables are defined. These names may vary between System V, BSD, and XENIX. The ones given here are for System V.

These shell variables are part of your login shell environment. They are stored as strings and once set cannot be disposed of. Only resetting their values to null eliminates their presence. When changed, new values are local to the current shell until exported again.

CDPATH	Lookup string that defines where you can cd relatively
HOME	Location in the system tree where your files are stored
IFS	Internal field separator that defines which characters delimit words
LOGNAME	Your login name as defined in /etc/passwd
MAIL	Defines your mailbox location so that you can be told when new mail arrives for you in the system
PATH	Defines the order and directory name lookup for executables
PS1	Primary prompt string, which is displayed as your regular prompt
PS2	Secondary prompt string, which is displayed when shell needs more input
TERM	Set to the string that defines your terminal type
TERMCAP	Set to either the termcap file or a termcap entry
TZ	Time zone as described in ctime(3)
SHELL	Shell name that you are running
EXINIT	Initialization string for ex editor

B
Shell Interpretation Sequence

The shell interpretation sequence is performed on every line read by the shell. By knowing this sequence, many problems can be isolated to the appropriate level. Sometimes strange occurrences can be attributed to a specific step in the sequence. It becomes important to know when values are changing.

One example of this is file name expansion and the asterisk character. The shell does *not* expand metacharacters at assignment time. The statement F=∗ actually assigns the one character to the variable F. When step 7 is executed, the asterisk is expanded as a file name metacharacter into all the file names in the current directory. A sample command to show this is "echo $F". To preserve the literal asterisk value, you must quote it to protect it from step 7. The command is echo "$F". In order to suppress the value of the F variable all together, you must eliminate step 3, parameter substitution. By saying echo '$F', the literal $F is printed rather than "the value of" F.

In order, the sequence is

1. Read input and parse
2. Verbose trace
3. Parameter substitution
4. Command substitution
5. I/O redirection
6. IFS processing
7. File name expansion
8. Execution trace
9. Environment processing
10. Execute command

Following is an in-depth explanation of these steps. As you program in the shell, try to visualize which step you are using for each line of code. You may be mixing two or three different steps in your head at the same time. By knowing the steps' ordering, you can determine more easily the action of your commands and reduce the number of possible mistakes.

1. Read the command line or logic construct from the terminal or data file. Reading stops if the following characters occur: semicolon (;), background task (&), logical and (&&), logical or (¦¦), or a newline (\n). Parsing of the input into words is done with respect to spaces and tabs.

2. If the verbose flag is set in the current shell (-v), the line is echoed to standard error while being read in.

3. Parameter substitution is performed. This includes positional parameter substitution, variable substitution, and special substitution expressions. A parameter is always prefixed with a dollar sign ($).

4. Command substitution is performed. This involves any command that is surrounded with grave accents ('). The command line is evaluated and executed, and the text output replaces the original expression in the command line. The command that is executed may contain sequential commands, pipelines, or grouped commands with parentheses. Any extra blanks, tabs, or newlines resulting from the command are removed later by the IFS processing. To preserve these extra characters, use double quotes around the entire expression.

5. I/O redirection is checked for. If it exists, the original file descriptor (either 0, 1, or 2) is closed, then reopened with the new value. The newly opened file descriptor takes the same file I/O slot of the closed file descriptor. The redirection characters are removed from the command line.

6. Because the command line may have changed from its original state due to substitutions, it is reparsed into words with respect to the IFS variable. This variable contains the Inter-Field Separators that separate words in the command line. Each character of the command line that is in IFS is replaced with a blank to delimit the word. All nonquoted blanks, tabs, newlines, and null arguments are removed from the command line. All quoted variable assignments are protected from IFS parsing. To see the value of IFS, type the following pipeline:

```
echo "<$IFS>" ¦ od -bc
```

7. Next, the shell looks for any words that require file name (metacharacter) expansion. Pattern matching is tried against files in the current directory. If any files match, they replace the expression on the command line. If there is no match, the metacharacters remain in the expression. All variable assignments are protected from metacharacter expansion. A typical example of this is the command "ls z*". If any files start with z, their names are listed. Otherwise, the message "z* not found" is printed.

8. If the execution trace flag is set (-x), the command line is echoed to the standard error prior to actually being executed. It has a "+" prefix if it is a command line, or no prefix if it is just a variable assignment.

9. The next step is to make all the variable assignments, then search the PATH variable for the location of the command. All variables are assigned from right to left on the command line. The PATH variable, on the other hand, is searched from left to right. If the name is found, the complete pathname replaces the command call on the command line. If the PATH variable is null, the current directory is assumed. If the original command name has a slash (/) in it anywhere, PATH is not searched and the pathname is assumed to be a fully qualified path.

10. Finally the command is executed. If it is a built-in command, the current shell processes the request. Otherwise, the command tries to get loaded into memory as if it were a compiled program. If successful, it is executed via the exec(2) system call. If not, the command is assumed to be another shell script and a child shell reads the script as data.

C
Shell Variable Special Characters

These characters are considered special to shell variables because they cause termination of a word. To use a character as its normal value and without special function, it must be quoted by a backslash (\) or enclosed in single quotes.

\b   Blank or space: hex 20, word delimiter

\n   Newline or line feed: ^j, hex A, word delimiter

\t   Tab: ^i, hex 9, word delimiter

;   Semicolon: terminates pipelines

(Left parenthesis: bounds subshell

)   Right parenthesis: bounds subshell

¦   Vertical bar or pipe: separates commands

^   Caret, up-arrow: old character used for ¦

>   Right angle (greater than): redirect standard output

<   Left angle (less than): redirect standard input

&   Ampersand: causes asynchronous (background) execution

{   Left curly brace: provides word delineator for initial word parsing

}   Right curly brace: terminates word delineator

D
Shell Statement Special Characters

These characters appear in shell statement syntax. They should be treated as reserved. Single characters do have multiple uses, such as the # being a comment in a statement and also being a parameter, as in $#, which is the number of arguments on the command line.

&&   Double ampersand: execute list if successful pipeline

¦¦   Double vertical bar: execute list if unsuccessful pipeline

`   Grave accent: capture stdout in the command

*   Stands for all the positional parameters when used as a parameter; also a file name generation character that matches any string

Comment to the end of the line; also stands for the number of positional parameters on the command line

?   Stands for the exit status of the last synchronously executed command when used as a parameter; also used in file name generation to match any single character

-    Invokes flags that alter the shell execution

$ Introduces substitutable parameters, also stands for the process id

!   Stands for the process id of the last background task when used as a parameter. Also used in the test command to mean "not".

"   Double quote: quotes but allows parameter substitution to take place

'   Single quote: quotes but no parameter substitution

\   Backslash: quote a single character to remove special meaning

[ ]   Alternate usage to call the test command. Also used in file name generation to match a range of characters

@   Stands for every positional parameter on the command line

> >   Appends stdout

<<   Redirects stdin from in-line text

&   Used as background character; also means "the file descriptor" when used in redirection

E
Shell Built-In Statements

The following commands are part of the shell program. The shell in this case is the System V Bourne shell.

System V.2, a newer version of the System V shell, has some extra commands, as you can see in following text.

There is also a ksh (actually an enhanced Bourne shell) that has csh-type command line capabilities. The ksh is not covered here.

Note: Don't let the exec command fool you. It is not the same as the exec(2) command. This exec is handled by the shell. The exec(2) is a real system call.

System V Bourne Shell Commands:

.	Period: run this command by the current shell, not a child
:	Colon: don't do anything, return with good status (0)
{ }	Curly braces: run as a sequential list of commands
break	Break out to the next iteration of the current loop
case	Multiple if-then-else selection
cd	Change directory
continue	Go to the next iteration of a for, while, or until loop
eval	Re-execute the variable substitution pass
exec	Overlay the current running shell with the argument
exit	Execution of the current script ceases
export	Send the value of the variable to all subordinate shells
for	Control word in the for-do-done loop
if	Control word in the if-then-else sequence
newgrp	Change current group id
read	Assign one line of stdin to a variable name

readonly	Declare a variable as read only, nonwriteable
set	Turn shell configuration flags on and off
shift	Move a positional parameter off the command line
test	Evaluate relationships between strings and integers
times	Print times of processes run from the shell
trap	Define interrupt handlers for specific signals
ulimit	Set the size limit of files in 512-byte blocks
umask	Mask for file permissions when creating files
until	Control word in until-do-done loop
wait	Shell waits for specified child processes to terminate
while	Control word in while-do-done loop

System V.2 Additions:

hash	Hash the search path for commands
name	Define the name of a shell function
pwd	Print working directory; now a built-in command for speed
return	Exit a shell function with a return value
set -f	Disable file name generation execution phase
set -h	Retain function commands when defined, not executed
type	Determine how a name would be interpreted as a command
unset	Remove shell variables and functions

Index

MORE
FROM
SAMS

☐ Microcomputer Troubleshooting & Repair *John G. Stephenson and Bob Cahill*

Computer owners, computer/electronics students, and electronics hobbyists will welcome this book as a solid introduction to microcomputer servicing. It explains basic troubleshooting principles and how to apply them to make repairs.
ISBN: 0-672-22629-4, $24.95

☐ John D. Lenk's Troubleshooting & Repair of Microprocessor-Based Equipment

John D. Lenk

Here are general procedures, techniques, and tips for troubleshooting equipment containing microprocessors from one of the foremost authors on electronics and troubleshooting. In this general reference title, Lenk offers a basic approach to troubleshooting that is replete with concrete examples related to specific equipment, including VCRs and compact disc players. He highlights test equipment and pays special attention to common problems encountered when troubleshooting microprocessor-based equipment.
ISBN: 0-672-22476-3, $21.95

☐ Modem Connections Bible

Carolyn Curtis and Daniel L. Majhor, The Waite Group

Describes modems, how they work, and how to hook 10 well-known modems to 9 name-brand microcomputers. A handy Jump Table shows where to find the connection diagram you need and applies the illustrations to 11 more computers and 7 additional modems. Also features an overview of communications software, a glossary of communications terms, an explanation of the RS-232C interface, and a section on troubleshooting.
ISBN: 0-672-22446-1, $16.95

☐ Printer Connections Bible

Kim G. House and Jeff Marble, The Waite Group

At last, a book that includes extensive diagrams specifying exact wiring, DIP-switch settings and external printer details; a Jump Table of assorted printer/computer combinations; instructions on how to make your own cables; and reviews of various printers and how they function.
ISBN: 0-672-22406-2, $16.95